# In the Feminine Mode

# In the Feminine Mode

*Essays on Hispanic Women Writers*

### Edited by
### Noël Valis and Carol Maier

Lewisburg
Bucknell University Press
London and Toronto: Associated University Presses

Associated University Presses
440 Forsgate Drive
Cranbury, NJ 08512

Associated University Presses
25 Sicilian Avenue
London WC1A 2QH, England

Associated University Presses
P.O. Box 488, Port Credit
Mississauga, Ontario
Canada L5G 4M2

The paper used in this publication meets the requirements
of the American National Standard for Permanence of Paper
for Printed Library Materials Z39.48-1984.

Library of Congress Cataloging-in-Publication Data

In the feminine mode: essays on Hispanic women writers/edited by
Noël Valis and Carol Maier.
    p.   cm.
Includes bibliographical references.
ISBN 0-8387-5160-1 (alk. paper)
    1. Spanish literature—Women authors—History and criticism.
2. Spanish American literature—Women authors—History and
criticism.   I. Valis, Noël Maureen, 1945–   .   II. Maier, Carol,
1943–   .
PQ6055.I6   1990
860.9'9287—dc20                                          88-43410
                                                             CIP

*A Gift For Marina Romero*

# Contents

8                              CONTENTS

# Acknowledgments

Our thanks go to the University of Michigan's Department of Romance Languages and staff headed by Barbara Wexall, and to Bradley University's Board for Research and Creativity, for their generous help and support in this project.

"3" by Eunice Odio, from *Open to the Sun: A Bilingual Anthology of Latin-American Women Poets*, ed. Nora Jacquez Wieser. Reprinted by permission of Perivale Press. Copyright 1979.

Permission to quote from the sampler of Lydia Coffin is granted by the Nantucket Historical Association.

Permission to quote from the poems of Marina Romero, from the collections *Sin agua, el mar*, *Midas*, and *Presencia del recuerdo*, is granted by Marina Romero.

Excerpts from the preface by Leonard Woolf in *A Writer's Diary* by Virginia Woolf, copyright 1953, 1954 by Leonard Woolf and renewed 1981, 1982 by Quentin Bell and Angelica Garnett, reprinted by permission of Harcourt Brace Jovanovich Inc.

Permission to quote from "Canción de jinete" by Federico García Lorca, in *Obras completas*, copyright 1963, is granted by the heirs of Federico García Lorca and Aguilar, S.A., Publishers.

Permission to quote from the epilogue and to reprint the poem, "Soy una y estoy sola," both by Gloria Fuertes, from *Historia de Gloria*, ed. Pablo González Rodas, copyright 1983, is granted by Ediciones Cátedra, Publishers.

Permission to quote from the poems of Clementina Arderiu, *Obra poètica*, Pròleg de Joan Teixidor, copyright 1973, is granted by Edicions 62, Publishers.

# Marina Romero

## NOËL VALIS

Marina Romero was born in Madrid, on 5 February 1908. A pupil from age four to ten at the International Institute for Girls in Spain, she later attended the Instituto Escuela, an offshoot of the famed Institución Libre de Enseñanza. She would also teach there for a few years. Her guardian was *institucionista* Luis Simarro, to whom she dedicated the first poem of *Nostalgia de mañana*. With grants from the Spanish Republic and Smith College, Romero undertook graduate studies in the United States in 1935. In 1937 she received the M.A. from Mills College. From 1938 to 1970 she taught Spanish literature at Douglass College in New Brunswick, New Jersey.

Her early poetry—*Poemas "A"* and *Nostalgia de mañana*—reflects the influence of the Generation of 1927, especially Pedro Salinas, in its rhetorical and lyrical playfulness and neopopular strains. In *Presencia del recuerdo*, *Midas*, and *Sin agua, el mar*, all written, significantly, in exile though published in Spain, Romero attains a greater luminosity and depth through a simplicity of style in this very personal and intimate poetry. Her last books are written for children. Marina Romero now resides in Madrid.

## Marina Romero's Works

**POETRY**

*Poemas "A"*. Madrid: Asociación de Alumnas de la Residencia de Señoritas. Imp. S. Aguirre, 1935, 34 leaves, n. pag.
*Nostalgia de mañana*. México: Rueca, 1943, 89 pp.
*Presencia del recuerdo*. Madrid: Insula, 1952, 98 pp.
*Midas. Poema de amor*. Madrid: Insula, 1954, 82 pp.
*Sin agua, el mar*. Madrid: Agora, 1961, 55 pp.
*Honda raíz*. Sonetos. Madrid: Torremozas, 1989, 62 pp.

ESSAY

*Paisaje y literatura de España. Antología de los escritores del 98.* Estudio preliminar y fotografías de Marina Romero. Prólogo de Julián Marías. Madrid: Tecnos, 1957, 430 pp. (Winner of the Premio INLE)

CHILDREN'S BOOKS

*Alegrías. Poemas para niños.* Preface by Eugenio Florit. Salamanca: Anaya, 1972, 150 pp. Madrid: Escuela Española, 1980, 55 pp. (a selection of 1972 ed.). In December 1979, 20 of these poems were adapted by composer Antón García Abril as a "Cantata-Divertimento" (at the Teatro Real de Madrid) for the International Year of the Child (see also RCA, Long Play, Emisión por Radio Nacional, 1982).

*Campanillas del aire. Poemas para niños.* Madrid: Escuela Española, 1981, 48 pp. Thirty poems from *Alegrías.*

*Churrupete va a la luna en busca de la fortuna. Teatro para niños.* Madrid: Escuela Española, 1985, 63 pp.

*Disparatillos con Masacha. Poemas para niños.* Madrid: Escuela Española, 1986, 47 pp.

*Poemas a Doña Chavala y Don Chaval que no están nada mal.* Zaragoza: Editorial Luis Vives, 1987, 64 pp. (Col. Ala Delta, 4).

*Cuentos rompecabezas.* Madrid: Escuela Española, 1988, 71 pp. (Col. Caballo de Cartón, 50).

UNPUBLISHED

*Arte, historia y literatura de Toledo (siglos XI al XX).* Antología.
*Poemas de ida y vuelta.*
*Viento en contra.*
*Lyric Anthology of the Young Galician Generation.*
*Las cuatro estaciones.* Pieza teatral para niños.

# After Words: A Preface

## CAROL MAIER

How to best dodge the dark
obsession of your soul
toward a "not loving you"
cleansed of your memory?
I will cover this name
with a false pseudonym
to prevent us from meeting,
extinguishing your trace,
while for myself, if I can
Marina like always,
though now to the leeward
of whatever befalls you.
And, who knows!
some day . . .
like Lazarus . . .

[¿Cómo esquivar la oscura
obsesión de tu alma
para un no quererte
limpia de tu recuerdo?
Me cubriré este nombre
con un falso seudónimo
resistente a tu encuentro,
apagando tu rastro,
y para mí, si puedo,
Marina todavía,
pero al socaire
de todos tus destinos.
Y, ¡quién sabe!,
algún día . . .
como Lázaro . . .]

(*Midas*, Poem 8)[1]

From the start it was clear to me that Marina Romero had "anticipated" this volume, but I was unaware of exactly how until I read Noël Valis's essay about her poetry, "The Language of Treasure," which appears at the

13

end of this book. I realized then that the stanza from *Midas* that Noël cites in her final paragraphs about women's assertion of "self through the diction of reticence" evokes Marina's participation in the beginnings of our collection. She was not present in person, of course, when we first discussed the idea of a *festschrift* for her (in fact, neither of us had seen her for years). But as Noël and I talked and corresponded about *In the Feminine Mode*, I learned that not only had Marina influenced our lives after we graduated from Douglass College, she also had influenced us both in an absent and doubly mysterious way.

This was particularly interesting to me because our actual memories of Marina are quite different. Noël has written of "a small woman, carefully arranged white hair, hands opening like the leaves of a prayer book." She sees herself in the front row of Marina's classroom, "veined serenity of the rose and the book enduring the same space." I too think of Marina's diminutive stance (how could I not, for, as an unusually tall student—also a pregnant one the semester we met—I seemed to dwarf her), but my images are more animated than serene. The roses I see are brightly colored and worked in cross-stitch, splashed over the front of a Mexican blouse, and the hands are in motion, extended, as Marina reaches out with them on the first day of class to greet individually each of the *chicas* taking her course. I remember the intense energy that flowed from her gestures, that prompted her rigorous standards (and therefore the repeated revisions of our papers), and that gave rise to impatience or even annoyance with students who were lazy or with those who were unable to attend the many extracurricular activities she sponsored in the Spanish House. A small compressed center of activity, Marina was a giant figure for me, and I sat timidly, even reverently, as she introduced me to the figures on her altar: Galdós, the Generations of 1898 and 1927—"the canon"—but also Carmen Laforet, Ana María Matute, and Elena Quiroga, whose work had not yet been widely studied.

As I recall that ceremony, or initiation (for Marina was indeed performing a ritual), Noël is seated near me, but we were not side by side since I was rarely confident enough to sit in the first row, and Noël was waiting for the unfolding of what she remembers as a quiet experience. We are, however, immersed in the same instant, and even though we now remember that instant with different images and did not talk about it until many years later—in fact we did not see each other for more than a decade—during those years we returned to it time after time as to a single moment of mystery. Like the "strong emotion" that Virginia Woolf poignantly describes in "A Sketch of the Past," the introduction to "being" through literature that Noël and I shared in Marina's classroom left "its trace within us," assumed an "existence that seems to be independent of our minds," and is always available to us when we try to "get ourselves again attached to it."[2]

Curiously enough, despite the fact that our anecdotal remembrance of Marina is so different and so sketchy, and despite our eventual decision not to focus on conventional biography per se in *In the Feminine Mode*, it was through biography that we returned to Marina and consciously attached ourselves to the mystery. Furthermore, once the book was complete and we were able to see it as a whole, we were both drawn to reflect on the relation between biography and elusiveness in writing by and about female authors. My thoughts were to be expected since we had agreed that I would write the introduction for the volume. Noël's, however, were unforeseen, and one of the greatest pleasures of this project was the virtual irruption into my text of her "Note on Marina Romero."[3]

Noël began that process of "reattachment" in the spring of 1984 when she sent me a letter and a handful of photocopied notecards about Marina and her work. She had recently gathered and read all of Marina's poetry in order to prepare the annotated entries about her for Carolyn Galerstein's *Women Writers of Spain: An Annotated Bio-Bibliographical Guide*.[4] Noël had also begun to work on some translations of Marina's poems, and she wondered if anyone had ever dedicated a collection of essays to her. She asked if it would be possible to prepare one and if I would like to help organize such a project. "When I think back, I can't imagine anyone more deserving," Noël wrote; I see now that she was already thinking back with considerable clarity. The task of summarizing Marina's poems and writing a brief biographical sketch had put Noël face to face with the double mystery I noted earlier: the mystery of our own initiation into Spanish literature and the sense of mystery that had always surrounded Marina herself.

Because Marina was both differ-

A few years ago I was asked to contribute to a dictionary of Spanish women writers. As I sat thinking about the project, I began to remember one writer in particular: Marina Romero. After I wrote a brief sketch for the volume, I found I couldn't leave the subject of Marina with a mere bio-bibliographical addendum to her life and writing. So I translated a few of her poems into English, and these would appear in Houston in a small literary magazine, *Touchstone*.[5] Yet even this seemed insufficient. There are presences in life that need to have their reverberations enumerated, in grateful praise of gifts freely given.

I wrote to Carol Maier and asked if she would like to do something for Marina Romero. Carol, like me, had been a student of Marina at Douglass College during the 60s. My spontaneous suggestion seemed right for us at that moment in our lives. We had both graduated from a women's college at a time when American women were beginning to wake up. Many of us (including myself) didn't even know we were waking up. We were the solidly

ent and the same in our mind's eye, the coincidence and the rather paradoxical nature of those two mysteries seemed fundamental to the purpose of our project: we wanted to honor the hauntingly present absence of a woman we both admired greatly but about whom we knew—and continue to know— very little. Neither Noël nor I was especially close to Marina during our years at Douglass and we did not keep in touch with her after graduation. (Marina and I have never corresponded, and Noël wrote to her only occasionally.) Consequently, when it came time to prepare the annotations for *Women Writers of Spain*, Noël found that she was pursuing an "insistent object" and a highly elusive one at that. Moreover, when she realized that in addition to the biographical data needed for the entry, she wanted to explore "the value of a woman's writing life," she discovered that— like the familiar stranger Marina has always been for us—in her writing she is also presented only obliquely. As I reflect on Noël's comments about women writers and on the life of women writing and working in academics, it seems as if, in addition to being an aesthetic strategy for writing about love and the end of a relationship, Marina's "dodging" was a very purposeful method for insuring her own survival—as both protection in the present and projection toward the future.[6]

In fact, as the coeditor of this volume and, to some extent, the reader addressed in *Midas*,[7] I can-

comfortable products of midcentury female education. We were women and we were educated, but most of us had little idea of what that really meant. There were no intimate associations made between these two possible notions of ourselves. There was no sense of future to be found in them. I cannot remember ever having questioned myself about the ideas that these statements imply in those days.

Yet I felt happiness as I remembered those wordless, unconscious moments when we waited for Marina to appear in the classroom. It didn't matter that we were blind to our own consequences, that our names (and other things) would change over the years, that we might forget one another. (So with Carol, whose name change would separate us for ten years.) We were linked by a small woman and her love for literature. She gave us seas—foreign and rich—of words to remember. Only in this way would we remember ourselves: as youthful swimmers surrounded by a glimmering, mysterious wave of expectancy. Somehow, the words pushed and pulled us in that movement *toward*. There was a pointing ahead to what we would be: a community of women cohering through the strength of words remembered and shared.

So it seemed perfectly natural to plan a book on women writers as our gift to Marina Romero. But Marina's persona could not be explained without her poetry. For me, the words she used in class and those I read in her books are in-not help but notice the irony of Marina's refusal to define herself explicitly in light of her use of a "diction of reticence" that Noël has shown to be a very definite, albeit indirect self-assertion. Clearly, despite her elusiveness as a person and the "disguise" employed in her poems, it is not a desire for self-effacement but rather a strong determination to endure that leads the speaker in *Midas* to address her lover-reader in the second person. The "covering up" mentioned and the refusal to meet will not only avoid and extinguish the lover but will also insure the lover's active participation in the poet's work (Marina's future life). This means, as Noël implies when she points out the ambiguity of the term "al socaire de" (meaning "leeward of" and also "enjoying the protection of"), that even as she tries to escape from her lover-reader, the speaker in Marina's poem apparently acknowledges and assures the reader's essential role in the poet's resurrection.

The speaker suggests that continued reading will be insured by a delicate interplay of intimacy and distance. The "quest" of the poem's second person is thus both thwarted and encouraged: the reader is steered away from a "dark obsession" for names and certainties and instead guided to the uncertain, "obscure" areas of pseudonyms and transformations.[8] There, albeit paradoxically and with great effort, the poet holds fast to her own identity ("Marina like always" ["Marina todavía"]) so that "some day. . . / like Lazarus. . ." ("algún día. . . como Lázaro. . .") she might find new life.

extricably connected, as mutual explanations of one another. Her poetry is the inner biography of the woman and teacher who gave me a love for Spanish literature. Later, I would read reviews of her work, reviews that frequently extolled her poetry as typically feminine and spoke of delicate and sensitive verses, of love poetry that was "authentically feminine." I wondered what reviewers meant by that. Can anyone define the feminine? This question and many others that occurred to me in the course of writing the essay on Marina led me to different theoretical considerations: namely, to the premise underlying feminist criticism, that writing about women authors is writing about women. Stated another way, feminist criticism is predicated on the notion of radical biography as a way of understanding women's writings. Hence to read Marina Romero's poetry is to read Marina Romero.

* * *

Noël and I did not discuss the poem from *Midas* or Marina's influence on our project as we planned *In the Feminine Mode*, but Marina's interweaving of reticence and self-assertion and her insistence on mystery as the source of continuity did seem to direct us. We decided almost immediately that none of the articles would be simply descriptive or biographical. Despite our realization that, as Constance Sullivan has recently pointed out[9]—and as Galerstein's *Women Writers* documents quite thoroughly— there is still much "detective work" of discovery, rediscovery, and reevaluation needed in Hispanic feminist criticism, we believed that we could best honor Marina not by resurrecting her and other women as unsung heroines but rather by focusing on the reading and writing processes themselves.[10]

Our first call for essays, distributed at the end of 1984, was quite general and described the volume as "a form of homage to the many Hispanic women who have enriched our lives through their writing as well as personal example"; but we soon drafted a more focused prospectus. In a second circular, recalling Marina's example and believing, like Emily Dickinson, she would undoubtedly prefer to "have her work rather than her life appreciated,"[11] we asked potential contributors not only to describe the life and work of women writers but also to re-view or revise that work in light of Hispanic literature and criticism. What we had in mind was a collection of essays that would make readers "think about the ways we approach women writers and about the ways writers change our perception of the feminine. Essays that revise our received ideas of the woman writer. . . . Essays that make us see again, and differently." We cited Adrienne Rich's definition of "re-vision" as "looking back, of seeing with fresh eyes, of entering the text from a new critical direction";[12] and we requested work that would be "speculative and/or creative in nature, essays/dialogues/meditations that do not sever the links between the writer as critic or woman (yourself, others) and the writer as imaginative being." Our hope was to encourage "connections" of a kind "generally discouraged by the orthodox critical tradition," since we believe that a vital, open continuation of tradition depends not merely upon solving the mysterious (perhaps not so mysterious) disappearance of "missing" women and upon the insertion of their names and work in the literary canon, but also upon an altered, unorthodox way of approaching the literary "mysteries" themselves.

At some point in the early stages of our planning, we chose "In the Feminine Mode" as a title, and we have stuck with it despite several reservations. In particular, we were concerned that the use of the definite article might lead readers to infer certainty—an alternate prescription or canon. We considered replacing "the" with an indefinite article or ending the title with a question mark. Both of those options seemed weak, however, and risked the suggestion of ambivalence instead of the interrogative, exploratory spirit we wanted. In the end we decided to let the definite article stand and ask the essays themselves to provide questions. If they truly reflected our purpose, we reasoned, they would do the "essaying" and as a group would make it clear that the feminine mode is an inclusive term of plurality, difference, and even contradiction. To some extent we expected contributors to work against our title, and we evaluated each submission with that requirement in mind. We wanted strong, thoughtful, critical voices. We also wanted a certain tentativeness, however, and we endeavored to avoid the rigidity of unexamined assumptions that (despite their unorthodoxy) prevent speculation and exclude readers rather than make possible new definitions.

I am tempted now, since these paragraphs will precede the essays we selected some months ago, to let them fill the conventional role of a preface and explain the ways in which we found each piece to essay or attempt the feminine mode. In fact, it would be all too easy to slip into the expected gestures of simulated beginning and to define, after the fact, the formation of the body of this book—to go "after" the essays in hopes of proving that they confirm the expectations we had for them.[13] Since I have gone to some length, however, to discredit definitions as limiting and prescriptive, it seems far more appropriate to let the essays speak for themselves and raise their own questions about women and writing in Hispanic literature. Consequently, I will add no more than a few words of explanation about the book's configuration.

The essays we have included were selected individually during more than a year's time. Although we realized that we were choosing contributions about both Peninsular and Latin American literature from varying genres and historical periods, it was only when we met to read and edit all of the essays that we became aware of the balance and coherence among them. On the one hand, this made it difficult to divide the manuscript into sections or chapters. On the other hand, however, we were able to discern quite easily several different concerns. We decided to arrange the essays according to those differences, adhering to a general chronological order. In the first section, "Writing the Self," we placed essays that discuss either works by relatively unfamiliar writers or new works by familiar writers, essays that explore in different ways the notion of feminine identity, and essays that take feminine experience and its representation as their point of departure. The studies in section two, "The Text of Subversion," explore some of the ways in which Hispanic literature and history are being, and have been, written by women. In the final section, "The Critical Space," the contributors look either at other critics looking at texts by Hispanic women writers or at their own critical work. Although we did not consciously frame the book in mystery, I find it appropriate that *In the Femi-*

*nine Mode* opens with a lost *romance* by Sor Juana Inés de la Cruz and closes with Marina's refusal to define the poet's self, which, according to Noël, is a "resurrectional act" that locates the "richness of women's writing" precisely in "biographical insufficiency."

Noël and Marina's affirmation of incompleteness and my realization that absence as much as presence, questioning, or even silence—as well as apparent plenitude—have determined my participation in Marina's survival, lead me to conclude this preface with two further observations about mystery and pursuit. The first continues my thoughts about Marina as a present absence with respect to several absences and ironies in this volume. One of those ironies surprises me somewhat because I am suddenly made aware that, despite my strong distrust of definitions, I have been expecting the essays to outline a definable—if not wholly definitive—profile of the "Hispanic woman writer." As I recognize this now, and catch myself looking for a completeness that was not part of our original purpose, I find myself making mental notes about several aspects of Hispanic feminist criticism that would need to be discussed if one were to attempt a comprehensive portrait. Two of those aspects seem particularly significant, and I mention them in the following paragraph lest their absence from *In the Feminine Mode* be considered either an oversight or an intentional omission.

The first is a consideration of work by Latina writers in the United States, consideration such as Luz María Umpierre has given to Sandra María Esteves and Norma Alarcón has given to Helena María Viramontes and Cherríe Moraga.[14] That work represents some of the finest Hispanic writing now being produced, and no portrait of the Hispanic woman writer is complete without it. The second aspect I should mention is the discussion of Hispanic feminist criticism itself and its relation to other critical practices. This discussion, which was barely audible when Noël and I initiated our project in 1984, has become increasingly vigorous and articulate, especially with respect to Hispanic America.[15] As Jean Franco notes, for example, the role of both literary critics and writers in Hispanic countries has tended to differ radically from that of their counterparts in the United States. Rather than focusing exclusively on stylistics, the primary concerns of Hispanics have been traditionally "ethical," and critics have demanded "sincerity of writers and adhesion to national and liberatory goals and to the cause of the poorer classes."[16] Consequently, critics like Sara Castro-Klaren warn against a fixed, universal definition of feminist writing, and many would agree with Franco that feminist theory fails unless it includes "a reading of culture that fundamentally alters the framework of the entire literary system and, at the same time, provides us with new instruments of analysis" ["una lectura de la cultura que altere sustancialmente los marcos del sistema literario y nos dé, al mismo tiempo, nuevos instrumentos de análisis"].[17] They would also join Castro-Klaren in warning against a fixed, universal definition of feminist writing and against the uncritical use of work by North American and European (particularly French) feminists in the study of Hispanic women writers.[18]

The concerns raised by Franco and Castro-Klaren are addressed only indirectly in *In the Feminine Mode*. At the same time, however, I believe that the essays work in a complementary way as they seek to solve what Reddy considers the real mystery for feminists: "the development of woman's character and her work in a patriarchal culture." Like the feminist mystery novels discussed in Reddy's review, the essays are therefore "fundamentally subversive, exposing at once the inadequacy of conventional understanding of psychology and the dangers of passive acceptance of dominant values."[19] Moreover, by engaging that process of development precisely as it occurs in and against words themselves, they examine some of the strategies Hispanic women have employed to question those dominant values and to create an understanding of the forces inherent in language that impede a counter or autonomous use of it.

What emerge from the essays, then, if not a portrait of the Hispanic woman writer, are portraits of Hispanic women writers in different countries and historical periods who have endeavored to work as subjects with language in a consistently paradoxical situation. As Nancy Newton has pointed out, the Hispanic tradition has "suffered from dependence and marginality," but it has also been prescriptive and "strongly conservative in its views of sex roles." This has led to the creation of "disjunctive practices" for writers of both sexes, and in particular to the painfully ironic position of Hispanic woman in relation to certain contemporary critics who, in Newton's words, identify woman as "any force 'other' to and subversive of the (patriarchal and phallocentric) status quo."[20]

As a collection, the essays in *In the Feminine Mode* recall Newton's speculations about "real" women as opposed to what Alice Jardine has called "the woman-in-effect." They indicate the need for further exploration of the position of women in countries that—like Spain in relation to the United States, or Latin America in relation first to Spain and now the United States—"have historically played the role of women."[21] By examining women's fictionalizing of female experience (as in the essays of Janet Gold and Janet Pérez), studying the subversion of canonical texts of a "marginal" tradition (Susan Kirkpatrick on Gertrudis Gómez de Avellaneda, Linda Gould Levine on Isabel Allende, Elizabeth Ordóñez and Maryellen Bieder on Emilia Pardo Bazán), and exploring some of the ways in which Hispanic women writers have been aware of and even collaborated with the work of other women (Amy Kaminsky on Sor Juana Inés de la Cruz,

Bernice Hausman on Victoria Ocampo and Virginia Woolf), all of the essays address the difficulties encountered by women as they struggle to capture language without being co-opted (Debra Castillo on Carmen Gómez Ojea, Marci Sternheim on Sara de Ibáñez), trivialized, or misread (Teresa Vilarós-Soler on Clementina Arderiu, Elsa Krieger Gambarini on Teresa de la Parra).

The image of women writing "after" words returns me to Marina and to my second observation about our pursuit of her work. In truth, the observation is yet another question, for, as *In the Feminine Mode* nears completion, I find myself wondering whether it will please Marina. I wonder if she will recognize her presence in these essays about other women writers, if she will find the blend of mystery and demystification appropriate, and if she will approve of the re-visions, the altered perceptions of reading and critical space. As I remember Marina's classes, I cannot help but recall that although she taught us to read actively, there was not a hint of what we now call resistance to the text. Perhaps the reversals suggested here will disturb or even offend her. My instinct, however, is that they will not, because—her reverence for literature not withstanding—Marina taught us to read independently, with the spirit of responsibility that Adrienne Rich has demanded of female students,[21] and with the same attention or *esmero* for which, in her essay, Harriet Turner thanked Joaquina Navarro. More importantly, Marina provided an example of competence, energy, and determination that would later encourage (here I will knowingly risk Noël's heaviness of sentiment) and inspire women to read as women—as subjects.

Furthermore, that example is linked to the same will to create and survive that gives rise to the resolution of transformation and disguise at the center of *Midas* ("I will cover up this name / with a false pseudonym" ["Me cubriré este nombre / con un falso seudónimo"]). Because of such explicit play with a writer's identity and because she draws attention to that play in the text of her poem, I suspect that Marina will discern analogies between her work, the studies in *In the Feminine Mode*, and the various strategies of representation and survival that both present. I also believe that she will find appropriate and gratifying the spirit of "essay" she represented and that we have made the central principle of this volume. With thanks to her, I conclude with a few words of thanks to me, written by Harriet Turner about "writing in the feminine mode" as directed, indirectly, by Marina Romero.

The essay is also a new endeavor because it takes root in my own experience; it's almost confessional with more of a personal stamp on it than anything I've done. The balance between the subjective and objective is always a challenge. . . . It seems to me the balance is struck, in a useful way.[23]

# Notes

1. Marina Romero, *Midas* (Madrid: Insula, 1954), pp. 20–22. These lines, in my translation, differ somewhat from the version provided by Noël Valis in her essay. I include them not in contradiction or correction but in the spirit of collaboration that has directed our work throughout the preparation of *In the Feminine Mode*.

2. Virginia Woolf, "A Sketch of the Past," in *Moments of Being*, ed. Jeanne Schulkind (New York: Harcourt Brace Jovanovich, 1976), p. 67.

3. Shortly after I mailed a photocopy of this preface to Noël, I received from her a brief note entitled "Marina Romero" and a question about including it in *In the Feminine Mode*. Our pieces had crossed in the mail, and I was struck by the confirmation they offered of *collaboration* as work done "in conjunction" (C. T. Onions, ed., *The Oxford Dictionary of English Etymology*, 1974 printing [New York: Oxford University Press], p. 190) and by the way Noël and I seemed to speak together about Marina. In an effort to capture the dialogue I experienced as we wrote and talked about this project, I suggested that we print side by side the sections of our essays that dovetailed most closely. The conversation that resulted includes approximately two-thirds of Noël's note about Marina; the other third became the biographical and bibliographical sketch of Marina that we placed at the beginning of the book.

4. Noël Valis, "Marina Romero Serrano," in *Women Writers of Spain: An Annotated Bio-Bibliographical Guide*, ed. Carolyn L. Galerstein, with nonCastilian materials edited by Kathleen McNerny (New York: Greenwood, 1986), pp. 277–79.

5. Marina Romero, "Presencia del recuerdo" ("Presence of Memory") and "En su forma la flor" ("In Its Form the Flower"), trans. Noël M. Valis, *Touchstone* 10, no. 1 (1985): 3–6.

6. In this context, it might be instructive to speculate further about mystery and "biographical insufficiency" as distinctly nonmetaphorical strategies, and to consider Marina's life in relation to the tales of women, writing, and academics as told by Amanda Cross (*Death in a Tenured Position* [New York: Dutton, 1981]; *Sweet Death, Kind Death* [New York: Dutton, 1984]; *No Word from Winifred* [New York: Dutton, 1986]), or by Joyce Carol Oates (*Unholy Loves* [New York: Vanguard, 1979]; "The Dead," *Marriages and Infidelities* [New York: Vanguard, 1972; Greenwich, Conn.: Fawcett Publications, 1973], pp. 380–409).

7. The second person, familiar *tú* or "you" is clearly the speaker's lover—what we could call the poem's "narratee." At the same time, however, that "you" cannot help but include the actual or real reader, making his or her relation with the speaker veer, like the lover's, between intimacy and distance.

8. It is important to note here that the *oscura obsesión* indicates both obscurity and darkness. The translator is forced to decide which of the two suggestions is closer to the Spanish and to choose between them. Noël has opted for "obscure" and I for "dark." I prefer "dark" because a "dark obsession" evokes the persistent, even sinister pursuit of Marina by the reader-lover; "obscure" suggests a vagueness or lack of precision that seems contrary to the idea of obsession. There is a contradiction in Marina's lines, but I find it in Marina's subversion or transformation of the reader-lover's obsession rather than in the obsession itself. By hiding behind a disguise, placing herself in the shadows, the poet guides the reader-lover from a dark (implicitly destructive) obsession intent on facts and meetings to a darkness that is rich in possibility. "Obscurity" is thus redefined, and the reader-lover is

forced to inhabit it on the poet's terms. Unfortunately, whether the translator chooses "dark" or "obscure," the full dimension of Marina's transforming obscurity is not conveyed in English. I should also note that Noël's choice of "obscure" enabled her to duplicate Marina's alliteration in "o." I have lost that, although the use of "dodge" to convey the poem's hide-and-seek between poet and reader-lover gives rise to an alliteration in "d."

9. Constance Sullivan, "Re-reading the Hispanic Canon: The Question of Gender," *Ideologies and Literature* 4, no. 16 (1983): 93.

10. There is a need for this kind of volume in Hispanic criticism because there are still far too few critical studies available about the work of Hispanic women writers. Some recent exceptions in this country—encouraging signs that much more work is being written and will soon be available—are the greatly increased number of sessions devoted to women writers at most major conferences, the existence of Feministas Unidas as an allied organization of the Modern Language Association, the independent existence of the Asociación de Literatura Femenina and the publication of its journal *Letras Femeninas*, the publication of *Third Woman*, and the now yearly attention paid to Hispanic women writers at the Wichita State University Conference of Foreign Literatures.

In addition, a wealth of new scholarship is indicated by the following (this list is far from exhaustive, especially because it is limited to books): Marjorie Agosín, *Silencio e imaginación: Metáforas de escritura femenina* (México: Editorial Katún, 1986); Marjorie Agosín, Elena Gascón-Vera, and Joy Renjilian-Burgy, eds., *María Luisa Bombal: Apreciaciones críticas* (Tempe, Ariz.: Bilingual Press/Editorial Bilingüe, 1987); Magdalena García Pinto, *Historias íntimas: conversaciones con diez escritoras latinoamericanas* (Hanover, N.H.: Ediciones del Norte, 1988); Evelyn Picon Garfield, ed., *Women's Voices from Latin America: Interviews with Six Contemporary Authors* (Detroit: Wayne State University Press, 1985); Patricia Elena González and Eliana Ortega, eds., *La sartén por el mango. Encuentro de escritoras latinoamericanas* (San Juan, P.R.: Ediciones Huracán, 1984); Asunción Horno-Delgado et al., eds., *Breaking Boundaries: Latina Writing and Critical Readings* (Amherst: University of Massachusetts Press, 1989); Susan Kirkpatrick, *Las Románticas: Women Writers and Subjectivity in Spain* (Berkeley: University of California Press, 1989); Robert Manteiga, Carolyn Galerstein, and Kathleen McNerney, eds., *Feminine Concerns in Contemporary Spanish Fiction by Women* (Potomac, Md.: Scripta Humanistica, 1988); Carmen Martín Gaite, *Desde la ventana* (Madrid: Espasa-Calpe, 1987) and *Usos amorosos de la postguerra española* (Barcelona: Anagrama, 1987); Doris Meyer and Margarite Fernández Olmos, eds., *Contemporary Women Authors of Latin America*, Vol.1: *Introductory Essays* (Brooklyn: Brooklyn College Press, 1983); Janet Pérez, *Contemporary Women Writers of Spain* (Boston: Twayne Publishers, 1988); Marta Ester Sánchez, *Contemporary Chicana Poetry: A Critical Approach to an Emerging Literature* (Berkeley: University of California Press, 1985); Aurea María Sotomayor, *De lengua, razón y cuerpo (nueve poetas contemporáneas puertorriqueñas): Antología y ensayo crítico* (San Juan, P.R.: Instituto de Cultura Puertorriqueño, 1987).

Biographical and bibliographical information about the lives of Hispanic women writers is also becoming more accessible, thanks to Carolyn Galerstein's *Women Writers*, Diane Marting's companion *Women Writers of Spanish America: An Annotated Bio-Bibliographical Guide* (New York: Greenwood, 1987), and Catherine Perricone's "A Bibliographical Approach to the Study of Latin American Women Poets," *Hispania* 71 (1988): 262–87. The inclusion of essays like Tey Diana Rebolledo's "The Maturing of Chicana Poetry: The Quiet Revolution of the

1980's," in Paula Treichler, Cheri Kramarae, and Beth Stafford's *For Alma Mater: Theory and Practice in Feminist Scholarship* (Urbana: University of Illinois Press, 1985), pp. 143–58, and Cherríe Moraga's "From a Long Line of Vendidas: Chicanas and Feminism," in Teresa de Lauretis's *Feminist Studies/Critical Studies* (Bloomington: Indiana University Press, 1986), pp. 173–90, indicates that work by Latinas is being read and considered by North American feminists. Also worthy of note are special issues of several journals: *Chicana Creativity and Criticism: Charting New Frontiers in American Literature*, ed. María Hererra-Sobek and Helena María Viramontes, special issue of *The Americas Review* 15, nos. 3–4 (Fall-Winter 1987); *Reading for Difference: Feminist Perspectives on Women Novelists of Contemporary Spain*, ed. Mirella Servodidio, special issue of *Anales de la Literatura Española Contemporánea* 12, nos. 1–2 (1987); special issue of *Revista Iberoamericana*, nos. 132–33 (July–December 1985), ed. Rosa S. Minc, which includes the proceedings of "Escritoras de la América Latina," a symposium held at Montclair State College, 16 March 1984, and *Woman of Her Word: Hispanic Women Write*, ed. Evangelina Vigil, special issue of *Revista Chicana-Riqueña* 11, nos. 3–4 (1983).

Finally, several studies and collections not limited to the analysis of writing by women must be mentioned as important contributions to the formation of Hispanic feminist criticism. See, for example, Bell Gale Chevigny and Gari Laguardia, *Reinventing the Americas: Comparative Studies of Literature of the United States and Spanish America* (Cambridge: Cambridge University Press, 1986); Ruth El Saffar, *Beyond Fiction: The Recovery of the Feminine in the Novels of Cervantes* (Berkeley: University of California Press, 1984); Sharon Magnarelli, *The Lost Rib: Female Characters in the Spanish-American Novel* (Lewisburg and London: Bucknell University Press, 1985); Beth Miller, ed., *Women in Hispanic Literature: Icons and Fallen Idols* (Berkeley: University of California Press, 1983); Gabriela Mora and Karen Van Hooft, eds., *Theory and Practice of Feminist Criticism* (Ypsilanti, Mich.: Bilingual Press/Editorial Bilingüe, 1982); and Carmelo Virgillo and Naomi Lindstrom, eds., *Women as Myth and Metaphor in Latin American Literature* (Columbia: University of Missouri Press, 1985).

11. For this quotation about Dickinson and a timely reminder that biography can be more distracting than illuminating, I am indebted to Eileen Phillips's review of four feminist biographies: "We Don't Need Another Hero," *Marxism Today* (June 1986): 45.

12. Adrienne Rich, "When We Dead Awaken," *On Lies, Secrets, and Silences* (New York: Norton, 1979), p. 35.

13. I am reminded here of Jane Gallop's assertion that an editor's introduction "is always a secondary revision (in the psychoanalytic sense of the term) of the unruly material of an anthology" ("Reading the Mother Tongue: Psychoanalytic Feminist Criticism," *Critical Inquiry* 13 [1987]: 327).

14. Luz María Umpierre, "La ansiedad de la influencia en Sandra María Esteves y Marjorie Agosín," in *Woman of Her Word*, pp. 139–47; Norma Alarcón, "Making *Familia* from Scratch: Split Subjectivities in the Work of Helena María Viramontes and Cherríe Moraga," in *Chicana Creativity and Criticism*, pp. 147–59.

15. See, for example, the following studies: Sara Castro-Klaren, "La crítica literaria feminista y la escritora en América Latina," in *La sartén por el mango*, pp. 27–46; Jean Franco, "Trends and Priorities for Research on Latin American Literature," *Ideologies and Literature* 4, no. 16 (1983): 107–20, esp. 119–20 and "Apuntes sobre la crítica feminista y la cultura hispanoamericana," *Hispamérica* 45 (December 1986): 31–43; Amy Katz Kaminsky, "Come to the Banquet: A Belated Invitation," unpublished paper read at "Hispanism as Humanism: An Internation-

al Symposium," Albany, N.Y., 21 March 1980; Gabriela Mora, "Las novelas de Isabel Allende y el papel de la mujer como ciudadana," *Ideologies and Literature* 2, no. 1 (Spring 1987): 53–61; Nancy Newton, "Mermaids and Minotaurs in Hispanic Literary Culture: Reflections on Sexuality and Ideology," unpublished paper read at the convention of the Midwest Modern Language Association, Bloomington, Ind., 2 November 1984; Elizabeth Ordóñez, "Inscribing Difference: *l'Écriture Féminine* and New Narrative by Women," *Reading for Difference*, pp. 45–58; Cynthia Steele, "Toward a Socialist Feminist Criticism of Latin American Literature," *Ideologies and Literature* 4, no. 16 (1983): 323–29; Constance Sullivan, "Rereading the Hispanic Canon," pp. 93–101.

Perhaps the most extensive effort to date in the United States to define the work of Hispanic feminist criticism was an international conference held 31 March–2 April 1988 at the University of Minnesota. The proceedings of that conference will make available an in-depth overview of current work by some twenty critics: *Cultural-Historical Grounding for Hispanic and Luso-Brazilian Feminist Literary Criticism*, ed. Hernán Vidal (Minneapolis, Minn.: The Prisma Institute, forthcoming).

16. Franco, "Trends and Priorities," p. 107. Franco writes about Latin America, but I believe that in this context Spain could be included as well.

17. Franco, "Apuntes sobre la crítica feminista," p. 32 (translation mine).

18. Castro-Klaren, "La crítica literaria feminista," p. 31; Franco, "Apuntes sobre la crítica feminista," p. 32; and Castro-Klaren, "La crítica literaria feminista," pp. 27–38.

19. Maureen T. Reddy, "She Done It," review of recent feminist mysteries, in *The Women's Review of Books* (December 1986): 8.

20. Newton, "Mermaids and Minotaurs," p. 3; italics added. In the last quotation, Newton is referring to Jonathan Culler, *On Deconstruction: Theory and Criticism After Structuralism* (Ithaca, N.Y.: Cornell University Press, 1982), p. 175. For a more thorough—and feminist—discussion of the phenomenon described by Culler, see Alice Jardine, *Gynesis: Configurations of Women and Modernity* (Ithaca, N.Y.: Cornell University Press, 1985), chap. 1.

21. Jardine, *Gynesis*, pp. 31–49; Newton, "Mermaids and Minotaurs," p. 3. Although she does not situate them in terms of contemporary literary criticism, Kaminsky also raises these same questions ("Come to the Banquet"). John Beverley provides a thorough discussion of Hispanism's "feminine" position as "one of the most marginal and least prestigious fields in the American academy." See "Can Hispanism Be a Radical Practice?" *Ideologies and Literature* 4, no. 16 (1983): 11. He does not, however, link that marginality with feminism, or even with women, although he does note (albeit apparently without seeing the irony of his comments) that "it is not by accident that it [Hispanism] has been a field attractive and open to women" (p. 11).

22. Adrienne Rich, "Claiming an Education," *On Lies, Secrets, and Silence*, p. 233.

23. Harriet's comments are from a letter dated 11 March 1986. I have printed them here with her permission.

In the Feminine Mode

# Part 1

# Writing the Self

# Nearly New Clarions:
# Sor Juana Inés de la Cruz Pays Homage
# to a Swedish Poet

AMY KATZ KAMINSKY

Among the encomia dedicated to the author of a book of poems published in Stockholm in 1713, one, signed in Mexico by a nun, seemed to the Swedes particularly exotic. In a 148-line *romance*, Sor Juana Inés de la Cruz pays homage to Sophia Elisabeth Brenner, "Polar Muse, One of the Marvels of the North."[1] Of the twenty-two texts of praise and congratulations that accompany the poems of Sophia Elisabeth Brenner in the *Poetiske Dikter* (Poetic verses), Sor Juana's comes from farthest away. It is grouped with two other panegyrics from the Spanish Empire—one in Latin by "Gusmán", signed in 1711, and the other an undated sonnet written by a highborn Spanish nun, Doña Catalina de Alfaro Fernández de Córdoba, from the Convent of the Holy Spirit in the Andalusian city of Alcaraz.[2]

Historians of Swedish literature have not failed to point to the Mexican nun's tropical tribute as proof of Fru Brenner's wide fame. But lacking knowledge of the language and literature of Spanish America, they were not able to appreciate the great value—or the great contradictions—inherent in this poetic document.[3] The *romance*, written in quatrains, that Sor Juana Inés de la Cruz dedicated to Sophia Elisabeth Brenner is characterized by a strong Americanism and a profound religious sense that proclaim the Mexican woman's independence. The poem's speaker claims that living in an Edenic America that provides all material comfort and having a religious vocation that precludes amassing wealth make her a disinterested profferer of homage, who wishes to gain nothing from the recipient of the poem (11–25). This disinterest, however, seems to degenerate rapidly into indifference. Not only does the speaker digress at length from the task of praising the other woman, focusing instead on the glories of the New World and the ennobling requirements of her own religious vocation, but to make matters worse, it turns out that the poet has used the same laudatory poem before. In the 1680s Sor Juana addressed a somewhat longer version of this work to Doña María Guadalupe de Alencastre,

31

duchess of Aveyro. In fact, Sor Juana does have a vested interest in re-working the poem, sending it, and having it published in Sweden, though her interest has nothing to do with material gain. By singing the praises of another woman poet, Sor Juana validates herself as a writer. Nor is Sor Juana indifferent to the poet she praises. A close reading of the text shows how, by rhetorical devices that first create and then overcome distance, the poet expresses real delight in finding another like herself.

It is not clear who asked Sor Juana to contribute a poem to Sophia Brenner's bouquet of encomia. Two Swedish literary historians who have studied Brenner's work hold differing opinions. Karin Westman Berg believes Sophia Brenner could have contacted Sor Juana directly, since Brenner learned Latin as a child and was well-enough versed in romance languages to write poems in French and Italian. Since Sor Juana's lost correspondence is known to have been extensive, Westman Berg's theory is not to be summarily discarded. However, I am inclined to share the opinion of Magnus Von Platen. He believes that Urban Hjärne and Sophia Brenner's husband Elias, who undertook to collect and publish Fru Brenner's poetry, sought out all the encomia, including Sor Juana's.[4]

What disposes me toward accepting Von Platen's explanation is the curious way in which the poet identifies herself at the end of the encomium. After insisting on her American identity throughout, Sor Juana startlingly claims her Visigothic ancestry, signing the poem "Sister Juana Inés de la Cruz, professed nun in the Monastery of Saint Jerome in the Imperial City of Mexico, Basque, from the mountains where there still remain notable relics and families of the pure Visigothic blood of Spain."[5] Not only does this statement undermine her professed allegiance to America, it rests on a heritage to which Sor Juana lays claim through her natural father, a Basque captain who abandoned her when she was a small child and whose name she rarely used. This unlikely signature makes some sense, however, if it is seen in the context of Elias Brenner's belief in Johannes Rudbeck's theory of the Swedish, and thus Gothic, origins of European civilization. Elias Brenner, as a disciple of Rudbeck, had a certain interest in supporting this ethnocentric theory with the evidence of the Visigothic roots of a Spanish-American poet. Gusmán also signed his eulogy with a reference to his Visigothic lineage: "Hispanus e sanguinare Visi-Gothico oriundus."[6]

Doña Catalina de Alfaro Fernández de Córdoba is the only one of the Hispanic contributors who does not claim this link with the Swedish poet and Rudbeck's theory. What connects her to this project is Sor Juana herself. The first volume of Sor Juana's collected works, published in 1689, contains a sonnet by Doña Catalina that eulogizes the Mexican poet.[7] This sonnet is an earlier version of the poem that the nun of Alcaraz offered to Sophia Elisabeth Brenner. Sor Juana was not the only one to revise a poem of praise and send it to Sweden.

Alfonso Méndez Plancarte, who compiled and published the most definitive edition of Sor Juana's works, was unaware of a second version of her poem addressed to the duchess of Aveyro. It is almost certain, however, that the variant he published was written before the version sent to Brenner. Although it is impossible to date either version with absolute certainty, it is very unlikely that Sor Juana would have been asked for the poem to Brenner before 1688, the latest date Méndez Plancarte will attribute to the variant he published.[8]

In 1688 Sor Juana's patron, who had requested she write a poem in praise of the duchess of Aveyro, returned to Spain with her husband, the viceroy. Two years later, Sor Juana's life changed when the bishop of Puebla published Sor Juana's *Athenagoric Letter*, a critical response to a sermon by the renowned Jesuit, Antonio Vieyra. With it, under the name of Sor Filotea de la Cruz, the bishop included an open letter admonishing Sor Juana to dedicate herself less to worldly letters and more to spiritual matters. Chastised by her bishop, Sor Juana also lost the protection of the new viceroys and underwent a radical change of fortune in which, as Octavio Paz has pointed out, not only her vocation, but her entire life was called into question.[9] In this state of spiritual siege Sor Juana constructed a two-tiered fortress: she composed the *Reply to Sor Filotea* (1691) as a defense of her intellectual life, and then, selling her library, her musical instruments, and her scientific equipment, she retreated into silence.[10]

Nevertheless, circumstances indicate that the version of the *romance* dedicated to Sophia Brenner was written well after the duchess of Aveyro received hers. Between 1670 and 1713, Brenner wrote 164 poems, thirty-two of which antecede the death of Sor Juana in 1695. Since Brenner dated all but eight of her works, we know that by 1690 Brenner had written only nineteen poems. The slow poetic production of the Swedish writer, who besides being a poet and housewife was the mother of seventeen children, suggests that Urban Hjärne and Elias Brenner began to request homages from her contemporaries several years after Sor Juana addressed her eulogy to the duchess of Aveyro.[11] There is also evidence internal to the poem, particularly the suppression of all reference to the eulogized object's beauty and a changed attitude toward the rhetoric of submission, that suggests the "Swedish" version of the poem was written after 1690.

Toward the end of her life Sor Juana struggled to suppress her aesthetic impulses and redirect her energy toward displays of religiosity. In the 1680s, before circumstances changed her life radically, Sor Juana was untroubled by the equation of physical beauty and virtue, or the use of rhetorical flourishes to declare her prostration before another human being, both of which appear in the Portuguese version of the poem.[12] In the 1690s these elements were no longer simply matters of rhetorical convenience. Selling her musical and scientific instruments was more than an act of obedience and charity; it was a sign of Sor Juana's withdrawal from the natural world as an object of intellectual pleasure and from the world of art as object of aesthetic pleasure.

Added to the unlikelihood of worshipping physical beauty under such circumstances was Sor Juana's lifelong conflicting feelings about her own beauty, first evident in the famous childhood incident in which she cut her hair off because, she believed, a head so slow to learn Latin was undeserving of adornment. That is, beauty and intellect are in conflict, and the former is subordinate to the latter.[13] In the revision of the eulogy, beauty is once again suppressed in favor of intellect: three of the stanzas praising the duchess of Aveyro's beauty disappear altogether in the revised poem and the one remaining sees physical charms converted into intellectual accomplishments (30). Since it was expected that any poem in praise of a woman would comment on her beauty, failing to mention it is not merely an effect of Sor Juana's ignorance of the Swedish woman's appearance, but a conscious choice.[14]

A second difference between the two variants of the poem is more subtle. Though in the first version of the poem Sor Juana plays games with the conventions of eulogistic language, she goes even further to diminish the passion with which she pays homage in the later version. In every instance of submission, Sor Juana tempers her humility before Sophia Brenner, as if such prostration, rhetorical though it may be, were not decent before another human being. No longer mere convention but rather the sign of true adoration that only God deserves, the language of submission recovers its meaning. The speaker who prostrates herself at María de Guadalupe Alencastre's feet will merely place herself at Sophia Brenner's hands (28). As a result, Sor Juana's homage to Sophia Brenner is less servile but more sincere than the one she wrote for the duchess of Aveyro. It is, ultimately, an artificial creation that participates consciously, and willingly, in the rite of poetic homage.

The following is the complete text of the *romance* that Sor Juana Inés de la Cruz dedicated to Sophia Elisabeth Brenner. This is the first reprinting of the text since its original publication in Stockholm in 1713. I have modernized the spelling but not the punctuation.

Aplaude lo mismo, que la fama en la
Sabiduría de la Señora Misoña
SOPHIA ELISABETH BRENNER.
Musa Polare
Una de las maravillas del Norte
Que encanta con su canto
y triunfa del olvido

Gran Minerva de los Godos!

Mejor, que la que triunfante
De Neptuno, impuso a Atenas
Sus insignias literales.  1
  Cifra de las nueve musas,
Cuya pluma es admirable
Arcaduz, por quien respiran
Sus nueve acentos suaves.  2
  Claro honor de las mujeres,
De los hombres docto ultraje
Que probáis, que no es el sexo,
De la inteligencia parte.  3
  Sois valida de Apolo,
Que de sus rayos solares,
Gozando de los plenilunios,
Mostráis las actividades.  4
   Clara sibila visigoda!
Más docta y más elegante,
Que las que en diversas tierras
Veneraron las edades.  5
  Alto asunto de la fama
Para quien hace, que afanes
Del martillo de Vulcano
Nuevos clarines os labren.  6
  Oíd una musa, que
Desde donde fulminante
A la Tórrida da el sol
Rayos perpendiculares.  7
  Al eco de vuestro nombre
Que llega a lo más distante
Medias sílabas responde
Desde sus concavidades.  8
  Y al imán de vuestras prendas
Que lo más remoto atrae
Con amorosa violencia
Obedece acero fácil.  9
  Desde la América enciendo
Aromas a vuestra imagen
Y en este apartado polo
Templo os erijo, y altares.  10
  Desinteresada os busco,
Que el afecto, que os aplaude,
Es aplauso a lo entendido,
Y no lisonja a lo grande.  11
  Porque para qué señora
En distancia tan notable
Habrán vuestras altiveces
Menester mis humildades?  12
  Yo no he menester de vos
Que vuestro favor me alcance
Favores en el consejo,
Ni amparo en los tribunales.  13

Ni que acomodéis mis deudos,
Ni que amparéis mi linaje,
Ni que mi alimento sean
Vuestras liberalidades.                    14
   Que yo señora nací
En la América abundante,
Compatriota del oro,
Paisana de los metales.                    15
   Adonde el común sustento
se da casi tan de balde,
Que en ninguna parte más
Se ostenta la tierra madre.                16
   De la común maldición
Libres parece que nacen
Sus hijos según el pan
No cuesta al sudor afanes.                 17
   Europa mejor lo diga,
Pues ha tanto, que insaciable
De sus abundantes venas
Desangra los minerales.                    18
   Y cuantos el dulce Lotos
De sus riquezas les hace
Olvidar los propios nidos,
Despreciar los patrios Lares.              19
   Pues entre cuantos la han visto
Se ve con claras señales
Voluntad en los, que quedan
Y violencia en los, que parten.           20
   Demás, de que en el estado,
Que Dios fue servido darme,
Sus riquezas solamente
Sirven para despreciarse.                  21
   Que para volar segura
De la religión la nave
Ha de ser la carga poca,
Y muy crecido el velamen.                  22
   Porque si algún contrapeso
Pide, para asegurarse,
De humildad no de riquezas
Ha menester hacer lastre.                  23
   Pues, de qué cargar sirviera
De riquezas temporales,
Si en llegando la tormenta
Era preciso alijarse?                      24
   Con que, por cualquiera de estas
Razones, pues es bastante
Cualquiera estoy de pediros
Inhibida por dos partes.                   25
   Pero! adónde de mi patria
La dulce afición me hace
Remontarme del asunto?
Y del intento alejarme?                    26

Vuelva otra vez mi señora
El discurso a recobrarse,
Y del hilo del discurso
Los dos rotos cabos ate.                    27
   Digo pues, que no es mi intento
Señora, más, que ponerme
A vuestras manos, que beso
A pesar de tantos mares.                    28
   Me informó de vuestras prendas
Como son pues quien las sabe
Siendo sólo tanto Homero
A tanto Aquiles bastante.                    29
   A la vuestra su doctrina
Alaba porque envidiarse
Se concede en las bellezas
Y desdice en las deidades.                    30
   Yo pues con esto movida
De un impulso dominante
De resistir imposible
Y de ejecutar no fácil.                    31
   Con pluma en tinta, no en cera
En alas de papel frágil
Las ondas del mar no temo,
Las pompas piso del aire.                    32
   Y venciendo la distancia,
Porque suele a lo más grave
La gloria de un pensamiento
Dar dotes de agilidades.                    33
   A la helada región
Llego donde las señales
De vuestras prendas me avisan,
Que allí mis rodillas estampe.                    34
   Aquí estoy a vuestros pies,
Por medio de estos cobardes
Rasgos, que son podatorios
Del afecto, que en mí arde.                    35
   De nada puedo serviros
Señora porque no soy nadie.
Mas, quizá por aplaudiros
Podré aspirar a ser alguien.                    36
   Hacedme tan señalado
Favor, que de aquí adelante
Pueda de vuestras criadas
En el número contarme.                    37

Sòror Juana Agnez de la Cruz monja profesa en el monasterio del Señor San Jerónimo de la Imperial Ciudad de México, viscaina, de las montañas adonde se quedan aún insignes reliquias y familias de la sangre limpia visigoda en España.

In Praise of the Fame in Knowledge
of SOPHIA ELISABETH BRENNER
Polar Muse

One of the Marvels of the North
Who Delights with her Song
and Triumphs over Oblivion


Great Minerva of the Goths!
Greater than she, who triumphant
over Neptune, imposed on Athens
her sect's insignia,                                          1
　　Emblem of the nine muses
whose pen is an admirable
conduit, through which they breathe
their nine soft accents,                                     2
　　Bright honor of women,
learned affront of men,
who proves that sex
is no part of intelligence,                                  3
　　You are the favored of Apollo
who by his solar rays,
full moon in possession,
reveals your talents.                                        4
　　Bright Visi-Gothic Sybill
more learned and more elegant
than those who in diverse lands
the ages venerated,                                          5
　　Exalted subject of fame
for whom the toil
of Vulcan's hammer
forges new clarions,                                         6
　　Hear a Muse who,
from where the thundering
sun beams perpendicular rays
to the Torrid Zone,                                          7
　　To the echo of your name
that reaches the most distant place,
answers with half-syllables
from her depths.                                             8
　　And the magnet of your gifts,
which attracts what is most remote,
with loving violence
weak steel obeys.                                            9
　　From America I kindle
scents to your image
and in this distant Pole
a temple I erect for you, and altars.                       10
　　Disinterested I seek you
for the feeling which lauds you
is praise for intelligence
not flattery for greatness,                                 11
　　Because, for what reason, lady,
at such notable distance
would your pride
need my humilities?                                         12

I have no need of you
that your favor might extend me
favors in council
nor protection in tribunals,                          13
    Nor that you accommodate my family
nor that you protect my lineage
nor that my nourishment
be your generosity,                                   14
    For I was born, Lady,
in abundant America
compatriot of gold,
countrywoman of metals                                15
    Where common sustenance
is given so freely
that in no other place
does Mother Earth boast more.                          16
    From the usual curse
her children seem born free
since bread does not cost them
the toil of their sweat.                               17
    Europe, and best I say it,
has for so long insatiably
bled the minerals
from her abundant veins,                               18
    And how many do
sweet Lothos' riches cause
to forget their own homes
and despise their native lands?                        19
    For among all who have seen her
with clear signs we see
willingness in those who stay
and violence in those who leave.                       20
    Besides, in the state
that God saw fit to grant me
her riches serve only
to be despised.                                       21
    Since in order for religion's ship
to fly secure,
the load must be light
and the sail full blown,                              22
    Because if counterweight it needs
for steadiness' sake
of humility, not riches
it needs must make the ballast.                       23
    For, what good would it do
to carry earthly wealth
if when the storm arrived
it was necessary to lighten?                          24
    So that, for any of these reasons,
since either is sufficient,
I am restrained from asking
your favors on two sides.                             25

But! Where does sweet
affection for my country take me,
withdrawing me from the matter at hand
and separating me from my intent?                    26
   Let my Lady pick discourse
up again, and the two loose ends
of discourse's thread
again be tied together.                              27
   I say, then, that none other is my intent
Lady, than to place myself
at your hands, which I kiss
despite so many seas.                                28
   I have learned of your talents
from one who knows them,
who alone is sufficient Homer
for such an Achilles.                                29
   This Homer your learning
praises, for envy
is conceded in beauties
and withdrawn in deities.                            30
   I then with this moved
by a dominating impulse,
impossible to resist
and not easy to execute,                             31
   With quill in ink, not in wax,
on wings of fragile paper,
I do not fear the waves of the sea,
I step on currents of air,                           32
   And conquering distance,
because the glory of a thought
often gives gifts of agility
to that which is most heavy,                         33
   To the icy regions
I come where the Signs
of your talents guide me,
that there my knees might leave their mark.          34
   Here I am at your feet
by means of these craven
lines that are envoys
of the feeling that in me burns.                     35
   In nothing can I serve you,
Lady, for I am no one.
Yet, perhaps by praising you
I may aspire to be someone.                          36
   Grant me the great
favor, that for now and evermore
among your maidservants
I might count myself.                                37

Sister Juana Inés de la Cruz, professed nun in the Monastery of Saint Jerome in the Imperial City of Mexico, Basque, from the mountains where there still remain notable relics and families of the pure Visigothic blood of Spain.

As a ritual of humility whose worth is directly related to the prestige of the writer affecting inferiority, eulogy embraces a paradox that Sor Juana exposes in this poem. The conventional language with which the speaker invokes the eulogized object suggests that this will be an encomium like any other. The fact that the same poem, even taking into account the variations, can serve for two individuals as different as Sophia Brenner and María de Guadalupe Alencastre, testifies to its conventionality. Sor Juana makes her poem's recipient a paper goddess, built of dying metaphors that, having not yet degenerated to the level of parody, still hold a quality of courtesy. She erects an American branch of this goddess' temple, whose distance from its object of adoration is crucial to charting its central task: bridging distances, be they geographic, spiritual, cultural, or formal. This task unifies the poem, but it attains only partial success, since it contravenes the poet's "deconstructive work" in which she exposes the genre of eulogy, opening a rift in the poem that she never mends completely.

The geographical distance between America and Europe allows the disinterest of the speaker that she both announces and with which she threatens to revoke her homage. Though she raises the expectation that she will list the noble attributes of her recipient (11–12), the speaker instead attends to her own humility in language that is less than truly humble (13–15). This in turn raises doubts about the true intention of the poem. The rhetorical structure breaks down, returning an interrogative meaning to what should be a rhetorical question: of what use is this (now possibly false) humility?

The implicit response to this question exposes the mechanism of the genre, revealing that through the speaker's pose of humility, the eulogized woman gains prestige she previously lacked. Certainly the efforts of Brenner's husband and friend to accumulate encomia from all over Europe indicate the truth of this. The diction of the lines further undermines convention. The prosaic syntax and direct, uncourtly language of lines like "Yo no he menester de vos / que vuestro favor me alcance / favores en el consejo / ni amparo en los tribunales," clash with the refined baroque elegance of earlier verses such as "Y al imán de vuestras prendas / que lo más remoto atrae / con amorosa violencia / obedece acero fácil." The carefully polished artificial language with which the poet evokes the eulogized object becomes an empty form, while the everyday language and simple structure surprise and shock; this is another of the paradoxes of the poem. Baroque hyperbaton, as well as hyperbole, lose their impact. In this poem verbal violence is not syntactic but semantic, affirming not the virtues of the eulogized but rather her impotence.

This procedure might be labelled a Newtonian rhetorical device that, taking the concept of disinterestedness to the extreme, could provoke a celebratory reaction of equal force, returning the text to the conventions of the encomium. Sor Juana used a similar technique in her *Athenagoric Let-*

*ter*, in which she argued that the greatest expression of divine love is the withholding of God's gifts, implying that it is preferable to love God without expecting any earthly reward. Similarly she might suggest in this poem that the purest eulogy is offered by the one who has the least to gain from it. But Sor Juana once again defies expectations; the speaker follows the logic of her own argument and drops the matter of eulogy altogether. Her proclaimed disinterest becomes actual indifference as the poem becomes a celebration of herself.

The speaker associates herself with the essence of the New World, evoking both its economic value and its Edenic qualities, and challenges Europe's crass appropriation of America. Her stunning patriotic fervor (15–20) ebbs only to give way to a contemplation of the religious journey she has chosen as her way of life (21–24); and together patriotism and religion bespeak her independence (25). Once this self-sufficiency is expressed, the speaker may return to the titular matter of the poem, i.e., praise of the European lady (28–37). The transition from self-affirmation to encomium underscores the division between the self-conscious author in control of the production of the text and the fictional speaker who, all unknowing innocence, declares her independence (26–27).

Apologizing for her inappropriate patriotic tirade, the speaker reveals that this subject matter, which supposedly sprang forth unexpectedly, is the true content of the poem. Moreover, her attempt to repair the rupture that her "unexpected" patriotic and religious eloquence produced demonstrates the impossibility of such a task. The poem remains irreparably torn, making manifest what is usually suppressed: the egocentrism of the writer of the eulogistic form.

After her forceful rending of the text, it is difficult to credit the speaker's submission before the eulogized object in the final section of the poem. However, there is a third, connecting level of the poem underlying both the conventional encomium (1–11 and 28–37) and the hymn of self-praise (13–26): the story of poetic sisterhood.

The reference to the gender of the poem's recipient reveals that a deeply felt commitment, not mere social or professional obligation, occasioned the writing of the eulogy. This commitment explains the sincerity exuded by the poem, but whose source is otherwise difficult to locate. One of the purposes of this text is to affirm that "no es el sexo de la inteligencia parte." This notion that intelligence has no gender is one of the themes of Sor Juana's life, and it increases in importance after the publication of the *Athenagoric Letter* when it becomes necessary to prove, to herself and to the world, that to be a learned woman doesn't require violation of the laws of nature. To assert this, Sor Juana arms herself with the irrefutable fact of the existence of learned women past and present. Thus her return to the homage is rendered believable.

Sor Juana manages this return in the poem by reining in her metric freedom. When the speaker in the Swedish version of the poem ends her religious and patriotic fervor, in which the stanza structure serves as a bare frame, she returns to the encomiastic task via three strictly controlled verses, each ending with a play of parallelisms and a closed distich (30–32). The effect of these stanzas is not merely a return to control, but an ostentatious display of the conscious effort such a return demands.

Once her egocentrism is reined by these controlled lines, the speaker loosens the structure and normalizes the syntax in a structural approximation of the sincerity that the simpler syntax of the poem's beginning connoted. Without losing the elegance of its baroque lines, the final stanzas acquire a simplicity that persuades the reader to accept on a grammatical level what he or she has learned to doubt on a rhetorical level. By now, it is impossible to believe the speaker's affirmation that she is a nobody whose only chance of recognition is to serve the eulogized object; nevertheless, the poem can be understood to say, "This eulogy reaffirms both of us as poets and defends us as learned women."

The speaker and eulogized object are reconciled at the moment that the former—or her spirit captured in the poem—completes her journey across the sea. This geographical journey is the poem's most obvious one, the most fully elaborated, and the one that is most nearly fulfilled. The motif of the speaker's desire to reach Heaven, which occupies the literal and figurative central space of the poem, echoes on a spiritual level the speaker's desire that her words reach from the New World to Europe. Ironically, even as Sor Juana links the spiritual journey to the physical one by means of figurative language, the former threatens to render the latter superfluous, given that the speaker declares that any boon received from the eulogized object is detrimental to her spiritual journey. Nevertheless, language provides a potential means of reconciliation among the three sundered sections of the poem. The spiritual journey is figured in nautical language, while the trip the poem is to take across the ocean is figured in the language of flight.

In the spiritual as well as the physical journey the speaker mixes air and water, sky and sea.[15] The speaker's soul must "navigate" the distance between Earth and Heaven, while the poem "flies" across the ocean. The maritime metaphor of the heavenly journey is extended through three stanzas, evoking a ship with its cargo, sail, and ballast weathering stormy seas (22–24). The nautical nature of a journey skyward is balanced in the final section of the poem when the encomium itself crosses the sea on wings and feathers. Sor Juana complicates this inversion by insisting on the artificiality ("alas de papel" [wings of paper]) or technological transformation ("pluma en tinta" [quill in ink]) that produces the physical object—the text—that crosses the sea both carrying and embodying the thought of the speaker. The feather/quill is used here in its linguistic function, since the speaker deliberately rejects the temptation to use it as a means of transport. She will attempt this journey "with feather in ink, not wax." Icarus's attempt to fly failed, and the speaker does not pretend, even metaphorically, to travel bodily to Europe. The verbal arrangement permits the speaker to cross oceans without having to humble herself physically before the eulogized object. This trip takes place by means of two incomplete metamorphoses: the feather that maintains its form and something of its alatory function when it is turned into a pen, and the poem as written text ("alas de papel frágil" [wings of fragile paper]) that literally crosses the ocean. The material text, which is the poetic voice concretized in ink and paper, is, finally, a homage to the European lady as tangible as the act of kissing the hem of her dress.

The distance the poet overcomes with her poem becomes even greater when the poem crosses cultural frontiers as well as the sea. The religious link, linguistic similarity, and the connection with the Mexican vicereine, facilitate communication between Sor Juana and the duchess of Aveyro. It is literary sisterhood, and nothing else, that connects Sor Juana to Sophia Brenner, even after she decided to lay down her pen.

The history of women's literary relations in Spain and Spanish America is yet to be written. But we can state with some certainty that Sor Juana's knowledge of other women writers, though incomplete, was of enormous importance to her. As Electa Arenal shows, Sor Juana's literary production occurs within a feminine context. Many of her poems refer to women, we owe the publication of her works to the efforts of her friend and protector, the countess of Paredes, and much critical work has been done on Sor Juana by women scholars.[16]

In the *Reply to Sister Filotea* Sor Juana refers to the inspiration she received from books that spoke of learned women of the Bible, of Greece and Rome, and of the Church. This inspiration had nothing to do with the themes of her writing or with the style she adopted, but with something far more basic.[17] With their example, Sor Juana could write without feeling that she was alone and unique in all the world; from these literary and intellectual mothers she received permission to write. But Sor Juana also had to heed the fathers, who, as real and potential representatives of the Inquisition, not only inhibited the sort of writing she was willing to risk, but also made it difficult for her to identify her literary sisters.[18] It was relatively safe for Sor Juana to speak of other learned nuns, and she defends her literary efforts by referring to three of her near contemporaries. The names of Saint Theresa, the nun of Agreda (on whom King Philip relied for spiritual and political advice), and the poet Sor María de la Antigua all appear in the *Reply to Sister Filotea* as examples of Church-approved writing nuns.

Sor Juana's intellectual autobiography reveals that she feared the Inquisition, which, among other things, banned the importation of novels to the New World. Though many novels did enter Mexico surreptitiously, we do not know if Sor Juana was aware of the novelist who most closely shared her protofeminist beliefs: María de Zayas y Sotomayor. It would have been imprudent to mention having read Zayas's *Novelas ejemplares y amorosas* (Amorous and exemplary tales) or her *Desengaños amorosos* (Love's disillusionment), and Sor Juana explicitly states that she wished to avoid problems with the Inquisition. This is a sad story no matter how we read it. If Sor Juana knew of Zayas's works she had to suppress her knowledge of this sister voice; and if the ban on prose fiction kept Zayas's work out of America, she did not even know that such a voice existed. For feminist critics and literary historians the story of Zayas and Sor Juana is emblematic of the fragmentation of women's literary history in the Spanish speaking world: two protofeminist writers, one Mexican, the other Spanish, whose works have survived, both wanted a community of women writers that would justify themselves, but a relationship between the two was prohibited.

This example demonstrates how narrow the Hispanic context has been for literary women. The creation of a community of women writers requires broader vision. Sophia Brenner was Swedish, Protestant, married, and the mother of seventeen. She lived on the other side of the world, but she shared with Sor Juana the desire to be remembered as a poet.[19] Ironically, the distance between Sor Juana and Sophia Brenner made their relationship, however tenuous, possible. Sor Juana would not have dared associate with a Protestant woman if the latter had lived closer. By revising one of her own poems and sending it across the ocean, Sor Juana could, without much apparent effort or risk, affirm a connection between herself and another woman poet.[20] This act represents Sor Juana's reintegration into the world of letters, a reintegration that depends on the inclusion of another woman writer. In the 1690s Sor Juana existed as a poet because Sophia Brenner existed. Just as Brenner is constituted as a poet by the act of writing and being read, and consolidated as a poet by a poem written in her honor, the writer of the laudatory poem in turn constitutes herself by writing it. It is bracing to realize that in Sweden Sor Juana exists only as the exotic nun who praised Sophia Brenner.

Thanks to Adrienne Rich the notion of re-vision has great resonance among feminist critics, who have taken up the term and used it to fruitful ends, seeing anew the works of women writers and the representation of gender in literature. Critics like Electa Arenal are reassessing Sor Juana's work in this way. The re-vision that Rich calls for, however, is not only critical but also creative. She calls on the writer as well as the critic to see the world anew, to create a feminist vision that will replace the worn-out patriarchal one.[21] In her re-vision Sor Juana did what Rich is asking writers now to do—to look at the world in a new way. Sor Juana, at the time she recast her poem, truly needed to do that. The literary and intellectual world she had so carefully constructed had come apart.[22]

The poem Sor Juana dedicated to Sophia Brenner underwent a literal, old-fashioned rewriting, as well as a Richian re-vision based on a particularly Hispanic sense of *revisión*. Rich, through her etymological archaeology on the English word, encourages critics not simply to take the received meaning of the word, whether it be the traditional one or the new Anglofeminist version. *Re* in Spanish is an augmentative prefix: thus to revise, *re-visar*, suggests not only a looking again, but also a seeing in depth.

As autobiography Sor Juana's poem was violently revised by the events surrounding it. Written to the duchess of Aveyro before 1688, during Sor Juana's years of intellectual stardom, it was a paean to Mexico, to clever women, and to the religion she and the duchess shared. The self-affirmation of that version was in many ways outdated. America was no longer the land of riches occupied by God's chosen. The excessive rains that struck Mexico in 1691 destroyed the harvest and left many starving. Famine affected the political balance and thus contributed to Sor Juana's fall. The verses of the poem concerning the need to divest oneself of one's worldly goods in order to gain Heaven took on new meaning now that Sor Juana had in fact impoverished herself. Imitating Christ's poverty as a rhetorical device was one thing, but actually giving all of one's possessions to the poor was quite another.

Sor Juana herself revised her poem, giving it new depth. Originally it was addressed to a pious, generous, and learned woman of Portugal; in its new version it became a celebration of the woman poet. Sor Juana wrote the first version of this poem to please her friend and patron, the vicereine of New Spain, Doña María Luisa Manrique de Lara, countess of Paredes and cousin of the duchess of Aveyro. The presence of Doña María Luisa, not only as a behind-the-scenes initiator of the encomium but also as a figure present in several of its stanzas, diffuses the focus of the work. The intimate friend, though present only briefly, becomes an alternative object of veneration in the poem. Once she is removed, both as the source of inspiration and as an object of homage, the poem focuses more sharply upon the actual object—now Sophia Brenner rather than the Portuguese duchess.

In his essay on apostrophe, Jonathan Culler notes the form's poetic waste, first discussed by Quintilian.[23] The apostrophe is not directed to the poem's judge but rather to a distant being who is unable to reward the poetic effort. Sor Juana knew this well—it is a fundamental motif of this poem. But apostrophe is one thing and homage is another, and the recipient of the former is not necessarily the recipient of the latter. In this poem, the duchess of Aveyro is the target of the apostrophe, while the countess of Paredes is the object of the homage.

The duchess of Aveyro functions as a screen that obscures the eulogy's true object—a screen upon which this eulogy is projected.[24] María de Guadalupe Alencastre is a medium that receives the eulogy only to reflect it back on the third figure, the judge whom the poet sought to please with the composition of the poem. It is worth noting that Sor Juana evokes the countess of Paredes with the same direct language she uses in her self-affirmation. It is unnecessary to compare the vicereine with classical goddesses because her name is its own hyperbole.

> La siempre divina Lysi
> aquella en cuyo semblante
> ríe el día, que obscurece
> a los días naturales;
> Mi señora la Condesa
> de Paredes (aquí calle
> mi voz, que dicho su nombre
> no hay alabanzas capaces.)
>
> [The ever divine Lysi
> in whose countenance
> the day laughs, who obscures
> nature's days;
> My lady Countess
> of Paredes (here I must silence
> my voice, for once her name is mentioned
> there are no praises high enough.)][25]

If the countess of Paredes is the true recipient of the poem, the hymn to America is not the insulting challenge that it seems on first reading. Though as vicereine, María Luisa Manrique is the representative of Spanish authority, as "Lysi" she is the friend and protector of Sor Juana in America. The egotistical charge of the poem is diffused since Sor Juana's patriotism would have been agreeable to the vicereine. Similarly, the encomium to the duchess of Aveyro must be sincere if it is to please her cousin. That Sor Juana did consider María de Guadalupe de Alencastre's charity, piety, and intellect worthy of praise is demonstrated by her invocation of the duchess as an exemplar of learned women in the *Reply to Sor Filotea*.

When the poem was revised to accommodate Sophia Brenner, the seven quatrains praising the beauty and charm of the vicereine in the original poem shrank to a vague and vestigial two stanzas (29 and 30), reducing the judge to a shadowy, genderless cipher. As the judge becomes vestigial and the screen figure is recovered as sole recipient of the eulogy, the focus of the poem shifts to the speaker's situation as a Creole and a Catholic. Tension arises between the poetic "I" who continually threatens to become the center of the work both as subject and object, and the "you," a stranger to whom the encomium is directed. But if Sophia Brenner cannot offer a tangible reward to Sor Juana, she can serve her in another way. Once the judge is gone, Sor Juana can use the eulogized object to constitute herself as poet. Culler describes how this works.

> We might posit [a] level of reading where the vocative of apostrophe is a device which the poetic voice uses to establish with an object a relationship which helps to constitute him. The object is treated as a subject, an I which implies a certain type of you in return. One who successfully invokes nature is one to whom nature might, in its turn, speak. He makes himself poet, visionary. Thus, invocation is a figure of vocation.[26]

In this case, the invocation of the woman poet to her counterpart, with its hyperbolic praise, consolidates the right of both women to claim the title "poet." The encomium to Sophia Brenner is another reaffirmation of Sor Juana's faith—faith in herself as American, Catholic, and poet. She affirms the first two by contrasting herself to the Swedish poet and the last by identifying with her. For her part, Sophia Brenner receives an encomium that establishes her in her own country as a poet known in the most far-flung reaches of the world.

Like a photograph and its negative, whose images have the same semantic content, the poem remains a celebration of the woman poet, whether we foreground the self-centered digressions or the eulogy to Brenner. Sor Juana's text is reminiscent of the familiar figure-and-ground optical illusions that by themselves subordinate neither figure nor ground. By leaving it to the reader to reconcile the struggle for supremacy or coexistence between the two, the poet sets up a must-win situation. If the tension is resolved in favor of coexistence, the oscillating images of two women poets remain, each empowering the other. If the reader insists on foregrounding either of them, she still finds the celebration of the woman writer.

The contrast between figure (the homage to Brenner) and ground (the celebration of self) is rendered in the gulf separating the two women. Not only does an ocean come between them, creating for the cloistered nun and the mother of seventeen an insurmountable physical distance, but the religious difference, to which Sor Juana calls attention by celebrating her status as a Catholic nun, implicitly defines them as enemies. Though the speaker does not make this religious animosity explicit, she does reveal another form of hostility. Brenner belongs to the Old World that the speaker blames for exploiting the riches of America. The speaker presents herself as a proud daughter of the New World, in opposition to a spent and decadent Europe.

The contrast between the poem's figure and its ground is deliberately sharp, but Sor Juana implicitly rejects any notion of contradiction between them. A traditional reading could easily condemn the poem for its apparent internal inconsistency. How can the speaker both praise Brenner and displace her by celebrating in herself those elements that differentiate her from the Swedish poet? A feminist reader, however, understands that a celebration of self need not occur at the expense of another. The familiar self/other split of Western thought, in which a separate self is formulated in opposition to a distinct and subordinate other, loses meaning when the "self" formulated is from the group culturally defined as "other."[27] In fact, in order to recognize the worth of women other than herself, any woman must recognize her own worth. Conversely, the success of another woman confirms the possibility of one's own success. The tension between the homage to Brenner and the celebration of self thus becomes energy that fuels both projects.

Sor Juana simultaneously affirms herself as an American and a nun and as a woman and a poet. Her celebration of her Americanness and of her religion affirm her identity by locating her in a particular community. Her place in the world as a woman poet is confirmed by her participation in another community—that of other women poets, who need be neither American nor Catholic. Her connection to Sophia Brenner is in no way diminished by their differences, since part of the strength of their connection derives from elements of their lives that do not coincide. Writing is the way to overcome these differences, though it does not eliminate them.[28] It is precisely because she can declare her individuality, indicating the places where she and Brenner diverge, that Sor Juana can affirm Brenner and herself as women and poets in a community of distinct but connected beings.

# Notes

1. Sor Juana Inés de la Cruz, "Romance," in *Poetiske Dikter*, by Sophia Elisabeth Brenner (Stockholm: Julius Georg Matthiae, 1713), my translation. The *romance* is perhaps the most common traditional Spanish verse form. It consists of an indeterminate even number of eight syllable lines with assonant rhyme in the even lines (abcbdb, etc.). The grouping of lines into quatrains, as Sor Juana does in this *romance*, is not a requirement of the form.

2. Doña Catalina was not a great poet (as her sonnet praising Fru Brenner reveals), but she serves as one more sign of the "subterranean" existence of Spanish women of letters. Doña Catalina's sonnet, with modernized spelling and punctuation, follows:

Alaba a la Señora
Sophia Elisabeth Brenner,
única poetisa wisi-goda
MUSA DECIMA
con este soneto

Décima musa Sophia hija muy fuerte
    de Apolo, y que las nueve aún más divina,
porque fuese del sol la Benjamina,
    le nació en la vejez de su norte.
¡Qué sutil, si discurre! ¡qué elocuente
    si razona! ¡si habla, qué atina!
y si canta de amor, cuerda es tan fina,
    que no se oye rozada en lo indecente.
¡Afrenta de Homeros! ese talento
    que no le desperdicias, que le empleas.
Aun le envidia mi amor que es lince a tiento.
    ¡O! ¡que enhorabuena peregrina seas!
por, si vago tal vez mi pensamiento
    encontrase contigo en sus ideas.


                Praising the Lady
            Sophia Elisabeth Brenner,
            Unique Visigothic Poetess
                TENTH MUSE
                with this Sonnet

Tenth Muse, Sophia, strong daughter of Apollo,
even more heavenly than the other nine,
because the youngest was daughter of the Sun,
born to him in old age, of his Northstar.
    How subtle when she talks! How eloquent
when she argues! when she speaks, how well she aims!
And when she sings of love, the string is so fine
that it is never heard plucked in indecency.
    Affront to all Homers! That talent you do not deny
that you employ, even my love, a lynx
groping in the dark, envies you it.
    Oh! May you go as a Pilgrim!
So, if my thought perhaps should wander
it might meet you in its Ideas.


3. I found the volume containing Sor Juana's text in the library at the University of Umeå, Sweden, after a conversation with Docent Tore Wretö, my colleague in the Department of Literature at that university. We had been talking about our literary interests when Mr. Wretö mentioned a curiosity that might interest me: a poem written by a Mexican nun that was published in a volume of poetry from the beginning of the eighteenth century. Half an hour later I was holding the 1713 edition of Sophia Elisabeth Brenner's poetry, and it contained what I had hoped to find: a poem by Sor Juana Inés de la Cruz. The ease with which I obtained Brenner's book was not repeated in my efforts to find Alfonso Méndez Plancarte's edition of Sor Juana's complete works. I wanted to see if I had found an unknown text. Despite the help of the excellent librarians in Umeå, it was almost two months before I obtained the necessary volumes.

4. In conversations with Karin Westman Berg and Magnus Von Platen, Umeå, Sweden, 1983.

5. Sor Juana Inés de la Cruz, "Romance."

6. Brenner, *Poetiske*.

7. Catalina de Alfaro Fernández de Córdoba, "Soneto," in *Inundación Castálida*, by Sor Juana Inés de la Cruz (Madrid, 1689).

8. There is no reference to the Swedish version of the *romance* either in Méndez Plancarte's prologue or his abundant notes. It is also to be noted that Méndez Plancarte discusses the probability of the existence of works by Sor Juana that he did not locate. It is not unlikely that an encomium buried in a Swedish volume might well have eluded him.

For dating of the variant, see Alfonso Méndez Plancarte, "Notas," in *Obras completas*, by Sor Juana Inés de la Cruz, ed. Alfonso Méndez Plancarte (México: Fondo de Cultura Económica, 1951), 1:412.

9. Octavio Paz, "Sor Juana Inés de la Cruz," in *Las peras del olmo* (México: Imprenta Universitaria, 1957), p. 35n. Sor Juana's life grows dark in this period. The canonizers paint chiaroscuro images of mortified flesh, rooms bare of their furnishings, a praying figure in the shadows of the chapel. Sor Juana suddenly reappears in 1695, in the midst of the epidemic disease that killed her, caring for her sisters in religion. Her death has been called glorious by scholars bent on seeing her life as a progression toward Christian perfection, and her ultimate sacrifice is proof to them that she attained a sort of imitation of Christ. Octavio Paz, in *Sor Juana Inés de la Cruz o Las trampas de la fe* (Barcelona: Seix Barral, 1982), on the other hand, concentrates on Sor Juana's forced submission to authority and on her consequent renunciation of her intellectual pursuits and writing. That accomplished, the actual death seems anticlimactic. Paz is coy when he talks about it, saying merely that he recognizes Sor Juana's lucidity in her death, hinting that she died a suicide (p. 599).

10. In the *Reply*, Sor Juana tells of how deprivation of books made her ill and how the attempt to keep her from thinking merely by removing her books and scientific equipment was misguided and simpleminded. These statements commonly have been read as indications of how necessary learning was to her, but they might also be understood as threats. Sor Juana knew that merely depriving herself of her books and instruments would not turn her into a mindless woman of simple faith, and her recollection of past illness that resulted from a lack of access to books suggests that selling them now would mean condemning herself to future physical suffering. Indeed, at about the same time she disposed of her library and scientific equipment so that the money might be given to the poor, Sor Juana gave herself over to self-flagellation, in what seems to have been an attempt to beat herself "senseless." These measures did not work perfectly, and she was drawn back into her old world. After her death a fragmentary poem written in 1692 was found in Sor Juana's cell. This text, in praise of the laudatory poets of the world, is a final justification of much of her own writing, including the poem dedicated to Sophia Brenner. Yet Sor Juana never really returned to writing or to the life of the mind. As Octavio Paz notes in *Sor Juana Inés de la Cruz* (p. 603) the text of Sor Juana's 1694 blood-signed reaffirmation of faith, the single public break in her silence, is devoid of spirit. It is as if the life blood had been drained from her writing to appear, melodramatically, as her signature.

11. The project of collecting homages took many years, and Urban Hjärne and Elias Brenner gathered them from all over Europe. The majority of these texts are undated, and of the few that are, almost all postdate Sor Juana's death. There is one, however, dated 1683. Sophia Brenner was not only Sweden's first woman poet, she was also the first Swedish poet of either gender whose work was collected and published during her lifetime. It must have been extremely important to gather as many encomia as possible to justify this break with a tradition that had reserved the consecration of the poet until after his lifetime. (I do not use the masculine pronoun generically here.)

12. Until a short time ago, the majority of critics believed that Sor Juana's confessor, Antonio Núñez de Miranda, abandoned Sor Juana after the publication of the *Carta Atenagórica*, but Aureliano Tapia Méndez's recent book, *Autodefensa espiritual de Sor Juana* (Monterrey, Nuevo León, 1981), reviewed by Octavio Paz in *Vuelta* 78 (May 1988): 46–49, shows that it was Sor Juana who broke with Father Núñez, nearly a decade before, in favor of a less strict confessor who would allow her to dedicate herself to writing for the court. Sor Juana's ability in effect to dismiss her confessor is an indication of the autonomy she enjoyed in the 1680s.

13. On the other hand, Sor Juana's beauty served her well,—first to gain favor in the viceregal court, and even after her death as generations of literary historians and critics have been entranced by her face as much as by her mind. Sor Juana's ambivalence toward her beauty is reflected in her attitude toward her portraits. She consented to be painted twice, in sumptuous dress, and used the portraits in her poetry as objects of meditation on the transitory nature of a beauty to which she consents.

14. In the Portuguese version she refers to portraits she might have seen of María de Guadalupe Alencastre.

15. The Spanish *cielo* means both "sky" and "Heaven."

16. Electa Arenal, "The Convent as Catalyst for Autonomy: Two Hispanic Nuns of the Seventeenth Century," in *Women in Hispanic Literature: Icons and Fallen Idols*, ed. Beth Miller (Berkeley: University of California Press, 1983), pp. 166–67.

17. Sor Juana Inés de la Cruz, *Respuesta a Sor Filotea de la Cruz, Obras completas*, ed. Alberto G. Salceda (México: Fondo de Cultura Económica, 1957), 4:440–75.

18. In the *Reply* Sor Juana claims she avoided theological writing in order to avoid problems with the Inquisition; this may have been an excuse to write the worldly sort of literature that most interested her. But her able rebuttal of Vieyra's sermon suggests that in more liberal times Sor Juana might have written more extensively on theological issues.

19. One of Brenner's poems, in *Poetiske Dikter*, p. 211, which is dedicated to a woman painter, catalogues the difficulties of being a woman artist but it concludes with: "Though art has cost us some few hours / There is no better way to be remembered. / Let envy sneer, let death's scythe pull / Your brushes and my pen fear neither" (my translation).

20. I would like to thank Cheri Register for pointing out to me that Sor Juana's device of using and rupturing hyperbolic convention, which makes it appear that her praise of Sophia Brenner is not genuine, minimizes the risk in praising this Protestant woman of letters; therefore both the poem's digressions and its feigned humility may be a kind of subversion.

21. Adrienne Rich, "When We Dead Awaken: Writing as Re-Vision," in *On Lies, Secrets, and Silence. Selected Prose 1966–1978* (New York: Norton, 1979), pp. 33–49.

22. Luckily, before that happened the countess of Paredes took Sor Juana's complete literary works back to Spain with her and had them published and the bishop of Puebla had troubled himself to print the *Carta Atenagórica*. The *Reply to Sister Filotea* was another fortuitous survival. It made its way to Spain and was published in 1700, along with the rest of Sor Juana's collected works. At least one of Sor Juana's essays—on music—has been lost, and her entire correspondence has disappeared.

23. Jonathan Culler, *The Pursuit of Signs. Semiotics, Literature, and Deconstruction* (London: Routledge and Kegan Paul, 1981), p. 135.

24. The concept of screen character comes from Shoshana Felman's excellent study of Balzac's *Girl with the Golden Eyes*, "Rereading Femininity," *Yale French Studies. Feminist Readings: French Texts/American Contexts* 62 (1981): 19–44.

25. Sor Juana Inés de la Cruz, "Romance 37," *Obras completas*, ed. Alfonso Méndez Plancarte (México: Fondo de Cultura Económica, 1951), 1:100–05; my translation.

26. Culler, *Pursuit*, p. 142. Culler refers here specifically to invocations of natural forces, but the invocation of another poet can be understood to function in this way as well.

27. Carolyn Whitbeck's "A Different Reality: Feminist Ontology," in *Beyond Domination: New Perspectives on Women and Philosophy*, ed. Carol C. Gould (Boston: Routledge and Kegan Paul, 1984), pp. 64–88, suggests replacing the familiar Western ontology, which defines the self as necessarily separate from, and by extension in opposition to, the other, with an ontology that places the self on a continuum that blurs, rather than defines, boundaries between self and other.

28. Audre Lorde, *Sister Outsider* (Trumansburg, N.Y.: Crossing Press, 1984), teaches us that we need to celebrate our differences, for in them we find our strength.

# Sara de Ibáñez: The Battle to Create

## MARCI STERNHEIM

The battle to create is one of the dominant themes in the poetry of Sara de Ibáñez (Uruguay, 1909–71), beginning with her first book *Canto* (Song, 1940; prologue by Pablo Neruda) and continuing throughout her eight subsequent works, including the *Canto póstumo* [Posthumous song] collection published in 1973. But it is in her beautiful and disturbing book-length poem *La batalla* [The battle, 1967] that this theme receives its most ardent treatment.[1] Here, Ibáñez explores the romantic myth of the artist who heroically and willingly suffers in the name of his vocation. Yet as the traditional glorification of the artistic agon patently ignores the fact that the female artist, too, does battle with her creative calling, Ibáñez seeks to reinterpret this struggle from a highly personal point of view.

In all of her poetry, Ibáñez searches for her own voice and place in the literary tradition. Seeking out female as well as male models for her poetry, Ibáñez read deeply into the work of the poets of her Hispanic heritage, as well as those of the French symbolist movement, only to be disappointed by the dearth of women's writing available. Despite her affectionate poetic references to the twentieth-century *poetisas* and a profound connection to Sor Juana Inés de la Cruz,[2] it is clear that the female canon was not broad enough to influence or inspire her. Thus of necessity, Ibáñez had to depend heavily on male models. The ambivalence, which I find poignantly apparent in her work, of being a woman writing in a largely male tradition, comes through in her consistent use of the male voice as her poetic persona. There is a compelling androgynous tension to her poetry since the mask of this masculine "yo" does not hide, and I believe, was never intended to hide, the female sensibility directing it. This tension becomes very clear in *La batalla*.

As Ibáñez is not a well-known poet, some background on her might offer a context within which to read the poetic analysis that follows. In her native Uruguay Ibáñez's poetry has been lavishly praised and awarded prizes, and she has attained the status of a national treasure. Elsewhere in the Hispanic world, however (despite the fact that she has been anthologized[3]), she remains largely undiscovered or unread.[4] The propitious circumstances of her literary connections—she was married to the Uruguayan critic Roberto Ibáñez and was discovered and promoted by Pablo Neruda—as well as her undeniable talent, should have assured her much more fame and critical attention than she has received in the last forty years. Nevertheless, she has been overlooked for two rather unfortunate reasons. First, Ibáñez is considered a "poet's poet": her rigorous baroque form and syntax coupled with her allusive symbolist- and surrealist-inspired imagery are so demanding that they defy the attempts of all but the most serious readers—students of esoteric poetry or poets themselves. To call her a poet's poet is a euphemistic way of saying that her work is too hermetic and difficult to be read for pleasure. While it is true that she is not immediately accessible, I contend that a slow, careful reading of Ibáñez's poetry reveals a profound, exciting talent and yields wonderful rewards.

The second and perhaps more significant reason that Ibáñez is not read is that her poetry has consistently defied the traditional categories of literary history. As a woman born early in this century in the Río Platense region of South America she should be considered part of the group known as the *poetisas*, which includes poets such as Delmira Agustini, Alfonsina Storni, Juana de Ibarbourou, and Gabriela Mistral. Ibáñez held a great respect for these women, and her poetry acknowledges a certain debt to them; yet her work is so different, stylistically and thematically, from theirs that she cannot be classed among them. Literary critics have ghettoized these women by removing them from the mainstream (i.e., male) literary tradition. Ibáñez has been further marginalized because she does not fit into the *poetisa* category and never has been considered seriously in any other way.

Ibáñez's poetry makes great sense when read in the context of twentieth-century Hispanic literature once we realize that she is neither an unreadable poet nor an inexplicable literary anomaly. As a student of the rich Hispanic avant-garde tradition that flourished in the 1920s, Ibáñez was directly influenced by the poets of this movement and their work. Like other poets of her generation—most notably José Lezama Lima—Ibáñez's literary consciousness was formed both by her reading of the avant-garde's reevaluation of baroque literature as well as by the vanguard tendencies (ultraism, creationism, surrealism, etc.) of the time. Like Lezama, Ibáñez is thus best defined as an "original epigone" of the avant-garde and is most properly categorized as a poet whose work reflects one of the most important literary traditions since the avant-garde: the neobaroque. The literary syncretism—an intermingling of various literary styles from several different periods—that is the hallmark of the neobaroque is a definitive feature of *La batalla*.

*La batalla* might be described best as a contemporary epic poem: it is Ibáñez's version of the *Iliad* for the twentieth-century poet-warrior. The poem begins and ends with reminiscences of classical Greek epic and dramatic poetry. The first poem, "Atalaya," recalls the opening of Aeschylus's *Agamemnon*, and the last, "Apoteosis," reinterprets the traditional deification of the hero who has died in battle—this time the poet-warrior is immortalized through his poetic creation (reminding the reader of the "apotheosis of Homer" theme popular in neoclassical art). At times the violent imagery of the battle that rages within the protagonist invokes Baudelaire's masochistic "L'Héautontimorouménos," itself a reference to a play by Terence. Even one of the poem's central images, the inscrutable sphinx, alludes to Sophocles. Yet thematically, in its depiction of the existential crisis faced by the artist in society, and stylistically, in its use of abstraction and multiple voices to express the various facets of a single consciousness, *La batalla* is a very modern work.

Because of its epic quality, this poem is also certainly the most anecdotal of Ibáñez's work and, thus, in many ways the most accessible. With the opening poem, "Atalaya," the reader enters *in medias res* and is introduced to the protagonist: a lonely, suffering warrior who seems to have no free will. Some other force, the ubiquitous "they," apparently rules his destiny.

### The Lookout

They have left me on this cold wall
with my shadow cinched to my throat
where a live song oppresses its bursting torment
until itself broken up into red-hot coals.
I, here while sleep strips them
and in dreams they eat their deceitful berry
rising up in the veins of the dawn
gray pablum of their futile smile;
I, here while the innocent wisemen
and the calm ones of the crackling house
sleeping below, and learning the cold,
rest in their narrow marble;
I am here tossed by the black wind
I, forsaken by the smell of night
my hair fused into roots
that open and open turbulent oozings;
I, alone among condemned planets
who in search of their bones commit transgressions
—the age of the world in this poor blood
that cries out among the breaks in its history—
I am here disturbed by the fierce peace
which appeases me with the wisdom of tympans
sensing, among the absent essences,
the hard frenzy of the swords;
I am here watching, the deserted eyes

burnt by the breath of nothingness,
the black ships and the black fields
empty of their gold and their defects.
I, here trembling in the blind vigil
surrounded by a dream of a hundred wings
clothed by my cry I kneel
while my blood flies in the airy snow.

On this cold wall they gather me up.
I hear the sound of their measured steps.
The night sings in flight for my death,
and the dawn emerges from my white face.

[Atalaya

Sobre este muro frío me han dejado
con la sombra ceñida a la garganta
donde oprime sus brotes de tormenta
un canto vivo hasta quebrarse en ascuas.
Yo aquí mientras el sueño los despoja
y en sueños comen su mentida baya
para erguirse en las venas de la aurora
pábulo gris de su sonrisa vana;
yo aquí mientras los sabios inocentes
y los tranquilos de crujiente casa
durmiendo abajo, y aprendiendo el frío
de sus angostos mármoles descansan;
Yo aquí volteado por el viento negro
que el olor de la noche desampara,
los cabellos fundidos en raíces
que van abriendo turbulentas lamas;
yo solo entre planetas condenados
que en busca de sus huesos se desmandan
—la edad del mundo en esta pobre sangre
que entre las quiebras de su historia clama—
yo aquí turbado por la paz bravía
que con sagaces témpanos me aplaca,
sintiendo entre las médulas ausentes
el duro frenesí de las espadas;
yo aquí velando, los desiertos ojos
quemados por el soplo de la nada,
las negras naves y los negros campos
vacíos de sus oros y sus lacras.
Yo aquí temblando en la vigilia ciega
rodeado por un sueño de cien alas,
vestido por mi llanto me arrodillo
mientras vuela mi sangre en nieve airada.

Sobre este muro frío me recobran.
Oigo el rumor de los medidos pasos.
Canta la noche en fuga por mi muerte,
y el alba sale de mi rostro blanco.][5]

This poem, consisting of blank verse endecasyllables—a Spanish form that imitates the noble severity of Greco-Latin poetry—divides naturally into stanzas of four lines that, although they are not indicated typographically, each express one complete thought. The complicated baroque syntax emphasizes the feelings of frustration, torment, and oppression experienced by the warrior who is held captive. In the first four lines, the coldness of the wall and the images of constriction contrast sharply with the "canto vivo," the live song that is about to burst out, like fiery embers, from the warrior's throat. Following this are seven reminders of the warrior's presence that insistently affirm his existence by projecting him into the void of darkness surrounding him. The anaphoric repetition of "I, here" ["yo aquí"], slightly varied by the single "I, alone" ["yo solo"] is a well-noted technique in modern poetry that Leo Spitzer in his classic monograph has identified as "chaotic enumeration" ["enumeración caótica"], and that Severo Sarduy, who finds it a distinguishing characteristic of neobaroque poetry, has called "absurd enumeration" ["enumeración disparatada"].[6] A technique that both Federico García Lorca and Pablo Neruda have used in their most surrealistic works, it indicates both the fervent desire and the frustrating inability to control the emotions and circumstances that have engendered the particular poetic situation. Ibáñez frequently uses the device in her work and achieves a considerable dramatic effect with it, as one can see in "Atalaya". The variation of "yo solo" disrupts the potential lulling effect of the repetition, and, because it stands out from the visual pattern, it also functions metalinguistically to reinforce the notion of the soldier's solitariness.

The battle of the poet-warrior is entirely existential in nature. He must be constantly on guard against "the breath of nothingness" ["soplo de la nada"] that threatens at any moment to snuff out his life—to extinguish his fiery "canto vivo." The existential aspect of the poem becomes even clearer when the soldier complains bitterly of his fate and contrasts it with the cruelly thoughtless activity of the rest of the world at the same moment. The others sleep in innocence or carry on with their lives, ignorant of the crisis at hand that requires the warrior to be both their "atalaya"— watchguard—and sacrificial victim. He does not have the luxury of simply closing his eyes like "the innocent wisemen" ["los sabios inocentes"] to awaken "in the veins of dawn" ["en las venas de la aurora"]. He must remain awake; he must see all and maintain his vigil. To assure this, the elements of nature make him appropriately uncomfortable: the cold chills him, the wind batters him, the darkness makes him tremble. Ibáñez is a master at not merely describing nature but using it as an animate force. Elsewhere she demonstrates her skill in celebrating the pastoral, benevolent side of nature;[7] here in *La batalla* she takes a much more cynical view of its powers.

One of the more curious images in this particular poem (13–16) implies that the wind has blown the warrior's hair in such a way that it has given him a horrific, even Medusa-like appearance. This subtle feminine reference to long hair and Medusa immediately is undercut by the jarring masculine "yo solo." The entire poem of La batalla (characteristic of all of Ibáñez's work) is replete with equally discreet but powerful references to an androgynous orientation on the part of the protagonist. This certainly is due to the influence of French symbolist and fin-de-siècle decadent literature. Yet while the decadents used the androgyne as a symbol of the way modern society has corrupted the natural relationship between man and woman,[8] Ibáñez's use of androgyny does away with all sense of decadent perversity. In La batalla the androgynous voice is a technical device that allows the "yo" as warrior to function as a trope for the poetic and existential struggle, while the "yo" as poet is the voice of Ibáñez inserting herself into the text.

Ibáñez uses several techniques to make known her female presence through the warrior mask. In the second poem of the section entitled "Prisoners" ["Prisioneros"], for example, the poet speaks of the enemy who rides "on a palfrey of fire" ["sobre un palafrén de fuego," p. 50]. The poem is a romance written in arte menor and typically uses repetition to enhance its sing-song rhythmic quality. Thus, "palafrén de fuego" is mentioned in every stanza, and the idea that "the enemy ignores me / and I am his prisoner" ["el enemigo me ignora / y yo soy su prisionero"] is repeated twice. Knowing from an earlier poem in the sequence, entitled "Intimate conflict" ["Intima lid"] and written in the self-deprecating manner of Baudelaire's "L'Héautontimorouménos," that the protagonist is his own enemy—"I and I, enemy and enemy / I fall in my fount and devour myself" ["yo y yo, enemigo y enemigo / caigo en mi fuente y me devoro," p.43], one can therefore assume that he is also a prisoner of himself. But Ibáñez's choice of a "palafrén" as the protagonist's mount reveals her identification with him, with the enemy, and with the prisoner. A "palafrén" is a palfrey, a particularly gentle breed of horse usually used by women. Ibáñez therefore indicates that she is the poet-warrior, she is her own enemy and her own prisoner of this battle.

The use of the soldier persona and masculine voice in La batalla attests to the fact that like all good baroque poets Ibáñez insists upon using a mask that distances her as a poet from her creation. Yet in her work as a whole, her symbolist and surrealist influences give that mask enough transparency so that the poetry conforms to the more contemporary trend toward confessionalism. Ibáñez's confessions, however, are not always easily deciphered. One theme consistently discernible throughout all of her work, and most apparent in La batalla, emphasizes the difficulty involved in creating poetry. Above all, Ibáñez's work is about writing itself. The obsta-

cles she alludes to are problems that all writers confront: lack of creativity
and the inability to articulate certain ideas, as well as doubts about the
existential value of creative work. Yet there are also more subtle references that suggest her status as a woman interferes significantly with the
creative process. This assertion is difficult to corroborate biographically
since her public image as a loving wife and devoted mother is unassailable,
given the dearth of personal material available on her. But a close reading
of all the poetry suggests that her domestic role inhibited her ability to
write. In the first poem of Ibáñez's first book *Canto*, the struggle to create
is already a salient theme in her writing. While Ibáñez does not couch her
poetic voice in the masculine, neither does she identify it as feminine. The
neuter or androgynous point of view she chooses is, however, belied by
references to the domestic claustrophobia that makes her work a battle:

Island on Land

To the north the cold and its broken jasmine.
To the east a nightingale full of thorns.
To the south the rose in its airy mines,
and to the west a withdrawn road.

To the north an angel lies muzzled.
To the east the weeping arranges its mist.
To the south my tender sheaf of fine palms,
and to the west my door and my care.

The flight of a cloud or a sigh was able to
trace this fine frontier
that unwaning, defends my refuge.

A distant punishing wave bursts out
and bites your stranger's forgetfulness,
my dry island in the middle of battle.


[Isla en la tierra

Al norte el frío y su jazmín quebrado.
Al este un ruiseñor lleno de espinas.
Al sur la rosa en sus aéreas minas,
y al oeste un camino ensimismado.

Al norte un ángel yace amordazado.
Al este el llanto ordena sus neblinas.
Al sur mi tierno haz de palmas finas,
y al oeste mi puerta y mi cuidado.

Pudo un vuelo de nube o de suspiro

trazar esa finísima frontera
que defiende sin mengua mi retiro.

Un lejano castigo de ola estalla
y muerde tus olvidos de extranjera
mi isla seca en mitad de la batalla.][9]

This impeccable sonnet must have seemed unintelligible when it was first published. It was probably thought of as an elegant yet mysterious artifact, a poem in which the impressively original images overshadowed and therefore excused the seemingly unfocused content. But in light of the poetry that followed, it became clear that this poem articulates, in cloaked fashion, the frustration that Ibáñez must have experienced as a housewife trying to fulfill her poetic vocation. The poem refers to an island on land; the four directions might be the four walls of a house, a study, or some other private space. The images in the first stanza begin as cruel and violent manifestations of nature. But in the third stanza there is a fanciful reference to the aerial quality of the rose—a typically baroque synaesthetic confusion has taken place between the second and third lines attributing the rose's thorns to the nightingale and the bird's capacity for flight to the flower. The rose, which appears constantly throughout Ibáñez's work, usually symbolizes poetic creativity. Sometimes the writing is thorny and difficult, but at other times it flows easily allowing its airy, ethereal mines to be tapped. The last line of this stanza offers personal insight into the poet's vocation: it is, for Ibáñez, a very lonely, introspective path.

In the second stanza the images of the north and east seem to refer to the struggle for self-expression. Curiously, however, all the images in this stanza also could be related to children. Thus the "angel [that] lies muzzled" ["ángel [que] yace amordazado"] might be either an inhibited muse or sleeping child, while the "weeping [that] arranges its mist" ["llanto [que] ordena sus neblinas"] might refer to either the urgent need to organize confused thoughts or the plaint of an unhappy child. Once again in this stanza the south refers to creativity since the "haz" easily could be a sheaf of papers. But in its tenderness and with the description of "fine palms" ["palmas finas"], it could also be a metaphor for the hands of a small child. The west is again self-referential: it leads to doors and to the poet's outside cares.

The third stanza describes the extreme tenuousness of this privacy: a passing cloud or sigh could easily break down the "fine frontier" ["finísima frontera"] (a door or wall) between the poet's creative work and her domestic concerns. The choice is not an easy one. In the last stanza a wave of guilt, of self-chastisement breaks over the poet as she realizes that she is a stranger in both the creative world and the domestic realm. At war with herself and her responsibilities, she seeks refuge in her island. The fact that it is dry makes its meaning ambiguous: a dry island is a safe place, but not necessarily an oasis of creativity.

The main difference between "Isla en la tierra" and *La batalla* has to do with the way in which Ibáñez moves away from the solipsistic interpretation of the difficulty of poetic creation to a more generous vision of the creative struggle. This follows the tendency of her work to become more civically and socially oriented as in *Canto a Montevideo* [Song for Montevideo, 1941], *Hora ciega* [Blind hour, 1943], and *Apocalípsis XX* [Apocalypse XX, 1970].[10] Ibáñez by no means withdraws herself entirely from her writing; on the contrary, she remains a very strong presence in the text. Yet even without wholly diminishing the personal aspect, she most certainly makes a shift to the outside, gestures toward the universal. Thus instead of concentrating on her immediate domestic situation, as in many of the poems in *Canto*, in *La batalla* Ibáñez employs more transcendent symbols for her imagery; the military battle and the warrior figure attest to this.

Another universal symbol that Ibáñez exploits is that of the sphinx. Part woman, part beast, this mythical creature embodies many of the poet's conflicts, thus becoming the physical representation of the poet-warrior's abstract enemies. Her presence is ubiquitous; try as he might, the poet-warrior cannot escape her.

> And in front of my face—cold combat—
> motionless cascade, furious light,
> the hard glance of the sphinx
> curdles my blood drop by drop.

> [Y ante mi rostro—duelo frío—
> cascada inmóvil, luz furiosa,
> el duro ojeo de la esfinge
> cuaja mi sangre gota a gota.]
> ("Combate oscuro," p. 11)

The sphinx is a symbol of enigma; she jealously harbors the secret of life's meaning. In this regard, her presence tortures the poet-warrior who, more than anything else, wants to understand and fulfill his purpose in life—the creation of poetry.

> Here I gasp for breath until I exhaust my blood
> my sad lance thrust into the song
> until the maternal sphinx hurls the fruit
> of her old womb to ruin.

> [Aquí jadeo hasta acabar la sangre
> clavada en la canción mi lanza triste
> hasta que el fruto de su viejo vientre
> lance al estrago la materna esfinge.]
> ("Combate imposible," p. 15)

Here the poet-warrior is wounded in his most vulnerable organ—his song, his poem. Unable to "write" himself out of danger, he realizes that he will be stuck until the sphinx destroys the fruit of her womb. But the sphinx is a mother image, and though she appears to be a grotesque monster of nature, she would never go against her maternal instinct. Thus the poet-warrior is condemned to an eternity in torturous limbo—unable to write, unable to die.

The sphinx as a central image works well with the poem's classical motif and also serves as a modern figure of sexual ambivalence. It once again reveals the influence of symbolist and decadent imagery on Ibáñez. The *fin-de-siècle* writers—influenced by the symbolists, especially Baudelaire, and disseminated in the Hispanic literary world through Darío and *modernismo*—changed the traditional notion of woman by making her other than feminine: the androgyne is a masculinized woman (or a feminized man); the *femme fatale* becomes a vampire-like creature.[11] Ibáñez's portrayal of the sphinx incorporates both her emasculating power and seductive character, making her, once again, both an enemy to and a part of the poet-warrior.

By the end of the poem, however, the poet-warrior dies: "God has seen him frequently in battle" ["Dios le ha visto frecuente en la batalla," p. 59] under all types of circumstances and sees him "dead, finally, of splendid wounds" ["muerto al fin, de espléndidas heridas," p. 59]. The warrior's apotheosis is quite different from what one would expect: it is recounted in the first person and it chronicles his falling away into oblivion rather than his rising up for deification. Certainly there is an existential irony here— the struggle, all that torture and suffering, yet the poet-warrior dies. There is some consolation to be found in the mesmerizing final lines of the poem, which consciously respond to both Huidobro's *Altazor* (1931) and Gorosti-za's *Muerte sin fin* (1939).

> My blood falls, finally, on the gaudy
> purple branches where the wind dies
> and, unravelling their wounded strength,
> the blind dahlias intone the night.
> I fall without end, gripped by a sweet sorrow
> like the sharp transit of the rose,
> and beneath my abolished knees
> oases explode, and lips
> sing in chorus of my return; ears,
> open in the midst of a meadow
> worked in musical gold, listen:
> —flowers rise up without fear—they listen
> to a single sound, and forever they listen.
>
> [Cae mi sangre, por fin, en las fastuosas
> purpúreas ramas donde muere el viento
> y desenvuelven su llagado brío

las dalias ciegas que la noche entonan.
Caigo sin fin, asido a un dulce duelo
como el tránsito agudo de la rosa,
y bajo mis rodillas abolidas
estallan los oasis, y los labios
corean mi retorno; los oidos
abiertos en mitad de una pradera
labrada en oro musical, escuchan:
—las flores suben sin temor—escuchan:
un solo son, y para siempre escuchan.]
("Apoteosis," p. 61)

Ultimately, death is not scorned here nor looked upon bitterly; the warrior's body might fail, but the poet's work lives on.

In *La batalla*, Ibáñez takes the reader through every aspect of a battle: there are different "combats" ["combates"], "challenges" ["desafíos"], a "bivouac" ["vivac"]; prisoners are taken, messages are transmitted, rounds are made. The warrior fights internal as well as external enemies, he is wounded, he dies, and he is resurrected through his poetic creation. Throughout the work Ibáñez dazzles readers with a stunning array of poems that invoke every great style in Hispanic literature. There are sonnets, *romances*, *cuartetos*, and free verse; she is alternately baroque, surreal, modernist, and mystical. Her poetic versatility is astounding—very few poets in this century have demonstrated such a remarkable capacity for rhyme, meter, and form. The use of so many different poetic forms and styles is integral to what Ibáñez has set out to do in *La batalla*.

Through her poetic virtuosity Ibáñez wages her own creative struggle on masculine territory: the verbal androgyny that is the hallmark of her poetry is set in strong relief as the poem's pervasive female sensibility. The result is a work in which Ibáñez boldly establishes her poetic presence in relation to the predominantly male tradition in which she wrote, achieving, in the maturity of her poetic voice, a compelling *ars poetica*. In a very real sense, Ibáñez fought splendidly in the battle and emerged victorious from the war.

## Notes

1. This essay is part of a larger study I am conducting on the neobaroque poetry of Sara de Ibáñez. I would like to thank Manuel Ulacia Altolaguirre and the late Emir Rodríguez Monegal, to whom I dedicate the essay, for their help and encouragement in its preparation.

2. Sor Juana was undoubtedly Ibáñez's touchstone poet as her fourteen-sonnet cycle, "Tránsito de Sor Juana Inés" (in *Las estaciones y otros poemas* [México: Tezontle, 1957], pp. 71–82), attests.

3. See, for example, Ginés de Albareda and Francisco Garfías, eds., *Antología de la poesía hispanoamericana: Uruguay* (Madrid: Biblioteca Nueva, 1968), pp. 401–409; Domingo Luis Bordoli, ed., *Antología de la poesía uruguaya contemporánea* (Montevideo: Universidad de la República, 1966), 2: 74–89; Helen Ferro, ed., *Antología comentada de la poesía hispanoamericana. Tendencias, temas, evolución* (New York: Las Américas, 1965), pp. 346–48; and José Olivio Jiménez, ed., *Antología de la poesía hispanoamericana contemporánea 1914–1970* (Madrid: Alianza, 1971), pp. 404–14.

4. The critical bibliography on Ibáñez—scant to say the least—consists of the following studies: Lídice Gómez Mango, ed., *Homenaje a Sara de Ibáñez* (Montevideo: Fundación de Cultura, 1971); Roberto Ibáñez, "Anticipo, Umbral y Envío," in *Canto póstumo*, by Sara de Ibáñez (Buenos Aires: Losada, 1973); Alejandro Paternain, "La raíz del fuego (la imagen en Sara de Ibáñez)," *Cuadernos Americanos* 164 (1968): 242–61 and "Sara de Ibáñez: La esfera cerrada (notas para *Canto póstumo*)," *Cuadernos Americanos* 184 (1972): 181–208; Sylvia Puentes de Oyenard, *Sara de Ibáñez: Testimonio lírico* (Montevideo: Intendencia Municipal de Tacuarembo, 1980); Eliana Suárez Rivero, "La invención barroca en dos poemas de Sara de Ibáñez," in *XVII Congreso del Instituto Internacional de Literatura Iberoamericana* (Madrid: Cultura Hispánica del Centro Iberoamericano de Cooperación, Universidad Complutense de Madrid, 1978), pp. 597–611; and Celia de Zapata, "Dos poetas de América: Juana de Asbaje y Sara de Ibáñez," in *XVII Congreso del Instituto Internacional de Literatura Iberoamericana*, pp. 257–67.

5. Sara de Ibáñez, "Atalaya," in *La batalla* (Buenos Aires: Losada, 1967), pp. 7–18. All subsequent quotations will appear in the text. As far as I know, Ibáñez's poetry has not been translated into English. The translations I have done for this essay are more literal than interpretive and are intended to aid the reader with Ibáñez's very difficult poetry.

6. See Leo Spitzer, *La enumeración caótica en la poesía moderna* (Buenos Aires: Facultad de Filosofía y Letras, 1945) and Severo Sarduy, "El barroco y el neobarroco," in *América Latina en su literatura*, ed. César Fernández Moreno (México: Siglo XXI-Unesco, 1972), p. 170.

7. See Ibáñez's *Pastoral* (México: Ediciones Cuadernos Americanos, 1948), as well as *Las estaciones y otros poemas*.

8. George Ross Ridge, *The Hero in French Decadent Literature* (Athens: University of Georgia Press, 1961), p. 128.

9. Sara de Ibáñez, *Canto*, prologue by Pablo Neruda (Buenos Aires: Losada, 1970), pp. 13–14.

10. Sara de Ibáñez, *Canto a Montevideo* (Montevideo: Intendencia Municipal, 1941); *Hora ciega* (Buenos Aires: Losada, 1943); *Apocalípsis XX* (Caracas: Monte Avila, 1970).

11. Ridge, *The Hero*, p. 141. See also Baudelaire's "Les Métamorphoses du vampire," *Les Fleurs du mal, Oeuvres complètes*, ed. Claude Pichois (Paris: Gallimard, 1975).

# Feminine Space in the Poetry of
# Clementina Arderiu

## TERESA VILARÓS-SOLER

One of the goals of certain feminist critics is to present texts written by women as significantly different from texts written by men. Sandra Gilbert and Susan Gubar, for instance, posit that because women live in a patriarchal society, their writing is bound to adopt a number of characteristic strategies in order to counterbalance patriarchal oppression.[1] The existence of feminine writing, though, is a notion that can be challenged. Annette Kolodny wonders whether the so-called "typically feminine" really enables women's writing to be labeled "writing in the feminine mode," and she goes on to say: "If we insist on discovering something we can clearly label as a 'feminine mode,' then we are honor-bound, also, to delineate its counterpart, 'the masculine mode.'"[2]

Kolodny's remark, although pertinent, does not question the very existence of those "typically feminine" features that clearly differentiate women from men. Julia Kristeva, on the other hand, does not accept such a distinction: "To believe that one 'is a woman' is almost as absurd and obscurantist as to believe that one 'is a man'" ["Se croire 'être une femme' c'est presque aussi absurde et obscurantiste que de se croire 'être un homme'"].[3] In "Féminité et écriture" [Femininity and writing] she says: "Nothing in women's past or present publications permits us to affirm that there is a feminine writing [écriture féminine]" ["Rien ne me semble permettre, des publications des femmes passées ou récentes, d'affirmer qu'il existe une écriture féminine"].[4]

A definitive answer to these questions cannot be given, which means that the door is open for a feminist rethinking of writing. Julia Kristeva herself admits that it is possible to find in most texts written by women recurrent thematic and stylistic patterns.[5] For one thing, as Patricia Meyer Spacks says, "women have characteristically concerned themselves with matters more or less peripheral to male concerns."[6] This trait, which in itself has encouraged the masculine critic to discredit women's texts, is especially notable in the work of women poets. Feminine poetry generally has been regarded by the masculine critic as "nonprofessional," a poetry busy with small, often trivial feelings alien to the interests and activities of the majority of men. This indeed has happened with the work of Clementina Arderiu. Although not completely forgotten by the traditional critic, her poetry until now has been interpreted and classified as plain, unimportant, and preoccupied only with everyday matters rather than with the lofty realm of the (masculine) Ideal.[7]

Admittedly, then, it is difficult and probably impossible to validate the notion of feminine writing. Nevertheless, a new world of interpretation opens up if one approaches a text written by a woman—Arderiu in my case—with a feminist will, that is, with a politically motivated intention to retrieve feminine experience from the text. I propose to consider Arderiu with this intention and to discuss her work as feminine according to Hélène Cixous's definition of the term: feminine texts are those that "work on the difference" ["travailler sur la différence"].[8] I will try to uncover what generally has been ignored or hidden from the traditional critic: I will call it "feminine" for the sake of simplicity, but one should keep in mind that "feminine" here relates to the feminine space, the space of difference from masculine-oriented discourse. The acceptance of feminine self-reflection in at least some texts written by women suggests new outlooks and perspectives. A feminist will may well open the way to an interpretation reaching beyond the mere feeling of alterity or otherness recognized by masculine critics.

Viewed in such light, Arderiu's poetry will no longer be considered nonproblematic, calm, and peaceful, which is how masculine critics have defined it. Consider for example the following comment by Joan Teixidor.

> In the poetry of Clementina Arderiu words are very close to the theme, and it is very easy to follow the underlying story, at times terribly clear, terribly defenseless (sic) otherwise. . . . In a very deep and not at all pejorative sense the poetry in question is almost that of an amateur writing at odd moments.

> [Llavors, és clar, les paraules són molt pròximes al tema i és molt fàcil de seguir l'argument subjacent, tan clar de vegades, tan indefens en altres. En un sentit molt profund i gens pejoratiu, és tracta gairebé d'una poesia d'aficionat que s'escriu a estones.]

And elsewhere he says that her poetry is like the illuminatis, untouched by earlier writers ["és excepcional: propi de criatures il.luminades, d'un do molt pur i gens mediatitzat per exemples previs"].[9] In spite of the ease that Teixidor claims in reading Arderiu, his comment reveals a crucial alienation from the texts. Surprised by an apparent and mystifying simplicity, he reacts by assuming it is nonprofessional, inexperienced writing; indeed he nearly apologizes for doing so.

Arderiu's themes are likely to appear amateurish to the masculine critic, if only because they are the themes with which a housewife is generally associated: husband, children, the house, births and deaths in the family, everything that surrounds her in a primary way, like trees, leaves, the sun, and the wind. Amazingly and puzzlingly, the difficult elements of Arderiu's private life—civil war and exile—do not seem to affect the calmness and peacefulness of her poetry, qualities often praised by her critics.[10] Vicente Aleixandre observes that no other poet has evoked the feeling "of a soothing atmosphere, a room where life is the story of long and understanding experience" ["de un clima tranquilizador, de una habitación donde la existencia es un relato de una larga experiencia entendedora"]. José Corredor-Matheos says that Arderiu's long life "does not show any sense of breach of continuity. It gives a clear impression of unity." ["Esta larga trayectoria no ofrece, sin embargo, cortes. La sensación de unidad es clara."] And Joan Fuster thinks that Arderiu's poetry "is of the kind born whole, complete, evidently maintaining the intimate consistency of its identity" ["és d'aquelles que neixen ja complertes i que manté evident la íntima consistencia de la seva entitat"].[11]

Another critical theme regarding Arderiu is the strong divergence between her life and her work: how did Arderiu develop her poetic trajectory in the normal sense, if her private life was not free of troubling complexities? The answer seems to be: because she is a woman. Only a woman, or only Teixidor's "illuminati," can go through life preserving "identity" and "unity," extracting from it only that which is spontaneous, pure, and good. Teixidor comments: "Without dismissing its moral significance, but rather implying it as an ultimate reality transforming everything, I would go so far as to say that this is good poetry." ["Sense fer abstracció d'aquella accepció moral, sinó implicant-la com una última realitat que ho transfigura tot, gosaríem afirmar que aquesta és una poesia bona."][12]

All these conflicts of interpretation indicate an alterity in Arderiu's poetry when set against the assumed poetic canon, a canon that has been defined by masculine standards. But I would rather cancel Arderiu's alterity. I suggest that some of the puzzles and conflicts of Arderiu's poetry would disappear if it is seen as an expression of feminine space—the space that has been given (or left over) to women, a space of difference that consequently remains stubbornly closed off to traditional critical discourse. Women, as Elaine Showalter says, have had to express themselves in a "typically oblique, displaced, ironic and subversive way. One has to read between the lines, in the missed possibilities of the text."[13] A feminist reader appropriates as familiar and her own that "missed possibility," the space of difference alien to the masculine reading.

For Alicia Ostriker the textual expression of feminine space usually has been articulated with a code disguising "passion as piety, rebellion as obedience."[14] Arderiu's work often has been defined as pious in nature. She herself has been described as a devout and—most significantly—submissive woman. I do not suggest we deny the presence of these qualities in her work, but I want to emphasize the anxiety, the sexual feelings, the rebellion, and the passion sometimes hidden under the apparent calmness, obedience, and piety of her poetry.

Arderiu's poetry, although shaped to some extent by Josep Carner, Ausias March, and Joan Maragall, does not follow definite textual-canonical models. It is influenced much more by a feminine and popular oral tradition—nursery rhymes for girls for example—than by specific authors. Rather than engaging previous literary patterns, Arderiu attempts to express a feminine experience, or an experience registered in the feminine space. It is not that she wants her poetry to remain apart from the male reader. Rather, she addresses all of us: "I have written human words . . . I have wanted them . . . clear, precise, for everybody." ["He posat paraules humanes. . . les he cercades. . . clares, justes i de tothom."] But she speaks to us as she can: "My life as a woman, as an ordinary woman like so many other women, has sung deeply and continuously." ["La meva vida de dona com les altres, com tantes altres, ha cantat profundament, continuament."][15] A feminist reading must seize upon that commonality of female experience to contest the masculine critic's claims for interpreting Arderiu's poetry as a poetry of serenity. That serenity that has been linked to identity and unity could be considered a mask capable of revealing the quest for tranquillity, for identity, and for unity. One does not sense calmness, but rather the specific (feminine) movement of the search.

Arderiu's poetry should not be regarded as born whole and complete. From the first poem to the last, there is a constant search for identity: the poet asks herself who she is, who she was, who she will be. As a young woman—"Clementina" in the text—she seeks contentment in sexuality. To achieve fulfillment she will need a man—her lover, her husband-to-be, the "mirror" Clementina cannot imagine herself without. The necessity of a male companion is one of the leitmotifs of Arderiu's work. This can be read as nothing else than submissiveness but it must be remembered that self-sufficiency is of the very essence of masculine power. In Arderiu's continual yearning for a sexually differentiated partner there is the inscription of the feminine space, a space of difference wanting difference. The theme of man as mirror does not suggest a will to identify with man. It does speak of identity encountered in difference, and it does so in the modes of obliquity, irony, and disguise, which for Showalter constitute the code of feminine writing.

The young Clementina writes of her exuberant sexuality in playful, joyful terms. In "El nom" [The name] (p. 36), Clementina depicts her shift from a timid and reserved sexuality to its acceptance as something marvel-

ous and splendid: "Clementina my name is, / Clementina my name was."
["Clementina em dic, / Clementina em deia."] The identity of the name
does not obviate the celebration of the change in being, a change accomplished through love. Not until her lover whispers it in her ear can
Clementina really believe she may still keep her old name. But should we
conclude then that her intimate self-recognition is dependent upon a man's
actions? Why not, if that man signifies celebratory difference and not
penetrating authority? Clementina comes to possess herself by means of
her Other, breaking out of the closure that defined her.

> That name which forged my timidity and later became a sweet whisper on my
> bare lips—I myself used to utter it; now it is my honor and my wonder. No other
> name is so beautiful on earth as this one that my lover sings in my ear and enters
> the hidden shelters of my soul and goes up to my brain and closes my eyelids.

> [Aquell nom que abans
> féu ma timidesa
> i es torna després
> una dolça fressa
> sobre el llavi nu
> —jo mateixa el deia—
> ara m'és honor
> i m'és meravella.
> Cap nom no és tan bell
> damunt de la terra
> com el que l'amat
> em canta a l'orella,
> i entra en els recers
> de l'ànima meva
> i em puja al cervell
> i em clou les parpelles.]

The poem contains obvious sexual imagery presented traditionally: the
name enters through the ear looking for the hidden shelters, etc; but it is
Clementina's name that makes the voyage, even if aided by the masculine
voice. Clementina's sense of wonder does not spring from a scene of
alienation: the experience is not to be translated into terms of power or
possession; the entrance of the name is not penetration. And self-
recognition is not to be interpreted in the fallen and insidious sense of
self-acquisition. Rather, self-recognition is that which moves toward the
cognition of the Other.

The poem that follows, "D'un mateix tany" [Of the same stem] (p. 38),
seems to be an earlier one possibly reflecting a previous experience.
Clementina is talking to her breast, still virgin but ready to be offered,
although already known and explored by her. It is a beautiful poem of
sexual impatience.

Because you are unknown by everybody but me, so shy that the mere mention of Love's name frightens you; because you only have the caress of a linen tunic, oh you, born crowned with a ruby; because you are soft and sweet—June made you ripe—and you remain on the branch and nobody comes to pick you; because yesterday I saw you sad, nearly languid, and because you are lightened up now, like roses and good wine, I will sing your glory, yesterday's and today's.

> [Perque sou inconegudes
> de tothom sino de mi,
> tan tímides que us esglaia
> fins el nom d'Amor veí;
>
> perque haveu sola carícia
> d'una túnica de lli,
> oh vosaltres, que naixíeu
> coronades d'un robí;
>
> perque sou suaus i dolces
> —juny us feia ammadurir—
> i resteu dalt de la branca
> sens que us vinquin a collir;
>
> perque ahir us veia tristes
> i al devora del llanguir,
> i perque ara sou enceses
> com les roses i el bon vi,
>
> cantaré la vostra glòria,
> la d'avui i la d'ahir.]

The movement of the poem, as it rushes syntactically towards its end, reveals a double gesture. By calling attention to and concluding with the last two verses and therefore privileging them as a conclusion, the poem makes the reader focus on that which is denied in the end. In other words, an all-too-obvious urgency directs the reader to question the urgency itself, thereby indicating that the direction of the textual movement may be a mask. The poem's guidance at the level of the *signifiant* turns out to be a misguidance; but then, once this is realized, the misguidance is revealed as a clue to the real textual meaning. This double gesture is in accord with the code of obliquity and irony characteristic of the feminine text.

The poem's conclusion refers to a dual glory of flesh. The glory—the flesh—has been doubled by some sort of temporal gap that is not clarified. There is a yesterday and a today, but the flesh that is ready for sexual enjoyment has not been taken yet. What is this "today" then, where a "lightening-up" can overcome the languidness of frustrated expectation? Notice that this overcoming is not a substitution: the wine and the roses still exist for somebody to respond to them. However, the poem's "today" creates a positive mood toward expectation. It may be that, today, mere waiting has become anticipation. Anticipation is made possible by the poem itself, or better, by the action of writing it, whereby a space is created that ensures that the metaphorical *hortus* of the poem is not to become a wasteland, but rather a home ready to receive a dweller. Writing, because it speaks of glory, transfigures melancholy into anticipation and transforms the empty wait into the expectation of a homecoming. What is awaited is the Other, the sexual difference that can, through its difference, give and take identity. Is the feminine space a space of anticipation? The space of difference is the space of glory.

Delighted anticipation is also at the heart of "Prefigurant" [Foreshadowing]: "I want, I want, I really want / this to be the day / and yet I don't know what I'll do nor would do / if today were the day." ["Jo voldré, jo voldré, jo voldria / que ja fos el dia, / que no se que faré ni faria / si avui fos el dia," pp. 38–39.] The nervous ambiguity of the mood expressed here is not meant to imply ambivalence towards the yielding of self on the wedding night. Rather, it expresses the moment of anxiety prior to the final accepting resolve. Anticipated self-fulfillment does not negate awareness of its finitude: "I present to the purest joy / a 'It doesn't last forever: / it is killed by an ache'." ["Presento a la joia més pura / un 'Sempre no dura: / la mata un dolor'," p. 38.] This awareness, in turn, has nothing to do with fear. On the contrary, it is the sense of intimate union with her beloved that makes possible the cessation of fear.

Path that takes me, when you leave this garden, will you still be as smooth as you are now? . . . Will you be a deadend on the other side and should I be counting my steps already? . . . Your ending would not hurt me any more because my sweet beloved would embrace me and you would take us both in one walking.

[Camí que em menes, quant surtis de l'hort
seràs encara suau com ets ara?
. . . . . . . . . . . . . . . . . . . . . . .
seràs potser a l'altre banda finit
i ja els meus passos podrien comptar-se?
. . . . . . . . . . . . . . . . . . . . . . . . . . . . . .
el teu finar no em doldria ja pus
que el dolç amat s'enllaçava a mes vores
i amb un mateix caminar te'ns enduus.] (p. 41)

The completed union of love has man and woman face-to-face, living in a realm where no worldly considerations seem to matter: "I am already yours and you are mine and the whole world is left outside." ["Jo ja sóc teva i tú ja ets meu, / i tot el món es queda fora," p. 54.] Curiously, it is from this moment that Arderiu's poetry becomes richer in themes and more intensely preoccupied with the expression of feminine experience. Supported by her love, the poet frees herself for the exploration and writing of her life as an ordinary woman.

Corredor-Matheos talks about Arderiu's poetry in terms of interior space.

> The poet has a space of her own: her inner world, sometimes identified with a house [her home]. . . . Inside herself she seems to feel out of danger. . . although her refuge is in reality a battlefield.

> [El poeta tiene un ámbito que le es propio: su mundo interior, que en ocasiones es identificado con su casa. . . . Dentro de ella misma parece sentirse a salvo. . . pero ese refugio mismo es, en realidad, el campo donde se libra el combate.][16]

The house is a metaphor for the poet's feminine space, but a metaphor that still must be constructed. This is no easy task: "With pain I was building my house, there is no other more skillful [female] worker." ["Amb dolor jo ma casa bastia / i altre obrera més habil no hi ha," p. 53]. Construction work is typically a man's job. The man builds the house that is then given to the woman who cares for it. But Arderiu reverses the convention with a pungency that is lost in translation by using the feminine gender in "obrera." "Casa" means both "house" and "home." House-building is also home-making. Arderiu displaces the traditional image according to which women may only inhabit a borrowed space. The house—the home—is of her own making, which in the first place means it is primarily her own space.

The house is a metaphor for her inner world. But the inner world, for a poet, is that which is expressed in poetry. House-building and home-making are both metaphors for writing. Writing, also traditionally a man's job, is therefore also displaced from its customary position: writing as house-building must relinquish its power to the claim of writing as home-making. Both coexist in fruitful but painful tension in Arderiu's textual space.

This tension is inscribed in the fact that Arderiu writes most of her poems on themes dealing with traditional female occupations and concerns. It is as if the very courage necessary to take on the act of writing, the weaving of texts rather than pullovers, becomes exhausted in itself and is not strong enough to reach out into the world—that outside world that is paradoxically closed off to women as mere inhabitants of the house, mere home-makers. But at this point it is inappropriate to talk of exhaustion and strength. Such talk would necessarily fall into a binary discourse, legitimizing anew the traditional masculine pretension that it takes something women do not have to face and master whatever is "out there."

On the other hand, a paradox must be acknowledged in Arderiu's text. In the assumption of writing—i.e., house-building—as writing—i.e., home-making—there is a sense in which "house-building" is an act of creation, whereas "home-making" situates itself in the order of preservation and care. Gilbert and Gubar have defined a woman's anxiety in the face of creation as a "radical fear that she cannot create, that because she can never be a 'precursor' the act of writing will isolate or destroy her."[17] The acceptance of "house-building" as the real or even primary name for writing situates woman in a position of subordination and necessary submission—just as another often-used metaphor, creation as insemination, places man as biologically better, gifted, and therefore privileged.

The fear of the radical impossibility of creation is indeed a part of Arderiu's work. And as such it is coupled with the textual recognition that creation—literary creation at least—belongs to man. Married to the renowned poet Carles Riba, Arderiu needed his support in order to write. She says: "when I was afraid of something" ["quan tenia alguna por"] her husband would tell her "Make verses. . . my friend, / you get better at it every day" ["Fes versos. . . amiga mia / que cada dia els fas millor," p. 58]. But again the irony and obliquity of Arderiu arise here in the self-mocking tone. By pointing out her submission to husbandly paternalism, she also denounces and thereby escapes it. Anxiety was there, but also writing—her writing.

The following verses, however, seem to imply no ambiguity:

> I write my verses for my husband, who welcomes them as offspring coming out of my body, where I have put in a lot of myself.

> [Jo faig els versos per l'espòs
> que me'ls acull com la fillada
> que fos sortida del meu cos
> i molt de mi hi hagués posat.] (p. 58)

Here is a straightforward declaration of surrender to her husband's horizon of acceptance. Arderiu's verses, as soon as they are born, are turned over to her husband; this turning over will reproduce a patriarchal possession. Arderiu compares her verses to her children and apparently gives both to her husband in similar ways. The familial terms used in the comparison (verses as offspring for the husband) establish a particular frame Arderiu could not avoid: the patriarchal bourgeois family that has existed since the nineteenth century. Therefore once this new space is created by Arderiu herself, her husband will inevitably appropriate and dispose of her verses as he would of sons: giving them a name, grafting onto them the mark of his possession. The notion of creation as delivery is clouded in these verses by the implication that there was a previous insemination carried out by her husband thus making the words possible. Arderiu, who had rejected

fear and resolutely embraced an authentic Otherness in her love relationship, gives in to masculine authority when writing is concerned. It
might seem, then, that Arderiu's feminine space of difference is lost when
articulated into a family situation because she yields to the fear of poetry as
creation. She jeopardizes her house and her home, surrendering her verses
to her husband and to the masculine appropriation implied.

On the other hand, perhaps surrender does not necessarily imply
appropriation. If, for example, Arderiu's turning over her verses to her
husband is seen as a gift rather than a dispossession, a whole different
meaning is provided. The line, "I write my verses for my husband" ["Jo
faig els versos per l'espòs"] states clearly that she makes her verses for him
and gives them to him. And by giving, an implicitly subversive move here,
she removes herself from all possible connections to masculine authority.
The paradox is solved by setting up a gift exchange system that, according
to Lewis Hyde, is mostly feminine: "Gift exchange is a 'female' commerce
and gifts a 'female' property."[18] Arderiu's is a total giving. As such, it will
move in a particular way. As Hyde writes, "the only essential is this: *the
gift must always move*," and it moves "from plenty to emptiness. It seeks
the barren, the arid, the stuck, and the poor." Two things are at stake for
Arderiu. First, in giving her verses to her husband as a gift and in comparing them to her children, she fills an emptiness instead of feeling one.
There is no insemination or submission because the setting is different.
Second, the motion of the gift requires that the husband should give her
verses to somebody else to be consumed or read (as Hyde says, "a gift must
always be used up, consumed, eaten").[19] When he does this, he in turn will
give up all authority and be engaged in the gift exchange system—that is,
in her space.

Arderiu did on occasion write about her husband: "Let him take care of
his own accounts, as I do mine" ["Que ell es dugui els seus comptes / com
me'ls duc jo," p. 59]. These two verses frequently have been cited as proof
of Arderiu's poetic independence with respect to her husband. At this
level, though, independence remains problematic and can only be adduced
at the cost of suppressing textual evidence that cannot be ignored. If the
verses are seen as arising from her feminine space, they might reveal that
what happens to her verses, ultimately, is not something she wants to control. She is definitely not willing to "play masculine." She will give (she will
write) but not by the masculine rules, as Arderiu herself states in another
poem, "Revolta" [Rebellion]. The poem, in my view, is the most radical of
her texts, and it discloses a refusal to give in to masculine law at a deeper
level.

Whether it was or wasn't necessary?—Poetry. Bound by unknown laws?
—Grimaces.

[Si calia no calia?
—Poesia.
Lligada per lleis ignotes?
—Ganyotes.] (p. 102)

('Ganyotes' also means 'faces' as in the expression 'to make faces'.) She is going to play her game according to her own rules, and the last irony is that there may be no rules at all. This, of course, raises the question of whether writing is possible. To that question there is only one answer in Arderiu's texts: *ganyotes*.

# Notes

I thank Noël Valis for all her encouragement and friendship. All citations in the text refer to Clementina Arderiu, *Obra poètica*, Pròleg de Joan Teixidor (Barcelona: Ed. 62, 1973).

1. I am referring here to the book by Sandra Gilbert and Susan Gubar, *The Madwoman in the Attic* (1979; reprint, New Haven: Yale University Press, 1984).
2. Annette Kolodny, "Some Notes on Defining a 'Feminist Literary Criticism'," *Critical Inquiry* 2 (1975): 78.
3. Julia Kristeva, "La femme, ce n'est jamais ça," *Tel Quel* 59 (Fall 1974): 20. All translations are my own.
4. Kristeva, "Féminité et écriture: En réponse à deux questions sur *Polylogue*," *Revue des sciences humaines* 168 (1977): 496.
5. Kristeva writes in "Féminité et écriture":

> In the long run, it is possible to distinguish, in books written by women, stylistic and thematic features which might suggest a woman's specific relation towards *écriture*. But it is difficult for me at present to tell if these features come from a specific femaleness, from a sociocultural marginality or, more simply, from a certain structure (i.e., hysterical) favored today in the way things function and having to do with the whole array of feminine possibilities.

> [Il est éventuellement possible de distinguer, dans des livres écrits par des femmes, des particularités stylistiques et thématiques, à partir desquelles on pourrait ensuite essayer de dégager un rapport spécifique des femmes à l'écriture. Mais il me semble difficile, actuellement, en parlant de ces particularités, de dire si elles relèvent d'une spécificité proprement féminine, d'une marginalité socioculturelle, ou plus simplement d'une certaine structure (par exemple hystérique) favorisée par le marché contemporain à partir de l'ensemble des potentialités féminines.] (p. 496)

6. Patricia Meyer Spacks, *The Female Imagination* (New York: Avon Books, 1975), p. 6.
7. The only critical approach I know of that does not follow the traditional pattern is the introduction by María Mercè Marsal, to be found in Arderiu's last anthology of poems, *Contraclaror* (Barcelona: La Sal, 1985).
8. Hélène Cixous, "Entretien avec Françoise van Rossum-Guyon," *Revue des sciences humaines* 168 (1977): 480. I should point out that Hélène Cixous does

reject the term "écriture féminine." Toril Moi, in *Sexual / Textual Politics: Feminist Literary Theory* (London and New York: Methuen, 1985), has written about her.

> Cixous is adamant that even the term *écriture féminine* or "feminine writing" is abhorrent to her, since terms like "masculine" and "feminine" themselves imprison us within a binary logic, within the "classical vision of sexual opposition between men and women" (Conley, 129). She has therefore chosen to speak either of a "writing said to be feminine" (or masculine) or, more recently, of a "decipheral libidinal femininity which can be read in writing produced by a male or a female" (Conley, 129). It is not, apparently, the empirical sex of the author that matters, but the kind of writing at stake (p. 108).

(Toril Moi is quoting Verena Andermatt Conley, *Hélène Cixous: Writing the Feminine* [Lincoln and London: University of Nebraska Press, 1984].)

9. Joan Teixidor, Introduction to *Obra poètica*, by Clementina Arderiu, p. 8.

10. Two collections of poems by Clementina Arderiu, *Sentiment de guerra* and *Sentiment d'exili*, explicitly deal with her experience with war and exile. Critics do not deny this fact, but they continue to consider her poems, as a whole, as an expression of tranquillity. Thus Vicente Aleixandre will say: "Clementina Arderiu gives us serenity" ["Clementina Arderiu nos concede seguridad"]. Of course, the term "us" refers primarily to men. (Aleixandre, "Clementina Arderiu, de cerca," *Insula* 95 [15 November 1953]: 1.)

11. Aleixandre, "Clementina Arderiu," p. 3; José Corredor-Matheos, Introduction to *Antología*, by Clementina Arderiu (Barcelona: Plaza y Janés, 1982), p. 11; Joan Fuster, Introduction to *Es a dir*, by Clementina Arderiu (Barcelona: Ossa Menor, 1959), p. 2.

12. Teixidor, Introduction to *Obra poètica*, p. 10.

13. Elaine Showalter, "Toward a Feminist Poetics," in *The New Feminist Criticism*, ed. Elaine Showalter (New York: Pantheon Books, 1985), p. 138.

14. Alicia Ostriker, "The Thieves of Language," in *The New Feminist Criticism*, p. 315.

15. Arderiu, *Obra poètica*.

16. Corredor-Matheos, Introduction to *Antología*, pp. 14–15.

17. Gilbert and Gubar, *The Madwoman*, p. 49.

18. I am using the notion of "gift" as it is described by Lewis Hyde in *The Gift. Imagination and the Erotic Life of Property* (New York: Random House, 1983). In the chapter "A Female Property" he discusses gender and sex in a gift exchange system. It is important to note that in qualifying the gift exchange as a "female" commerce, I am restricting the term to the monogamic family structure of Western culture. As Hyde says, "gift exchange is not aboriginally, nor yet universally, a 'female' commerce. There have always been times and there are still places where both men and women are sensitive to the functions of gift exchange, and where a man in particular may acquire his masculinity, or affirm it, through the bestowal of gifts" (p. 104).

19. Hyde, *The Gift*, pp. 4, 24, 8.

# Plant Imagery, Subversion, and Feminine Dependency: Josefina Aldecoa, Carmen Martín Gaite, and Maria Antònia Oliver

## JANET PÉREZ

Since the publication of *Tiempo de silencio* [Time of silence] in 1962, certain important Spanish novelists have striven to expose the falseness and corruption of traditional Spanish literary language (e.g., Juan Goytisolo in *Reivindicación del Conde don Julián* [Revindication of Count Julian]). An underlying aim has been to demonstrate the extent to which Spain's moral, political, and socioeconomic institutions are based upon a euphemistic rhetoric that conceals a closed culture and a system of relationships of exploitation and dependency or submission. Whether attacking official political rhetoric directly (cf. Ramón Nieto in *La señorita* [Young miss]) or exposing dependence upon conventional signs (cf. Delibes in *Parábola del náufrago* [Parable of a shipwreck]), "mainstream" novelists of the post-neorealist era call attention to underlying forces that negate freedom and threaten the achievement of true autonomy. Certainly, sexual inequality is one of these forces, and both female dependency and the universe of discourse that buttresses masculine supremacy are targeted in the three works analyzed here. The extent to which their effect and impact depend upon the subverting of a specific aspect of dominant discourse brings Aldecoa, Martín Gaite, and Oliver together with those cited and with others of similar bent in the assault upon traditional language and its underlying presuppositions.

Plant and flower images frequently are used by a male-defined culture to disguise or idealize feminine dependence and psychosocial restrictions upon the female. From the pale wildwood flower to the shrinking violet, clinging vine, and the blushing rose (not to mention the wallflower), botanical metaphors for the female are a common part of daily communication. Somewhat more aggressive, erotically charged, edible images allude to girls or women as objects ready for devouring: a real peach, a cute tomato, a hot potato. The list might be endless, but the point is that in the oral tradition as in popular culture, such patronizing depiction by the reigning hierarchy has been for centuries a recurrent sign of woman's less-than-equal status. Examples of such imagery are numerous enough that to examine even a representative sample might constitute a book-length study. This essay is limited to an examination of how three very different Spanish women writers use plant imagery as metaphors or analogues of the feminine condition, with particular reference to the problem of feminine dependence versus female autonomy. In each of the works examined, the problem is related specifically to singleness (not necessarily spinsterhood, for one woman is a widow, two are separated from their husbands, and another—who later marries—has rejected provincial domesticity to become a university student). The equation of women and plants, while common to all three writers, differs in degree of development both quantitatively (i.e., extent and visibility) and qualitatively (i.e., subtlety versus specificity, and whether the metaphoric relationship remains figurative or becomes literal). In all cases, the plant imagery points to dependency as a barrier to autonomy, self-realization, and satisfaction.

La enredadera[1], the first novel of Josefina R[odríguez] Aldecoa, published in 1984, provides the most extended and varied use of the patronizing and paternalistic "clinging vine" image. Enredadera is defined on the frontispiece of the novel: "a voluminous or climbing plant which becomes entangled in other plants, trees, or any support whatever" ["planta de tamaño voluble o trepador que se enreda en matas o arbustos o en un soporte cualquiera"]. The phrase "any support whatever" is most relevant to the novelist's implicit (and occasionally explicit) symbolism—an artistic representation of woman's dependence upon man, be it economic, psychological, legal, emotional, or otherwise. This phrase assists in unveiling the ideologies underlying the text, subtly illuminating the protagonists' struggles with tradition.

Aldecoa (who took a seemingly unfeminist step in adopting her late husband's surname) presents the somewhat parallel biographies of two women, Clara and Julia. Their lives are not absolutely parallel, for at some points they converge (e.g., they live in different centuries in the same house; each is separated from her husband and estranged from her only child; and they have similar perceptions and sentiments). In other ways, the two women differ significantly: they live very different lives almost one hundred years apart. Nineteenth-century Clara has only one love, the husband who abandoned her when she was unable to bear more children; twentieth-century Julia—who has left her husband to pursue her own career and self-realization—has had many lovers. Clara's inability to give her husband a son rendered her life a failure (in the eyes of her husband, her father, much of society, and ultimately herself). Julia bore a son, but lost him for reasons not entirely clear: alienation, lack of communication,

lack of commitment. Despite variations in levels of consciousness and abili-
ties to cope, both women are torn by ontological anxieties, riddled by internal contradictions, and bound by restrictive codes that obstruct self-
definition. Both struggle during adolescence with the desire to reject the
constraints of the feminine condition, eventually making accommodations
thereto. Both marriages end in alienation and estrangement, and both
struggle through midlife crises precipitated by problems of female aging.
However, Clara is inactive, unworldly, resigned, and dies young, while
Julia—active, willful, worldly, and involved—barely shows signs of aging
at forty. The convergences and divergences of the two women's lives are
reinforced artistically by flower imagery. Convergences emphasize generic
or archetypal aspects of the feminine condition, while divergences point
out how that condition has changed through generations.

Flowers abound in the novel, as do flower scents and colors. Often, they
function as objective correlatives of significant experiences or events. Elsewhere, they serve as a contrast that ironically highlights half-conscious
feminine sentiments of alienation, or as intensifiers that underscore loneliness, isolation, helplessness. Aldecoa refers to an impressive variety of
plants and flowers, and frequent descriptive passages attest to her garden-
ing knowledge (e.g., "drops of water trembled on the terse petals;
thousands of tiny tight nipples which emerged from the stalk to reach their
dome-like perfection" ["Las gotas de agua temblaban en los pétalos tersos;
millares de apretados pedúnculos que emergían del tallo hasta alcanzar su
perfección de cúpula"], p. 117). Although sometimes the flowers seem to
exercise a largely decorative function, elsewhere they are artfully and
completely integrated into the action and repeatedly intervene in the outcome. It is not on this level that the plant imagery is most significant,
however; rather, it is via a subtle, implicit subversion of traditional discourse, a demythification of ossified concepts of the feminine role, and a
break with archetypal patterns of silent submission that plant and flower
imagery becomes part of Aldecoa's most subversive statement.

Specific, overt identifications of the feminine with flower imagery occur
with sufficient regularity to prevent misreading by even the most naïve
reader. These are found especially in relation to Clara, whose husband, a
millionaire *indiano*, spared no cost in planning a sumptuous park and
botanical garden for all seasons:

> . . . because you must always be surrounded by flowers, Clara. Primroses on the
> April lawn. Fuchsias, *lantanas*, roses in summertime. Every possible color of
> roses for you, Clara, flowers year-round, yet none a more beautiful flower than
> you, Clara.

> [ . . . porque tú, Clara, siempre has de tener flores a tu alrededor. Prímulas, en el
> césped de abril. Fucsias, lantanas, rosas en verano. Rosas de todos los colores

para ti, Clara; flores todo el año, aunque ninguna flor mejor que tú, Clara.] (p. 123)

As if this identification were not sufficiently explicit, Andrés (an amateur botanist) names a hybrid rose that he has invented in honor of his bride: "Red outside and progressively lighter-colored toward the centre. Andrés named it 'Clara'." ["Roja por fuera y cada vez más clara por dentro. 'Clara', la bautizó Andrés."] (p. 60)

Since Julia is more autonomous and independent, equating her with flowers is accomplished more subtly and implicitly. For example, she needs sunshine and hates the cold (pp. 17, 28, 48), a trait shared with Clara (cf. p. 14). Elsewhere, fading flowers ("two fainting red chrysanthemums" ["dos crisantemos rojos . . . desmayados"]) become a mirror for Julia's fatigue and signs of aging (p. 195).[2] Not only are the female protagonists themselves identified with blossoms, but the reverse is also true (i.e., flowers are perceived as women). Julia perceives the greenhouse as a harem, where the insect who violates its privacy will die: "it will die without escaping the harem" ["morirá sin salir del serallo"] (p. 64). Continuing her inversion of the metaphoric equation, she likewise views the greenhouse as a nunnery:

> The door enclosing the suffocating interior, the flowers, the painful sensation of being in a cloister made her think of a church. "Nuns," she decided absurdly, "they look like young nuns, inviolable beauties enclosed forever."

> [La puerta cerrada, sobre el sofocante interior, las flores, la angustiosa sensación de claustro, le hizo pensar en una iglesia. "Monjas," decidió absurdamente, "parecen monjas jóvenes, bellezas inviolables, encerradas para siempre."] (p. 64)

Although the foregoing metaphor humanizes the flowers, in other rhetorical figures the transformation makes of plants an abstract, menacing force: "a vegetal fate" ["destino vegetal"] (p. 18); "a vegetal siege" ["asedio vegetal"] (p. 48); "a vegetal aggressiveness" ["agresividad vegetal"] (p. 64). Aldecoa thus extends the bounds of conventional imagery and clichés that reflect constrictions upon women and constructs a mirror for the imprisoning forces with which traditional society has surrounded the female. The negative side of the coin is revealed, with a range of ominous and menacing connotations that are threatening by virtue of their abstractness. This abstract rhetorical operation portrays love as a plant (p. 202), and the death of Clara's father is made visible via a description of the unkempt, neglected garden of her paternal home (p. 144). These examples illustrate the extent to which Aldecoa has interwoven flowers, trees, and other plant imagery with the fabric of the narrative.

Certain equations between Clara and roses are of symbolic interest, serving as contrapuntal emphasis for the two most important moments of her life, which can be equated retrospectively with triumph and despair, fertility and sterility, plentitude and emptiness: the yellow silk dress covered with lifelike, handmade roses (designed by Andrés for Clara) is linked inseparably with fulfillment of love and realization of her male-defined role of child-bearer:

> When Andrés helped me to undress and the dress stretched out at my feet like a carpet of roses, I took advantage of the opportunity to announce the hope, the first suspicion, the almost-certainty that his love had blossomed in my womb.
>
> [Cuando Andrés me ayudaba a desvestirme y el traje se quedó extendido a mis pies como una alfombra de rosas, aproveché yo para anunciarle la esperanza, la primera sospecha, la certeza casi de que su amor se había cumplido en mis entrañas.] (p. 140)

These yellow roses are the favorite flower of Lucía, Clara's daughter (p. 60). Given the symbolic correspondence between Clara and the rose, it becomes possible to dilucidate the otherwise hermetic significance of Andrés's final gift. After years of estrangement when Clara was left sterile by complications following Lucía's birth, Andrés sought a reconciliation with his still-beautiful, ever-faithful wife. He presents a brooch as a token of his sentiment that is described by Clara years later as "a hardened rose of rubies" ["rosa cuajada de rubíes"] (p. 184). Clara's aversion to this gem appears to be rooted in her association of its scarlet glint with the drunken light in her husband's reddened eyes, which "for the first time seemed to me hard and malevolent" ["me parecían por primera vez duros y malvados"] (p. 185). Although she does not verbalize her insight, Clara understands that the brooch emblemizes her sterility, and that she, too, is a stone flower that has only cold beauty but will never bear fruit. Thus Clara interprets the brooch as an accusation: "Andrés left you because you couldn't give him a son" ["te dejó Andrés porque no le diste hijo varón"] (p. 186).

It is not only women who are portrayed through botanical images. Trees, many in bloom, are not simply an addition to the flower motifs but function as a complementary metaphor of maleness. Besides being a phallic symbol, the tree represents protection and support. Furthermore, its symbolic masculinity is recognized in popular, male-dominated phrases such as "strong as an oak" or "the sheltering pine." The two men who play the most important roles in the novel—Clara's husband and Julia's lover—are each associated at first with trees and repeatedly thereafter with the activity of planting them: "'I'm going to plant some trees', Andrés would say" ["'Voy a plantar árboles', decía (Andrés)"] (p. 29). In a similarly metonymic activity, Juan first appears straightening young trees blown down by a recent storm: "I'm going to plant more [trees]. This whole side . . ." ["Voy a plantar más. Toda esta ladera . . ."] (p. 25). Both Andrés and Juan (his grandson) are further identified with trees by having abandoned civilization and family disappointments for refuge in the forest solitude of Braña Nueva.

The imagery of woman as a clinging vine and man as a supportive tree reflects perceptions of a male-dominated society that justifies its limitation of feminine options and freedoms in the name of protection and support. Julia becomes latently aware of this early on, at first reacting positively to paternal sheltering but later refusing to continue to pay the tribute of submission and dependency. As a child, Julia imagined herself to be a squirrel, taking refuge in a huge tree trunk (i.e. patriarchal protectiveness). "The tree—hickory, oak, chestnut—meant solidity and refuge, a challenge to visible enemies, wind, rain and snow." ["El árbol, haya, roble, castaño, significaba solidez y abrigo, desafío a los enemigos visibles, el viento, la lluvia, la nieve."] (p. 32) A few years later, Julia—who from adolescence rejected the monotonous domesticity and servitude she perceived as the prevailing lot of women in the provinces—wrote a schoolgirl essay explaining why she would like to be a tree (pp. 83–84) (i.e., assume masculine strength and power). This essay finds its complement in the lecture that she struggles to compose following her break with Juan. "To be a woman in a man's world; that was the idea which had pursued her continually from the moment she agreed to give the lecture." ["Ser mujer en un mundo de hombres; ésa era la idea que le perseguía todo el tiempo desde que había aceptado la conferencia."] (p. 181) At this same juncture, Julia mutely identifies herself with a vine wrenched from its supporting tree by autumn storms (pp. 102–103).

Women, however, have no monopoly on vulnerability, and trees are repeatedly felled by storms (cf. pp. 25, 75). It is also especially relevant that a vine can tighten its grasp to the point of choking a tree or destroying the structure supporting it. Julia perceives the destructive potential of such relationships, and this realization underlies the break with her son, Bernal.

> She had left voluntarily, for the sake of not holding on to her son, to let him breathe and grow, and not clasp him like a clinging vine. Once the gardener told her that when the ivy totally covered the greenhouse, it would end up pulling down the gutters, destroying the very thing which had supported it with a terrifying force.

> [Ella había desertado voluntariamente, por no agarrarse al hijo, por dejarlo respirar y crecer, por no abrazarse a él como una enredadera. Una vez el jardinero le había dicho que cuando la enredadera cubre totalmente la casa del invernadero, acaba arrancando las tuberías, destruye lo que era su soporte con una fuerza aterradora.] (p. 37)

Aldecoa's integration of tree and flower motifs with the action and descriptions of the novel is not merely an exercise in ingenuity or an oblique ironic meditation upon popular speech; it is the vehicle for the feminist theme announced by the title metaphor. The *enredadera* and its variants (clinging vines including bougainvillaea, ampelopsis, honeysuckle, roses, and ivy) become part of a powerful statement of the feminine condition, an implicit denunciation of the constraints that perpetuate or intensify dependency. Both heroines of the novel equate the *enredadera* with *ataduras*—feminine bondage (the titular metaphor of Martín Gaite's work). Rejecting Juan's offer of a permanent relationship, Julia reasons: "I don't want ties, bonds, chains, entanglements." ["No quiero lazos, ataduras, zarzas, enredaderas."] (p. 118) Her almost obsessive need for freedom inhibits Julia's relationship with Juan from the outset, rendering her unable to respond to him: "She couldn't say, 'I'd love to stay', because it wasn't true. 'I'm dying to be alone, to check and make sure that I'm still free, that nothing is tying me down'." ["No podía decir 'Me gustaría quedarme', porque no era verdad. 'Estoy deseando comprobar a solas que sigo libre, que nada me está atando'."] (p. 79) For similar reasons, Julia always has preferred an unconventional, even antisocial, type of man: "She was attracted by men who wanted to stay on the margin, the unclassifiable or *declassés*, far out. People who don't imprison you because they themselves are beyond bars." ["Le atraían los hombres que deseaban permanecer al margen, los inclasificables, desclasados, *far out*. Seres que no aprisionan porque ellos mismos están rejas afuera."] (p. 84)

Julia cannot escape social conditioning to the extent of avoiding matrimony, yet her need for freedom ultimately destroys an otherwise happy marriage, bringing voluntary separation from the man who had been her great love. Reflecting upon their past together and her present solitude, Julia equates herself with a honeysuckle torn free by the wind: "The honeysuckle which covered part of the main façade tore loose and the branches shook in the rain. 'Without a support, without a wall', thought Julia, 'just as I am, torn loose and free'." ["La madreselva que cubría parte de la fachada principal de la casa se desprendió y las ramas tremolaban bajo la lluvia. 'Sin sujeción, sin muro', pensó Julia, 'como yo misma, desgajada y libre'."] (pp. 102–103) Loneliness and anguish are the price of her freedom: "A lack of support beneath her feet, the well-known fear of falling, the vertigo of anguish attacked Julia. . . . Once again, the tower of her self-sufficiency had collapsed in ruins." ["Una falta de apoyo bajo los pies, la conocida ansiedad del vacío, el vértigo de la angustia asaltaron a Julia. . . . Una vez más, la torre de la autosuficiencia se había convertido en un montón de ruinas."] (p. 119)

However, Julia is unable to live in complete independence, without love; so she depends for emotional support upon a series of transient lovers, of whom Juan is probably typical. Sharing certain characteristics with the author,[3] Julia appears to be economically liberated; being a professional and perhaps of independent means, she is able to travel more or less freely and maintain a second home. She is sexually liberated as well, insofar as her actions are concerned, having left her husband and having had a series of lovers. On a more intimate level, however, Julia is considerably less liberated than her lifestyle suggests, and constantly must resist her need for companionship and psychological support, and combat existential inertia.

Nineteenth-century Clara is not at all liberated, although she has a measure of economic independence (her wealthy husband deeds her the house and lands after abandoning her). But she is unable to leave home even temporarily—though she daydreams about world travel—because she clings to the remote possibility of Andrés returning.

> Here is Marta and here am I, she is poor and I am rich. Yet both of us are alone, souls in torment. And how different it would be if we were men. I'd say to her, "Marta, close up the house this very minute, grab a few things, and let's go out into the world to live adventures in other lands, meet new people, seek companionship, parties and joy far away from here. . . ."
> The bonds we women have aren't broken that way, so easily.

> [Aquí está Marta y aquí estoy yo, ella es pobre, yo rica. Pero solas las dos, almas en pena las dos. Y si fuéramos hombres, qué distinto. Yo le diría, "Marta, ahora mismo, cierra la casa, coge cuatro cosas, vámonos por el mundo a vivir aventuras a otras tierras, a conocer personas diferentes, a buscar compañía y fiestas y alegría lejos de aquí. . . ."
> Las ataduras que tenemos las mujeres no se rompen así, tan fácilmente.]
> (p. 133)

Logically, the most poignant evocations of the feminine condition are Clara's reflections on her own situation and memories of her mother.

> Scenes in which Mama is sad, murmurs I can't quite decipher, sighs, severe gestures by my father, Mama's clasped hands begging for something she needs, a promise, an excuse, something which my father isn't going to give her because he gets up brusquely.

> [Escenas en las que mamá está triste, murmullos que no acabo de descifrar, suspiros, gestos adustos de mi padre, manos entrecruzadas de mamá suplicando algo que necesita obtener, una promesa, una disculpa, algo que mi padre no le va a dar porque ya se levanta bruscamente.] (p. 143)

Perhaps Aldecoa's message in part involves a slow improvement in the condition of women across the generations, since Clara's husband does not subject her to this sort of tyranny, although he does leave her for another woman whose only apparent attraction is her ability to reproduce.

Confined to bed by a progressively deteriorating asthma, the sometimes childlike Clara indulges in retrospection that might otherwise seem out of character. In fact, Clara exhibits a well-developed Peter Pan complex, as is clear from her reaction to an observation that she is growing up.

> "I don't want to grow up, Mama, I don't want to be a woman." "Woman" was a word she heard a lot. "Poor woman." It seemed to me that it was difficult and dangerous and sad to be a woman. Everybody talked either pitying or attacking women. It seemed that being a woman was a misfortune like being lame or blind or infirm.

> ["Yo no quiero crecer, mamá, no quiero ser mujer." Mujer era palabra que oía muchas veces. "Pobre mujer." Me parecía que era difícil y peligroso y triste ser mujer. Todos hablaban compadeciendo o atacando a las mujeres. Parecía que ser mujer era una lástima como ser cojo o ciego o poco sano.] (p. 170)

Sensing the pervasive preference accorded male children, Clara's daughter Lucía, as a child, also rejects traditional feminine roles planning to be a warrior: "'If there were a war, I'd go, dressed as a soldier so Papa would be happy and proud of me'. . . ." ["'Si hubiera guerra yo me iría vestida de soldado para que papá estuviera contento y orgulloso de mí'. . . ."] (p. 171) Like her father, she rejects and avoids her mother until the night she accidentally overhears his bungled attempt at reconciliation: "'It doesn't matter that Lucía isn't a man, Clara . . . at least she will do for producing other men'. . . ." ["'No importa que Lucía no sea hombre, Clara . . . por lo menos sirve para hacer hombres'. . . ."] (p. 185) Lucía returns to the convent school for her final year of *bachillerato* [secondary school equivalency], never again to leave the cloister. Clara interprets Lucía's decision as vengeance against Andrés, but also sees it as another of her own (Clara's) failures: "Lucía left you because she wasn't willing to be the next victim, the next one in line to fail, by bearing a daughter. . . ." ["Te dejó Lucía porque no estaba dispuesta a ser la víctima siguiente, la próxima embarcada en el fracaso de parir hijas. . . ."] (pp. 186–87)

Unable to take a similarly decisive action, Clara lives an increasingly restricted, enclosed existence, like the blossom that constricts and shrivels after the flower has bloomed. As a flower (specifically, she is identified with the rose), Clara literally withers on the vine after Andrés abandons her. Confined to bed more and more by a condition that, if not purely psychosomatic, has been aggravated by her psychological state, she withdraws from the world. Not even Lucía in the convent is more cloistered. No longer the simple personification of the archetypal clinging vine, Clara becomes an example of the most extreme feminine dependency, since her very life hinges upon Andrés to such an extent that, when deprived of his presence, she collapses like a vine deprived of support.

As her illness progresses, Clara identifies herself more consciously with flowering vines. One of her semidelirious monologues, an extended metaphorical meditation, integrates the *enredadera* and several other images in self-submersion into the plant world. Comparing her life to the *enredadera* and correlating with it the image of the male as supportive tree, Clara envisions the stages of her existence as seasons in the year.

I was born in April, and my childhood was all covered with juicy green leaves, and I soaked it up like a sponge, clinging to those parents who never let me fall. . . . Then summer came, and flowers grew all over my body in the arms of Andrés. I coiled around him, holding on; like a clinging vine I climbed up my post, my tower, my column, my Andrés. But suddenly everything was autumn and down came the branches and the leaves, still burning with color. He tore them from their moorings. . . the clinging vine thrown to the ground. . . thirty-eight years old, and Clara, the clinging vine, was already dead.

[Nací en abril, mi infancia estuvo toda cubierta de hojas verdes y jugosas, me esponjaba abrazada a aquellos padres que nunca me dejaron caer. . . . Vino luego el verano y me crecieron flores por todo el cuerpo en los brazos de Andrés. Yo me enroscaba a él, me sujetaba; como la enredadera, yo trepaba por mi poste, mi torre, mi columna, mi Andrés. Pronto todo fue otoño y abajo se vinieron las ramas y las hojas que ardían todavía. El las arrebató de su soporte . . . la enredadera tirada por el suelo. . . con treinta y ocho años y ya muerta, Clara, la enredadera.] (pp. 190–91)

All of the images that Julia applies to Andrés are phallic: tree, post, tower, column. But she does not attempt to demythify the patriarchal figure, nor does recognition of her debilitating and potentially fatal dependency inspire a desire for change. For Clara, as for Julia, the *enredadera* uprooted or torn free symbolizes her solitary and unsupported condition. She is "always supported by others and now without anything to retain or support, [fallen] on the ground" ["siempre apoyada en otros y ahora sin sujeción ni apoyo, por los suelos"] (p. 191). But Clara cannot go on living alone, unsupported. She cannot cope with the freedom thrust upon her; others have decided for her, ordered her actions, and she only had to obey. Docile and submissive since childhood, Clara never dreamed of rebellion: "I liked to obey. It's marvelous to have somebody tell us at every moment what we should do." ["Me gustaba obedecer. Es maravilloso que alguien nos diga lo que en cada momento debemos hacer."] (p. 61) She had no experience in decision-making or action: "Nobody told me, 'the door's open, you're free'." ["Nadie quiso decirme, 'abierta está la puerta y eres libre'."] (p. 191) Clara's sole decision, exemplifying the ultimate existential limit situation, is her refusal to go on living: "this time nobody else is choosing for me; I want to die, and I'm going to die. . . ." ["Esta vez nadie elige por mí, quiero morirme y voy a morir. . . ."] (p. 193) Clara lived her entire life for others—parents, husband, child. Only death belongs to her alone. One of her final reflections brings the topos of death as the great equalizer into the context of male/female relations: "Death is the only thing which makes men and women equal." ["La muerte es lo único que iguala al hombre y a la mujer."] (p. 205) That this should seem true—even in extremis and to an archetypal female of a century ago—is a telling indictment of traditional values and mores, a denunciation of constrictive ideologies that is not weakened by artistic subtlety.

The crucial difference between Clara and her twentieth-century counterpart is the element of choice or self-determination. Julia chooses her lonely search for self-definition. As if to demonstrate Clara's error in submissively accepting the restrictions that shape and doom her, Julia exhibits egalitarian behavior and growing self-awareness in at times parallel circumstances some three generations later. Believing that "only in solitude can we truly be ourselves" ["sólo en la soledad podemos ser nosotros mismos"] (p. 205), Julia remains alone by choice, lonely but moving toward emotional self-sufficiency. Just as she sacrificed her marriage in the quest for self, she breaks off her love affair with Juan to end her nascent dependency. Like Clara's death, this separation occurs in November; the dying plants and dying year are mirrors for Julia's extinguishing the flame of love: "Next to the greenhouse, the façade of the house which only a few days before burned with the fire of the autumnal vine, grew darker by the minute." ["Junto al invernadero, la fachada de la casa que hace unos días ardía con el fuego de la enredadera se oscurecía por momentos."] (pp. 205–206) Since Julia associates the *enredadera* with dependency (as do Clara and Aldecoa), it is doubly significant that its death coincides with her own quasi-cyclic liberation from yet another dependent relationship. The smell of rosemary, an objective correlative of her honeymoon and associated by Julia with erotic love, is at this point transformed to another image of death: "rosemary and lavender, growing beneath her bridal window" ["romero y lavanda, plantados bajo su ventana de novia"] (p. 135), losing the honeymoon connotations when Julia returns following her last visit to Juan and "the odor of dried rosemary hit her in the face" ["el olor de romero seco la golpeó"] (p. 207).

The erotic idyll—perhaps her last—has ended, and once more Julia must pay the price of self-affirmation and independence with loneliness and vulnerability. As autumn rains chill summer's ardor, Julia's eyes fall upon another metaphoric equivalent of the *enredadera*, another symbol of feminine bondage: "the ampelopsis was twisting, torn loose in pieces from the wall." ["La ampelopsis se retorcía desprendida a trozos de la pared."] (p. 208) Julia's tears reveal that her freedom is purchased at the price of anguish and emptiness, and she retreats into her work. Her forthcoming lecture contains a reflection that not only reveals and encapsulates her motivation, but connects the lives of the two women in the novel: "The sentiment of love, the absorbing plenitude of motherhood, the fear of being alone. Those [feelings] are the real entanglement. . . ." ["El sentimiento del amor, la absorbente plenitud de la maternidad, el miedo a la soledad. Esa es la verdadera enredadera. . . .."] (p. 211) Clara had no defense against the void, while Julia—like the legendary fox—is able to choose freedom even at the price of self-mutilation.

The title of Carmen Martín Gaite's short story collection, *Las ataduras* (The bonds),[4] also employs a symbolic correlation between the clinging vine and feminine bondage, but the metaphor is minimally developed, barely insinuated in a manner that might prove hermetic if not for Aldecoa's extended development of identical images. Martín Gaite's correlation probably was left implicit because of the prevailing censorship in 1960. Written in an era that Martín Santos's widely discussed novel aptly termed a "time of silence," Martín Gaite's novelette makes use of silences, omissions, and ellipses to communicate her nonconformity.[5] In this story, the symbolism of the clambering vine is conveyed through ironic juxtapositions and the incongruity of the heroine's reaction. It is unclear to what extent the novelist relied upon an implied intertext (i.e., fixed phrases of popular discourse) as an aid for the reader's interpretation.

Like Julia, Alina of "Las ataduras" is an intelligent, studious girl who rejects traditional domesticity during her adolescence, longing for the broader experiences offered by a university education. Alina and Julia are also similar in another way: at the university Alina becomes involved with an unconventional man who seems to offer a free, happy lifestyle. Martín Gaite's heroine elopes to Paris with the quasi-bohemian French artist, Philippe. Despite his professed nonbelief in marriage, she finds herself trapped in the type of situation that she wished to avoid: in financial difficulty, and with small children and an arbitrary, temperamental common-law husband who at best is patronizing, and at worst, tyrannical. Her adolescent desire to escape the marriage trap, symbolized by another *enredadera*, is portrayed in the farewell scene when Eloy, her best friend in earlier years, leaves for America, to what Alina envisions as a life of adventure and liberty. Male freedom is contrasted with the female's corresponding lack of autonomy in a subtle, allusive dialogue in which Eloy insinuates that Alina's future holds provincial domesticity. Passing a run-down house overgrown with a trailing vine that always has revulsed the heroine, Eloy offers her one of the flowers in a symbolic gesture equating her with the rooted plant.

Up along the balcony of rotting wood climbed a passionflower vine, strange flowers like painted-up flesh, with a grotesque, moribund grimace looking like the faces of old female clowns. Alina, who was afraid of nothing, feared these flowers, and she had never seen them anywhere else. Eloy stopped and picked one.

"Take it."

"Me take it? Why?" she shuddered without reaching for the flower her friend held out.

"No reason, kid. Because I'm leaving; a present. You're looking at me funny, as though you were afraid. Why are you looking at me that way?"

[Por el balcón de madera carcomida, subía una enredadera de pasionarias, extrañas flores como de carne pintarrajeada de mueca grotesca y mortecina, que parecían rostros de payasa vieja. A Alina, que no tenía miedo de nada, le daban miedo estas flores, y nunca las había visto en otro sitio. Eloy se paró y arrancó una.

"Toma."

'¿Que tome yo? ¿Por qué?" se sobrecogió ella sin coger la flor que le alargaba su amigo.

"Por nada, hija. Porque me voy; un regalo. Me miras de una manera rara, como con miedo. ¿Por qué me miras así?"] (p. 50)

The inexplicably negative reaction by Alina, whose fearlessness has been stressed repeatedly, obviously is intended to draw attention to the significance of the incident. Clearly, she associates the flowers with feminine stagnation and aging: "painted-up flesh," "a grotesque, moribund grimace," "faces of old female clowns" ["carne pintarrajeada," "mueca grotesca y mortecina," "rostros de payasa vieja"].

The fear of entrapment and of wasting her life in provincial squalor is underlined by the fact that the flower incident is juxtaposed with the death of Alina's grandfather, who for both Eloy and Alina symbolized freedom as a spokesman of choice and self-determination (cf. p. 51). Ironically, Alina's "escape" is short-lived, for she is caught by her own sexuality and maternity, and finds herself in a situation not too different from the one she sought to avoid in her adolescent rebellion. Lacking the autonomy that education, a career, and two decades of social change provide for Julia, Alina manages only to change her geographical location, but in so doing she intensifies her isolation and alienation by distancing herself from supportive parents.

Because Martín Gaite wrote under strict censorial control by a regime distinguished for its hostility to feminism and the liberation of women, the symbolic import of this story is less visible than that of Aldecoa's novel. The full significance of the vine must be extrapolated from the relationship of the metaphor to the title of the novelette ("Las ataduras"), which is also the title of the short story collection as a whole. Seemingly unrelated titles were sometimes utilized as clues to a work's allegorical meanings (concealed from the censors), and this tale provides a good example of the technique.

While each of the three works considered here is a narrative employing plant imagery to express woman's dependent condition, the stories differ greatly in plot, characters, and atmosphere, and each takes a different narrative form: full-length novel, long short story or novelette, and the television drama or dialogued novel (televised). Maria Antònia Oliver[6] explains the differences as primarily a matter of narrative perspective or point of view.

> In television, the camera is decisive, and therein lies the biggest difference between a literary product and a television production. The camera takes over the functions of the reader's visual imagination, and occupies the optic field of the theater spectator. Comparing a published novel with a televised one, we might say that the camera is the narrator of the story, and it is the camera that describes the setting and visualizes the emotions.

> [En televisó, la càmera mana, i en això rau la més gran diferència entre un producte literari i un producte televisiu. La càmera fa les funcions de la imaginació visual del lector, i del camp òptic de l'espectador de teatre. Comparant una novel.la publicada amb una novel.la televisada, la càmera és, como si diguéssim, la narradora de la història, la descriptora del paisatge, la visualitzadora de les emocions.] (p. 8)

The script for the five-part "telenovela" *Vegetal* (Plant) retains a good deal of its spoken, theatrical character, frequently approaching the dramatic monologue. There is only one setting, a Barcelona apartment, and only one important character. Except for the indefinite time, the program fulfills the dramatic unities. The secondary characters are entirely subordinate to the protagonist and convey to the reader (or audience) data relevant to the protagonist's relationship to external reality.

Marta, the protagonist, is a conventional, bourgeois widow of approximately fifty years, economically comfortable but ill at least psychologically. After two years of widowhood she has not freed herself from the patronizing, paternalistic tyranny of her late husband, en Joan, who still influences many of her conscious and unconscious acts. She has not adopted a female-defined perspective but continues to live within male inscribed boundaries. Marta appears first as an obsessively neat housekeeper, cleaning every speck of imaginary dust from furniture she secretly detests, having tolerated it through thirty years of marriage because it was chosen by en Joan. Her monologue is punctuated with references to en Joan: what he would have said, done, or thought as a result of each of her actions or reflections. Each evocation of the departed husband summons his shade that recites exactly what she imagines he would have said or enacts what she has said he would have done. Although the stage directions specify that there is no malice in him—he speaks "with fatherly affection" ["amb tendresa paternal"] (p. 18)—it becomes clear that Marta never was allowed to think for herself or make decisions. Patriarchal control of her life was nearly absolute, and Marta's feeble attempts at revolt were smothered with patronizing tolerance.

The title, the work's major symbol, derives from Marta's defeat in her mute struggle for self-expression. A recurring battle between Marta and en Joan, which she lost time and time again, involved her having plants, especially in the bedroom. Early appearances of en Joan reiterate his disapproval: "What a mania has taken hold of you with these plants, dear." ["Quina mania que t'ha agafat amb les plantes, estimada."] (p. 19) "It isn't healthy to have plants in the bedroom, Marta." ["No és sa tenir plantes dins el dormitori, Marta."] (p. 18) Actually, Marta's husband objected to any semblance of initiative or personal opinion on her part, and because en Joan smoked to such an extreme the air was poisoned and the plants died.

Two years of solitude barely suffice for Marta to become autonomous enough to purchase plants again and to rearrange the furniture to accommodate them. Like Clara, Marta was totally dependent on her husband; even though both women were left financially secure, the psychological dependence and years of accommodation to paternalistic domination resulted in personalities seemingly incapable of independent decisions or actions.

With the advantage of living a century later, in an age of rapid social and moral change, Marta at least is able to struggle to break out of her confinement, while Clara could not. Once the decision is made to purchase the first plant, other such decisions follow almost uncontrollably. However, as she symbolically breaks the constraints of her submissive role, Marta also loses the support it provided. She has no experience in decision-making or independent living, and the transition to autonomy leaves her utterly vulnerable. Already talking to herself on first appearance, Marta begins talking to the plants, responding to their replies (audible only to her), and thereby evincing her emotional instability. Searching for self-definition, she repeatedly changes the apartment, finally disposing of the despised dark, heavy furniture that symbolized the subjugation of her decorating taste.

After a visit from her only son, Carles, when she reacts badly to his invitation to meet his live-in fiancée, Marta calls her best friend Fina, who proves unsympathetic. Feeling rejected by Carles and hurt by Fina's indifference, Marta confesses to the plants her jealousy of Julia (Carles's fiancée); she finds consolation in caressing the plants: "Now I can touch the plants whenever I want . . . before I had to be on the lookout during the days I felt unhappy." ["Ara ja pu tocar les plantes sempre que vulgui . . . abans havia d'anar alerta durant els dies dolents."] (p. 26) Plants, her only friends, are positioned so that they, too, can watch TV. Two other bulwarks of Marta's archetypal role (as bourgeois wife and mother) have vanished from her life with the disaffection of Carles and Fina and, while she remains poised precariously on the brink of autonomy, she reaches out desperately for support. Her generation had little exposure to ideologies that might offer a theoretical support and because she is unequipped to enter the workplace, Marta is especially open to feelings of loneliness and alienation. Although Oliver makes no specific reference to menopause, Marta also may be suffering the physical and psychological crisis of feminine aging. There is little in her background or personality to augur a favorable outcome, though she continues to struggle.

Some time later, Marta has transformed her apartment completely, and the shade of en Joan no longer appears. What was once a dark enclosure crowded with somber, heavy furnishings has become a light, airy, almost empty space: "Yes, I'll have to bring a few pieces of furniture for us . . . and these curtains will have to go! We'll make over the gallery into a garden room." ["Sí, hauré de treure uns quants mobles perquè faran nosa. . . i aquestes cortines, també fora! i convirtirem la galeria en un jardín."] (p. 29) Exchanges with the plants reveal that Marta has no other pastimes, such as reading, for her husband did not approve: "Nobody ever encouraged me to read books. . .John used to say that reading was a waste of time." ["Ningú no m'ha ensenyat a llegir llibres . . . En Joan deia que era perdre el temps, llegir."] (p. 30) The extent to which Marta and the apartment have changed is underscored by Fina's shock when she drops in unexpectedly with her small grandsons. The children bring Marta to the verge of hysteria by defoliating her favorite azalea. Fina reacts: "'It isn't as though it were a person, girl, instead of a plant'. Marta is at the point of saying that it is the same as a person, but she doesn't say a single word." ["'Ni que fos una persona, noia, i no una planta'. La Marta està a punt de dir que és igual que una persona però no pronuncia ni un mot."] (p. 34) The visit ends in an argument after Fina suggests that it is unhealthy to be shut in constantly with plants; this provokes a violent outburst from Marta. Here, the secondary characters function to heighten the visibility of increasingly neurotic behavior. Marta's effort to become her own person clearly is fraught with danger, even if partially successful. While she has become more autonomous and less dependent on her friendship with Fina, she has become emotionally dependent upon the plants. Her internal contradictions and anxieties manifest themselves in behavior that symbolically converts the plants first to friends, then to family.

An indefinite time afterwards, Marta appears dressed in flowered cretonne, and the plant population continues to increase. The changes in her appearance provide visible evidence of her continued search for self-definition, but her emotional instability is shown by the proliferating plants and an increase in what the other characters perceive as bizarre behavior. The protagonist has begun to collect all sizes and shapes of clocks, mirrors, and calendars, strategically placed so the plants can see them (and look at themselves). Except the final scene, the remainder of the action consists of a periodic increase in the numbers of plants, clocks, mirrors, and calendars—the last three items relating to the passage of time and the aging process.

The time motif is reinforced by Marta's reading aloud to the plants from Virginia Woolf's work in Catalan translation, *Els anys* [*The Years*]; she reads a passage concerning a funeral. Her commentary reveals a previously suppressed relief at the death of en Joan: "When John died, I didn't feel any pain at all. . . and during the funeral I paid attention to all kinds of stupid things and wasn't able to think about him for a minute." ["Jo, quan es va morir en Joan, no sentía cap dolor. . . i al funeral em fixava en tot de coses banals i era incapaç de pensar en ell."] (p. 44) Marta's confession reveals a marriage that resulted from societal conditioning and her own submissive acceptance of a role created by a male-dominated culture. She was not in love with en Joan, perhaps not even deeply attached to him, but she mechanically played her role, wearing the mask expected of her and feeling little more than numbness when en Joan's death terminated the performance.

When Carles and Julia pay a surprise visit and are invited to dinner, they are disconcerted to discover that the kitchen too is overflowing with plants. Having argued with her son because of his refusal to live with her, Marta appeals to Julia, explaining that she has only the plants to fill her time and keep her company.

> All my life I've been like them. . . stuck in a flowerpot like a plant to look pretty, or keep someone company. . . and that's all. That's why we get along so well, because we're alike. . . but if I don't watch out, I'll turn into a plant completely, a fuchsia, or ivy, or a ficus. . . .

> [Tota la vida he estat com elles. . . posadeta dins un test com un estaquirot, per fer bonic, per fer companyia. . . i res més. Per això ens avenim tan bé, perque som iguals. . . però si no vaig alerta em tornaré com una planta de debò, una fucsia, o una heura, o un ficus. . . .] (p. 61)

This is a key speech for understanding the work as a whole, especially Oliver's daring use of metamorphosis in the denouement. It underlines the essential parallel Marta perceives between herself and the plants and sets forth the "object" nature of both, kept for a lifetime in a planter to look pretty and provide company. Despite recognition of the danger inherent in her situation, Carles rejects her contention that she has devoted all her life to him, pointing out that she should have begun long ago thinking of herself and having her own activities. Thus Oliver not only shows the long-term effects of the wifely role as decorative possession, but suggests that maternal self-sacrifice is a deleterious and ultimately self-defeating quality. Marta's final, desperate appeal to Julia places the latter in the uncomfortable position of having to choose between her future husband or mother-in-law, and as she wavers, disconcerted, Marta insults her and throws the young couple out.

In subsequent scenes the protagonist attempts to find employment, not for the income, but as a way of being useful and also escaping the encroaching menace of the plants. A job, even if not a career, would bolster her self-esteem and aid in self-definition. But no one in the outside world wants her, not even as a neighborhood volunteer, and the one offer Marta receives is clearly a scam whose operators wish to exploit her social standing to bilk her neighbors and acquaintances.

Turning to a priest for counsel, Marta is advised not to be selfish but to be content with the life she has lived: "What do you mean, live your life, Marta? You've already lived it, you've lived your life while you were with your husband and your son. . . . The memory alone should satisfy you, my daughter, and suffice to fill up the hours of your old age." ["Què vol dir, viure la teva vida, Marta? Tu ja l'has viscuda, la teva vida, amb el teu marit i el teu fill. . . . Només el record ja t'hauria de bastar, filla, per omplir totes les hores de la teva vellesa."] (p. 55) The surrealist symbolism of Marta's many clocks, mirrors, and calendars takes on added significance with the rector's reference to "filling the hours" of her old age, a gerontological allusion that leaves the protagonist outraged and indignant. Thus, the Church not only fails to provide support, but intensifies her suffering by adding to Marta's feminine alienation and solitude an awareness of the aging crisis. The Church here appears in its traditional, stereotypical role as a patriarchal institution and reaffirms the code of male sexual dominion and female subordination. Woman's existence is reduced by the vicar to that portion of her days that she is able to devote to the men in her life (husband and son); Marta should content herself with having been able to serve as wife, mother, and housekeeper. Oliver makes clear that the Church is firmly against liberation or even a broadening of women's sphere of activity. Even though there has been no prior indication of Marta's religiosity, her failure to find support or refuge in the Church removes another potential means of escape.

Failing in several attempts to integrate herself into the outside world, Marta is obliged to recount her adventures and defeats to her plant family and to face the realization that only they want or need her.

> Clearly, since I don't know how to do any work, then I'm no good for anything. . . I'm tired, worn out. . . and it isn't my fault that I lost, because I tried . . . . [Listening to a plant that speaks to her] Yes, you're right, I was afraid of all of you. . . I was afraid of stagnating among you, of becoming completely like you. . . and I tried to run away. . . but I'm no longer afraid now.

> [Es clar, com que no sé fer res, doncs no serveixo per a res. . . estic cansada, fastiguejada. . . i per mi no s'ha perdut, no, que jo ho he intentat. . . . (Escolta una planta que li parla) Sí tens raó, us tenia por a totes vosaltres. . . Tenia por d'estancarme entre vosaltres, de tornar de debò com vosaltres. . . i he intentat fugir. . . però ja no en tenc, de por.] (p. 61)

With her confession that she no longer fears becoming a plant, Marta begins to lose the battle. Oliver prepares the audience for the notion of metamorphosis by emphasizing change over an indefinite period of time in which each day brings modifications in Marta's appearance or in that of her house. When she returns home once more in defeat, having failed again to find a job, the suggestion is emphasized more strongly: not only has Marta's life been like that of a decorative plant, she has now lost her fear of becoming part of the plant world. In losing the battle for autonomy and self-definition, she is also losing her instinct for self-preservation as her sense of identity weakens. It is thus part of a logical progression that on Marta's next appearance she wears a leafy, flowery garment and her hair is full of leaves. Serenely, she plans to discard and burn the few remaining possessions—clothes, papers—that tie her to the past, thereby freeing herself to become fully a plant. The metamorphosis becomes visible in her color: "Don't you think I can see what color I am?. . . The green of a new leaf. . . Yes, I'm a plant. . . ." ["Que no ho veieu, quin color tinc? . . . Verd de fulla tendra, transparent . . . sí, sóc un vegetal. . . ."] (p. 64)

A final visit from Fina confirms Marta's sentiments: she is not simply retreating from an unfeeling world but rather is defiantly rejecting the constraints of a lifetime as a bourgeois wife in which she was unable to be herself, to behave spontaneously, or to express her own feelings; she was obliged to dress, act, and think to please her husband and to conform to social conventions and expectations. She clearly states her rejection of her former lifestyle: "All that has ended now. . . I don't ever again want to be a. . . lady" ["Això ja s'ha acabat. . . no vull ser més una. . . senyora."] (p. 67) The contrast between Marta and Fina, who is conformity personified, is heightened by visual ploys, especially the ease with which an increasingly vinelike Marta lolls on the floor, while Fina is uncomfortable with the lack of furniture. Though it may appear that Marta is in the process of achieving a measure of liberation, actually, the reverse is true. Her change in attitudes and mannerisms simply shows accommodation to her situation, just as she accommodated to paternalistic domination. Retreating from the freedom that she is psychologically unprepared to handle, Marta prepares to embrace the one alternative open to her.

But since the solution of metamorphosis still might be too radical, too final, one more attempt is made to find a conventional escape. Marta plans a trip around the world as a last effort to assert her will.

I don't want to be like you [plants]. . . if I can't be good for anything but looking pretty or hanging things on, I'd rather go see something of the world[ . . . ] I feel more and more like a plant all the time . . . and it's pleasant, yes, very pleasant- . . . but I don't want it. I don't.

[No vull ser com vosaltres [. . .] si només serveixo per a fer bonic o per a enganx-ar segesells, més m'estimo anar-me'n a córrer món [. . .] de cada vegada em sento més vegetal . . . i és agradable, sí, molt agradable . . . pero no vull. No vull.] (p. 69)

This is the only time that Marta clearly rejects her end, but it is too late. When the camera last focuses on her, she is preparing a bonfire in the living room, burning those objects that bind her to her former life, placing the plants out of danger, her forgotten half-packed suitcase visible in a corner. In the final scene some time afterward, Carles and Julia fruitlessly seek Marta in the cold, silent apartment. The pile of ashes and open suitcase are the only clues; in the bedroom is a strange new plant—apart from the others. Julia's femininity enables her to explain the transformation: "'She told us it would happen, she warned us about it'. . . . And Marta, now changed into a polypodacia [fern], remains in the room, solitary and serene. . . .'" ["'Ella ja ens ho havia dit, ens ho havia advertit'. . . . *I la Marta, convertida en falguera, roman damunt la peanya, solitària, sere-na. . . .*"] (p. 72)

Oliver's metamorphosis, more daring and extreme than Aldecoa's metaphors, is probably at greater risk of misinterpretation. Given the objective nature of her medium (the camera does not comment or inter-pret, and symbols must be conveyed nonverbally), much more depends upon the interpretive powers of the viewer; undoubtedly, some interpret the ending not as a feminist statement but as a kind of science fiction epi-sode. The more conservative viewer might conclude that Marta simply had been driven insane by the loss of her nurturing, paternalistic husband. Clearly, neither of these interpretations accords with Oliver's intent. Mar-ta, somewhat like Augusto Pérez in *Niebla* (Mist), is a character in search of self, annihilated by general indifference (which communicates the mes-sage that she does not exist as a meaningful entity) and by her inability to cope, her lack of preparation for any but one archetypal role. Hers is a tragedy without an identifiable villain; the culprit is traditional society that prepared her for only a single role in life (wife and mother) and has no use for her when she is no longer needed to fulfill that role. Marta—a person of upright character—struggles against overwhelming odds; it is a silent tragedy that society ignores or is unprepared to perceive either as wrong or as tragic. After all, as the vicar observed, Marta had a "good" life: she was not abused, murdered, raped, or starved, and did not even have to work for a living. Her personality, her individuality were stifled, however, since marriage, probably since childhood. What she might have contributed to the world as an original intellect will never be known.

It is simple to apply Marta's plight beyond the feminist context to the situation of the senior citizen in most of the Western world. In both cases, those who no longer prove useful or productive are relegated to a second-class status, forgotten by society and often even by family members, or they are considered a burdensome responsibility to be avoided whenever possible. Marta's loneliness and solitude are constants of twentieth-century life. Oliver's message is not debilitated by its broadness, and the powerful symbol with which she ends the work has the necessary ambiguity to permit varying interpretations. As a feminist statement, the denouement constitutes a powerful call for attention to the dehumanizing effects of total dependency—with no autonomous existence, being reduced to a possession, a mere extension of someone else (in Marta's case, en Joan's wife and Carles's mother). Marta humanizes the plants and seems to show more concern for what she imagines to be their feelings than appears to have been accorded hers.

Comparing Oliver's protagonist with Aldecoa's Julia, near contemporaries (Marta is less than a decade older, and both live in present-day Spain), the difference is striking. Despite living in a large city during the twentieth century, Marta is more similar to rural nineteenth-century Clara than to the more or less liberated members of her own generation. All three have lost their husbands (Julia by an act of will) and are estranged in varying degrees from an only child. All three have a measure of financial security, belong to the upper-middle class, and are middle-aged. At that point, the similarities end: Clara and Marta dream of world travel but never leave home; Julia appears to be quite well-traveled. Clara and Marta are at the mercy of fate or the whims of others; Julia decides her own future. The crucial differences between the three women are a university education and a profession; Julia has both and the other two have neither. Martín Gaite's Alina differs from the others in being considerably younger and in having small children at the story's end. She lacks the potential for independence since she abandoned her university studies to elope with her lover; she is thoroughly trapped in the domesticity she sought to escape. The plant imagery selected by Martín Gaite—the passion-flower vine, equated with *ataduras* or bonds—is almost identical with Aldecoa's *enredadera* or climbing, clinging vine (the latter constitutes a class of plants to which the former belongs). Such images clearly imply dependency or the need for support, and suggest that such support binds the dependent female, curtailing her liberty, as is underlined by the references to encloisterment, domestic enclosure, and the predominance of indoor settings (with the exception of Julia, whose freedom allows a variety of outdoor scenes). Two of the women's stories are closed: Clara and Marta cannot exist alone. The other two are inconclusive, for Alina appears unhappy with her entrapment, while Julia struggles for her freedom.

Aldecoa, Martín Gaite, and Oliver employ botanical images to symbolize the feminine condition, with few variations: the first two use the clinging vine image to denounce the plight of women educated solely for the roles of wife and mother, and Oliver uses the decorative houseplant for an identical purpose. Unquestionably, Oliver's development of the metaphor is more dramatic—the identification of woman and plant that is merely figurative in Aldecoa and Martín Gaite becomes literal for Oliver. Characters do identify themselves with plants, Clara with the *enredadera*, Julia with the ampelopsis torn free by the wind, and Marta with a more generic term ("sóc un vegetal. . . ," p. 64), although she includes vines among the plants she predicts she may become: *fucsia, heura, ficus* (p. 51). As women who have managed to escape the "plant" state by virtue of education and professional activities, the three writers are well aware of the importance of such factors but too realistic to suggest that all problems for women can be overcome so simply. Biological urges and social conditioning continue to exert powerful influences and, as Julia's struggle indicates, "being a woman in a man's world" requires uncompromising effort and vigilance. If the fate of Martín Gaite's Alina is ultimately less grim than that of Marta and Clara, the reader deduces that it will be because of her escape from Spain to a reputedly more progressive and egalitarian society.

The *enredadera* and its variants symbolize immobility and the lack of options for women who have but one support, which is at the same time a form of restraint or constriction. Because plant imagery is so much a part of daily discourse, it is less startling and less visible than more unusual rhetorical devices. But its familiarity creates a subtle, subliminal effect, explaining why these three writers have chosen to subvert it, utilizing botanical figures both as symbols of the feminine condition and as a means of exposing male-centered dominant discourse.

# Notes

1. Josefina R[odríguez] Aldecoa, *La enredadera* (Barcelona: Seix Barral, 1984). All citations from Aldecoa refer to this first edition and will be documented by page numbers. English translations from Aldecoa and throughout the essay are my own.

2. Similarly, Clara in her final, lingering illness characterizes herself as "a helpless clinging vine, curled around a smooth trunk" ["enredadera desvalida, rizada sobre lisos troncos"] (p. 193).

3. For example, both women possess graduate degrees, have similar professions, family and social backgrounds, and attitudes; there are also demographic and geographic similarities.

4. Carmen Martín Gaite, *Las ataduras* (Barcelona: Destino, 1960). All references to Martín Gaite are to this first edition and will be documented by page numbers.

The tale "Las ataduras" [Bonds], more than sixty pages in length, is the longest piece of the collection, and because of length and structure it is classifiable as a short novel or novelette.

5. See Janet Pérez, "Functions of the Rhetoric of Silence in Contemporary Spanish Literature," *South Central Review* 1, no. 2 (1984): 108–130, for a full treatment of these techniques and their purposes. Methods of circumventing censorship are also treated in Janet Pérez, "Techniques in the Rhetoric of Literary Dissent," *Selected Proceedings. Third Louisiana Conference on Hispanic Languages and Literatures* (Baton Rouge: Louisiana State University, 1984), pp. 216–30, and in Janet Pérez, "The Game of the Possible: Francoist Censorship and Techniques of Dissent," *The Review of Contemporary Fiction* 4, no. 3 (Fall 1984): 22–30.

6. Maria Antònia Oliver, *Vegetal i Muller qui cerca espill* (Barcelona: La Llar del Llibre, 1984). Subsequent citations from Oliver are documented by page numbers.

The frequent ellipses in the citations from Oliver are part of the original text. On the one or two occasions that I have deleted part of a quoted passage, it is indicated by ellipses within brackets.

# Frame Tale: Carmen Gómez Ojea's *Otras mujeres y Fabia*

## DEBRA A. CASTILLO

The protagonist of *Otras mujeres y Fabia* [Other women and Fabia], the second novel of the Asturian author Carmen Gómez Ojea, is a thirty-six-year-old single woman, a teacher of literature "who had explained too often the nature of metonymy" ["(que) había explicado demasiadas veces en qué consistía una metonimia"].[1] Fabia's life is changed by a chance occurrence when she wins the lottery. Using the prize money, she resigns from her teaching position, takes an apartment in a ghetto neighborhood, and devotes herself to watching and eavesdropping on the housewives who live in the crowded tenements, alternating these periods of voyeurism with imaginary conversations with the framed pictures of her foremothers on the wall. Physically suspended between "those above" ["los de arriba"] ("an ineffable family circle" ["un cercle de famille, inefable"], p. 21) and "those below" ["las de abajo"] ("two midcentury sisters" ["dos hermanas demi-siècle"] p. 23), Fabia is suspended as well between her apartment and the house of her childhood, between the window frame and the picture frames, between everyday activities and nightly insomnia during which she struggles to comprehend what it means to be a woman—what it means to be part of an indissoluble chain of women who must consciously or unwittingly negotiate day after day what Blau calls the "tricky econometrics of repression."[2] Fabia conducts her inquiry against the background of this tricky repression. Seeping into her carefully constructed edifice of meaning is the corrosive suspicion that neither time nor space offers answers to her probing, that memory is valueless, the present inexpressive, and the anticipation of a future impossible. Fabia is left at the end of the novel with what she has at the beginning: her grey hairs, her voices from wall and window, her shabby, restricted apartment.

This econometrics of repression in *Otras mujeres y Fabia* is framed by the problem of a woman's relation in and to history. But which history? Fabia is ambivalent. She realizes that "such a bewildered city would never

101

be able to listen to the aged voices of its history" ["una ciudad tan aturdida jamás podría escuchar las viejas voces de su historia"] (p. 48), but is skeptical about the possibilities of remedying this problem. Men's history, the history of the battles of the Spanish Civil War, is clearly irrelevant. More useful, perhaps, is the feminine counterhistory of the period: "through the hushed voices of women—mothers, grandmothers—. . . the unwritten, unadulterated history was not buried along with so many other corpses. . . ." ["A través de esas voces acalladas de mujer—madres, abuelas— . . . no bajó a la tumba, junto con tantos cadáveres, la historia no escrita, la historia no amañada. . . ."] (p. 30). Yet Fabia shows no facile turning from masculine (bad) to feminine (good) history: her insights are far clearer and less simplistic. While society chooses to ignore the "aged voices" ["viejas voces"] of an unwritten history, now revealed as female, those soft historical voices are not inimical to accepted views of history. Official history often infringes perilously on the methods and functions of myth, on uncomplicated representations, on clear, pure meanings valid for all time. The unattended female voices, repressed as indistinguishable background noise, serve a clear, even necessary, social function by blurring the sharply defined perimeters of official reconstructions of the past that would otherwise seem closely allied to the production rather than the discovery of truth—to the construction rather than the chronicling of power. Pure meaning can be counterproductive beyond a certain point. As Barthes notes, "Society, it seems, mistrusts pure meaning"—even the pure meanings imposed by official versions of the past; "it wants meaning, but at the same time it wants this meaning to be surrounded by a noise . . . which will make it less acute."[3] Even antagonistic voices can be co-opted into accepted history, provided those voices are muted into the background.

The role of women's history is co-opted in another, more frightening sense. Women, Fabia knows, are the carriers of culture: "Thanks to those mothers and grandmothers, through the umbilical cord of their words, children could claim the past for themselves, even though it had been falsified by tones of passion, coldness, or ignorance" ["Gracias a esas madres y abuelas, a través del cordón umbilical de sus palabras, los niños pueden hacer suyo el pasado, aunque esté falseado por tonos de pasión, frialdad o ignorancia"] (p. 80). Unattended voices are tolerated—even required—as noise that reflects meaningful structure but, as Barthes further observes, "at the limit, *no meaning at all* is safer."[4] What the straining ear, struggling for unique meaning behind the static, hears in the whispers ranges from gibberish to a slightly perverted tale that underscores rather than undercuts official history. The feminine noise acquires meaning through convergence with a single historicized structure. Oral women's history offers no genuine alternative to official male history; both restrict the child with the ropes of custom, the umbilical cords of civilized behavior. Fabia's sardonic repetition of anecdotes chosen from oral feminine history illustrates this point perfectly. She recalls a paradigmatic anecdote, the history of the war told by one of her aunts.

Aunt Rosana had lost her only son in the war, a nineteen-year-old interim second lieutenant. Before he left she had embroidered for him a half-dozen handkerchiefs with his initials, cross stitching them in red swastikas. "Oh," she exclaimed, "that novelty became a big hit among my friends."

[La tía Rosana había perdido a su único hijo en la guerra, un alférez provisional de diecinueve años. Antes de partir le había bordado media docena de pañuelos con sus iniciales en rojo, a punto de cruz gamada. "Oh," exclamó, "aquello fue una novedad que hizo furor entre mis amigas."] (p. 88)

The sheer triviality of women's history provokes Fabia's hostility. Suspended between two realities, she can find no firm base from which to launch her criticism, and her helplessness only intensifies her anger. She too is implicated in this false history, tied by the umbilical cord of her foremothers' words; her only recourse is in the stylized ironic distortions she deploys while she compulsively speaks and writes, "launching into one topic after another, wandering in and out of the trite expression of the stupidest clichés" ["lanzando tópico tras tópico, entrando y saliendo en lugares comunes de las más estúpidas frases hechas"] (p. 67). Recipes, fashions, children, handkerchiefs with initials "cross stitched in swastikas" ["a punto de cruz gamada"]—Fabia recalls, and savagely and sympathetically details all the meager substance of daily life.

Fabia's reflections on the rigid rules of woman's role in society and, by extension, on her own role framed by convention, are further expressed in the evocation of la señora Efe, her cousin and "other self".[5] Efe, like Fabia, is well-educated. Unlike Fabia, her place in the econometrics of repression is unambiguous. While in society's terms, Efe is a woman who has everything—education, money, a husband, children—"nevertheless, there was something very, very bitter in her" ["sin embargo había algo en ella amargo, amargo"] (p. 55). Her perfect husband, her ideal home, her impeccable children are the very essence of society's code of contented domesticity, yet Efe suffers from murderous dreams and a barely repressed rage. While her husband finds fulfillment in a well-paying job and comes and goes at will, la señora Efe is planted, like a flower, in the restricted space of her home, increasingly frustrated by the continuous tasks of housekeeping that sap her energy and blunt her sharp intelligence. "'Look at me', she tells her cousin, 'here I am, a broken, faded flower'" ["Ya me ven, aquí estoy, una fleur tronchada, fané"] (p. 55). Efe's bitter denunciation of this unendurably empty existence provides the perfect counterpart to the distanced reflections of the unmarried Fabia.

Fabia, the ironist, the voyeur, is irresistibly drawn to the sad detritus of the housewife's life—the ugly cycle of the "sordid, millenary, ancestral customs, whispered in the ears of generations and generations of little girls, who later became women in charge of the hubbub that fills each morning" ["costumbres ancestrales, milenarias y sórdidas, susurradas al oído de generaciones y generaciones de niñas, que después se hicieron mujeres y organizaban el alboroto de cada mañana"] (p. 10). Looking through her window, Fabia sees a girl who should have been young and beautiful but is aged beyond her years, trapped like her mother and grandmother by marriage and its inescapable duties. She is increasingly dehumanized by her marriage, "her sweet hands hardened, just like her heart, and turned into enraged claws" ["sus dulces manos se endurecieron, lo mismo que su corazón, y se hicieron garras enfurecidas"] (p. 41). The emptiness of her life remains, and her already limited possibilities are foreclosed by the birth of children. Hardened by poverty life, the young mother ignores the sufferings of her child: "Who could feel tenderness or pity for such a blindly irritated creature?" ["¿Quién podría sentir piedad y ternura por semejante criatura ciegamente irritada?"] (p. 32). Thus, the ignored little girl who receives no tenderness grows up into a tired mother with no love to give; and inevitably, she must come to terms with her own stifling entrapment. "Start the day well, Poil, start off well" ["Empieza bien tu día, Poil, empieza bien"], adjures the absent mother, as old images and old roles are passed heedlessly from generation to generation. "And after picking up what needed picking up would come the putting away of what needed putting away" ["Y después del recoge que te recogerás, empezaba el pon que te pondrás"] (p. 28). But eventually the tired realization comes: "And life was so stupid" ["Y la vida era tan estúpida"] (p. 44).

Nowhere is the stupidity of life more clearly and concisely portrayed than in the story of a mother who keeps house for her taciturn son, feeding him her own despair with the meals she prepares.

> The son ate pots of heart with potatoes, which his mother cooked for him with her heart pierced by four wounds. . . . : four wounds opened by four swords bathed in oil from the Garden of Olives and lemons from the hot, tragic south to dress a bitter salad—mother and son in the Golgotha of most livid sadness—bathed as well with drops of vinegar, which were tears, which were blood.

> [El hijo comió cazuelas de corazón con patatas, que le guisó su madre con el corazón traspasado por cuatro llagas . . . . : cuatro llagas abiertas por cuatro espadas bañadas en aceite del huerto de los Olivos y limones del sur caliente y trágico para aderezar una amarga ensalada—madre e hijo en el Gólgota de la más lívida tristura—bañada con gotas de vinagre también, que eran lágrimas, que eran sangre.] (pp. 38–39)

The mother is faceless and nameless, subsumed in the mass of all sacrificing, sacrificed mothers back to the mother of Christ. Her function is to nourish; her son's, to consume her. Yet what the child consumes of the mother is not the tender poetic spirit once housed in her body, but the broken-hearted bitterness left by the process of her acculturation. She offers her lifeblood; it is a cup of gall.

At her window, Fabia watches the cycle of housework, continually repeated in thousands of households day after day. She watches as well the equally inexorable cycle of a woman's life: crying infant, repressed child, submissive wife, pitiless mother, savage old age. In that ugly, inhospitable neighborhood, Fabia (as she notes with her characteristic irony) "had learned to see things she had never noticed before and that were useful and instructive" ["había aprendido a ver cosas en las que jamás había reparado y que resultaban aleccionadoras e instructivas"] (p. 104). Powerless against the debasing system that destroys them, yet unconsciously vindictive in teaching their daughters to take on unsatisfyingly restrictive roles, the women of the *barrio* do indeed teach Fabia a great deal.

As Fabia turns from window frame to picture frame she also turns from a contemplation of the present to a meditation on the past, from the shrill voices of the tired ghetto mothers to the whispering admonitions of long-dead foremothers. Equally attracted and repulsed, Fabia studies the portraits of literary and literal foremothers with concentrated attention. As in her description of the moving pictures framed by her window, her examination of the portraits is a frustrated mixture of bitter acceptance and rejection, her barely repressed hostility constantly in evidence. Thus, while Fabia admits that "ladies who wrote things that were published and well-known . . . in their self-portraits . . . seemed unsettling" ["las señoras que escribieron cosas conocidas y divulgadas. . . a través de sus retratos . . . resultaban inquietantes"] (p. 75), she fails to recognize that it is her determined iconoclasm that gives them the peculiar uneasiness she describes. What space and what frame, if not those of her books, contain the essence of the woman writer? Fabia does not even address the question rhetorically. Instead, she perversely turns from the faceless pages of the books to the painted or photographed faces of their authors, pausing before each image. "Mme de Sévigné," she finds, "was too big-busted. And all women with large breasts, as she had been noticing, were inclined to sing, to be gossips, to talk to themselves while they ironed or polished a console" ["Mme de Sévigné era demasiado pechugona. Y todas las pechugonas, según había ido comprobando, sentían inclinación a cantar, a ser parlanchinas, a hablar consigo mismas mientras planchaban o daban cera a una consola"] (p. 75). The writer regresses into the housewife, with a housewife's tasks. Rosalía de Castro, similarly damned by interpretation of her works through an analysis of her portrait, is dismissed as "homely" ["malencarada"]. Such women, says Fabia, "generally wrote lyrics for *saetas* and tried to make everyone else share their anguished existences" ["escribían por lo general letras para saetas e intentan que todos los demás participen de sus angustiosas vivencias"] (p. 75). Literary transcendence is once more suppressed under Fabia's ruthless banalization, the universality of the poet's work buried in the singularity of her portrait. Only Emilia Pardo Bazán escapes the condemnation; significantly, her portrait is not described in the text.

As Fabia proceeds in her investigations from the faceless writings to the faces of her literary foremothers in her search for a literary heritage, so too, in a reverse manner, she goes from the portraits of her mother, her grandmother, and her great-grandmother to the faceless faces of her remote ancestors, searching for a literal genealogy. She follows the whispering voices of the chain of women, hands clasped, back to the shadowy Mother of them all. "That Mother of mothers, from which she came, was imposing and diffuse, and at times she inspired her with respect and fear" ["Esa Madre de madres, de la que ella venía, era imponente y difusa, y a veces le inspiraba respeto y temor"] (p. 17). This mother-daughter chain, like the portraits of women writers, is evoked in an effort to understand those past experiences that affect Fabia's present existence. Fabia's shabby room, lit only by moonlight—another figure of the Great Mother of mothers—fills slowly with these other women, fills with the "things that told the story of the women who had carried one girlchild after another in their wombs until it was her turn" ["cosas que contaban la historia de las mujeres que se habían llevado en el vientre una a otra hasta llegar a ella"] (p. 17), fills with their whispering voices recriminating her for her sterile womb, empty of daughters, ridiculing her yearning to bear a daughter into the chain (pp. 19–20). Through the picture frames holding photographs of her great-grandmother, her grandmother, and her mother, Fabia reaches to memories of a past that cannot be recalled, counterposing this insomniac nighttime vision of an unbroken linear succession implicitly with her daytime voyeurism on the cyclical housekeeping activities of the neighborhood.

Yet this chain, too, is a cycle of sorts. Underlying Fabia's recognition of the community of women, and their common history and common destiny, is the fear that the frames of the past and the present are subsumed in one frame, that Fabia can see the whole picture at a glance without the duality of day and night, mother and daughter, present and past. As part of the chain and part of the neighborhood despite her detachment, Fabia fears not only her mother's fate but also her mother's self. In her impulse to frame, Fabia is also framed. In her eschewal of history, Fabia becomes a part of history. In rejecting her childhood home, Fabia is drawn back through the window/picture frame (which metaphorically becomes the opening of the birth canal) into the suffocating night of her mother's tightly shuttered womb. And she finds herself part of an unwilling communion. "Didn't I already have my/your lips?" asks Luce Irigaray. "And this body open on what we would never have stopped giving each other, saying to each other?" Thus Fabia hears the whispering voices and sees the silent, enigmatic smile on the lips (which lips?) of the Great Mother. Irigaray's lyric evocation continues, recalling "this breach of silence where we constantly reenvelop ourselves in order to be reborn. Where we come to relearn ourselves and each other, in order to become women, and mothers, again and again." Mothers and daughters are revealed as extensions, continuations of each other, whose speech (whispered or shouted, spoken or written) is silenced in the stilled portrait, the human still life of the frame tale. "But we have never, never spoken to each other," Irigaray concludes. "And such an abyss now separates us that I never leave you whole, for I am always held back in your womb. Shrouded in shadow. Captive of your confinement."[6]

Not surprisingly, Fabia expresses a desperate desire to abort the past—"to erase it until she felt a sharp pain deep within" ["borrarlo hasta que sintiera un vivo dolor en las entrañas"] (p. 90). Neither in the window nor in the picture frames can she find the self she wants to be. Those women, molded into womanly form by pressures past and present, are alien to her. Nevertheless, frighteningly, in the mothers' voices she hears her own voice and in their faces sees herself mirrored, framed, historicized, her body converted into an anatomized, two-dimensional image. Their flatness, made hideous by Fabia's obscure captivity within, fills her sight, forceably occupies the site of her meditations. The engorgement of her time by their images block memory and thought with burgeoning countermemories that falsify thought and interpretation. "History is hysterical," says Barthes in a radically paradoxical formulation. "It is constituted only if we consider it, only if we look at it—and in order to look at it, we must be excluded from it."[7] Excluded as daughter from mother, yet drawn back by the fugitive witness of old voices testifying to shadows and confinement, Fabia gazes upon portraits of hysteria (madness, or merely the typical condition of womanhood) and decries the "constitutive" function of historical/hysterical interpretation. There is no comfortable place left in the world for her, no frame that will give meaning to her life.

Fabia's physical isolation in her tiny apartment in a sordid area of the city correlates to this psychological constriction of possibilities. She arrives in the neighborhood "shortly after the death of her mother, after the old house was torn down" ["a poco de morir su madre, después de que la antigua casa fuera demolida"] (p. 104)—two events that are metaphorically one, representing the destruction of the past—and struggles to maintain her detached view of the daily activities of the women in nearby apartments. As she hopefully (hopelessly?) repudiates present and past, so too she spurns the future. Single, without a lover at age thirty-six, she will have no daughters. Like Peter Pan and the Lost Boys, who according to Fabia have lost their innocence,

> [Fabia and her friends] had reached the border. From here they would not go on. They would only wrinkle. They would fold in upon themselves like pieces of paper, like handkerchiefs. And Tinkerbell had lost the magic dust from her wings and neither she nor anyone else would ever fly again.
>
> [. . . habían llegado a la frontera. De ahí ya no pasarían. Sólo se arrugarían. Se doblarían sobre sí mismas como un papel, como un pañuelo. Y Campanilla había perdido el mágico polvo de sus alas y ni ella ni ninguna jamás volaría.] (p. 100)

Tinkerbell's fairy wings become flightless chicken wings, and the tired, deathless cycle stretches into infinity.

But despite her intermittent dismissal of history, of woman's history as well as man's, Fabia's motives are far from clear—her desire for cancellation of the past linked to a strong (if undefined) sense of self, her disgust at the present undermined by compulsive voyeurism, her negation of the future weakened by periodic "mental disorders" ["desarreglos mentales"] (p. 21) of hormonal drives pushing her toward the maternity she abhors. Above all else, Fabia wants to *know*; thus she emphasizes direct perception (with the eyes) of spatialized "framed" gnostic history, a history curiously fashioned by her revulsion against time and death despite recognition of Peter Pan's inevitable transformation. Like the historians she rejects, Fabia wants to achieve a stasis in which nothing happens and time is frozen like the pictures fixed in their frames.

In the singlemindedness of this desire, Fabia fails to consider the unavoidable dualities that frame her own tale, dualities perceptively explicated by Barthes in *Camera Lucida.* "The Photograph belongs to that class of laminated objects whose two leaves cannot be separated without destroying them both: the windowpane and the landscape, and why not: Good and Evil, desire and its object: dualities we can conceive but not perceive. . . ."[8] It is the critical role of conception—"we can conceive but not perceive"—that the protagonist of this novel elides; ironically, Fabia's emphasis on seeing clouds her perception. She knows, but forgets or represses the sight (site) framed by her moving (window) and still (photograph) portraits. Barthes does not. He warns: "Whatever it grants to vision . . . a photograph is always invisible: it is not it that we see."[9] Fabia's error lies in the belief that if she only looks long enough and hard enough she will really *see*; other options are excluded or repressed. This "lying against time" (Bloom's phrase) in the preference of perceiving over conceiving (which is not to know, but to actively create and form within the self) is a direct consequence of the same impulse that leads her to reject (kill) her mother and withdraw into the maternal womb (room).

The first word of the novel, "¡Edepol!" points to a psychoanalytic interpretation of the antihistorical impulse. "Oedipal," suggests the narrator, is the only possible word to describe correctly (or frame) the picture of an old woman who "twisted the neck of a fat chicken" ["(que) retorcía el cuello de un gordo pollo"] and later "picked her nose parsimoniously, afterwards wiping her finger in the feathers of that helpless creature she had strangled so inconsiderately" ["se hurgaba la nariz con parsimonia, para limpiarse a continuación el dedo entre las plumas de aquel desvalido bicho tan desconsideradamente estrangulado"] (p. 9). Children are conceived with the same grotesque action: "Maybe she was picking her nose while she conceived them, or maybe she was so tired she didn't even notice. . . ." ["Acaso se estaba hurgando la nariz, mientras los engendraba, o se encontraba tan cansada que ni se enteró. . . ."] (p. 11). The chain of association is complete as la señora Efe, Fabia's alter ego, confesses her love for Fabia's mother, admitting that "what fascinated [Efe] most was [Fabia's mother's] way of fluttering her hands" ["lo que más le fascinaba de ella era su modo de *aletear* las manos"] (emphasis added), ending her confession with the exclamation "¡Edepol!" once again (p. 63). Fabia's mother is alternately the fat chicken cruelly strangled and the suffocating, careless woman who strangles her chick, her child; she is strangled and strangling with love, with hate.

Fabia errs only in calling this composite scene "Oedipal", another example of her "lying against time." It is more strictly pre-Oedipal, part of the mythic time of the all-powerful mother and the intense love-hate relationship between the nurturing woman and the suckling child. A time belonging to what Freud called the prehistoric "Minoan-Mycenean" substratum behind the civilization of Greece,[10] the pre-Oedipal phase is associated not only with the paradisal attachment to the mother but also with the "surprising, yet regular dread of being killed (?devoured) by the mother" (p. 196). The child, however, is more than a helpless chicken about to be devoured. She or he also hungers and Freud finds that "the person the child wants to devour is the mother who nourished him" (p. 206).[11] Tinkerbell or Wendy, the little girl (old woman) kills her mother (her child) and wipes her nose on the pathetic flightless wings, thereby engendering other chicks, other children, other mothers.

The transition from the pre-Oedipal phase to the Oedipal complex is the transition that Fabia—with her deliberate spatialization of knowledge, her rejection of history, her rejection of relationships with father figures—does not make. Obsessively lying against time, Fabia perceives her world from behind the shutters of the prenatal period and constitutes reality from experiences drawn from the timeless time before weaning. Her desire for transcendence goes no further than the limits of the Minoan-Mycenean prehistory described by Freud, and the image that most frequently haunts her is derived from a modern myth. Again and again Fabia returns to her copy of *Gone with the Wind*, ignoring the implications of the title. Although Fabia rereads the end of the book, it is the framed still of the final scene in the movie that offers the underlying pictorial invocation to dream. Fabia, who turns (returns) to a maternal room (womb), mimics Scarlett O'Hara's return to Tara at the end of the novel and the movie. Likewise, Fabia's story ends with a repetition of Scarlett's words: "after all, tomorrow is another day" ["después de todo mañana será otro día"] (p. 109). More truly than she can conceive of, her will to knowledge is blocked by a lie, by her refusal to recognize the effects of the passage of time.

Because Fabia's associations are pre-Oedipal (mythic, spatial) rather than Oedipal (historical, temporal), her obsessive quest for self is doomed to failure, because she denies the guilty Oedipal knowledge of love and lack, of law and language. As Besançon notes, it is "the Oedipal complex [that] constitutes the raw materials for comprehending the social world, the chief category for historical understanding."[12] Fabia bypasses the raw materials necessary for her self-framing in refusing (quite rightly, on ideological grounds) men's historical interpretations, while at the same time belittling or undercutting the oral history given in the "tales and stories from the war by mothers and grandmothers" ["cuentos e historias de la guerra por madres y abuelas"] (the submissive Oedipal women); she sees women's history as "somewhat more instructive and revealing than a hundred round tables, where knights who had absolutely nothing to do with King Arthur carried on heated discussions" ["algo más instructivo y revelador que cien mesas redondas, donde caballeros que en absoluto tenían que ver con el rey Arturo discutían acalorados"] (p. 81). Women's history may be more instructive than male myths, but its value is relative. As Fabia shrewdly suspects, the oral tales merely ape the dominant historiography at several removes of ignorance; both are products of the civilized, civilizing force of Oedipus.

By repudiating "Oedipus-as-structure"[13] as a productive force, Fabia opts for dispersal in her life and in her text. Like the moon with which she strongly identifies, in her rebellion against cultural frames she consciously refuses any mode of existence except pure contingency. Though aware of the intolerable constraints of the role of wife and mother, this knowledge masks a refusal of knowledge that makes her recognition trivial and invalidates her assumed independence. She does not have the courage or the decisiveness to step outside the role decreed for women by the mores of social structure, nor to struggle actively against that role. Thus, her assumption of contingency stands revealed as a form of framing reality rather than a force for change, her separation from society reflecting the immature and egoistic alienation of a spoiled child. Contingency, then, becomes an adopted pose similar in effect to the photographic poses of her foremothers. As with la señora Efe, Fabia's frustrations are buried under tiny eccentricities and ironic rhetoric that, to her, compensate to some degree her submission to conventions. Ultimately, tellingly, she accepts Scarlett as a model—the little girl who never grew up—over Wendy, the premature mother of Peter Pan, and assuages guilt with dreams of a never-never tomorrow.

Fabia's history—for it is a history despite her attraction to pre-Oedipal myth—is, like all history, compromised by the necessity to perceive and frame the raw materials in what might be called the (Oedipal) production of truth, a truth that is highly vulnerable to the infrastructure of thought. Fabia's passion to know and to perceive turns from the external observation of social interaction to the interior contemplation within a closed room of framed pictures depicting her personal history. Between the two forms of perception Fabia creates a changing identity that is projected onto the work, a written work, *Otras mujeres y Fabia*, where the nameless "other women" ["otras mujeres"] are given a weighty first place in the title, but the emphasis falls on the single name, "Fabia." In this fictional autobiography that is a social history, the frames coalesce and the spectacle of meaning is revealed as a mirror frame: the book becomes a double of the self.

Many questions raised by this study remain unanswered, of course: questions about the relation of history (male or female) to repression, to the production of truth, to desire, and the desire for power. Clearly, the vulnerability of history to thought and perception will overdetermine any answers that might be proposed. Can identity remain fluid within the structures of a written, autobiographical text, and is the radical alterity of oral, woman's history compromised by the writing of it? In a book burgeoning with images of maternity, how can Fabia's anti-genealogical impulse be satisfied? Why is seeing given primacy over conceiving, and how does this preference relate to the comparative absence of fathers, sons, and brothers (who appear briefly but are seldom given voice) in the text?

Finally, the woman who reads this novel and writes about it must face the problem of evaluating what kind of frame theory can provide for a spatialized history-as-myth. Michel de Certeau, in a discussion of the work of Lafitau, makes the following suggestions.

This metamorphosis and occupation of the space of the Other by theoretical writing presents three characteristics which are to be found whenever reason transforms into a myth the real on which a belief depends; for the believable is substituted the readable/visible; for the historical, the speculative; and for non-coherence of different wishes (or beings), the coherence of principles by which a thought gives itself, as in a mirror, its own project.[14]

Despite her anti-Oedipal care, Fabia's disaffected historicism does revert to the mythologization of the real in the novel; the shadowy, virile Great Mother occupies the place of the law, the place of the Father, and provides the punishing frame that contains all that is visible, and hence readable— Fabia's speculative, specular fiction. What is the price of such a text in the hidden economy, the female's econometrics of repression?

# Notes

1. Carmen Gómez Ojea, *Otras mujeres y Fabia* (Barcelona: Argos Vergara, 1982), p. 99. Further references will be documented by page number within the text.

2. Herbert Blau, "Disseminating Sodom," *Salmagundi* 58–59 (1982–83): 222.

3. Roland Barthes, *Camera Lucida*, trans. Richard Howard (New York: Hill and Wang, 1981), p. 36.

4. Ibid., p. 38.

5. Other details support this interpretation of Efe as Fabia's fictional alter ego. Besides the first initials—Fabia, Efe, "F", Fleur, Flor—educational backgrounds, and general outlook, Fabia shares with her cousin more intimate traits such as the tendency to sprinkle her speech with Latinisms and French. At times, it is difficult to decide which of the cousins is speaking in the text.

6. Luce Irigaray, "And the One Doesn't Stir Without the Other," trans. Hélène Vivienne Wenzel, *Signs* 7 (1981): 67.

7. Barthes, *Camera Lucida*, p. 65.

8. Ibid., p. 6.

9. Ibid.

10. Sigmund Freud, *Sexuality and the Psychology of Love*, ed. Philip Rieff (New York: Collier, 1963), p. 195. Further references will be documented by page number within the text.

11. In terms of the frame tale, Freud's perception might complement Barthes' statement that "Death is the *eidos* of that Photograph" (p. 15); i.e., Fabia is actively seeking death—her own and that of her mother—in her obsession with the photographic record.

12. Quoted in Christine Fauré, "Absent from History," trans. Lillian S. Robinson, *Signs* 7 (1981): 76.

13. Gilles Deleuze and Felix Guattari, *Anti-Oedipus: Capitalism and Schizophrenia*, trans. Robert Hurley, Mark Seem, Helen R. Lane (1972; reprint, Minneapolis: University of Minnesota Press, 1983), p. 107.

14. Michel de Certeau, "Writing vs. Time: History and Anthropology in the Works of Lafitau," *Yale French Studies* 59 (1980): 56.

# Part 2

# The Text of Subversion

# Gómez de Avellaneda's *Sab*: Gendering the Liberal Romantic Subject

## SUSAN KIRKPATRICK

Gertrudis Gómez de Avellaneda's novel *Sab* was the first abolitionist novel to be published in Spanish.[1] Two details—the gender of the author and the date of publication in 1841, a key year for Spanish romanticism—point to another achievement as well: *Sab* attributes to female characters the new paradigm of subjectivity that emerged with Spain's romantic movement. The novel's condemnation of slavery is intimately related to its representation of women as the subjects of romantic experience, and this connection is made possible by a particular intersection of Spanish romanticism and liberal ideology.

Mariano José de Larra addressed the relation between the new literary movement and the liberal attempt to transform Spanish society in his essay on "Literatura." Writing in January 1836, when Mendizábal's reforms were no more than promises, Larra expressed the link between art and society only in terms of hope, rather than reality: "Let us hope that soon we will be able to lay the foundations of a *new* literature, the expression of the *new* society that we have become, a literature made up of *truth* just as our society is made of *truth*." ["Esperemos que dentro de poco podamos echar los cimientos de una literatura *nueva*, expresión de la sociedad *nueva* que componemos, toda de *verdad* como de *verdad* es nuestra sociedad."][2] Larra squarely identified the renovative force in Spanish society with liberalism: the motto of the age, he tells us, is freedom of commerce, freedom of industry, freedom of conscience. Thus, Larra sets forth the fundamental project of his literary generation: to create a literature appropriate to liberal Spain.

Larra links liberalism and emerging romanticism in his essay, arguing that artistic freedom, freedom from rules, precepts and schools is simply part of the liberal program. But he also points to a much deeper level on which the new literary and political movements join. That "new truth" that he refers to in the passage just cited requires the use of italics to suggest that he is giving the words a special, new meaning. Not surprisingly he combines syllogism and paradox in his attempt to further define "truth": "In politics man sees only *interests* and *rights*, that is, *truths*. In literature, consequently, he can look for nothing but *truths*. . . . Because what is imagination itself, if not a more beautiful *truth*?" ["En política el hombre no ve más que *intereses* y *derechos*, es decir, *verdades*. En literatura, no puede buscar por consiguiente sino *verdades*. . . . Porque la imaginación misma, ¿qué es sino una *verdad* más hermosa?"] (p. 133). The discrepancy between the various terms that he equates with truth—self-interest, rights, passions, imagination—can be resolved only if one understands that the new reality on which Larra expects to ground society, politics, and literature is the individual subject. In effect, Larra's essay articulates the new model of the subject that both liberalism and romanticism assumed, that both movements elaborated and propagated at different levels of social activity. Subjectivity in the form of self-interest, bearing with it unalienable rights, became the reality that economic and political structures must allow to be expressed; that same reality when represented in art appeared as passions, fantasies, and imagination. In Larra's formulation desire is the crucial form of subjectivity: the project for his generation is to make space for the individual subject to express its desire in economic, political, and artistic practice.

While Larra clarified the basic assumptions of progressive consciousness of his day, it was his friend José de Espronceda who offered the most complete poetic formulation of the new, liberal-romantic paradigm for subjective experience. His evolution as a poet can be read as the working out of an increasingly complex representation of the subject in relation to its world. Starting with "La canción del pirata" [Pirate's song] in 1835, Espronceda used the first person in an entirely different way than he had in his neoclassical poetry. In that earlier phase, the poetic voice implied a universal, conventional perspective, with emphasis upon the object of its discourse, often an element of nature, as in "A la noche" [To night] and "Al sol" [To the sun]. His romantic poetry written after 1835, by contrast, implies a speaker that is fully personalized and located in a particular time and space: it might be a pirate, singing the joys of his free life on the sea; or a poet who, while addressing some other being, describes his personal history, his state of mind, his fantasies and desires. Indeed, the lyrical self becomes the poem's true theme. The poem exists to embody subjectivity, the individual's passions and imagination that according to Larra form the cornerstone of a new social reality for Espronceda's generation.

In 1838 Espronceda published two key lyrical poems, "A una estrella" [To a star] and "A Jarifa en una orgía" [To Jarifa in an orgy], offering a fully developed paradigm of subjectivity that opposes the creative forces of the inner self to the power of material reality. "A Jarifa en una orgía" shows clearly how the poet articulates the elements of romantic subjec-tivity. A dialectic between self and world is set in motion by desire, which generates illusion when projected upon external reality.

> I want love, I want glory, I want a divine delight like I
> imagine in my mind, like nothing that exists on earth. . . .
>
> [Yo quiero amor, quiero gloria,
> Quiero un deleite divino,
> Como en mi mente imagino,
> Como en el mundo no hay. . . .]³

The world's failure to correspond to desire precipitates the mood of bitter frustration with which the poem opens. Since Espronceda conceives sub-jectivity as a temporal process above all, he shows the dynamics of his malaise by reviewing his spiritual history. In the first stage, the imaginative powers born of desire propel him out into the world to find the objects of his fantasy.

> Like a speeding comet, I threw myself on the wings of my
> ardent fantasy: my headlong, restless mind thought it
> found happiness and triumphs everywhere.
>
> [Yo me arrojé, cual rápido cometa,
> En alas de mi ardiente fantasía:
> Do quier mi arrebatada mente inquieta
> Dichas y triunfos encontrar creía.] (p. 52)

The subjective powers of imagination and desire produce the values marked as positive throughout the poem, while the real, external world encountered in the search for such values is perceived in negative terms.

> Then I sought with eager and delirious love
> For virtue and glory on earth,
> And stinking dust and crumbling slag
> Was all my weary spirit found.
>
> [Luego en la tierra la virtud, la gloria,
> Busqué con ansia y delirante amor,
> Y hediondo polvo y deleznable escoria
> Mi fatigado espíritu encontró.]
> . . . . . . . . . . . . . . . . . . . . . . .
> And I saw my illusions wither, my desires were
> eternal and insatiable. I touched reality and hated
> life. I believe only in the peace of the grave.
>
> [Y encontré mi ilusión desvanecido
> Y eterno e insaciable mi deseo:

Palpé la realidad y odié la vida.
Sólo en la paz de los sepulcros creo.] (p. 53)

In Espronceda's paradigm, the gap between subjectively generated positive values and the object world is absolute; as if by definition, reality cannot correspond to desire, illusion leads to disappointment. Subjectivity,
then, is both the source of positive value and the repeated experience of
frustration and pain. Furthermore, desire is unrelenting; only in death does
the poet hope to find peace from its insatiable compulsion. This dilemma
generates the poem's point of departure, since the poet goes to the brothel
to seek a kind of small death in drink and sex. But because desire can
neither be repressed nor satisfied, the poem itself reenacts the ever repeated process of subjectivity: desire, illusion, disappointment, disgust.
The brothel, of course, provides an apt metaphor for the experience
Espronceda wishes to represent.

For Espronceda, mankind is characterized by an insatiable aspiration
toward something that does not exist; the discrepancy causes a fall into
despair and rebellion. The presentation of Satan as the voice of man in the
introductory canto of *El diablo mundo* [The devil world] clearly exemplifies this paradigm. Yet, like so many of the mental configurations
through which Western culture claims to represent universals, Espronceda's image of the human psyche is identified with masculine consciousness.
In "A Jarifa," he marks subjectivity as male by figuring the relationship
between self and world as the erotic connection between a masculine subject and a feminine object. In this poem—and in all the other poems he
composed between 1838 and 1841—the beloved or desired woman stands
for the object world that fails to correspond to the values imagined and
desired by the lyrical, masculine subject. Jarifa represents the "other,"
that which is not identical to the poetic self. This difference from the lyrical
subject, Jarifa's otherness with respect to his desire, leads the poet to push
her away in disgust after he has called her to him. "Leave me, woman: I
detest you" ["Huye, mujer: te detesto"] (p. 51), he tells her, and then
explains:

> Why does my heart, foolishly perhaps, swoon over phantom
> women, if later, instead of meadows and flowers, it finds
> arid deserts and thorns . . . ?
>
> [¿Por qué en pos de fantásticas mujeres
> Necio tal vez mi corazón delira,
> Si luego, en vez de prados y de flores,
> Halla desiertos áridos y abrojos . . . ?] (p. 52)

The inability to find in the concrete woman, Jarifa, the infinite object projected by his desire prompts the poem's reflections on the inadequacy of reality to imagination. These reflections, in turn, take woman as a primary exhibit of reality's deficiency.

> I saw clean, virginal women in white clouds of celestial
> light; I touched them, and saw their purity turn to
> smoke, to mud and rot.

> [Mujeres vi de virginal limpieza
> Entre albas nubes de celeste lumbre;
> Yo las toqué, y en humo su pureza
> Trocarse vi, y en lodo y podredumbre.] (p. 53)

Woman's status as object, her otherness from the subject that desires her, equates her with materiality and justifies the tension between attraction and disgust that structures the movement of the poem. The germinal figure of the poem—the prostitute in her brothel—becomes a metaphor for the object world through which the subject inevitably fails to realize his infinite desires.

The image of woman as split between a positive male projection and a negative material reality is not unique to "A Jarifa." It recurs in Espronceda's work, notably in "Canto a Teresa" [Song to Teresa]: "But, oh, a woman is either a fallen angel / Or merely a woman and filthy mire" ["Mas, ¡ay! que es la mujer ángel caído / o mujer nada más y lodo inmundo"] (p. 188). In the same stanza the reference to the biblical fall of man implies that woman is the source of human unhappiness.

> Yes, for the devil in lost Eden burnt the first woman
> with fire from the deep and, alas! that fire has since
> been her children's legacy.

> [Sí, que el demonio en el Edén perdido
> Abrasara con fuego del profundo
> La primera mujer, y ¡ay! aquel fuego
> La herencia ha sido de sus hijos luego.]

Thus he warns "the burning heart" ["el corazón ardiente"] not to drink at the fountain of love, "for hell has poisoned its stream" ["que su raudal lo envenenó el infierno"] (p. 189). This imagery identifies woman with the impurity of the world that poisons every attempt to slake the thirst of human desire.

Espronceda's new poetic paradigm for subjectivity represents women not as subjects in their own right, but rather as emblems of a vitiated object world. This should come as no surprise, especially when Espronceda's poetic project is viewed in the context of the political and economic thought in his generation. The Spanish liberals who sought freedom for individual rights and the pursuit of self-interest left no place for women in their concept of political expression. Political equality for women simply was not conceived as a possibility in early nineteenth-century Spain. Indeed, Larra, the theorist of the connection between liberal ideology and romantic subjectivity, became quite caustic in his review of Dumas' *Anthony* about the idea that women should claim rights and freedoms that might undermine the institution of marriage.

In this literary and ideological context, Gómez de Avellaneda's novel has a very particular place. Contemporaneous with Espronceda's lyrical poems (*Sab* was begun in 1838 and completed the following year), the novel incorporates romantic and liberal values. Indeed, Gómez de Avellaneda's images of the interaction of self and world and of inner, subjective experience closely parallel those of Espronceda. However, Avellaneda reverses the gender positions in this paradigm: women become the subjects rather than the objects of desire. Consequently, her depiction of the external world's hostility to inner feelings and hopes focuses on a very concrete injustice—the impotence and oppression of women and slaves who are excluded from the social structures of power.

The plot of the novel revolves around two interlocking love triangles: Carlota, heiress of a sugar plantation, and Teresa, her orphaned cousin, both love Enrique, the son of an English merchant; Carlota is loved both by Enrique and by Sab, a mulatto slave who is part of her household. This conventional pattern changes, however, as the romantic themes of the novel unfold and the plot traces the impact of a cold, commercial, unjust society on those characters blessed—or cursed—by a superior capacity for feeling. By the end of the novel, Sab, Teresa, and Carlota form a new triad unified not by rivalry for love, but rather, by shared values and common experiences of powerlessness within the social structure.

To illustrate the contrast that differentiates Teresa, Sab, and Carlota from the other characters, let us first consider the case of Enrique Otway. In an interesting reversal of male romantic narratives, his role is that of object—the object of feminine desire; Carlota and Teresa are both in love with him when the novel opens. Although the narrator explores Enrique's feelings and thoughts occasionally, his subjectivity has no impact on the external world of the novel. Instead, his behavior and his emotions are determined from without—by his father's demand that he abandon Carlota or by learning the information that Carlota has won a lottery prize. Furthermore, he is closely associated with the material world, for he concerns himself primarily with business, commerce, and money—values inherently alien to the inner life of the other three main characters. Enrique, then, together with his father, represents the public world of the market, and his feelings obey the laws and norms of that world. For this reason, though ultimately she is devastated by her husband's relentless pursuit of material interests, "Carlota could not, in strict justice, condemn the behavior of her husband, nor complain of her lot." ["Carlota no podía desaprobar con justicia la conducta de su marido, no debía quejarse de su suerte."][4] Enrique is not presented as an evil man; he is simply the human embodiment of a social structure whose values the novel challenges.

The three other main characters belong to a different category, established early in the novel:

> There are on this earth superior souls, privileged with regard to feeling and unrecognized by common souls; souls rich in affections, rich in emotion—for whom are reserved unbridled passions, great virtues, overwhelming sorrows—but . . . Enrique's soul was not one of them.

> [Hay almas superiores sobre la tierra, privilegiadas para el sentimiento y desconocidas de las almas vulgares; almas ricas de afectos, ricas de emociones—para las cuales están reservadas las pasiones terribles, las grandes virtudes, los inmensos pesares—y . . . el alma de Enrique no era una de ellas.] (p. 74)

Carlota is quickly identified as belonging to this privileged category because of her sensibility and the passionate blindness of her love for Enrique. Teresa also, though described as outwardly dry and impassive, has a soul that "was not incapable of great passion; was in fact made to feel it" ["no era incapaz de grandes pasiones, mejor diré, era formada para sentirlas"] (p. 55). Sab reveals his spiritual nature in an internal monologue in which he compares himself to his privileged but unemotional rival, reflecting that Enrique has no idea that the slave has the superior soul, "capable of loving, capable of hating" ["capaz de amar, capaz de aborrecer"] (p. 78). This inversion of social and spiritual status is common to the three exceptional souls—they all occupy inferior positions in the social hierarchy. And the correspondence between the social destiny of the black slave and that of the two women becomes the covert message of the novel.

While all three "superior souls" exemplify the basic romantic paradigm of subjectivity found in Espronceda—the fall from the illusions of the passionate imagination to the bitter knowledge of alienating reality—it is Carlota's experience that most fully embodies this trajectory. The most startling feature of this representation of romantic consciousness in a woman is that Carlota's destiny is tragic, even though the external world grants her all that should make a woman happy. As Teresa observes, "adored daughter, beloved mistress, future wife of the man you have chosen, what could make you unhappy, Carlota?" ["Hija adorada, ama querida, esposa futura del amante de tu elección, ¿qué puede afligirte, Carlota?"] (p. 51). Yet Carlota does suffer, for the fatal romantic chasm between illusion and reality yawns inescapably in woman's social destiny.

Marriage takes Carlota from the virginal garden presented as an externalization of her personality and places her in her husband's sphere, the world of the marketplace where there is no room for love, beauty, and feeling. Consequently, Carlota languishes after her marriage.

> Carlota was a poor poetic soul thrown among a thousand materialist existences. Endowed with a fertile and active imagination, ignorant of life in an age when existence is no more than sensation, she found herself obliged to live according to calculation, reflection and convenience. That mercantile and profit-seeking atmosphere, that incessant concern with material interests dried up the lovely illusions of her young heart.

> [Carlota era una pobre alma poética arrojada entre mil existencias positivas. Dotada de una imaginación fértil y activa, ignorante de la vida, en la edad en que la existencia no es más que sensaciones, se veía obligada a vivir de cálculo, de reflexión y de conveniencia. Aquella atmósfera mercantil y especuladora, aquellos cuidados incesantes de los intereses materiales marchitaban las bellas ilusiones de su joven corazón.] (p. 213)

Carlota's disillusionment teaches her the truth about her place in the world of social facts and power. She discovers that her father-in-law has falsified her own father's will, so that upon his death the inheritance goes to her alone instead of being divided with her sisters. Determined to rectify this injustice, she asks Enrique to give her sisters their fair share. When he refuses, treating her request as childish nonsense, she realizes the full extent of her powerlessness.

> Carlota struggled uselessly for several months, afterward she kept silent and seemed to resign herself. For her all had ended. She saw her husband as he was; she began to understand the realities of life. Her dreams dissolved, her love fled with her happiness. Then she touched reality in all its nakedness, in all its pettiness, . . . and her soul . . . found itself alone in the company of those two earthbound men.

> [Carlota luchó inútilmente por espacio de muchos meses, después guardó silencio y pareció resignarse. Para ella todo había acabado. Vio a su marido tal cual era; comenzó a comprender la vida. Sus sueños se disiparon, su amor huyó con su felicidad. Entonces tocó toda la desnudez, toda la pequeñez de las realidades, . . . se halló sola en medio de aquellos dos hombres pegados a la tierra.] (p. 215)

The key to Carlota's disillusionment is found in the words "luchó inútilmente": the gap between her desire and the world cannot be bridged because women's subordination enforces the radical separation between feminine feeling and male action.

Clearly, Gómez de Avellaneda departs from the conventional women's fiction that her novel at first seems to resemble; instead of demonstrating that women's true happiness is found in their socially assigned role, *Sab* exposes that belief as an illusion. At the same time, the Cuban-born novelist infuses the romantic paradigm of consciousness with radical new content by attributing it to a female subject. In Espronceda's lyric poetry, the lack of social explanation for the subject's alienation and the frustration of his Promethean desire implies a metaphysical determination;[5] but Carlota's story, insofar as it reenacts the romantic syndrome of despair in terms of a woman's experience of what society offers as her optimal destiny, attributes alienation to social injustice. Thus, the novel places the romantic model of subjectivity and the socially prescribed model of femininity in a dialectical confrontation from which neither emerges intact.

The subjectivity of those treated by the social hierarchy as objects is further demonstrated in the characters of Teresa and Sab, both of whom occupy a disadvantageous position in society—Teresa was born out of wedlock and Sab was born a slave. The range of the social critique is in this way extended to include slavery and racism, along with marriage and the subjection of women.

Teresa is presented as a soul capable of passion and feeling, but, "humiliated and swallowing her mortification in silence, she had learned to dissimulate, becoming ever more glacial and reserved" ["humillada y devorando en silencio su mortificación, había aprendido a disimular, haciéndose cada vez más fría y reservada"] (p. 55). In a self-protective effort, Teresa has repressed her deeply felt emotions; the unique lucidity stemming from the detachment she imposes on herself permits her to see Sab's secret love in actions that remain opaque to the other characters. When he reveals to her the extent of his passion and suffering, she is able to grasp the true value of his spirit. It is she who formulates the novel's primary code of ethics by deciding to protect Carlota's illusions about Enrique rather than destroy them with the truth—that he intends to break off their engagement because her dowry is too small. She exhorts the world in general:

Oh, you who have seen it all! . . . Respect these pure brows which have not been stamped with the seal of disillusionment; respect these souls . . . rich in hope and powerful in their youthfulness; let them keep their delusions, which will do them less harm than that fatal clairvoyance you would give them.

[¡Oh, vosotros, los que ya lo habéis visto todo! . . . Respetad esas frentes puras, en las que el desengaño no ha estampado su sello; respetad esas almas . . . ricas de esperanzas y poderosas por su juventud; dejadles sus errores, menos mal les harán que esa fatal previsión que queréis darles.] (pp. 146–47)

She prevails upon Sab to accept this code of ethics, persuading him to abandon his plan to expose Enrique's materialistic calculations and instead to use his winning lottery ticket to make Carlota rich and thus renew her fiancé's commitment.

Teresa's sublimated passion becomes compassion, which is at the top of the novel's scale of values. Both Sab and Carlota turn to her for sympathy and comfort in their anguish. Sab tells her: "May God bless you! . . . Were it not for you, I would have gone through life as if through a desert, alone with my love and my misfortune without encountering one look of sympathy or compassionate word!" ["¡Bendígate Dios! . . . ¡A no ser por vos, yo hubiera pasado por la senda de la vida como por un desierto, solo con mi amor y mi desventura, sin encontrar una mirada de simpatía ni una palabra de compasión!"] (p. 174). Romantic consciousness, according to Gómez de Avellaneda, sees happiness as an illusion, an impossibility in reality. But the novel offers a compensatory value: the sympathy of another feeling soul eases the frustration of desire, confirming the existence of spiritual values despite the exterior world's hostility. Creating a select fellowship of "superior souls" becomes a way of mitigating the isolation of the feeling subject in an alien world.

The value of intersubjective relations as compensation for the failure of the subject-object relation is dramatized in Teresa's final act. As she lies on her deathbed, Teresa gives Carlota the letter in which Sab had revealed his true feelings as he was dying. She offers this testament as a consolation for her friend in the lonely years to come.

> Perhaps you will find nothing great or beautiful to solace your tired heart. Then you will have this paper; this paper is a complete soul; it is a life and a death. . . . When you are reading this paper you will believe as I do in love and virtue.

> [Acaso no hallarás nada grande y bello en que descansar tu corazón fatigado. Entonces tendrás ese papel; ese papel es toda un alma; es una vida, una muerte. . . . Mientras leas ese papel creerás como yo en el amor y la virtud.] (p. 218)

The lesson that Teresa teaches is that compassion and love, the shared subjectivity of the oppressed, provide the only consolation in a hard, commercial world, the only antidote to solitary despair.

If the sublimation of passion into compassion, the abstraction of a philosophy from pain, are processes of the psyche explored in Teresa, Sab represents the movement of primary emotion. His soul, preserved like a life-giving balm in his letter, has "the fragrance of a heart that died without drying up" ["el aroma de un corazón que moría sin marchitarse"] (p. 218). He believes that his love for Carlota fully justifies his life: "My flame has been pure, immense, inextinguishable! It does not matter that I have suffered, for I have loved Carlota. . . ." ["¡Mi llama ha sido pura, inmensa, inextinguible! No importa que haya padecido, pues he amado a Carlota. . . ."] (p. 171). And Teresa agrees: "the heart that can love like this is not a common heart" ["el corazón que sabe amar así, no es un corazón vulgar"] (p. 173). Sab is all heart, all passion. In contrast to Teresa, he cannot sublimate feeling; when he has sacrificed his passion by assuring Carlota's marriage to Enrique, his psychic substance has been spent and he simply dies.

However, there is more to Sab's emotion than passionate love, for he supplies what so far has been lacking in Gómez de Avellaneda's representation of female subjectivity as romantic consciousness—a sense of outrage, the Promethean impulse to revolt. The fifth chapter of the novel links Sab with a rage that, echoed and magnified by nature, escapes the bounds of his character. Accompanying Enrique through the forest as a dangerous thunderstorm approaches, Sab stares somberly at Carlota's fiancé, trying to perceive his innermost thoughts. Suddenly, as if he has seen the truth— that Enrique intends to jilt Carlota because her dowry is insufficient— Sab's face changes, crossed by "a bitter, scornful, inexplicable smile" ["una sonrisa amarga, desdeñosa, inexplicable"] (p. 76). At this moment the storm breaks out in all its fury: "The sky splits open, spewing fire through innumerable mouths; lightning describes a thousand burning angles; its bolts fell even the largest trees and the blazing atmosphere is like a vast bonfire" ["El cielo se abre vomitando fuego por innumerables bocas; el relámpago describe mil ángulos encendidos; el rayo troncha los más corpulentos árboles y la atmósfera encendida semeja una vasta hoguera"] (p. 76). The object of this violence is Enrique, struck from his horse, bloody and unconscious; Sab, standing over him, is identified with the storm: "the gleam emitted at that moment by his jet black pupils was somber and sinister, like the blazing storm . . ." ["sombrío y siniestro, como los fuegos de la tempestad, era el brillo que despedían en aquel momento sus pupilas de azabache . . ."] (p. 77). Sab finally subdues the murderous storm in his breast and takes his rival to safety. Still, this episode reveals great anger in Sab's soul, as if the character were the channel for a threatening energy latent in the atmosphere of the island paradise.

Indeed, Sab concretizes the historical threat felt by Cubans during the century following the Haitian revolution insofar as he protests the social order that makes his dream of love an impossible fantasy. In his long conversation with Teresa, he reveals that he harbors fantasies of a slave uprising.

I have thought, too, of arming against our oppressors, turning the chained hands of their victims against them; raising in their midst the terrible cry of liberty and vengeance; bathing myself in the blood of white men; treading their corpses and their laws under my feet, and perishing myself among the ruins.

[He pensado también en armar contra nuestros opresores, los brazos encadenados de sus víctimas; arrojar en medio de ellos el terrible grito de libertad y ven-

ganza; bañarme en sangre de blancos; hollar con mis pies sus cadáveres y sus
leyes y perecer yo mismo entre sus ruinas.] (p. 157)

At another point in the novel Sab evokes the image of slave revolt, this
time reporting the words of Martina, his surrogate mother, who claims to
have descended from the now extinct indigenous population: "the descen-
dents of the oppressors will be oppressed, and the black men will be the
terrible avengers of the red men" ["los descendientes de los opresores
serán oprimidos, y los hombres negros serán los terribles vengadores de los
hombres cobrizos"] (p. 133).

In this vengeful talk, Sab distinguishes himself from the female "superior
souls." Although the cases of Teresa and Carlota imply a social critique,
exposing the heartlessness of a society ruled by the marketplace as well as
the impotence of women who preserve the human value of love, they do
not condemn or denounce social injustice, nor do they register any thought
of rebellion. Yet the three characters are so closely associated that the
anger suppressed in Carlota and Teresa speaks in Sab's violent fantasies.
And in the end, Sab takes on the submission exemplified by the two
women. Just as his violent rage during the tempest eventually is subdued,
so the thoughts of rebellion are carefully constrained. Sab disavows the
desire to rebel, though he fully appreciates the necessity of revolt. "Don't
worry," he tells Teresa, "the slaves are patiently wearing their chains; to
break them they need to hear perhaps only one voice crying to them: 'You
are men!' but that voice will not be mine, you may rest assured" ["Tran-
quilizaros, los esclavos arrastran pacientemente su cadena; acaso sólo
necesitan para romperla, oír una voz que les grite: '¡Sois hombres!' pero
esa voz no será la mía, podéis creerlo"] (p. 153). At the conclusion of his
letter to Teresa, Sab piously asserts that the oppressed must not act, but
trust God to raise the throne of justice upon the ruins of the old society.

In contrast to the clarity of his indictment of society, Sab's reasons for
not acting upon his political awareness appear vague, revealing a narrative
divided against itself as it attempts both to justify and to contain Sab's
anger. At the end of the novel in Sab's letter to Teresa, an equation between the destiny of women and that of slaves makes manifest the link
between the women characters and Sab's angry protest. Sab's letter to
Teresa is passed on to Carlota as a condensation of the secret awareness
shared by three souls endowed with superior subjectivity; it also recapitu-
lates Gómez de Avellaneda's identification of the romantic subject with
marginalized gender and race. Through the letter, Carlota discovers Sab's
inner soul, which harbored a sublime passion that she has come to think
impossible. Yet Sab's last words emerge less as a declaration of love than
as a powerful attack on the injustice of slavery and a condemnation of
society.

Sab begins his letter with a long description of his early reflections on virtue. In his youth he rejected the Church's teaching that "the virtue of he slave . . . is to obey and be silent, to serve his legitimate owners with humility and resignation, and never to judge them" ["la virtud del esclavo . . . es obedecer y callar, servir con humildad y resignación a sus legítimos dueños, y no juzgarlos nunca"] (p. 220). Virtue must be the same for all men, he argues, protesting that the God-given harmony of nature has been perverted by human society. Above all, he indicts a social structure that, because he is a slave, prevents him from using his superior talents.

If destiny had opened me any path whatsoever, I would have taken it. . . . [I] had the aptitude and determination to do anything. I lacked only the power! I was a mulatto and a slave.
How many times have I dreamed like the pariah of great, rich, populous cities, cities of culture, those immense workshops of civilization where the man of genius finds numberless opportunities!

[Si el destino me hubiese abierto una senda cualquiera, me habría lanzado en ella. . . . [P]ara todo hallaba en mí la aptitud y la voluntad. ¡Sólo me faltaba el poder! Era mulato y esclavo.
¡Cuántas veces, como el paria, he soñado con las grandes ciudades ricas y populosas, con las ciudades cultas, con esos inmensos talleres de civilización en que el hombre de genio encuentra tantos destinos!] (p. 226)

Sab's letter rings with echoes of liberalism; he adopts the arguments of an aspiring bourgeoisie that accuses a system of inherited privilege of excluding those who possess talent and demonstrate merit: "it is men who have forged this destiny for me, . . . for they have raised a wall of error and prejudice between themselves and the destiny God designed for me" ["son los hombres los que me han formado este destino, . . . si ellos han levantado un muro de errores y preocupaciones entre sí y el destino que la providencia me había señalado"] (p. 226). Significantly, when Sab reaches this culminating point of his denunciation, he becomes aware of the shadow of death pressing in and a vision of Carlota, at the point of consummating her marriage, interrupts the flow of his argument. "It's she, it's Carlota, with her wedding ring and her virgin's crown—but she is followed by a squalid and hateful troop! They are disillusionment, tedium, regret—and behind them comes that monster with the sepulchral voice and the iron head—the irremediable" ["Es ella, es Carlota, con su anillo nupcial y su corona de virgen—¡Pero la sigue una tropa escuálida y odiosa!—son el desengaño, el tedio, el arrepentimiento—y más atrás ese monstruo de voz sepulcral y cabeza de hierro—lo irremediable"] (p. 227). The words that immediately follow this prophesy of Carlota's fate suggest that Sab's discourse on slavery actually has been about *women's* destiny:[6] "Oh, women! Poor, blind victims! Like slaves, they patiently wear their chains and lower their heads under the yoke of human laws" ["¡Oh!, ¡las mujeres! ¡Pobres y ciegas víctimas! Como los esclavos, ellas arrastran pacientemente su cadena y bajan la cabeza bajo el yugo de las leyes humanas"] (p. 227). He deemphasizes the finality of a slave's fate in comparison to a married woman's, arguing that slaves at least can buy their freedom.

> [B]ut woman, when she raises her wasted hands and her battered head to ask for freedom, hears the monster with the sepulchral voice shouting: 'In the tomb.' Don't you hear a voice, Teresa? It's the voice of the strong who say to the weak: 'Obedience, humility, resignation—these are virtue'.

> [Pero la mujer, cuando levanta sus manos enflaquecidas y su frente ultrajada para pedir libertad, oye al monstruo de voz sepulcral que le grita: 'En la tumba.' ¿No oís una voz, Teresa? Es la de los fuertes que dice a los débiles: 'Obediencia, humildad, resignación—ésta es la virtud'.] (p. 227)

With this reference to his starting point, Sab includes women in his entire condemnation of society's oppression of slaves.

Indeed, the dominant theme of Sab's letter suggests that the issue of slavery is secondary to that of women. In general, society's blighting of Sab's ambitions and talents is protested more than the oppression of a general class of human beings. While the letter begins with an argument against slavery derived from the assumption of natural human equality, the concrete proof of slavery's iniquity—both in Sab's letter and in the novel as a whole—is found in the denial of an outlet through which Sab's innate superiority might express itself. This focus reveals the true target of the denunciation of oppression. The fictional slave's outrage vents the frustration of the author, a young colonial woman who aspired to pour out her subjectivity in writing and win recognition in the great European centers of civilization and culture, but who was told to be silent and resign herself to those virtues prescribed for women.

Gómez de Avellaneda began to write *Sab* at her stepfather's family home in Galicia in 1837. An autobiographical document written two years later describes the conflict that immediately ensued between the young woman and Spanish expectations of feminine conduct. In Cuba her mother had more or less indulged her literary aspirations, but her stepfather's people in the very traditional city of La Coruña were appalled by her preference of books to housework.

> They said I was an atheist, and the proof they gave was that I read Rousseau. . . . [T]hey said . . . that I wasn't good for anything because I didn't know how to iron, or cook, or darn stockings; because I didn't wash windows, or make beds, or sweep my room. . . . They also ridiculed my fondness for studying and called me *the lady scholar*.

[Decían que yo era atea, y la prueba que daban era que leía las obras de Rousseau. . . . [D]ecían . . . que yo no era buena para nada, porque no sabía planchar, ni cocinar, ni calcetar; porque no lavaba los cristales, ni hacía las camas, ni barría mi cuarto. . . . Ridiculizaban también mi afición al estudio y me llamaban la Doctora.][7]

To ease the domestic tension, Gómez de Avellaneda was allowed to travel with her younger brother to her deceased father's birthplace in an Andalusian village. There, too, her relatives' main concern was that she conform to the Spanish ideal of womanhood and marry a local *hidalgo* (p. 75). Firmly resisting all attempts to domesticate her, Gómez de Avellaneda expressed throughout her autobiography the "horror of marriage" ["horror al matrimonio"] (p. 63) that informs Sab's final outburst. In Sab, she projected her aspirations for self-realization and through his mouth dared to condemn the social institution that would inflict upon women the role of passive resignation to powerlessness that Sab protested. And through *Sab* she defied the social conventions of gender hierarchy and realized her desire to step into man's world of literary publication: the publication of *Sab* and her *Poesías* in 1841 signaled her success.

It was her determination to write, to claim her place in the public world and her right to express her inner passions and fancies, that led Gómez de Avellaneda to assert in *Sab* that woman, too, can be that liberal and romantic subject characterized in the writing of contemporaries such as Larra and Espronceda. By applying the romantic paradigm of desire and despair to those excluded from the freedom and equality claimed by liberal ideology, she gave that paradigm a social specificity that it lacked in other formulations. This was her achievement in the novel: pointing to concrete inequities that inflicted alienation and anguish on those in her society who were neither male nor white.

However, the limitations of Avellaneda's perspective are also patent in the novel. In a sense she colonized the mulatto slave's subjectivity to suit her own purpose when she characterized him as willing to sacrifice both his freedom and his people for his impossible love of a white woman. That a bourgeois white woman's representation of a mulatto was conditioned by the interests of her class and race is hardly surprising. But the fact that this female author wrote the first Hispanic antislavery novel as a vehicle for an oblique feminist protest reveals something less predictable: Gómez de Avellaneda found it easier to express abolitionist sentiments—which were considered so subversive by the Spanish colonial government in Cuba that it would not permit *Sab* to be published there—than to broach directly the issues of sexual inequality. This paradox may remind contemporary readers of the power of the cultural taboos that Gómez de Avellaneda faced as she challenged the male monopoly of literature.

# Notes

1. In Cuba another abolitionist novel, *Francisco. El ingenio o Las delicias del campo*, by Anselmo Suárez y Romero, was finished in 1839, the same year in which the manuscript of *Sab* was completed. Suárez's novel, however, was not published until 1880, while *Sab* appeared in Spain in 1841. See Alberto Gutiérrez de la Solana, "*Sab y Francisco*: Paralelo y contraste," in *Homenaje a Gertrudis Gómez de Avellaneda*, ed. Gladys Zaldívar and Rosa Martínez de Cabrera (Miami: Editora Universal, 1981), pp. 301–303.

2. Mariano José de Larra, "Literatura," in *Obras de Mariano José de Larra*, ed. Carlos Seco Serrano, Biblioteca de Autores Españoles 127–30 (Madrid: Editorial Atlas, 1960), 2:133–34. Subsequent page references to this essay will be included in the text.

3. José de Espronceda, *El diablo mundo. El estudiante de Salamanca. Poesías*, ed. Jaime Gil de Biedma (Madrid: Alianza, 1966), p. 52. Subsequent page references to this edition will be included in the text.

4. Gertrudis Gómez de Avellaneda, *Sab*, ed. Carmen Bravo Villasante (Salamanca: Anaya, 1970), p. 213. Subsequent references to the novel will be included in the text.

5. See Thomas E. Lewis, "Contradictory Explanatory Systems in Espronceda's Poetry: The Social Genesis and Structure of *El diablo mundo*," *Ideologies and Literature* 4 (1983): 44.

6. This observation has also been made by Pedro Barreda Tomás in "Abolicionismo y feminismo en la Avellaneda: Los negros como artificio narrativo en *Sab*," *Cuadernos Hispanoamericanos*, no. 342 (1978): 613–26.

7. *Autobiografía y cartas de la señorita doña Gertrudis Gómez de Avellaneda*, ed. Lorenzo Cruz de Fuentes (Madrid: Imprenta Helénica, 1914), p. 72. Subsequent references to this work will be included in the text.

# Between Genre and Gender:
# Emilia Pardo Bazán and *Los Pazos de Ulloa*

## MARYELLEN BIEDER

When Emilia Pardo Bazán published *Los Pazos de Ulloa* [The manor house of Ulloa] in 1886, the diversity of competing genre models placed contradictory demands on the shape of the narrative. The writer whose work would emerge as the seminal novelistic presence in late nineteenth-century Spain, Benito Pérez Galdós, had already begun to define the contours of Spanish realism in his own novels, while the theories and novels of Emile Zola were being debated in literary circles in a polemic to which Pardo Bazán herself added no little fuel with her reasoned but unflinching presentation in *La cuestión palpitante* [The critical question] (1883). Against these two emergent models stood the tradition of the prevailing genres that had given shape to the Spanish narrative throughout the nineteenth century: romanticism, *costumbrismo* or regional sketches, the sentimental novel, and such enduring genres as hagiology. Pardo Bazán stands at the confluence of these literary impulses, some in ascendancy, others on the wane, and charts the path of her novel through the largely male-defined and male-dominated waters. In adopting the realist-naturalist mode, she also positions herself within a male genre tradition without entirely disengaging her fiction from the influences of either male-voiced *costumbrismo* or the female-voiced sentimental novel.[1]

Pardo Bazán forges her novel from the conjunction of *costumbrista* set pieces, realistic portrayal and plotting, sentimental exaltation of motherhood, and naturalist observation of man and nature. Fashioning her response to the claims of competing genre traditions, she builds a synthesis of referential representation (realism), detached observation (naturalism), and moral suasion (sentimental novel).[2] Within this resolution of conflicting genre imperatives, *Los Pazos de Ulloa* manifests an underlying gender-linked tension. This tension arises from Pardo Bazán's subversion of the boundaries of gender differentiation marked out in the varying modes on which her novel draws.

On a thematic level the structure of *Los Pazos de Ulloa* owes a debt to popular fiction. At the same time, Pardo Bazán manages to free this thematic borrowing from its rigid cautionary framework and rework it within her own novelistic vision. Recognizing the synthetic nature of this novel, Nelly Clémessy has attempted to identify the motifs that interlock to form the intensely dramatic structure: the servant girl-mistress, the adulterous husband, the enamored priest, excessive maternal love, the degeneration of a family line, and the social climbing of the rural proletariat.[3] The resulting structures fall into two classes: inversion of the class hierarchy of a traditional society and violations of gendered societal or moral norms governing individual conduct. In Pardo Bazán's treatment of the disruption of normative social patterns, the attention shifts from the restoration of the moral order, as in much sentimental fiction, to a probing of the underlying gender differentiation. On the other hand, the set pieces of naturalist description, infused with elements of *costumbrismo*, reproduce the defining forces and events of the isolated, self-contained world of the Pazo. The dinner hosted by the priest of Naya, the political intrigue, the hunting trips, even the scene of the rabbits in heat,[4] depict the sphere of male activity and influence and offer a display of male language, male mobility, and male bonding. This male world of hunting, politics, and the priesthood is, moreover, exclusionary and closed to women.

At first glance the narrative voice in *Los Pazos de Ulloa* appears to respond primarily to the conventions of the realist-naturalist mode. First person discourse only rarely disrupts the dominant third person narration. More significantly, within the undramatized, unobtrusive narration there emerges an identifiable voice characterized by the elaborations, explanations, information, and values that it enunciates. This culturally determined, value-bound voice invokes the common assumptions and knowledge shared by narrator and narratee (that readerly presence within the narrative itself), even as it marks the distance that separates them. The temporal referents, the appeal to broad cultural and psychological patterns, and self-reflexiveness define the narrative voice in the novel, but without gender-linked associations. In contrast, other distinguishing features of the narrative function to situate it squarely within the conventions of male-gendered narrative discourse. The displays of scientific information, the invocation of expert opinion, the knowledge of foreign cultures, the references to archaic language and customs, the privileging of exclusively male activities and space, all assert—too strenuously it might be argued—the identity of a gendered narrative voice. In speaking the language of education, science, art, sports, medicine, the Casino (gentlemen's club), and bourgeois morality—spheres defined and dominated by men in the nineteenth century—the narrative voice positions itself within a male-defined world.[5]

In contrast to the assertively male-voiced narrative conventions and the privileging of male culture, the narration itself largely is filtered through the subjectivity of the characters. Omniscient narration yields continually to the limited visual and conceptual perspective of the characters. This is not simply a matter of narrative point of view but rather, to borrow Gérard Genette's useful distinction, of focalization, since in *Los Pazos de Ulloa* the narration frequently adopts the limitations of the individual character's field of vision and perceptual frame of reference. Focalization is the relationship between "the agent who sees and what he sees."[6] In focalized narration the visual field narrows to coincide with the defined perceptual and conceptual framework of a focalizer. Dramatized or not, the focalizer is "the presence—. . . the consciousness—through whose spatial, temporal, and/or psychological position the textual events are perceived."[7] The predominant focalizer in *Los Pazos de Ulloa* is the young priest, Julián, although at intervals the narration shapes itself to other characters' visual and mental representation of their world.[8] Throughout most of the novel the shifts from one perceptual frame to another occur without any overt marking by the narrator. But this variable focalization disappears abruptly in an overt shift towards the end of the novel when the young child Perucho becomes focalizer.

In addition to its conventional male voice, the narration frequently narrows to follow the gaze and emotional responses of a gendered focalizer. The reader follows this dual-focused narration, reading both the narrative voice and the focalizer's perceptions of the world of the Pazo. Having blurred traditional genre boundaries in the synthetic configuration of her novel, Pardo Bazán also moves to juxtapose male-voiced narrative conventions to the subjective vision of the individual character. This gender identity of the viewing perspective constitutes one of the distinctive features of narration in *Los Pazos de Ulloa* and helps focus the broader question of gender identity within the novel. At the same time that male-voiced discursive strategies shape the overt features of the narrative voice, the narration probes the subsurface tensions within rigid gender definitions. In this way the subversion of dominant male-voiced narration through focalization carries over into the subversion of gender boundaries within the narration.

Illustrative of this subversion and resulting tension, the initial scene of *Los Pazos de Ulloa* echoes one of the most famous dramatic openings in Spanish literature, a literal "falling into" the world of the text. In Calderón de la Barca's Golden Age drama *La vida es sueño*, the young noblewoman Rosaura is thrown from her horse and falls into the wilds inhabited by the untamed prince Segismundo. To free herself from the strictures on female action, Rosaura has dressed as a man ("a traveler" ["hombre de camino"]) for her journey into the male world. Thus appearance and nature clash: the "male" traveler masks a lady, the forbidding mountain houses a prince, and gender identity is repeatedly subordinated to the demands of the social order. Pardo Bazán reworks this opening scene in her novel, as the young priest Julián finds himself powerless to control the horse that propels him into the world of the Pazo of Ulloa. The Calderonian intertext functions not only in the dramatic plotting—impetuous horse, unsure rider, precipitous journey—but more significantly in thematizing displaced identity. A female cloaked in male identity, Rosaura sets in motion her own plot within the conflicting desires and loyalties of a patriarchal social structure. As with Rosaura, nature and appearance clash in Julián, the male attire in conflict with the feminine sensibility and "the weakness of his lymphatic-nervous, purely feminine temperament" ["la endeblez de su temperamento linfático-nervioso, puramente femenino"] (p. 26).[9]

In the male world of the Pazo, Julián cuts an androgynous figure, neither wholly integrated into the male experience nor totally excluded from it. The statue of Saint Julian in the church at Naya graphically displays the tension inherent in the saint's namesake.

> [T]he blessed Saint Julian . . . with his credulous face, his ecstatic little smile, his tight-fitting waistcoat and short pants, his white dove in the right hand, and his left hand delicately resting on the ruffle of his shirt.

> [[E]l bienaventurado San Julián . . . con su carita inocentona, su extática sonrisilla, su chupa y calzón corto, su paloma blanca en la diestra, y la siniestra delicadamente apoyada en la chorrera de la camisola.] (p. 52)

The innocence of a Saint Julian, also observable in Julián since his seminary days (p. 26) and reconfirmed by his naive misunderstanding of the Pazo household, is linked externally to female reactions. In Julián's case, the predominance of female role models in his childhood along with a physiologically "feminine" character, form these patterns. Both his profession and his temperament allow Julián to mediate between the female and the male spheres, moving freely between them without belonging fully to either.

Through the intertextuality of the opening paragraph, Pardo Bazán has introduced an androgynous tension into a gender-determined narrative. From the outset, the slippage between external form and internal self is dramatized. Identity has both a physical and a social dimension, and the conflicting impulses of self and society create a tension that defines not only Julián but Nucha and other characters as well. While adopting narrative conventions of the realist and naturalist modes, Pardo Bazán problematizes the identity of individual characters at their most essential level of being, thus calling into question the normative definitions of "male" and "female."

The two central characters in *Los Pazos de Ulloa*, Julián and Nucha, experience a failure to reconcile their sexual and emotional selves with socially imposed roles. Julián may enact the role of chaplain at the Pazo, but his emotional self rewrites experience in the language of hagiology. Nucha, on the other hand, consistently is viewed as the embodiment of the maternal. Indeed, the male world sees her exclusively as a mother, from her brother Gabriel (for whom she has served as a mother), to her father (for whom she is mistress of the household and future housekeeper to Gabriel), to Julián (for whom she always and exclusively represents the Virgin mother), and to her husband Pedro (for whom she is the potential bearer of a son and heir).[10] Nucha has no real being outside that of mother—substitute, potential, real, or virginal—and when she fails to fulfill the female obligation to patriarchal society, that of giving Pedro a legitimate male heir, she has no role, no reason for existence. Neither Pedro, nor her father, nor her beloved brother offer a re-definition of the superfluous Nucha's role after the birth of her daughter. With no self-generated identity to offset this externally imposed definition of flawed motherhood, Nucha withers and dies.

The Pazo of Ulloa is a patriarchal world in which the female is assigned a defined, limited role determined by her relationship to the male.[11] Instead of authenticating Nucha's identity as mother, the experience of physical motherhood defines her as a failed mother. If the value of the female in this male-centered world lies in the mother-son bond, mothering women are curiously absent from the novel. Julián's mother, although unseen, ministers lovingly to her son, but as a housekeeper, she is at the service of the entire De la Lage household as well. Sabel, herself motherless, is a disinterested mother at best, while the wet nurse, in taking up her duties in the Pazo, has lost the possibility of mothering her own child.[12] Nucha's incarnation of her female identity thus merely distances her further from the world in which the mother is so underrepresented. The sentimental representation of motherhood is undermined by the story of Pedro's own mother, who suffered the violation of her enclosed female world and the physical violence of a brutal robbery. Her hoard of accumulated money constituted an abuse of the male prerogative of economic control, an abuse that invited violent male retaliation unchecked by moral restraints.

At the other extreme from motherhood, the ancient Limioso sisters live an anachronistic, desiccated existence, suspended in a time and a way of life long disappeared outside their *pazo*. They are spinsters, literally spinsters, ceaselessly spinning their monotonous life thread, unaffected by the passing of the era in which women of their class spent their days with the spindle and distaff. In Nucha's eyes, they represent a scene straight out of the world of fiction, having no analogue in her urban experience (p. 147).[13] Only the youthful Molende sisters replicate the activity and the female chatter that remind Nucha of the sororal community in which she grew up. They are also the only neighbors who are not at home when Pedro and Nucha call, and they do not appear directly in the narrative field of vision. Their life contrasts sharply with the life of a married woman such as Nucha who is bound by the restraints of a patriarchal world.[14]

By highlighting the incompatibility between the masculine world of the Pazo and the androgynous priest who stumbles into it, Pardo Bazán suggests the inadequacy of patriarchal definitions and the exclusionary male perspective. The choice of Julián as focalizer of the unfamiliar world of rural Galicia serves a number of functions—primarily the problematizing of stereotypical sexual roles. But Julián, with his feminine temperament and sensibility, and Nucha, ever "virginal" even in marriage, suggest androgynous identities that cannot mesh with normative social judgments. Nucha's sisters, Rita and Manuela, also violate patriarchal norms for female conduct and physiognomy; one displays independence of action and the other has the beginnings of a moustache, both suggestive of an inadmissible sexual ambiguity. The narrator's characterization of Manolita most clearly expresses this androgynous tension: "a masculine trait combined with feminine charms, facial fuzz which was growing into a moustache, a hairline which extended down along her ear until, in descending the length of the jaw, it was trying to become not just modest sideburns but rather a bold beard" ["un carácter masculino mezclado a los hechizos femeniles, un bozo que iba pasando a bigote, una prolongación del nacimiento del pelo sobre la oreja, que, descendiendo a lo largo de la mandíbula, quería ser, más que suave patilla, atrevida barba"] (p. 88). Rita's flaw is less visible than her sister's but more devastating for being silenced; Julián cannot even name it. "How could he make even the most superficial and slightest mention of that 'business' about Miss Rita which, if maliciously interpreted, could prove so harmful to her honor?" ["¿cómo indicar ni lo más somero y mínimo de 'aquello' de la señorita Rita, que, maliciosamente interpretado, tanto podía dañar a la honra?"] (p. 97). Pedro has already detected the vivacious and piercing glances with which she responds to her male admirers. Rita is trapped by the duplicity of men who freely express their admiration while condemning her for responding to it. The men of the Casino openly approve of her allure, beauty, and shapely body but silently disapprove of her as a potential partner in marriage. They convey their silent verdict in words that "taken literally carry no malice but which held up to the light can convey everything. . . ." ["tomadas al pie de la letra, no llevan malicia alguna, pero vistas al trasluz pueden significarlo todo. . . "] (pp. 101–102). Only a foreigner would not detect the unnameable "flaw" in Rita.[15]

From opposing social and environmental contexts, diametrically opposed judgments emerge. The urban society of Santiago values decorum, self-effacing modesty, and above all, the absence of self-assertion or obtrusiveness. Rita's crime in the eyes of the Casino males is her individuality, not her superb physicality but her awareness and enjoyment of it. At the other extreme, the rural doctor, Máximo Juncal, judges Nucha not as an incarnation of modesty and self-effacement but as a flawed reproductive system; his criteria are anatomical and physiological. Both societies pass judgment on women but their value systems conflict. Pedro marries Nucha for her irreproachable virtue, having decided that "he liked piety in a woman very much" ["le agradaba mucho la religiosidad en las mujeres"] (p. 98). But during the critical period of childbirth, his thoughts turn to the robust Rita, convinced now that "a woman should be suitable principally for the propagation of the species" ["la mujer debe ser principalmente muy apta para la propagación de la especie"] (p. 155). The same Rita who at best gave the appearance of immodesty in the stifling conformity of Santiago now suggests to him "the robust stock" ["el robusto tronco"] (p. 155) ideally designed to bear healthy fruit.

Pardo Bazán's novel dramatizes the lives, not of those who achieve a harmonious self-definition, but of those individuals who have no independent identity, only that imposed on them by others. This lack of self-definition, this absence of interiority, sets Nucha and Julián apart from the others. Raised by his widowed mother, subordinated to a household dominated by the De la Lage daughters, trained and ordained in the devotion of the Virgin Mary, Julián displays an idealized veneration of women even as he shares their world. Like Nucha, Julián's identity is externally imposed on him by individuals and institutions to whom he is subordinate as the son of a servant and as a priest.

Since childhood Nucha's family has defined her as mother, mother to her youngest sibling, Gabriel. Nucha accedes to the will of the male to whom she is subordinate—brother, father, husband and, to some extent, priest. Of Nucha the self-defined individual, one sees nothing. Pedro values her for attributes external to her self: her inheritance from her mother, the expected inheritance from her aunt, and the capacity to bear him a son and legitimate heir to his estate. (Note that Pedro himself is not the legitimate heir to the title Marqués de Ulloa, although he willingly accepts the designation.) Pedro marries Nucha as a means to an end—the resurrection of his estate and the regeneration of his succession; and she fails him on both counts, by losing the designation as heir to her aunt and then by bearing Pedro a superfluous female child. Displaced by Sabel in Pedro's bed and by Sabel's male child in his projection of the future, Nucha becomes a useless encumbrance. Having accepted the demands first of father and then of husband, she finds her uncentered existence incomprehensible: "Tell me, Julian, have I failed in my duty in any way?" ["Dígame usted, Julián, ¿he faltado en algo?"] (p. 263). After the birth of her daughter, she lives an isolated life mothering her child, a being so devoid of significance to others that she is not named in the text. Without purpose and without relationship to the world that surrounds her, Nucha wastes away until she ultimately disappears. Even her death is absent from the text, unobserved and undramatized. Ignored in life, she is unlamented in death. Even the memory of Nucha has disappeared from the Pazo in the ten-year interval, so tenuous was her passage there. She remains, of course, alive in Julián's suppressed memory as an extension of the memory of his own experience, becoming more dependent on him in death than in life.

Perhaps it is Nucha's very name that constantly invokes the dependent status of her existence both in her father's house and in marriage. Not a name at all, Nucha is a diminutive ending disassociated from the individualizing name, as she is constrained to explain to Pedro: "'My name is Marcelina. . . . But my sisters always call me Marcelinucha or Nucha. . . .'" ["Me llamo Marcelina. . . . Pero éstas me llaman siempre Marcelinucha o Nucha. . . ."] Pedro first calls her "'Miss Hucha, or whatever your name is. . .'" ["doña Hucha, o como te llames. . ."] (p. 84), further severing the link with the original name. Like her name, Nucha herself always seems to be a derivative, appended, and undifferentiated self. Only Julián recognizes that this odd name is more appropriate for a dog than a person (p. 99). And only Julián names her, addressing her always as "señorita Marcelina," respecting her autonomy as a person (and her superior social status). The repetition of "Nucha" throughout the narration reinforces the sense of her nonbeing and the marginality that characterizes her existence.[16]

Julián fails in his obligations to the household of the Pazo as surely as Nucha does, but he retains his externally defined identity. Patriarchal authority, in the form of the bishop, disposes of Julián's life as a husband or a father disposes of a woman's. While Pedro loses all interest in the commodity that so flagrantly failed to meet his expectations and Nucha's father fails to respond to this neglect of his daughter, the bishop never ceases to exercise his authority over Julián. Julián's life retains its intrinsic value for the bishop who finds him redeemable. Hardship and exile regenerate Julián, subordinating the feminine aspects of his character and building a controlled self. His lymphatic nervous temperament subjected to the harsh reality of a mountain parish, Julián sheds the visual markers of his feminine dimension. The new Julián is externally altered, but he is a hollow shell emptied of a part of himself; he is alive but not whole.

To reinforce the absence that characterizes Nucha's life, her experiences largely are focalized through Julián. He observes her, listens to her, interprets her, and collaborates with her. Her presence in the text is mediated in part through Julián's eyes and understanding. Since childhood Julián has always viewed Nucha adoringly as the sympathetic *señorita*; to him she is an angel. In contrast, the emotionally uninvolved Pedro views her dispassionately as "'somewhat cross-eyed . . . and skinny. . . . She only has pretty hair and a good disposition'" ["algo bizca . . . y flaca. . . . Sólo tiene buen pelo y buen genio"] (p. 97). But in Julián's eyes she is a living representation of the Virgin, a perception grounded in artistic referents. Pregnant, she recalls paintings of the Visitation of the Virgin: "The placement of her hands, spread over her abdomen, as if to protect it, completed the analogy with paintings of so tender a subject." ["La colocación de sus manos, extendidas sobre el vientre, como para protegerlo, complementaba la analogía con las pinturas de tan tierno asunto."] (p. 148).

At significant moments in her life, however, Nucha ceases to be the viewed object and becomes the viewing subject who gives shape to the narration. In one of the most powerful scenes of the novel, Nucha waits for Pedro in the nuptial chamber, an enclosure that in her mind replicates the awesome mystery of the wedding chapel.

It seemed to her that that room in which so imposing a silence reigned, in which such tall and solemn lights burned, was the very same temple in which less than two hours ago she had knelt down. . . . Vigorous footsteps, the creaking of brand-new boots, were heard in the corridor, and the door opened.

[Parecíale que aquella habitación donde reinaba tan imponente silencio, donde ardían tan altas y graves las luces, era el mismo templo en que no hacía dos horas aún se había puesto de hinojos. . . . Oyéronse en el corredor pisadas recias, crujir de botas flamantes, y la puerta se abrió.] (p. 114)

The impersonal "were heard" ["oyéronse"] closes the chapter and reinforces the absence of self, the alienation of Nucha's emotional self from her physical presence in the room. Nucha's perceptions at this highly charged moment dramatize from within her psyche the sacrificial nature of her marriage to Pedro. The narration has already prepared the parallels between altar and bed by fusing the atmosphere of bedroom and church in the language of its descriptions. Pedro, metonymically represented by his resounding boots, approaches the kneeling figure of Nucha as a conquering hero. As viewed through Nucha's experience, the union is the unequal conjunction of a dominant presence and a subordinate absence.

Nucha also functions as focalizer during the obligatory social calls on the "neighboring aristocracy." The criteria for evaluating the attire and demeanor of the wife of Cebre's judge, for example, are Nucha's; the absurdity and inappropriateness of the situation emerge from her survey of the scene. Nucha shares her perceptions of the experience with Julián, kindred spirit in an alien world, not with her new husband: "Shyly she smiled at Julián, indicating to him with an undetected wink the necklaces, lockets and brooches which were displayed on the lady's neck." ["A hurtadillas sonrió a Julián, mostrándole con imperceptible guiño los collares, dijes y broches que lucía en el cuello la señora."] (p. 142) The two displaced observers share the experience of the unfamiliar world and its traditions. Nucha is on firm ground here, the Santiago lady certain of her superior sense of fashion and good taste, and she exhibits an assured sense of self in this female defined context. The judge's wife, the archpriest's sister, Ramoncito Limioso's ancient aunts—all are subject to Nucha's gaze and perceptions on one of the few occasions when she penetrates the world outside the Pazo. Specifically, it is the female neighbors who are viewed through Nucha's eyes, one woman experiencing the world of women, however alien to her. And yet in this case as in others within the Pazo itself, the world that Nucha's eyes record is the enclosed domestic world of women's space.

Devoid of self-definition, Nucha cannot cope with the purposelessness of her life in the Pazo. Having always attended dominant males, she conceives of the world in patriarchal terms; and because she is isolated from external authority, she feels a heightened sense of enclosure and isolation. When Julián reads aloud to her from *El Año Cristiano*—note that Nucha listens to Julián's reading, she is not the reader herself—she participates vicariously in the persecution and martyrdom. The conventions of hagiographic literature transform adversity and self-denial into the "glorious and epic denouement of martyrdom" ["desenlace glorioso y épico del martirio"].

Such readings produced a fantastical effect, especially at nightfall in the harsh winter afternoons, when the dry leaves of trees were whirling about as if dancing, and the dense, cottony clouds passed slowly in front of the glass of the recessed window. There, in the distance, the perpetual sobbing of the millpond could be heard, and the carts creaked under the weight of cornstalks or pine boughs.

[Tales lecturas eran de fantástico efecto, particularmente al caer de las adustas tardes invernales, cuando las hojas secas de los árboles se arremolinaban danzando y las nubes densas y algodonáceas pasaban lentamente ante los cristales de la ventana profunda. Allá, a lo lejos, se oía el perpetuo sollozo de la represa, y chirriaban los carros, cargados de tallos de maíz o ramaje de pino.] (p. 171)

Outside Nucha's enclosed world, life continually evolves and changes. Her romantic reading of both the lives of martyrs and of nature is clearly etched in the repeated use of the pathetic fallacy. As a romantic reader, Nucha identifies with the lament of the natural world in its autumnal decline and with the visions of torture and martyrdom. Julián's models of Christian martyrdom evoke an urgent sense of her own vulnerability and of danger to her daughter in the unresponsive patriarchal world enveloping them.[17]

If Nucha's insistence on fleeing the Pazo with her daughter is a manifestation of hysteria and a sign of mental instability, as the narrator insists

(p. 261), it is also an enactment of a model prepared by the narrative and predicated on the perceived danger to her child. Nucha reads her experience in dramatic terms as incipient persecution and martyrdom, while Julián recognizes a different model for his role in the projected escape from the Pazo: that of Joseph. Nucha's is the archetypal maternal response, authenticated by the child of her own flesh: the protection of her daughter. To Julián the flight of the Virgin mother with child, accompanied by her chaste companion, enacts a familiar biblical response to persecution and suggests a relationship that has not altogether escaped his consciousness. Julián's dream of bringing to the Pazo Christian matrimony following the model of the holy family has been transmuted into a disturbing literal replication of that model: "the holy group was dissolved; Saint Joseph was missing from it or else a priest was standing in for him which was worse" ["el santo grupo estaba disuelto; allí faltaba San José o le sustituía un clérigo, que era peor"] (p. 177).

Pedro also projects a triangular reading of the scene he witnesses in the chapel, as Julián and Nucha prepare to escape with the child. Contextualizing the moment in melodramatic terms, Pedro acts out his role as defender of his sullied honor. In Pedro's eyes, Julián violates patriarchal authority and claims to property. The narrative voice anticipates Pedro's accusations of "snatching a daughter away from her father and a legitimate wife away from her master" ["arrebatando una hija a su padre y una mujer legítima a su dueño"] (p. 266). The privileging of daughter over wife and the claim to ownership assert society's appraisal of female chattel. The language of power and property corresponds to a very different code from the religious one that Julián and Nucha seek to activate. As possessions of a feudal lord, Nucha, her daughter, and even the chaplain are subordinate to the patriarchal structure of the Pazo and are acting against it in their attempt to redefine themselves and enact a textual model. Pedro's own reaction is, of course, shared and prepared by the world of the Pazo; his factotum, Primitivo, for example, will stage manage the dramatic denouement. Only the child, Perucho, responds to the dramatic scene with his own interpretation, enacting a model derived from his experience of family violence and his recent witnessing of Primitivo's death. His reactions unfold like the motifs of a fairy tale: recognition of danger, escape with his baby half-sister, refuge in the corn crib, delight in the possession of his "treasure," and story telling to keep reality at bay. Perucho's enactment functions not only at the level of action but also at a verbal level, as he holds his sister's attention with a story of his own, a variant of the ogre tale in which the threat of death is conquered by love (pp. 279–80).

In *Los Pazos de Ulloa* Emilia Pardo Bazán probes the normative definitions of gender identity within the emerging realist genre. Indeed, her novel could be characterized as a study of alterity and androgyny. Maleness is defined both from within by the closed, male confraternity, and from without, by Julián and by the female audience. Similarly, Nucha views herself as different from other women, confined within the role of mother to the exclusion of other self-definitions, while men arouse in her the fear of the unknown. The standards by which a patriarchal world assesses the value of the female belong to a long tradition in literature. Most surprising in Pardo Bazán's novel is the appraisal of Pedro voiced by the narrator: "and as he was then at the height of his attractiveness, which was masculine rather than manly, the female participants in the election intrigue prided themselves on sending such a handsome young man to the Congress" ["y como estaba entonces en el apogeo de su belleza, más bien masculina que varonil, las muñidoras electorales se ufanaban de enviar tan guapo mozo al Congreso"] (p. 225). A practiced female eye maintains the carefully drawn distinction between "manly beauty" and "masculine beauty," the former being more refined, more aesthetic, and hence more desirable to women than the uncontrolled male form. Earlier Pedro is described approvingly by the narrative voice as "unkempt in a manly way" ["varonilmente desaliñado"] (p. 13), but he has lost some of his aesthetic appeal while retaining his physical attraction. Pedro's viewers are clearly less discerning and less demanding than the narrator in judging male attractiveness. If patriarchal society has evolved normative judgments of female beauty and virtue, the female perspective upholds its own normative standards of male beauty as well.

As a female novelist writing predominantly within genre traditions established by male writers, Pardo Bazán might be expected to mark her difference by expressing her fictional world through a female narrator or privileging female experience.[18] Instead, in *Los Pazos de Ulloa* she appears to work consistently within the conventions already shaped by her male contemporaries. And yet, beneath the ostensibly male narrative voice and the male-dominated vision there is a discernible female presence and, more significantly, a female voice that subverts the boundaries of male and female experience and vision. The female presence is secondary and subordinate in the novel, the female world is interior and enclosed, the female voice is silenced, the female is externally defined and dependent—it is precisely these features constituting the vision of the feminine that Pardo Bazán incorporates into the novel. Julián's insistent comparison of Nucha with artistic representations of the Virgin underscores this view of woman: she is pre-viewed, pre-read, pre-determined. Her essence is imposed essence, her identity responds to external definition. That is, the process of reading is in itself a preshaped experience, prepared by our expectations and knowledge of genres and readers.[19] Pardo Bazán utilizes reader expectations not only in her reworking of familiar thematic material but in challenging the boundaries of male and female spheres while appearing to retain the conventions of the male narrative voice and shared male world.

In short, Pardo Bazán achieves what Ann Robinson Taylor defines as the goal of both Charlotte Brontë and George Eliot: "to find a voice that would transcend sexual stereotypes of the age."[20] By openly challenging normative definitions Pardo Bazán foregrounds traditional gender stereotypes and lays bare the cruel isolation and destructive silencing inherent in them.[21] *Los Pazos de Ulloa* thus raises radical questions about the stiflingly rigid definitions of gender identity inscribed in the generic modes that Pardo Bazán reworked.

# Notes

1. Critics have tended to privilege genre, especially naturalism, in their reading of Pardo Bazán's novel. See, for example, Carlos Feal Deibe, "Naturalismo y antinaturalismo en *Los Pazos de Ulloa*," *Bulletin of Hispanic Studies* 48 (1971): 314–27; Mary Lee Bretz, "Naturalismo y feminismo en Emilia Pardo Bazán," *Papeles de Son Armadans*, no. 261 (Dec. 1977): 195–219; Maurice Hemingway, "Grace, Nature, Naturalism, and Pardo Bazán," *Forum for Modern Language Studies* 16 (1980): 341–49; Alfred Rodríguez and Joan Lefkoff, "An Aesthetic Use of the Grotesque in Emilia Pardo Bazán's *Los Pazos de Ulloa*," *Revista de Estudios Hispánicos* 15 (1981): 275–81; Maurice Hemingway, "*Los Pazos de Ulloa*: Naturalism and Beyond," in *Emilia Pardo Bazán: The Making of a Novelist* (Cambridge: Cambridge University Press, 1983), pp. 27–41; Darío Villanueva, "*Los Pazos de Ulloa*, el naturalismo y Henry James," *Hispanic Review* 52 (1984): 121–39; and Clark Colahan and Alfred Rodríguez, "Lo 'gótico' como fórmula creativa de *Los Pazos de Ulloa*," *Modern Philology* 83 (1985–86): 398–404.

2. Noël M. Valis examines Pardo Bazán's resolution of these competing genre impulses by distinguishing between technique (surface realism) and vision (subterranean romanticism) in her study of the novel that immediately preceded *Los Pazos de Ulloa*, *El Cisne de Vilamorta* [The Swan of Vilamorta]: "Pardo Bazán's *El Cisne de Vilamorta* and the Romantic Reader," *MLN* 101 (1986): 298–324.

3. Nelly Clémessy, *Emilia Pardo Bazán como novelista (de la teoría a la práctica)* (Madrid: Fundación Universitaria Española, 1981), 1:228.

4. The dramatized scene of male rabbits lured by the scent of the female and visions of ecstasy into the moonlit clearing and the range of the hunters' guns replicates Pedro's personal trajectory. See *Los Pazos de Ulloa*, 3rd ed. (Madrid: Alianza, 1981), pp. 207–209. (All further references will appear in the text.) Pedro himself voices the parallel with reference to his mistress, Sabel: "every day I have to hunt her out as I would a rabbit" ["cada día tengo que cazarla como a una liebra"] (p. 71). The female is the agent of the male's destruction, but the catalyst in the process of self-annihilation is the male desire for gratification. In straying from social restraints and larger self-interest, Pedro dissipates himself in a waste of passion that simply makes him prey to those, like Primitivo, in whom controlled self-interest prevails.

5. In an article that appeared after I completed this essay, Carlos Feal Deibe argues that the narrative voice of *Los Pazos de Ulloa* expresses "a markedly feminine, or better yet, feminist attitude"; see "La voz femenina en *Los Pazos de Ulloa*," *Hispania* 70 (1987): 214. I find Feal's interpretation convincing, although I approach the gender identity of the narrative voice through genre.

6. Mieke Bal, *Teoría de la narrativa (una introducción a la narratología)*, trans. Javier Franco (Madrid: Cátedra, 1985), p. 110. Bal and other critics build on the distinction Gérard Genette draws between voice and vision in "Discours du récit," in *Figures III* (Paris: Seuil, 1972), pp. 183–267.

7. Susan S. Lanser, *The Narrative Act: Point of View in Prose Fiction* (Princeton: Princeton University Press, 1981), p. 141.

8. Darío Villanueva examines the narrator's "selective omniscience," concluding that the narrative voice limits itself almost exclusively to Julián's perspective (*"Los Pazos de Ulloa*, el naturalismo," p. 130).

9. Alfred Rodríguez and Newell Morgan have examined the Calderonian model for this passage in their note, "A Calderonian Resonance in *Los Pazos de Ulloa*," *Romance Notes* 19 (1978): 33–37. They stress Pardo Bazán's parodic echo of the Golden Age play rather than the destabilization of gender identity, although they make note of the disorder conveyed by "equivocal" sexual identity and the disguise motif.

10. In a new study of Nucha, Elizabeth Ordóñez identifies the genre patterns that underlie male roles in the novel: "The plot structure of *Los Pazos* emerges largely as a consequence of an intractable persistence of archaic patriarchal discourse in nineteenth-century mores: feudal epic, baroque drama, and clerical treatises on women"; see "¿Y mi niña?: Another Voice in *Los Pazos de Ulloa*," *Discurso Literario* 3 (1985–86): 121–31.

11. The world of the Pazo embodies the attitude, challenged by Pardo Bazán in an essay on women, that grants women "a purely relative destiny" ["un destino de mera relación"], and does not consider her "in herself, or for herself, but in others, by others and for others" ["en sí, ni por sí, ni para sí, sino en los otros, por los otros y para los otros"]; Emilia Pardo Bazán, "Una opinión sobre la mujer," *Nuevo Teatro Crítico* 2, no. 15 (March 1892), quoted by Carlos Feal Deibe, "Religión y feminismo en la obra de Emilia Pardo Bazán," in *Homenaje a Juan López-Morillᵃᶜ* (Madrid: Castalia, 1982), p. 206.

12. As Carlos Feal rightly observes, Nucha and Sabel are equally victims c triarchal authority exercised by husband and father ("La voz femenina," p. 218).

13. Two points emerge from this observation. First, Nucha makes a clear distinction in her mind between fiction and life, a distinction she blurs later on. Secondly, her urban experience is so distant from the world of the Pazo that she can contextualize it only with reference to literature. This literary contextualization foreshadows her later response to a growing sense of fear and vulnerability.

14. I omit the netherworld of the Pazo with its kitchen sisterhood gathered around Sabel and María la *Sabia*, a community that serves as a counterpoint to Nucha's isolation in a male-defined world.

15. Indeed in the sequel to *Los Pazos de Ulloa*, *La madre naturaleza* [Mother Nature] (1887), Rita has married an Andalusian engineer—Andalusia being as foreign to Galicia as geographically possible within Spain—perhaps suggesting that only the modern man of practical science can meet the challenge of Rita's womanliness and spontaneity. The contrast between Rita and Rosario, the object of desire of another young engineer, Pepe Rey in Galdós's *Doña Perfecta* (1876), is instructive. The pull of genre, the romantic tradition in Galdós's case, is both stronger and more consciously manipulated in the earlier novel.

16. Nucha is, of course, christened with the name of her aunt, but as Nucha she becomes so distanced from this original identity that she ultimately loses the inheritance from her aunt.

17. Nucha also sees her experience in the Pazo as a female gothic novel in the tradition of Anne Radcliffe (cited by Pardo Bazán in *La cuestión palpitante*). Feal lucidly has explored Pardo Bazán's use of gothic conventions ("La voz femenina," pp. 217–18). See also Colahan and Rodríguez, "Lo 'gótico' como fórmula creativa," pp. 398–404.

18. This is, of course, what Pardo Bazán does in *Insolación* [Sunstroke] (1889), published after *Los Pazos de Ulloa* and its sequel. In one of the first contemporary feminist readings of Pardo Bazán's fiction, Ruth A. Schmidt persuasively develops *Insolación* as "a 19th-century feminist's version of a traditional love story"; see "Woman's Place in the Sun: Feminism in *Insolación*," *Revista de Estudios Hispánicos* 8 (1974): 70.

19. Sharon Magnarelli has recently made a similar point with reference to the Spanish-American novel: "each reading and our subsequent reaction (to a text) has been predicated on and conditioned by a previous reader, by the other. Thus the female is not only inevitably other, but even our experience of her is shaped by yet others"; *The Lost Rib: Female Characters in the Spanish-American Novel* (Lewisburg/London: Bucknell University Press, 1985), p. 187.

20. Ann Robinson Taylor, *Male Novelists and Their Female Voices: Literary Masquerades* (Troy: Whitston Publishing Company, 1981), p. 103.

21. Unfettered by such social proscriptions, the child Perucho moves spontaneously to enact the protective maternal role towards his half-sister in the confusion surrounding the dramatic denouement of Nucha and Julián's failed script. The natural androgyny of childhood presents no challenge to the patriarchy, while in adulthood the androgynous blurring of rigid gender differentiation provokes margination and social condemnation.

# Revising Realism: Pardo Bazán's *Memorias de un solterón* in Light of Galdós's *Tristana* and John Stuart Mill

## ELIZABETH J. ORDÓÑEZ

By the time Emilia Pardo Bazán published *Memorias de un solterón* [The memoirs of a confirmed bachelor] in 1896, she could have become a very discouraged woman. Long committed to the instruction and enlightenment of Spanish women by means of her fiction, numerous publishing projects—including Spanish translations of works by Mill and Bebel—and the example of her own experience, Pardo Bazán's efforts were met repeatedly with indifference at best, hostility at worst. Considering this plight toward the end of her career, she quipped: "I have proof that if there were to be a plebiscite for the purpose of deciding whether to hang me or not, the majority of Spanish women would vote yes!" ["Tengo la evidencia de que si se hiciese un plebiscito para decidir ahorcarme o no, la mayoría de las mujeres españolas votarían ¡sí!"][1] But Pardo Bazán remained undaunted; although chastened by the trying consequences of her feminism, this tenacious reformer made yet another attempt through *Memorias* to sell her message. Continuing the family saga of *Doña Milagros* in this novel, the author directs her attention to the everyday struggles of the novel's female characters. As Nelly Clémessy has suggested, the novelist hoped that by means of another engaging tale, she could sweeten her lesson and finally insinuate it into the hearts of her female readers.[2]

Persistently vexed with the fate of fictional female protagonists when Galdós published *Tristana* in 1892, Pardo Bazán was uneasy with the failure of his protagonist and wrote her polemical critique of the work. Later, in *Memorias*, she responds to what she saw as the overwhelmingly pessimistic vision of Galdós's work. However, Maryellen Bieder, identifying a structural similarity in the two novels—their resolution in marriage—has suggested that Pardo Bazán also shied away from the consequences of her protagonist's search for freedom. Bieder charges that Pardo Bazán's critique of *Tristana* ("that it promised something else" ["que prometía otra cosa"]) could apply just as well to her own novel.

But the novels display too many differences; fine and subtle distinctions between them discourage a reading of converged meaning simply because both end in marriage. Given her disappointing track record as a feminist reformer in Spain, Pardo Bazán could hardly afford to challenge openly the dominant tradition. So she skirted the demands of such cultural authority while appearing to conform to it. Though conceding to the conventional marriage ending, Pardo Bazán molds her spouses to insure that her version of matrimony will be grounded on revised values and attitudes. In this way, she inscribes into *Memorias* what current literary theory has called "double-voiced discourse," a text containing at once a "dominant" and a "muted" story—a concession to literary convention that at the same time contains the story of its subversion.[3] This strategy was attractive to women writers during the last century, encircled as they were by restrictive ideological and social boundaries as well as by literary convention. Their technique of speaking out of both sides of the mouth at once results in what Nancy Miller has called "reinscription," a renunciation of the "logic of either/or" in favor of the "sign of both-and."[4] According to such revised logic, the female protagonist of *Memorias* can be both free and married. But before considering how Pardo Bazán accomplishes such a subversive sleight of hand, Galdós's *Tristana* should be reconsidered as a source for Pardo Bazán's rewriting of literary and social convention.

Neither Galdós nor Pardo Bazán spared their criticism of what Noël Valis has aptly described as "the rotting fabric of Spanish Restoration society."[5] But in *Tristana* and *Memorias* each author chose to highlight different threads of the fabric. Galdós assumed a thoroughly pessimistic perspective—especially in his view of woman's potential—while Pardo Bazán illuminated more constructive and modifiable aspects of female experience. As Pardo Bazán communicated to Galdós in one of her letters: "When you write, you're so nihilistic. . . I'm not as pessimistic as you." ["Cuando tú escribes, eres tan nihilista. . . yo no soy tan pesimista como tú."][6]

Though conditions for women in Spain during the latter part of the nineteenth century were by no means ideal, they were without doubt in a state of crisis and profound change. Significant numbers of women began to serve as teachers, nurses, mail and telegraph workers, librarians, typists, salespersons, and in other vocations now generally labeled as "women's work." Margarita Nelken, a friend of Galdós, described the unfortunate working conditions of women but lauded them as "so valiant, so honorable" ["tan valientes, tan íntegras"]. Contemporary historians also judge these modest advances by nineteenth-century women into the working world as definite progress.[7] And Pardo Bazán herself, writing about an international exposition of women's work to be held in Chicago during the 1890s, laments the absence of exhibits from varied sectors of the female economy: "In my country women plough, dig, prune, reap, irrigate, chop firewood, haul soil and rocks, and even break ground to form roadbeds!" ["En mi país la mujer ara, cava, poda, siega, riega, hace leña, arrastra tierra y piedra, ¡y hasta la rompe para formar la caja de las carreteras!"][8] Those exhibits that are destined for the American shore she assesses as testimony of "the first step on a road that must expand day by day" ["el primer paso en un camino que ha de ensancharse todos los días"] (ME171)

So when Saturna advises Tristana that "those who wear skirts can pursue only three professions" ["sólo tres carreras pueden seguir las que visten faldas"],[9] she is far from seeing things as they are, far from fully understanding "the possibilities that contemporary society offered woman" ["las posibilidades que la sociedad contemporánea ofrecía a la mujer"], as Germán Gullón has argued. It is certainly true, as Gullón says, that "Saturna observes life without the blitheness of the sentimental novel and the melodramatic serial" ["Saturna observa la vida sin las gaitas de la novela sentimental y del folletín dramatizante"], but her discourse is rooted in other literary conventions, those of realism.[10] Galdós's view of reality in *Tristana* may create the illusion of mimesis, yet it, too, is mediated by a different set of aesthetic conventions as well as by the idiosyncrasies of the author's own subjective view of life. As a consequence of Galdós's choices, less visible, more progressive strands of the social fabric remain obfuscated.

The salient characteristic of *Tristana* is that all the principal characters are the objects of Galdós's biting irony: don Lope, for being a decadent amalgam of the Calderonian gentleman, don Juan, and don Quixote; Tristana for being a female Quixote and an incurable romantic; her mother for being another quixotic throwback to a more idealistic past; Horacio for being at heart a petit bourgeois with conventional ideas about women and a soul too narrow to accommodate Tristana's highblown fancy.[11] Cervantine irony pervades the novel even to its very lexical level, as Galdós unrelentingly proves his fidelity to the Cervantine model by shaping a plot of "systematic disillusionment." In this theoretical context, Tristana's failed feminist ideals are but a part of her doomed utopian tendencies, a corollary to the fading of her excessive idealization of Horacio, indeed of her personal goals and ambitions. Her feminism is thus more quixotic, less an actual reflection of rational, late nineteenth-century social thought; she is more kin to Emma Bovary—for whom "dreams are destined, at the touch of reality, to wither into lies"—than she is to Concepción Arenal or even to Pardo Bazán.[12]

Like her quixotic predecessor, Tristana is caught in a web of borrowed and imposed texts, coming to see herself as several shifting and slippery fictional figures other than herself—Beatrice, Francesca da Rimini, Crispa, or Señá Restituta—"lyrical expressions that varied every few days" ["expresiones líricas que variaban cada pocos días"] (T90). But Tristana's subjugation to alien texts often is gender specific and indicative of woman's relationship to male—especially paternal—authority and authorship. As the object of borrowed identities, Tristana suffers from "anxiety of authorship" when she tries to write the text of herself.[13] But can she write, if she remains a prisoner within a male-inscribed mode? "The bad thing is I don't know how to write" ["Lo malo es que no sé escribir"], she says, and Saturna's response is ironically telling: "that is for men to do" ["eso es para hombres"] (T30). "De papel" [of paper], to be inscribed upon, Tristana, as Valis has pointed out, comes to signify a literary objet d'art or tabula rasa to be imprinted and erased over and over again.[14] She is a writing surface, and her male authors possess the metaphorical pen.

A modern Galatea, Tristana is inanimate object come to life: "the stuffing of the doll turned into the blood and marrow of a woman" ["se cambiaba en sangre y medula de mujer la estopa de la muñeca"] (T27). But even after the moment of her animation, Tristana's words and imagination continue to emanate from her Pygmalion, "the seedbed of her lover" ["semillero de su amante"] (T28). This, together with the epithet used to name her, "slave of don Lope" ["esclava de don Lope"] (T42), discloses how she is both generated and imprisoned by paternal authority. When Tristana nervously stumbles over her confession to Horacio about her true relationship to don Lope ("I'm not married to my husband. . . I mean, to my father. . . , I mean, to that man . . ." ["No estoy casada con mi marido. . . digo, con mi papá. . . , digo, con ese hombre . . ."], T63), the confusion of terms ironically reveals how utterly ubiquitous is don Lope's power over his charge. Alternately or simultaneously exercising the roles of all three—husband, father, generic male—he has pervaded Tristana's body, soul, and brain, undermining forever any definitive resistance on her part to paternal or patriarchal authority. Any claims to self-authorship she may attempt to make will be blocked by this deeply rooted, insidiously internalized conditioning.

Although Tristana often expresses herself with soaring brilliance in her epistles to Horacio, her relationship to texts remains largely passive throughout the novel. She alternately is written, read, and read to by the two principal men in her life. Even when she is creating, her ideas pass through the ideological filter implanted by these influences. To Lope, Tristana is an open book, a transparent text that his wily, corrupted wisdom easily deciphers: "for days I have been reading it in you. . . in your face, in your voice" ["hace días te lo leo. . . en la cara, en la voz"] (T66). This accords him a power that surfaces and resurfaces, even during the period of Tristana's greatest rebellion—a power and authority encoded by his gaze:

"Don Lope dominated her. . . and fascinated her with such mysterious authority. . . . Fixed on her, the penetrating eyes of don Lope, frightened her, dominated her" ["Don Lope se le imponía. . .y la fascinaba con tan misteriosa autoridad. . . . Los penetrantes ojos de don Lope, clavados en ella, la sobrecogían, la dominaban"] (T66–67). Lope's eyes become a rather transparent metaphor for phallic possession, or in a broader sense, as Dianne Sadoff suggests by way of Lacan, this kind of penetrating male gaze serves as a metaphor for man's potency, mastery, and dominance over woman.[15] Consolidating his power on all fronts ("I consider you wife and daughter, as it suits me" ["Te miro como esposa y como hija, según me convenga"], T69), Lope insures that any serious impertinence on the part of his wife/daughter will be suppressed or censored. All he has to do is wait. Nature (or the metaphorically phallic power of the male pen) will eventually castrate Tristana, make of her "a half-bodied woman, a bust and nothing more" ["una mujer de medio cuerpo, un busto y nada más"] (T164). Returning to the shadows of silence, Tristana will become totally and undisputedly the object of the male text ("Subdued forever!" ["¡Sujeta para siempre!"], T144).[16] Her letters to Horacio will dwindle away, and Lope again will speak for her.

Even when Tristana speaks or writes beyond her father/husband's control, her language often originates from the pens of other men. Horacio, whose "sole literary passion" ["única pasión literaria"] (T89) is Dante, reads to her from *The Inferno* and *The Purgatorio*, filling her with the words of "bel parlare." In a matter of weeks she has internalized the ill-fated Francesca and the idealized Beatrice. Absorbing and assuming roles from readings under the tutelage of her young lover, Tristana reiterates their tropes and lays claim to their imaginary, ethereal transmutations of amorous emotions: "you're becoming pure spirit, an intangible being" ["te me vuelves espíritu puro, un ser intangible"] (T114). It is ironic that Tristana should so effectively and quixotically identify with and incorporate the texts of the Italian poet that Horacio finally becomes her fantasy lover while she performs the role of a feminine Dante. She thus becomes a pawn in the game of objectification, playing out her moves through haphazard and naive readings of the master texts of patriarchal culture.

It is interesting to ponder how Galdós selected certain texts by women to incorporate into *Tristana*. As A. F. Lambert and Gilbert Smith have discovered, the letters of Galdós's mistress Concha-Ruth Morell are a key element of *Tristana*. Describing Morell as "an impulsive and strong-willed woman, intensely emotional and given to self-dramatisation, at times hysterical," Lambert reveals character traits remarkably similar to those of Tristana. Also like Tristana, Concha-Ruth was "an attractive woman given to depressions and impulsive enthusiasms." Lacking self-confidence, prone to belittle herself, and finally unsuccessful, Concha-Ruth provides the script for Tristana's "I know not what I think nor what I write" ["no sé lo que pienso ni lo que escribo"] (T104), for her masochism ("I deserve your scoldings and blows" ["merezco que me riñas y me pegues"], T99), and for her complete dependence on the male to shape her destiny ("I do whatever you command, and I obey you" ["hago lo que me mandas, y te obedezco"], T107). Though Smith hesitates to interpret the novel in light of the numerous and striking correspondences he discovers, he does comment on how these letters shed light on Galdós's "cynical attitudes toward a personal relationship with a woman."[17]

Since Galdós and Pardo Bazán were, for a time, lovers and exchanged correspondence, it is noteworthy that less of Pardo Bazán's words and attitudes make their way into Tristana. Perhaps her strength and forthrightness were inconsistent with the portrait of womanhood that Galdós's text demanded. In a letter she tells Galdós: "I have always held something back from you: I was restrained by the fear of harming you, a certain impulse of physical protection on the part of the stronger toward the weaker" ["Contigo me he reprimido siempre: el temor de perjudicarte, y no sé qué sentimiento de protección física del más fuerte al más débil me contenían"] (C82).[18] Pardo Bazán also declares in her letters her emancipation from paternal protection, her unselfconscious absorption in her work, and she writes—as she herself describes—with a brutal frankness and integrity. Had he borrowed from Pardo Bazán's articulations of self-confidence and self-sufficiency, Galdós would have undermined his ironic plot of disillusionment. So cynicism, if Smith's assessment is correct, may have determined—at least in part—the epistolary intertext of Tristana.

The intertextual borrowings in Tristana illuminate how this novel clearly is a result of both aesthetic and ideological choices. As Susan Kirkpatrick has proposed, Galdós appropriates and rewrites Concha-Ruth Morell's textualization (more than he does Pardo Bazán's), with the result that Tristana's protagonist becomes a hysterical woman, a figure of female castration, a sign of woman's inherent lack.[19] Or, in Gilbert and Gubar's terminology, these authorial choices create a Tristana who joins the ranks of other nineteenth-century male-authored women defined as "'self-less,' wholly passive, completely void of generative power."[20] In a parody of "happy endings" ("Were they happy, one with the other? . . . Perhaps" ["¿Eran felices uno y otro? . . . Tal vez"], T182), Tristana ends up almost inert, marrying don Lope "with indifference" ["con indiferencia"] (T182), accepting this determination of her destiny as "an act imposed by the outside world" ["un hecho impuesto por el mundo exterior"] (T182). Tristana's marriage takes place wholly without her active participation. Her sudden aging and Lope's final infantilization complete the process of woman's passive insertion into traditional Spanish domestic life. She goes piously to church and cooks up delicacies; he tends his garden and gleefully consumes her concoctions. And so the novel closes with a familiar paradigm indeed.[21]

Almost everything in *Memorias* points away from *Tristana*. The Pardo Bazán novel is narrated by a relatively young architect—a designer of the future—whose favorite escape from the boredom of provincial Marineda and his own methodical habits is reading and fantasizing, among other things, about "emancipated heroines" ["heroínas emancipadas"].[22] An Anglophile, he has remained a bachelor not only because he prefers the comforts of solitude and doing things his own way, but because he is averse to subjugating women: "Because I love that tender companion I do not wish to see her turned into a housewife, a servant or a weary and ill-humored wetnurse" ["Porque amo a esa tierna compañera no quiero verla convertida en ama de llaves, en sirvienta o en nodriza fatigada y malhumorada"] (M451). In sharp contrast to don Lope, who claims paternal authority ("I invest myself with authority. . . I declare myself father." ["Yo me revisto de autoridad. . . me declaro padre."], T68), Mauro is characterized by an absence of paternal desire and an ideological rejection of the evils of paternity: "paternity is incompatible with the fulfillment of moral law" ["la paternidad es incompatible con el cumplimiento de la ley moral"] (M451).

The reader immediately grasps the antithetical differences between don Lope and Horacio (mired in the past and conventionality), and Mauro (directed toward the future) as indicative of divergent male attitudes in a changing Spanish society. When Mauro first meets Feita he recoils into the vestiges of his traditional conditioning, but later, unlike Horacio and his growing coolness toward Tristana's desires for freedom, Mauro feels increasingly attracted to Feita as a vision of a new world: "Feita was the new woman, the dawn of a society different from that which exists today" ["Feita era la mujer nueva, el albor de una sociedad distinta de la que hoy existe"] (M494). She fascinates him for several reasons: she prefers to think of books rather than adornments, enthusiastically earns money with honorable, intellectual work, speaks to men with firmness and resolution (and a self-possessed yen to show off her learning), and generally eschews romantic illusion and mystery. She is class conscious and critical of the Spanish tendency to avoid work.[23] Finally, and not without significance in comparison to Tristana (with her amputated leg), Feita enjoys walking alone on a strong and healthy pair of legs, which remain that way. Completely taken with this genuine emancipated heroine, Mauro comes to admit that "everything in Feita which at first seemed to me reprehensible and even ludicrous and comical, later came to seem lofty and sublime, worthy of admiration and applause" ["todo lo que al principio me pareció en Feita reprobable y hasta risible y cómico, dió en figurárseme alto y sublime, merecedor de admiración y aplauso"] (M494).

Although the theme of female emancipation is central to *Memorias*, as in *Tristana* this issue is only part of the story. *Memorias* also is concerned with the limits and possibilities of woman's (and man's) relationship to texts. In his sensitive study of *Memorias*, Maurice Hemingway presents the following thesis: "Side by side in *Memorias* there are two entirely contradictory conceptions of the novel—on the one hand, a story full of striking events, and, on the other, a study of psychic phenomena."[24] These "striking events" often incorporate conventional or traditional textual elements that beg transformation or elimination (like the seduced and abandoned plots of Feita's sisters and the melodramatic vengeance plot of Feita's father); the story of Mauro's and Feita's psychological growth as individuals, on the other hand, suggests revisions in the text. As the protagonists shape themselves, they inscribe into nineteenth-century narrative fresh possibilities for the portrayal of man, woman, and even marriage.

The psychological thread of the novel initially is centered around Mauro, who gradually comes to experience a love capable of drawing him out of his meticulously ordered and tranquil bachelor's existence. To achieve this growth, Mauro must learn to read women—like texts—with accuracy. Though he seems to have little difficulty with sophisticated, worldly, free heroines, he fears, above all, misreading the traditional, silent woman. To illustrate this fear, he tells a story of a ball at which girls wait to be invited to dance. One waits quietly for a particular young man to fetch her, but he chooses a certain Natalia, leaving the waiting girl to suffer silently, holding anguished cries of disappointment within her. Then along comes Mauro and, asking her to dance, he unleashes an unfortunate chain of events: she accepts, thinking of the other, eventually marries Mauro, bears his children, all the while thinking of the other. Based on this hypothetical anecdote, Mauro, considering himself a poor reader of the feelings of women ("I . . . who was unable to read the young woman's heart" ["yo. . . que no pude leer en el corazón de la muchacha"], M459), rejects marriage out of the fear that he may misread woman and exploit her silence. As long as woman remains for him an inscrutable, passive, dissembling text ("I have been unable to rend the veil of her dissimulation" ["no he sabido desgarrar el velo de su disimulo"], M459), Mauro avoids bringing about a situation in which he may violate her deepest desires.

Some change must be brought about then, in order that Mauro may develop emotionally, may escape from a male existence that has been "trivialised by social prejudices as much as the female characters' lives."[25] For Mauro is misread, too, by the narrow minds of his town: "All Marineda condemns me. One might say that I have offended and injured that which is called 'esprit de corps', the point of honor of the community. . . . The community cannot forgive my individualism" ["Toda Marineda me anatematiza. Diríase que he lastimado y herido eso que se llama 'espíritu de cuerpo', el punto de honra de la colectividad. . . . La colectividad no me perdona mi individualismo''] (M456). So the function of Feita not only is to defend her own right to be free, but to help prepare a place for the new man, where redefined or self-defined man may read and write a renewed plot of male-female relationships. The Neira family will be Mauro's school for outworn plot devices; Feita will be his teacher of revised ones.

The first thing Feita teaches Mauro (and the reader) is that the nineteenth-century female character may escape the polarities of the conventionally feminine, wordless, passive woman—like her sister Rosa or Mauro's hypothetical dancer—or the grotesquely masculine, independent, and articulate woman—like Malvina, the English teacher in *Tristana*. Rosa, obsessed with clothes and willing to sacrifice her good name to get them, serves as a foil for the revised image of Feita. Early on, Mauro sees Rosa as "a supreme beauty" ["una belleza soberana"] (M463), but ironically, he also notices that she has few unique characteristics and that the blank emptiness of her expression makes her resemble "the perfect wax dolls that can be seen in the shop windows of hairdressers" ["las perfectas muñecas de cera que se ven en los escaparates de las peluquerías"] (M463). In contrast, Feita has just enough masculine characteristics to make her a bright, charming, healthy, animated individual.

> Her face, rather than that of a young woman, [is] that of a sharp and clever young boy, [and] offers piquant and original characteristics. . . her eyes are small, green, of a clear hue, shameless, direct in their gaze, eyes that question, that compel, that scrutinize, eyes of understanding. The body of Feita is free, agile. . . . Her hair lives in perpetual insurrection.

> [Su cara, más que de doncella, de rapaz despabilado y travieso, ofrece rasgos picantes y originales. . . sus ojos son chicos, verdes, de límpido matiz, descarados, directos en el mirar, ojos que preguntan, que apremian, que escudriñan, ojos del entendimiento. El cuerpo de Feita es suelto, ágil. . . . Su pelo vive en perpetua insurrección.] (M468–69)

Feita is unhampered and dynamic, every part of her being infused with vitality and verve; her youthful masculinity enhances her charm and forms an implicit, though sharp, contrast to a common stereotype of the masculine nineteenth-century intellectual woman, "dry and mannish" ["seca y hombruna"] (T110), like Malvina. This description of Feita already encodes the revised "sign of both-and" that will inform the plot of Mauro and Feita's growing intimacy: Feita's androgynous qualities transcend the "logic of either/or" upon which so much of the nineteenth-century's portrayal of women is grounded.

Feita proceeds to overturn the masculine control of woman by reversing several key elements identified in *Tristana*. She appropriates the privileged

position of male speech, expressing herself with a directness that apparently shocks, but at bottom delights, the narrator.

> [It was] the voice of Feita. And not muffled, not timid, not choked by emotion,
> but on the contrary, clear, sharp, well modulated. . . .
> "Well, inform him. . . . Inform him immediately. . . . I would enter: but God
> knows if he's in his drawers. . . ."
> This is what she said: this unseemly word was pronounced by the mouth of the
> savage. . . .

> [(Era) la voz de Feita. Y no velada, ni tímida, ni ahogada por la emoción, sino
> al contrario, sonora, aguda, bien timbrada. . . .
> "Pues avísale usted. . . . Avísale en seguida. . . . Yo entraría: pero sabe Dios
> si está en calzoncillos. . . ."
> Esto dijo: esta palabra inconveniente pronunció la boca de la salvaje. . . .]
> (M478)

Entirely unaffected and marginal to coquetry, Feita ignores conventional
gender restrictions on expression. Hers is the voice of an equal, not a subordinate: "Thanks, Pareja: on such an occasion the offer of your little
white hand is proof of friendship and sympathy, of the grandest sort!"
["Gracias, Pareja: en tal ocasión el ofrecerme la blanca manita es una
prueba de amistad y de simpatía ¡de las mayores!"] (M508) Her address
sounds like that of one man to another; but she refers to Mauro's hand as
a man would to a woman. In short, she repeatedly subverts the gender
markings of conventional discourse. Feita speaks directly and frankly but
is conscious of how she pierces through convention: "I am speaking as
young ladies do not speak" ["Estoy hablando como no hablan las señoritas"] (M504).
    As seen in her physical description, Feita also reverses the power rela-
tions encoded by the gaze; Mauro explains: "she faced me, gazing at me in
such a way that captivated with its clarity and firmness" ["se encaró con-
migo, mirándome de un modo que subyugaba por lo límpido y firme"]
(M504). Since, as Sadoff reminds us, the female gaze communicates a desire for mastery and dominance, it could be read as threatening by the
male.[26] But Feita's gaze is an essential part of her vitality and righteous
indignation about the sordid events occurring in her family; so, though
Mauro indeed is dominated by it, he reacts with increasing admiration,
enthusiasm, even passion. He longs to give himself, willingly, in an almost
feminine gesture to Feita's impassioned energy: "I did not want to struggle: I longed to surrender" ["No quería combatir: ansiaba entregarme"]
(M507). Mauro's confession thus enunciates, metonymically, a virtual reversal of the sexual economy that usually undergirds nineteenth-century
realism.
    Both Mauro and the reader are drawn into an inventory of diverse plot

options or literary conventions that are not to be appropriate in this emergent revised text and cultural context. Feita rejects the ploys of the cape and sword melodrama, laughing at Mauro's attempt to hide her presence from the town gossip, Primo Cova.

> "Feita should hide there, where she can," pointing out at the same time the escape door that led from my parlor to the dining room and the library. . . Feita came up to me, roaring with laughter, mocking me and my fears with all her might.
> "Come in, Cova, come in," said the girl, without recovering her seriousness and aplomb.
>
> ["Que se esconda Feita por ahí, donde pueda," señalando al mismo tiempo a la puerta de escape que desde mi sala conducía al comedor y al cuarto de los libros. . . me alcanzó Feita, riendo a carcajadas, burlándose a todo trapo de mí y de mis recelos.
> "Pase, Cova, pase," decía la muchacha, sin conseguir recobrar la seriedad y el aplomo.] (M480)

On another occasion Feita reiterates her aversion to false ritual and histrionics: "I'm not keen on incense and farces" ["soy poco amiga de incienso y de farsas"] (M488). The chivalric text is no longer functional either, as Mauro realizes when he better knows Feita. He cannot be another don Quixote or even don Lope, for those are men of fiction whose existence is made meaningful by their imagining, protecting, and even governing passive, dependent women. Mauro finds that Feita, unlike the chivalric prototype,

> was unprotectable and when people neither need nor want our support, it takes away our desire to become knights-errant, protectors of widows and orphans. Feita was a vigorous being, armed for life, without sentimentality, without infantile fears of any kind.
>
> [era improtegible y cuando las gentes ni necesitan ni quieren nuestro apoyo, se nos quitan las ganas de meternos a caballeros andantes, amparadores de viudas y huérfanas. Feita era un ser vigoroso, armado para la vida, sin sentimentalismos, sin temores pueriles de ninguna especie.] (M493)

The plot developing between her sister Rosa and the aged rake Baltasar Sobrado is revolting to Feita: "Where might one find a more immoral book than that of my family? That is why I don't wish to read it. I close it. If I could, I would burn it. Rosa was predestined to such a denouement" ["¿Dónde habrá libro más inmoral que mi casa? Por eso no quiero leerlo. Lo cierro. Si pudiese, lo quemaría. Rosa estaba predestinada a este desenlace"] (M505). Sobrado's son Ramón ultimately changes the course of this undesirable plot. By forcing his father to rid himself of his reputation as a philanderer through marriage to the young man's mother, he indirectly frees Rosa from her entrapment in the mercenary "seduced and abandoned" convention so common in nineteenth-century literature.

Finally, another seduction plot between "that seductive hysteric, María Ramona, that 'Divine Argos'" ["aquella seductora histérica, María Ramona, 'Argos divina'"] (M461) and the two-faced rake, Mejía, climaxes predictably in the melodramatic slaying of the seducer by the victim's father. Shortly thereafter, even though legally protected with an alibi of Mauro's invention, the already impotent father dies under the weighty guilt of his bloody act. In two strokes, the figures of cynical seducer and ineffectual father are dealt a mortal blow, leaving the sisters free to take up alternate revised plots. Rather than legitimizing the rake figure (as *Tristana* does with Lope), these subplots (consisting of what Hemingway has called "striking events") serve—as in the fiction of another woman writer, Jane Austen—as "monitory images" for Feita, Mauro, and the reader.[27] As in the works of Austen, the story of the rake is told without being perpetuated—those figures are either subsumed into responsibility or completely eliminated. Other more practical, constructive, and revised roles await the women the rakes have deceived.

The library and Feita's relationship to it provide an image of possibility, a source of ideas for revision. Though Feita suffers from the deficiencies of a haphazard education ("her instruction has been, as it usually is with persons of her sex, confused, hasty, incoherent, and with lacunae and deficiencies" ["su instrucción ha sido, como suele la de las personas de su sexo, confusa, precipitada, incoherente, y con lagunas y deficiencias"] (M469), these gaps allow room to mold herself, provide spaces to fill with a variety of texts according to her choosing. What Feita lacks in formal training, she supplants with her independent will, frequenting every library that her limited environment offers her: "every other day she came punctually to examine the library of the duchess of Piety, alternating this examination with that of another library, public and well-stocked, that of the port" ["cada dos días venía puntualmente a registrar la librería de la duquesa de la Piedad, alternando este registro con el de otra biblioteca, pública y muy copiosa, la del Puerto"] (M483). All her scholarly activity is self-directed and motivated, unlike the similarly haphazard but less independent reading activities of Tristana.

Feita is so persevering and so single-minded in her pursuit of learning that when she is in the process of reading and taking notes, she shuts everything else out—even Mauro, whose rooms are adjacent to the library she frequents. Seriousness and concentration in a woman are qualities unfamiliar to Mauro and, at first, are difficult to accept. Feita's independence and dedication irritate Mauro's masculine pride: "It also ruffled my masculine pride that on the other side of a thin wall was a woman dedicated to serious work, to an intellectual task, without thinking more of me than of the first chemise she wore" ["Chafaba también mi amor propio masculino que tabique por medio se encontrase una mujer dedicada a un serio trabajo, a una labor intelectual, sin acordarse de mí más que de la primer [*sic*] camisa que vistió"] (M484). But these are the very attributes he later comes to admire, indeed love, as he learns to accept Feita's difference.

When the decadent paternal text of the Neira family becomes obsolete and can no longer be written ("my father is another generation" ["mi padre es de otra época"], M506), and the elder Neira must perish after taking melodramatic vengeance on Argos's seducer in a fit of "fanaticism of fatherly love" ["fanatismo de su amor paternal"] (M525), it is left to Feita and her newly emancipated companion Mauro to fill in the textual and cultural gaps. Feita assigns roles to the remaining members of her family with energetic assurance; unlike Tristana, she metaphorically becomes the writer of—not written into—this new plot of her family's life. Her ability to put them all to work in appropriate fields as members of a nascent, productive middle class, and her choice of marriage to form the managerial unit that will supervise the family's activities, reinforces the goals and ideology of progressive, nineteenth-century bourgeois society: the development of personal, individual talents and responsibility.[28] If the text of woman is thereby inscribed with freedom, it is with an intellectual freedom, a self-defined authority exercised within the bounds of existent— albeit reformed and revised—institutions.[29] When Feita finally decides to become Mauro's wife, and he considers himself blessed to have been chosen "Feita Neira's husband" ["esposo de Feita Neira"] (M527), *Memorias* points definitively toward change in text and context.

To read the marriage ending as capitulation, undermining all the revisions leading to that denouement, would be to misread the theoretical difference of *Memorias* as a realist text authored by an independent and determined woman. Pardo Bazán deviates from the Cervantine plot of "systematic disillusionment," choosing for the psychological strand of this novel a paradigm derived from the rational, even enlightenment memoir or diary, a recounting of the intellectual, emotional, and spiritual growth of an individual.

It is very likely that an important inspiration for this novel may be found in the works of British philosopher John Stuart Mill. Pardo Bazán's admiration of the relationship between Mill and Mrs. Harriet Taylor, his friend and later his wife, clearly filters into her conception of Mauro and Feita.[30] Feita's personal qualities are strikingly reminiscent of Taylor's, as Mill described them: like Harriet, Feita seeks "self-improvement" with "ardour," possesses a "penetrating and intuitive intelligence," combines "genuine modesty with the loftiest pride; a simplicity and sincerity which [are] absolute; the utmost scorn of whatever [is] mean and cowardly, and

ɔurning indignation at everything brutal or tyrannical, faithless or dishon-
ɔurable in conduct and character."[31] Feita's thirst for knowledge, her
penetrating directness and youthful wisdom of her speech, her appearance
and manner, and her indignation before the illogical and immoral morass
ɔf her family's predicament closely fit Mill's glowing and devoted description of Mrs. Taylor. Feita's "outrageous eccentricities" ["inauditas excen-
tricidades"] (M469) seem to fly in the face of popular opinion ("because of
her. . . we'll be the talk of the town" ["por ella. . . vamos a ser la fábula
de la población"], M473), just as Mill advised they should in On Liberty:
"Precisely because the tyranny of opinion is such as to make eccentricity a
reproach, it is desirable, in order to break through that tyranny, that people should be eccentric."[32] And Mill's gratefulness that the widowed Mrs.
Taylor finally "consented to become my wife" (A129) seems echoed in
Mauro's delight that he will soon be the husband of Feita Neira.

The marriage of the philosopher and Mrs. Taylor moved Pardo Bazán
profoundly as she wrote of its benefits: "they cooperated, joining their
intellectual efforts and profiting mutually thereby" ["cooperaron, reunien-
do sus esfuerzos intelectuales y beneficiándolos mutuamente"] (ME127).
She bolstered her own defense of enlightened marriage with Mill's en-
raptured praise for a more egalitarian arrangement in which intellectual
development is an ongoing process: "What a sweet piece of paradise is
the marriage of two cultivated persons, who can take turns enjoying the
pleasure of guiding the companion along the path of intellectual development!" ["¡Cuán dulce pedazo de paraíso el matrimonio de dos personas instruidas, que pueden. . . gozar por turno del placer de guiar al
compañero por la senda del desarrollo intelectual!"] (ME124–25). In
Mill's liberal imagination, Pardo Bazán apparently discovered or confirmed the model that would eventually and definitively reshape the conception of marriage in Memorias.

In light of this influence, it seems doubtful that Feita will merely "return within the bounds of traditional society" to "become a provincial
matron," as Bieder has predicted. Believing, as did Pardo Bazán, that
more important than law in the subjugation of women was custom, Mill
proposed that woman be educated to support herself before marriage, thus
making marriage a pairing of "coequals" joined together only by affection,
not as superior and inferior or protector and dependent.[33] Given Feita's
intellectual development and financial self-sufficiency before marriage ("I
have the security of being able to earn my bread on any spot of the globe"
["Tengo la seguridad de ganarme el pan en cualquier punto del globo"],
M487), the union of Feita and Mauro promises to become just the sort of
coequal union imagined by Mill. It certainly will contrast the marriage between the silent, submissive, and dependent Tristana and don Lope.

The marital arrangement envisioned by Mill, in which "the family, justly constituted, would be the real school of the virtues of freedom,"[34] is echoed by Mauro in his first proposal of marriage: "In intimate relationships, in the stable society of the home, you will find that equality which does not exist in the world" ["En la vida íntima, en la asociación constante del hogar, encontrará usted esa equidad que no existe en el mundo"] (M510). Like Mill, who argues that the conditions of marriage be arranged by "mutual consent" and the modification of "general custom" (S38), Mauro is ready to revise custom and proclaim that Feita is his "equal in condition and in rights" ["igual en condición y en derecho"] (M510). Though Mauro at times may be unreliable as a narrator—he is prone to rationalize and misjudge his deepest feelings—there is no reason to believe that his declaration is anything but honest and sincere. When, in her introduction to La esclavitud femenina [On the subjection of women], Pardo Bazán criticized idealists like Dante and don Quixote, favoring the rational realist Mill "and those that think and feel as he does (how few they are still!)" ["y los que como él piensan y sienten (¡cuán pocos son todavía!)]" (ME124), she planted the seeds for Mauro, a character who will trade the quixotic or Dantean fantasies of a Tristana or a Horacio for the nononsense reality of a Feita—a character who may increase the ranks in Spain of men like the British philosopher Mill.

The underlying theory of Memorias is located, then, in this rational, constructive territory rather than in the "angst" of romantic disillusionment that permeates Tristana. Indeed, Pardo Bazán's letters to Galdós corroborate this reading of theoretical difference in Memorias: "let us construct, through the freedom of art, the situation that society could give us already made" ["construyamos, con la libertad del arte, la situación que la sociedad podría darnos hecha"] (C91). In her article on Mill, Pardo Bazán reiterates her faith in the burgeoning effect of reform beginning at the individual level.

> That which is in the most educated and most intelligent individual consciousness, will soon be in the general enlightened consciousness, afterwards in the universal consciousness, and, finally, or better said at the same time, in custom, in art, in laws.
>
> [Lo que está en la conciencia individual más educada y más inteligente, estará pronto en la conciencia general ilustrada, después en la conciencia universal, y, por último, o mejor dicho a la vez, en la costumbre, en el arte, en las leyes.] (ME131)

According to this philosophy, she would view Memorias as a preliminary step toward profound social change.

By shaping a double-voiced discourse at once inside and outside prevailing convention, Pardo Bazán is able to create an ending for Memorias that

ubverts dominant tradition without entirely overturning textual and cultu-
al expectations: the marriage ending remains intact, but the customs
underlying the social institution and the textual device are substantially
ransformed. In this way, *Memorias* seems grounded on the belief that
eason, domestic freedom, and responsibility—all directed toward a better
uture—are necessary elements when the woman writer sets out to revise
he realist text for her own benefit and that of her readers. She employs
"that practical sense and that exact notion of reality that woman needs and
ossesses" ["ese sentido práctico y esa noción exacta de la realidad que
ecesita y posee la mujer"],[35] exemplifying Mill's observation that "a
woman usually sees much more than a man of what is immediately before
er" (S78).

Curiously, Mill's and Pardo Bazán's gender-linked distinctions are being
econsidered today, and the recent theories of Carol Gilligan suggest a
ocus for future discussions about the possible differences between texts of
Galdós and Pardo Bazán, indeed between those of men and women: "the
male pattern' of fantasy . . . leads from enhancement to deprivation . . . to
n irreparable loss. But the pattern of female fantasy traces a path which
emains largely unexplored, a narrative of deprivation followed by en-
ancement in which connection is in the end maintained or restored."
While Tristana becomes "castrated" into submission (irreparably derived), Feita joins Mauro to make of her family a school for individual
rowth and development (enhancement). As Hemingway concludes, the
marriage of Feita and Mauro "is not a capitulation," but rather "a creative
ngagement with the situation they have been thrust into."[36] *Memorias*
hus demonstrates that the finest goals of individualism and liberal,
ourgeois feminism may have offered woman, as writer and protagonist, a
romising potential for inscribing ongoing female (and male) growth into
he nineteenth-century realist text. By keeping a watchful eye on the mul-
farious strands of the contemporary social fabric, *Memorias* made a
romise it was able to keep.

## Notes

1. Cited by Nelly Clémessy, *Emilia Pardo Bazán como novelista*, trans. Irene
Gambra (Madrid: Fundación Universitaria Española, 1981), 1:258, from El Caba-
ero Audaz, "Nuestras visitas. La Condesa de Pardo Bazán," *La Esfera* 7 (1944).
2. Ibid., 260.
3. Elaine Showalter, "Feminist Criticism in the Wilderness," *Critical Inquiry* 8
1981): 204.
4. Nancy K. Miller, "Emphasis Added: Plots and Plausibilities in Women's
iction," *PMLA* 96 (1981): 43.

5. Noël M. Valis, "Art, Memory, and the Human in Galdós' *Tristana*," *Kentucky Romance Quarterly* 31 (1984): 218.

6. Emilia Pardo Bazán, *Cartas a Benito Pérez Galdós (1889–1890)*, ed. Carmen Bravo Villasante (Madrid: Turner, 1975), p. 81. Subsequent references to this work will appear in the text and will be indicated by C.

7. Anabel González et al., *Los orígenes del feminismo en España* (Madrid: Zero, 1980), pp. 128–38.

8. From Pardo Bazán's "La exposición de trabajos de la mujer," *Nuevo Teatro Crítico* 3 (March 1893): 142–56. Reprinted in Emilia Pardo Bazán, *La mujer española y otros artículos feministas*, ed. Leda Schiavo (Madrid: Nacional, 1976), p. 165. Subsequent references to this work will appear in the text and will be indicated by ME.

9. Benito Pérez Galdós, *Tristana* (Madrid: Alianza, 1969), p. 29. Subsequent references to this work will appear in the text and will be indicated by T.

10. Germán Gullón, "*Tristana*: Literaturización y estructura novelesca," *Hispanic Review* 45 (1977): 20.

Harry Levin has cured readers of the naïve notion that realism necessarily sets a faithful mirror up to nature, arguing persuasively that realism creates the "illusion of reality" precisely by attacking previous literary illusions. Harry Levin, *Gates of Horn: A Study of Five French Realists* (New York: Oxford University Press, 1966), p. 43.

11. See Edward H. Friedman's "Folly and a Woman: Galdós' Rhetoric of Irony in *Tristana*," in *Theory and Practice of Feminist Literary Criticism*, ed. Gabriela Mora and Karen S. Van Hooft (Ypsilanti, Mich.: Bilingual Press, 1982), pp. 201–28, for a detailed analysis of the varieties of irony at work in *Tristana*.

12. Levin, *Gates of Horn*, pp. 48 and 263. In this sense I agree with Gullón and Valis that feminism, as a historical issue, is not of central importance in *Tristana*. Instead, the feminist theme is subsumed into the overall theoretical function of the text.

13. The term is borrowed from Sandra M. Gilbert and Susan Gubar, *The Madwoman in the Attic: The Woman Writer and the Nineteenth-Century Literary Imagination* (New Haven: Yale University Press, 1979).

14. Valis, "Art, Memory, and the Human," p. 209.

15. Dianne Sadoff, *Monsters of Affection: Dickens, Eliot and Brontë on Fatherhood* (Baltimore: Johns Hopkins University Press, 1982), p. 127.

16. Friedman attributes the silencing of Tristana to Galdós or to his authoritative narrative persona for whom Tristana's failure is a thematic imperative.

17. A. F. Lambert, "Galdós and Concha-Ruth Morell," *Anales Galdosianos* (1973): 40, 42; and Gilbert Smith, "Galdós, *Tristana* and Letters from Concha Ruth Morell," *Anales Galdosianos* 10 (1975): 117.

18. Bravo Villasante (Pardo Bazán, *Cartas*, p. 82) believes that Tristana's insistence on emancipation is a transcription of Pardo Bazán's ideas on the topic. While this may be so, Concha-Ruth Morell also declared her desire to be self-sufficient. The principal difference is that Pardo Bazán was more successful in achieving her desires than were Concha-Ruth or Tristana.

19. Susan Kirkpatrick, "Pardo Bazán Reading *Tristana*" (Paper delivered at the Modern Language Association Convention, Washington, D.C., 28 December 1984).

20. Gilbert and Gubar, *The Madwoman in the Attic*, p. 21.

21. It is difficult to accept Leon Livingstone's argument ("The Law of Nature and Women's Liberation in *Tristana*," *Anales Galdosianos* 7 [1972]: 93–100) that

the marriage of Tristana and don Lope exemplifies the working of natural law. This marriage is instead a cynical parody of natural law (which characteristically unites young and implicitly fertile people in a match based on love or a healthy attraction between the sexes) and is far from uniting equals in unforced union, as Livingstone concludes. Tristana has been beaten, metaphorically castrated, and placed in captivity and is hardly part of a union of "comparable and compatible equals" that Livingstone's optimistic reading suggests follows the course of natural law. Less optimistically, Friedman announces that *Tristana*'s ending "cries for revision" (p. 222).

22. Emilia Pardo Bazán, *Memorias de un solterón*, vol. 2 of *Obras completas*, ed. Federico Carlos Sainz de Robles (Madrid: Aguilar, 1964), pp. 448–527. Subsequent references to this work will appear in the text and will be indicated by M.

23. Here Feita parallels the views of her author who praises Paris for its reason and hard work in contrast to Madrid, which she sees ruled by uneducated caprice. See Robert Hilton, "A Spanish Francophile: Emilia Pardo Bazán," *Revue de littérature comparée* 26 (1952): 244–45.

24. Maurice Hemingway, *Emilia Pardo Bazán: The Making of a Novelist* (Cambridge: Cambridge University Press, 1983), p. 140.

25. Ibid., p. 142. Hemingway also believes that in *Memorias* "the feminist argument is part of a broader argument" (Ibid.).

26. Sadoff, *Monsters of Affection*, p. 129.

27. Gilbert and Gubar, *The Madwoman in the Attic*, p. 119.

28. This requires argument with Maryellen Bieder's assumption that "work is clearly viewed here as punishment" (p. 103). See her "Capitulation: Marriage Not Freedom. A Study of Emilia Pardo Bazán's *Memorias de un solterón* and Galdós's *Tristana*," *Symposium* 30 (1976): 93–109.

29. Pardo Bazán saw no need to overturn existent institutions to win rights for women. She preferred to focus on the reform of customs: "Our laws are absolutely broad: It is our customs that are moldy" ["La ley, entre nosotros, es de completa amplitud: las costumbres son las que tienen moho"], *La vida contemporánea (1896–1915)*, ed. Carmen Bravo Villasante (Madrid: Novelas y Cuentos, 1972), pp. 84–85.

30. Pardo Bazán wrote a stunning and moving prologue to her edition of John Stuart Mill's *On the Subjection of Women*, published separately in *Nuevo Teatro Crítico* 2 (May 1892): 41–76. Reprinted in *La mujer española y otros artículos feministas*, pp. 113–34.

31. John Stuart Mill, *Autobiography of John Stuart Mill*, ed. John Jacob Coss (New York: Columbia University Press, 1948). Subsequent references to this work will appear in the text and will be indicated by A.

32. John Stuart Mill, *On Liberty* (New York: Bobbs-Merrill Co., 1956), p. 81.

33. Bieder, p. 102; F. A. Hayek, *John Stuart Mill and Harriet Taylor: Their Correspondence and Subsequent Marriage* (Chicago: University of Chicago Press, 1951), p. 64.

34. John Stuart Mill, *On the Subjection of Women*, ed. Susan Brownmiller (Greenwich, Conn.: Fawcett, 1971), p. 63. Subsequent references to this work will appear in the text and will be indicated by S.

35. Emilia Pardo Bazán, *Lecciones de literatura* (Madrid: Editorial Ibero-Americana, n.d.), p. 104.

36. Carol Gilligan, *In a Different Voice* (Cambridge: Harvard University Press, 1982), p. 48; Hemingway, *Emilia Pardo Bazán*, p. 162.

# A Passage to Androgyny: Isabel Allende's
## *La casa de los espíritus*

### LINDA GOULD LEVINE

Imagine a familiar childhood scene: it is bedtime and your parents, wear
of adult realities, momentarily shed their grown-up burdens and enter th
enchanted world of fairy tales and fables engraved in their souls and th
souls of their parents before them. They place before you a cast of charac
ters who will become your soulmates during your formative years an
whose actions will undoubtedly influence your own: Cinderella, Rapunzel
Prince Charming. Now imagine a different scene. It is again the bedtim
hour in an unnamed country in South America. A mother reads to he
young daughter tales from the Brothers Grimm, Perrault, Hans Christia
Andersen. But instead of the beloved figures of Little Red Riding Hood
Sleeping Beauty, valiant dragon slayers, and princes, she offers her child
new cast of characters: a prince who sleeps for one hundred years, a damse
who fights dragons single-handed, a forlorn wolf who is unexpectedly dis
emboweled by a little girl.[1] For those who were comforted and sustaine
during the childhood years by the "orthodox" version, this new scenari
elicits a disquieting response. Disquieting, because it prompts specula
tion that present-day outlooks would differ had they been nurtured on suc
unusual tales.

If all imaginations do not stretch far enough to envision this alternative
Isabel Allende's certainly did. In her electrifying saga of a Latin America
family, *La casa de los espíritus*[2] (*The House of the Spirits*), her characte
Blanca reads or "rereads" traditional tales to her young daughter Alba
Her rendition is so original that it inspires Alba to "reread" her own famil
history and record in a journal her opinions of important events. Alba'
literary pursuits in turn represent a miniature version of Isabel Allende'
creative rewriting of patriarchy and male authorship. This network c
mutual influences and revisions suggests a tantalizing beginning for
feminist reading of the novel as well as an examination of the author

concept of androgyny. Allende's novel is not only a mirror in which tales are retold and female characters struggle against patriarchal oppression; it is also a forum in which male and female are joined together in a "spirit of reconciliation between the sexes."[3] Or to use a phrase from the novel itself, *La casa de los espíritus* is "a kaleidoscope of jumbled mirrors where everything and anything could happen" (p. 72) ["un caleidoscopio de espejos desordenados donde todo podía ocurrir"] (p. 78), including the unusual merging of the real and the magical, the fictitious and the historical, the spoken and the written, the politically exigent and the Utopian possibility, the male and the female.

Like the "casa" itself with its labyrinthian tunnels and unusual contours, Allende's novel invites readers to wander into one room that might be called "feminist," occupied by the women of the del Valle lineage; discover another door labelled "patriarchy," inhabited by Esteban Trueba; and then enter a narrow passageway between them, called "androgyny," in which many of the characters periodically reside. This essay will meander through these three textual spaces and journey through literary influences and mirrors, in an attempt to discover the ingredients and proportions of Allende's rich fusion of the sexes.

Perhaps a basic recipe for the author's unique literary "concoction" might be as follows: 1/4 cup of García Márquez, 1/4 cup of fairy tales, 1/2 cup of women's diaries, a tablespoon of Pablo Neruda, a teaspoon of the Marquis de Sade, a dusting of Karl Marx, a pan coated with an ample dose of imagination, good humor, and contemporary politics purchased in Latin America. Blend together until the mixture achieves a solid form. Set aside in a mold for sixty-five years. Carefully remove and serve. I suspect that if one tried to follow this recipe, the result would be a culinary and literary disaster, not nearly as flavorful as Allende's dish. Nonetheless, the recipe still would be more or less accurate. The only difference would be that while most would "read" the instructions as stated, Isabel Allende deliberately has "misread" them,[4] a necessary act of distancing that contributes to the originality of her style.

The most obvious recreation is of course that of García Márquez's *Cien años de soledad* (*One Hundred Years of Solitude*), a tantalizing precedent that has provided Allende's critics with countless opportunities for analysis. Recent articles and papers about her novel include stimulating discussions about the presence of magical realism in the two works, "with its calculated use of repetition, its circularity and its symbolic plotting";[5] an informed study of Allende's "dialectical response" to García Márquez's novel, as suggested by the comparison between Aureliano's ant-eaten child at the end of *Cien años* and Alba's awaited child at the close of *La casa*;[6] and a description of the Colombian's "apology of the so-called metaphysi-

cal virtues of housewives," contrasted with the "critical . . . revision of th
condition of women in Latin American society" as depicted by the Chilea
author.[7]

I would venture to add one more essential difference that underline
Allende's creative revision of García Márquez. The Colombian author'
novel is a mirror reflection of a male-authored world penned by one ma
(García Márquez), restated by another (Melquíades), and finally inter
preted by a third (Aureliano) in a "room of his own" from which wome
are zealously excluded. Allende's text, on the other hand, is a mirro
reflection of a female-authored world. Isabel Allende now occupies th
seat of García Márquez, while Clara, the spiritual grandmother whose ric
imagination and prophetic gifts mirror those of Melquíades, gently pushe
the gypsy aside to transcribe her own tale. Finally, Alba's mission, like tha
of Aureliano, is to read the tale. But while Aureliano's text disappears i
the cataclysm that annihilates Macondo, Alba's continues and is regener
ated by her pen and her womb—writing and gestation—an androgynou
fusion of traditional male and female symbols.[8]

Perhaps by destroying his text and its male-authored world, García Már
quez inadvertently has paved the way for the reemergence of the forgotte
goddesses and matrilinear realms that Allende clearly evokes even as sh
avoids engaging in any act of literary "parricide." For if she does not seer
to be trapped in the predicament of "killing" her literary "father" or c
exorcising him from her mind, I suspect it is because she recognizes that "
woman writing thinks back through her mothers" and "her fathers a
well." "Only male writers can forget or mute half their heritage."[9]

Certainly, the presence of Allende's "mother" or "grandmother" loom
larger than life in her text. Allende has stated that the model for Clara an
her notebooks is based on reality, though exaggerated by the lens o
fiction.[10] It almost would appear that these two benevolent muses—Clar
and García Márquez—guided Allende as she wrote her tale, gentl
coaching her as she gave birth to her narrator Alba. This character intro
duces another variation of the writing process, one that is a mirror reflec
tion of her author's creative fusion. Her tale, presented to the reader as th
novel itself—a literary device that recalls a "Chinese box construc
tion"[11]—is also a combination of male and female influences, narrate
primarily in the third person with occasional glimpses of Alba's first-perso
reality.

Most significant of these influences are Clara's journals. They not onl
set the tone for the intense thematic relationship between life and fiction
but also reinforce another concept central to the novel—the transforma
tion of life by fiction. For example: Clara is so concerned with preservin
the clarity of her diaries that she refuses to name either of her two son
Esteban, since "repeating the same name just caused confusion in he

notebooks that bore witness to life" (p. 99) ["los nombres repetidos crean confusión en los cuadernos de anotar la vida"] (p. 107). That is, life (the fictional one presented as real in Allende's novel) will be molded by the exigencies of fiction (Clara's re-creation of life in her notebooks), an emblem for the power of the written word that characterizes Clara's presence in the text. Yet, even as Clara remolds reality with her pen, she is acutely aware of the force behind her spoken words. She fears that Rosa might have died because "she had said she would" (p. 33). She uses silence as a means of establishing autonomy over her life and husband and, near the end of the novel, she urges Alba to write "a testimony that might one day call attention to the terrible secret she was living through" (pp. 351–2) ["un testimonio que algún día podría servir para sacar a la luz el terrible secreto que estaba viviendo"] (p. 362).

Clara's implicit belief that woman's words will survive history is underscored dramatically through Allende's narration of the mass burning of books that accompanied the early days of the military takeover (i.e., the Pinochet dictatorship). The books that are destroyed in the "infamous pyre" (p. 341) ["pira infame"] (p. 352) are Jaime's medical texts and his edition of the complete works of Karl Marx, Uncle Marcos's collection of magical tales, the esoteric treatise written by Nicolás, and Esteban's opera scores—all male-authored texts that noticeably exclude Clara's journals. These "miraculously" escape, not unlike Pascual Duarte's manuscript during the Spanish Civil War or *Don Quixote* itself, shuffled amidst a group of wares in a Toledian market. While this is a convenient and familiar literary ploy to make the reader believe in the reality of the text and its unusual odyssey from political turmoil to literary history, it also reflects Allende's view of the potency of women's words, words that cannot be silenced by oppressive regimes. In her preface to *Other Fires*, an anthology of short fiction by Latin American women, Allende writes:

> This anthology demonstrates that Latin American women have their own vision of the world and know how to express it, in their own personal, irreverent, furious, fantastic, ironic and poetic language. They tell us of the multiple forms of violence they suffer and, in doing so, violate the first rule imposed upon them since birth: the rule of silence. They do not accept it, they do not bow their heads; they do not resign themselves; they are not silent.[12]

Neither are the women of her own novel silent. Like Demeter of the classical world, Clara is powerless to save her offspring from rape in the Latin American version of Hell—Pinochet's torture chambers. She can, however, give her the power of words to "reclaim the past" (p. 368) ["rescatar las cosas del olvido"] (p. 380), a power that is pitted against the military's attempt to change "world history, erasing every incident, ideology and historical figure of which the regime disapproved" (p. 325) ["la historia universal, borrando los episodios, las ideologías y los personajes que el régimen desaprobaba"] (p. 337). Yet, even as Alba incorporates Clara's voice into her mission as writer, one senses the presence of a male-authored text that also contributes to her creative endeavors: the fairy tales she inherited from her great-uncle Marcos—the threshold to the world of the fantastic, read first by Clara, then by Blanca, and finally retold by Alba to children in the concentration camp.

The pervasiveness of reading, combined with Clara's journals, epitomize the joining of the male and female in *La casa de los espíritus* or the historically fictitious (the Brothers Grimm, Perrault) with the pseudo-fictitious (Clara's notebooks); but they also reveal one of the underlying principles of this novel: the Bloomian hypothesis that "you are or become what you read."[13] Alba exudes strength, perseverance, and imagination partly because of the influence of literary models. Similarly, one might speculate that the count's pornographic fantasies are a product of his readings in the Marquis de Sade and that Jaime's passion for social justice has been nurtured by Karl Marx. In a less literary vein, it also appears that Colonel Esteban García's intense rancor and hatred toward his twisted destiny can be ascribed in part to the stories his grandmother told him when he was young.

> His grandmother, Pancha García, had managed before she died to poison his childhood with the story that if only his father had been born in place of Blanca, Jaime or Nicolás, he would have inherited Tres Marías, and could even have been President of the Republic if he wanted. (p. 162)

> [Su abuela, Pancha García, antes de morir, alcanzó a envenenar su infancia con el cuento de que si su padre hubiera nacido en el lugar de Blanca, Jaime o Nicolás, habría heredado Las Tres Marías y podría haber llegado a Presidente de la República de haberlo querido.] (p. 170)

By juxtaposing one grandmother's tale of dispossession and humiliation (Pancha's) with the other grandmother's tale of self-possession and authority (Clara's), Allende artfully creates a compelling thesis for the perditious or felicitous effects of the word on human fate. Or to use Carmen Martín Gaite's terminology, she suggests a disquieting contrast between "la narración [narration] 'tanathos',' which leads to sterility and destruction, and "la narración 'eros',' which creates pleasure[14] and, in the case of her own novel, forgiveness. For in one sense, it appears that Alba's final response to her rape and victimization by Colonel García is a reaction, not to her real life experience, but to Clara's notebooks and other documents that she has on hand upon her release from jail. In those writings, she finds transcribed the story of Pancha García's rape by her grandfather, Esteban, and the sordid beginnings of Colonel García, who tries to rewrite his own history through his rape of Alba. To this degree, her decision to reverse the cycle of hatred and vengeance generated by Pancha's rape is a direct result of her metamorphosis through fiction. The following passage captures this sense.

When I was in the doghouse, I wrote in my mind that one day Colonel García would be before me in defeat and that I would avenge myself on all those who need to be avenged. But now I have begun to question my own hatred. Within a few short weeks, ever since I returned to the house, it seems to have become diluted, to have lost its sharp edge. . . . I feel its flame going out as I come to understand the existence of Colonel García and the others like him, as I understand my grandfather and piece things together from Clara's notebooks, my mother's letters, the ledgers of Tres Marías, and the many other documents spread before me on the table. It would be very difficult for me to avenge all those who should be avenged, because my revenge would be just another part of the same inexorable rite. (pp. 367–68)

[En la perrera escribí con el pensamiento que algún día tendría al coronel García vencido ante mí y podría vengar a todos los que tienen que ser vengados. Pero ahora dudo de mi odio. En pocas semanas, desde que estoy en esta casa, parece haberse diluido, haber perdido sus nítidos contornos. . . . Siento que se apaga en la medida en que me explico la existencia del coronel García y de otros como él, que comprendo a mi abuelo y me entero de las cosas a través de los cuadernos de Clara, las cartas de mi madre, los libros de administración de Las Tres Marías y tantos otros documentos que ahora están sobre la mesa al alcance de la mano. Me será muy difícil vengar a todos los que tienen que ser vengados, porque mi venganza no sería más que otra parte del mismo rito inexorable.] (p. 379)

Just as Sancho Panza is altered in part 2 of *Don Quixote* by the knowledge that he has been immortalized as a "presonaje" (i.e., *personaje* [character]) in Avellaneda's text, Alba's view of herself is filtered by the powerful written word. Her role as pardoner rather than avenger springs from a deliberate revising of her family epic, similar to Blanca's "misreadings" of fairy tales or Rosa's recreation of classical mythological creatures. Thus, while Alba's forgiveness of Esteban García may evoke a feminist or political response of anger or confusion, it is the only conclusion that seems harmonious with the rest of the novel and with Alba's optimistic personality.[15] It also exemplifies Allende's implicit desire to rewrite traditional literary and historical patterns, even one as highly charged as woman's attitude toward rape.

This question of reader response evokes still another consideration of the construction of the novel and its merging of male and female. Traveling from one physical and textual space to another in this work, we become acutely aware of two different voices, with two different ideologies, which we identify at the novel's close with Alba and with her grandfather Esteban. This union or coexistence of Alba's and Esteban's voices presents a refreshing version of what critics have called the "double-voiced discourse" of women's writings—a discourse in which the "dominant" voice is male and the "muted" story, female.[16] In Allende's novel, the dominant voice is obviously Alba's, a discourse composed of her own voice, Clara's, and many others, while the secondary voice, certainly not as resonant, is Esteban's.

Yet if Allende creates a narrative imbalance between male and female discourse and limits Esteban's participation to approximately forty-four pages of her 380 page novel, the fact that he writes at all and urges Alba to do the same is a tribute to Clara's influence over him. Just as Don Quixote is "Sanchified" in Cervantes's novel, Esteban gradually is "Clarified" ["aclarado"] in Allende's work, precisely because of Clara's presence in his life. At the moment of her death, he is literally (and figuratively) the same size as she, a symbol of his shrinking as a man and his entrance into the zone of androgyny. He also follows her custom of wandering through the house like a spirit and ultimately adopts her gesture of writing as a means of leaving testimony upon her death: "I can't talk about it. But I'll try to write it" (p. 248) ["No puedo hablar de eso. Pero intentaré escribirlo"] (p. 259).

This fusion of characters or mutual reflection of the two sexes in the "kaleidoscope of jumbled mirrors" permeates the text, creating that narrow passageway that at times suggests androgyny, as Mario Rojas has noted,[17] or simply another perspective regarding the bonds that unite Allende's seemingly disparate creations. Characters as different as Férula (Esteban's sister) and the Count (Blanca's husband) are joined in the reader's mind through their mutual attraction to unusual disguises and fabrications of fictitious selves. Esteban Trueba is united with the prostitute and brothel owner Tránsito Soto not merely on a sexual level, but through her ambition that at once evokes his own. Clara and Esteban Primero García are inexorably linked through their magical qualities and supernatural gifts that "move" tables and ants. Finally, Alba and her father Pedro Tercero García are related, not merely by blood, but through the mutilation of their right hands and their powerful will to continue creative endeavors with their left ones.

An additional component of this mergence of male and female is underscored through Allende's juxtaposition of her characters' destinies. Amanda tells her younger brother Miguelito that she would give her life for him and fulfills that promise years later during the military takeover. On the other hand, Pedro Segundo García dreams of sacrificing himself for Clara del Valle without being given the chance to realize his wish: "like an adolescent, there were times when he fantasized about giving his life for her" (p. 142) ["como un adolescente, a veces fantaseaba con la idea de dar la vida por ella"] (p. 149).

Through this spiral of mirror images that merge into one another and link characters of different sexes, ideologies, and social classes, Allende offers an unusual rewriting of Latin American reality. Her version not only suggests the restructuring of the continent's patterns of "dependency and dominance" as Engelbert has observed,[18] but also a revision of the traditional dichotomy between the sexes. If this interpretation denotes a utopian reading of the text, or Allende's utopian writing of it, such vision is clearly part of the novel's political and sexual dialectics. Sweeping the reader along in her whirlwind narrative, she gracefully moves from the "killing" of Rosa—the myth, "the angel of the house"[19]—to the antithetical realm of Pinochet's hell and the rebirth of hope at dawn in Alba's creative and synthetic gesture.

> I want to think that my task is life and that my mission is not to prolong hatred but simply to fill these pages while I wait for Miguel, while I bury my grandfather, whose body lies beside me in this room, while I wait for better times to come, while I carry this child in my womb, the daughter of so many rapes or perhaps of Miguel, but above all, my own daughter. (p. 368)

> [Quiero pensar que mi oficio es la vida y que mi misión no es prolongar el odio, sino sólo llenar estas páginas mientras espero el regreso de Miguel, mientras entierro a mi abuelo que ahora descansa a mi lado en este cuarto, mientras aguardo que lleguen tiempos mejores, gestando a la criatura que tengo en el vientre, hija de tantas violaciones, o tal vez hija de Miguel, pero sobre todo hija mía.] (pp. 379–80)

Is this a female version of Aeneas's odyssey through the underworld? Perhaps, but more likely it is a mirror image of Adrienne Rich's poetic description of the woman artist's journey "through the cratered night of female memory to revitalize the darkness, to retrieve what has been lost, to regenerate, reconceive and give birth."[20] For if Aeneas was able to apprehend only the shadows of his loved ones, without transforming them into living beings, Alba's creation of flesh and words at the close of the novel suggests the possibility of a new Elysian fields, both feminist and androgynous in nature. There may pass another sixty or one hundred years of solitude before this union of different spheres is realized. Until then, might we not follow Allende's footsteps and bequeath this entrancing dream to be told and retold to our children as their bedtime draws near?

# Notes

This article was completed with support from the Montclair State College Separately Budgeted Research Program.

1. This rendition of traditional tales is a paraphrase of Magda Bogin's transla-

tion, *The House of the Spirits* (New York: Alfred A. Knopf, 1985), p. 258. All subsequent quotations in English are from Bogin's translation.

2. Isabel Allende, *La casa de los espíritus*, 8th ed. (Barcelona: Plaza & Janés, 1983). All references in Spanish are from this edition.

3. Carolyn Heilbrun, *Towards the Recognition of Androgyny* (New York: Alfred A. Knopf, 1973), pp. x–xi. For a further discussion of androgyny in *La casa de los espíritus*, see Mario Rojas, "*La casa de los espíritus* de Isabel Allende: un caleidoscopio de espejos desordenados," *Revista Iberoamericana* 132–33 (July–December 1985): 917–25.

4. Harold Bloom, *A Map of Misreading* (New York: Oxford University Press, 1975), p. 3.

5. Magda Bogin, "The Magical Feminism of Isabel Allende" (Paper delivered at the Seventh Annual Conference on Latin American Literature, Montclair State College, Upper Montclair, N.J., 16 March 1984), p. 16.

6. Jo Anne Engelbert, "The Anatomy of Dominance: Isabel Allende's *The House of the Spirits*" (Paper delivered at the Modern Language Association Convention, New York, 27 December 1984), p. 16.

7. Juan Manuel Marcos, "Isabel viendo llover en Barataria," *Revista de Estudios Hispánicos* 19, no. 2 (1987): 131. For additional perspectives on Allende's strong concept of female characterization, see the articles by René Campos, Marcelo Coddou, Nora Glickman, Gabriela Mora, Juan Manuel Marcos, and Teresa Méndez-Faith included in Marcelo Coddou, ed., *Los libros tienen sus propios espíritus* (México: Universidad Veracruzana, 1986). Also see Marjorie Agosín, "Isabel Allende: *La casa de los espíritus*," *Revista Interamericana de Bibliografía/Inter-American Review of Bibliography* 35 (1985): 448–58.

8. See Sandra Gilbert and Susan Gubar, *The Madwoman in the Attic: The Woman Writer and the Nineteenth-Century Literary Imagination* (New Haven/London: Yale University Press, 1979), p. 7; Elaine Showalter, "Feminist Criticism in the Wilderness," in Elaine Showalter, ed., *The New Feminist Criticism: Essays on Women, Literature and Theory* (New York: Pantheon Books, 1985), pp. 250–51.

9. Edward Said, *Beginnings: Intention and Method* (New York: Basic Books, 1975), p. 209; Judith Fetterly, *The Resisting Reader: A Feminist Approach to American Fiction* (Bloomington: Indiana University Press, 1978), p. xxii; Virginia Woolf, *A Room of One's Own* (New York: Harcourt, Brace & Co., 1929), pp. 168–69; Showalter, "Feminist Criticism," p. 265; Ibid.

10. Isabel Allende, "Los libros tienen sus propios espíritus," in Coddou, *Los libros*, p. 16.

11. Robert Alter, *Partial Magic: The Novel as a Self-Conscious Genre* (Berkeley: University of California Press, 1975), p. 187.

12. See Alberto Manguel, ed., *Other Fires: Short Fiction by Latin American Women* (New York: Clarkson N. Potter, Inc., 1986), p. xiii.

13. Harold Bloom, *Kabbalah and Criticism* (New York: Seabury Press, 1975), p. 96.

14. Carmen Martín Gaite, *El cuento de nunca acabar* (Madrid: Editorial Trieste, 1983), p. 324.

15. For a further analysis of the controversy generated by the ending of Allende's novel, see two articles by Gabriela Mora: "Ruptura y perseverancia de estereotipos en *La casa de los espíritus*," in Coddou, *Los libros*, pp. 71–78, and "Las novelas de Isabel Allende y el papel de la mujer como ciudadana," *Ideologies and Literature* 2, no. 1 (1987): 53–61.

16. Susan S. Lanser and Evelyn T. Beck, "'Why' Are There No Great Women Critics?", in Julia A. Sherman and Evelyn Torton Beck, eds., *The Prism of Sex: Essays in the Sociology of Knowledge* (Madison: University of Wisconsin Press, 1979), pp. 79–91. Lanser and Beck describe the "double-voiced discourse" of women's writings as follows: "The writings of women who are struggling to define themselves but have not yet given up a patriarchal frame of reference may betray a tension so strong as to produce a virtually 'double-voiced' discourse" (p. 86). I have used this term in a somewhat different sense when applying it to Allende's novel. Rather than an illustration of the struggle between the male and female voice within one writer, Allende's text is an example of the coexistence of the two distinct voices; see also Showalter, "Feminist Criticism," p. 263.

17. Rojas, "*La casa de los espíritus,*" pp. 923–24.

18. Engelbert, "The Anatomy of Dominance," p. 16. See also William Ferguson, "Tradition and Modernization: A Latin American Perspective" (Paper delivered at Clark University, Worcester, Mass., 15 July 1985), pp. 21–22.

19. Rosario Castellanos, *Mujer que sabe latín. . .* (México: Sop Diana, 1979), p. 7; Virginia Woolf, "Professions for Women," in *The Death of the Moth and Other Essays* (New York: Harcourt & Brace, 1942), pp. 236–38.

20. Adrienne Rich, "Re-forming the Crystal," in *Poems: Selected and New, 1950–1974* (New York: W. W. Norton, 1975), p. 228.

# Part 3

# The Critical Space

# The Male Critic and the Woman Writer: Reading Teresa de la Parra's Critics

## ELSA KRIEGER GAMBARINI

The unexpected popularity of the work of Teresa de la Parra (Ana Teresa Parra Sanojo, 1899–1936) provoked a critical exuberance characterized by both excessive adulation and censure. A profusion of "critics without criticism," impelled at times by literary fashion and at times by the desire to "put in their two cents worth" about every book, showered the work of the Venezuelan author with, in the words of the creator of Mamá Blanca, "a white shower" ["aguacerito blanco"] of trivial essays of no substance. In 1980, Velia Bosch selected and published some of the more thoughtful critical essays, choosing an average of three writers to represent each decade.[1] The selection offers an interesting chronological panorama of "la crítica teresiana," revealing changes in tone and taste, as well as certain uniformities in the critical reading of her work. The critics comment on the author's life and work, or they respond to previous criticism, either to corroborate it or to disagree and correct it.

It is not my purpose to repeat in detail what all of these essays—the authors of which are almost exclusively male, until the 1970s—say about Teresa de la Parra. Rather, I would like to focus on the less obvious aspects of the critical text, on what it assumes without accounting for the range and implications of what it affirms. Some of the more valuable contributions of this critical literature will be used in this study, especially those that reveal changes in the treatment of de la Parra's work.

I will begin by suggesting that just as the unconscious infiltrates the conscious mind, the body of critical analysis—representing conscious activity—is penetrated by its own unconscious, which it contains within itself as the possibility of its own subversion. The most significant aspect of the criticism of Teresa de la Parra is how it unconsciously problematizes the feminine. The male critic confronts the difficult problem of how to locate himself before what culture has construed as otherness, and how to respond to this otherness when it manifests its problematic desire, when it speaks as a subject, when it writes a literary text. Before this arduous (if

177

not impossible) task of overcoming cultural constructions and constrictions, what critics achieve is to direct an "empty Word" at the novel/novelist, with whom they maintain an Imaginary relationship.[2] She (text and author) becomes the projection of an imago (cultural construction of the feminine) that in fact does not truly exist.[3]

What does exist is the feminine subject who writes in all her complexity; it is the feminine text that speaks with all its ambiguity. The critic, however, addresses a less problematic figure: the feminine enveloped by patriarchal constriction, where the feminine responds to an imaginary configuration. The critic stands in a mirror relation to the feminine text, which functions as a slave serving his desires, particularly his desire for recognition. He exercises authority over the feminine text with a dominating, magisterial discourse that seeks its own satisfaction above all else.[4] In other words, the (male) critic reads in Teresa's work that which Barthes has named the *texte lisible*, a fundamentally univocal aspect of the text that the reader understands and assimilates. The *texte lisible* represents that aspect of the text that is significant because it is recognizable; because, in effect, the reader has already read it.[5]

This *texte lisible* is none other than the return of the same. Clearly there is nothing less objective than this type of reductive critical reading, because in it the reader simply rediscovers him or herself, confirming his or her intellectual and cultural tradition in endless repetition. That which the male critic understands, that which is significant because it is recognizable in de la Parra's work, that which is rediscovered, is the feminine as understood by traditional culture. Unconsciously, in directing his discourse to the novel/novelist, the male critic attributes to it what he understands as the feminine. In the literary critical discourse addressed to de la Parra and her texts, there is resistance (in the psychological sense of the word) to allowing that feminine otherness to pass from the category of imago-object to that of subject, from the Imaginary to the Symbolic order, finally, to assume its place as subject in language.[6]

French critic Francis de Miomandre's prologue to the novel *Ifigenia* (published in 1924) is the model that various critics came to repeat.[7] In a kindly tone, Miomandre rejoices over the success of the book, whose merits he could "appreciate beforehand" ["apreciar de antemano"] because he had read it in manuscript form. He proceeds to emphasize what he considers "the most evident and most precious gift of Teresa de la Parra, her ingenuousness" ["el don más evidente, y el más precioso también, de Teresa de la Parra, la ingenuidad"]. This ingenuousness is the *texte lisible* the critic finds in the novel. Although Miomandre translated *Ifigenia* into French (for a collection that also included the works of Katherine Mansfield and Virginia Woolf), the ironic intention of this apparent ingenuousness escaped him. It is this ironic intention, however, that links de la Parra's work with a long literary tradition passing from Saint Paul, Socrates, Shakespeare, Cervantes, and Swift, to the present. When read carefully, this irony deconstructs the *texte lisible*; if he had done so, Miomandre would not have found his imago of the feminine confirmed by the text.[8]

Warned by the first "ingenuous" critical reactions, de la Parra stated in a letter:

It seems to me that another thing they hold against *Ifigenia* is this: they do not perceive in it the real intention of the irony. . . . Irony . . . is adulterated in our medium, exaggerated, deformed, reduced to the category of insult; they consider it a lesser form of insult and nothing more. True irony is not this. True irony, the real mccoy, is like charity—it begins at home; it must always have a smile of kindness, and the scent of indulgence.

[Otra cosa que me parece descubrir contra *Ifigenia* es ésta: el de no sentir allá la verdadera intención de la ironía. . . . La ironía . . . se falsea siempre en nuestro medio, se la exagera, se la deforma, la rebajan a la categoría de insulto, la consideran insulto atenuado y nada más. La verdadera ironía no es ésa. La verdadera ironía, la de buena ley, es aquélla que al igual que la caridad bien entendida, empieza por sí misma; la que debe tener siempre una sonrisa de bondad y un perfume de indulgencia.][9]

Not all readers of this period missed the ironic intention of the work, however. De la Parra recounts in another letter the reactions of one reader.

The Infanta Eulalia, the king of Spain's aunt, a charming person and a writer herself, enjoyed *Ifigenia* so much that she had me brought to her home. . . . She told me, in front of everyone, she had never smiled and laughed so much as when she read the needlework scene with the table cloth and the discussion. It seems it was at night, and she was reading in bed. Her chambermaid, hearing her laugh in that way, became extremely alarmed and hurried in to see what had happened.

[A la infanta Eulalia, la tía del rey de España, que tiene un espíritu encantador y es escritora, le gustó tanto *Ifigenia* que hizo que me llevasen a su casa. . . . Contó delante de todo el mundo la risa immensa, las carcajadas que la habían acometido al leer en *Ifigenia* la escena del calado con el mantel y la discusión. Según parece era de noche, estaba en su cama leyendo y su camarera al escucharla reír de tal modo vino alarmadísima a ver qué le pasaba.][10]

In another commentary intended to praise, Miomandre says, "Teresa de la Parra says everything that passes through her head, that pretty head as well-made on the outside as it is on the inside." ["Teresa de la Parra dice todo cuanto le pasa por la cabeza, esa bonita cabeza tan bien hecha por fuera como por dentro."] He adds that *Ifigenia* "is a confession for a select society" ["es una confesión para sociedad escogida"]. This last comment, as Benjamín Carrión remarked in the thirties, "belittles the work."[11] The critic, whose intention is to praise, actually diminishes the writer and devalues her work, leaving intact his feminine imago, whose reflection is pretty and ingenuous. The resulting criticism is ambivalent—it extols and devalues simultaneously—but through it the critic evades the difficult problem of taking a stand before the feminine subject, before the less accessible *texte scriptible*.[12]

In the same decade, Lisandro Alvarado read the novel in a narrow and censorious manner, claiming that it deals with a "domestic conflict that is simply reduced to the proselytizing of contemporary philosophical beliefs, limited in this case to a daring feminism and to the violent reactions of the fashion" ["un conflicto doméstico, que sencillamente se reduce al proselitismo de las creencias filosóficas contemporáneas, limitado en este caso a un osado feminismo y a las reacciones violentas de la moda"].[13] He does not hesitate to clarify his own position in this conflict, stating that María Eugenia, "the protagonist of the novel, is a pretty young woman, . . . a bluestocking, disdainful, arrogant, lacking will in certain ways, disoriented in everything" ["la protagonista de la novela, es una bella joven, . . . marisabidilla, desdeñosa, presumida, abúlica en ciertos aspectos, desorientada en todos"]; María Eugenia writes a diary of a time in her life in which "instigated by her own egoism, she undertakes the task of explaining the miniscule psychological analysis of her personality, of her manner of adapting to her fiancé and her marriage" ["instigada por su propia egolatría, emprende la tarea de bosquejar el minucioso análisis psicológico de su personalidad, de su manera de adaptarse al noviazgo y al matrimonio"]. Alvarado suggests, finally, that it would be better "to leave this thorny problem to the maternal teacher; and pray to the immortal gods for the suffering soul of María Eugenia" ["dejemos el problema peliagudo a la didáctica materna; y roguemos a los dioses inmortales por el alma lacerada de María Eugenia"].

Perhaps this critic is so disgusted and irritated because he senses the precariousness of his limited *texte lisible* of the feminine, as the novel dramatizes the subtle manner in which society forces woman to submit herself to the masculine construction of the feminine. In this respect, the critical scene becomes a repetition of the scene dramatized in the text.[14] The critic takes sides, joining with those who would confine the problem of the rebellious woman to the maternal teacher, that figure who has internalized the patriarchal message and is its most effective disseminator.

At the end of the first decade in which *Ifigenia* ran the gauntlet of male criticism, the Ecuatorian Gonzalo Zaldumbide, in an article praising the novel, expressed doubts about the novelist's artistic future.

Woman that she is, she probably won't be able to create another full-bodied and soulful heroine like this one, who could be her sister. Women are better at confessing than telling stories, and there is no way they can get around that fact. Is she destined to be a one-book writer, even though she may very well produce others, and very good ones at that? If this is the case, it could be worse.

[Como mujer que es, no llegará tal vez a crear, de cuerpo entero y alma ingénita, otra heroína que ésa, que se le parece como una hermana. Las mujeres, más que contar, saben confesarse; y no hay disfraz que no las traicione. ¿Será la mujer de un libro aunque produzca varios y muy hermosos? Menos mal que sea el que es.][15]

Unintentionally, Zaldumbide's critical commentary repeats the dramatic scene of the text. *Ifigenia* is a novel in the form of a diary, a confession, and María Eugenia tells the story of a "gradual step-by-step process" that results "in the annulment of her personality and the cease-fire of her rebellion" ["esa graduación, esa dosificación. . . [que resulta] en el proceso de anulación de su personalidad, de claudicación de todas sus rebeldías"].[16] María Eugenia, the protagonist of the novel, is the "woman of one book"; in it she records how and why she will not write again. By succumbing to a cultural construction of the feminine, Zaldumbide confuses the issue, displacing the drama of the novel onto the life of the novelist. Teresa de la Parra did write again (despite Zaldumbide's prediction), and as is well known, her novel *Las Memorias de la Mamá Blanca* is not *Ifigenia* in disguise.[17]

This sample of criticism from the 1920s shows how critical opinion oscillates between censure and praise mixed with grave doubts. Critical reception changed with the passage of years, however, and in some cases corrected the criticism that preceded it, specifically in the way that the "critical text" problematizes the feminine (the *texte lisible*). Yet these corrections often only repeat the problem in a different manner.

The criticism of the thirties began with an article by Benjamín Carrión that functions (in part) as a response to the preceding decade. Noting Miomandre's insistent references to Teresa de la Parra's ingenuousness, this critic claims that "rather than ingenuous, her work is wise, intelligent, elegant, and ironic" ["antes que ingenua, su obra es sabia, inteligente, elegante e irónica"]. Carrión responds to Lisandro Alvarado's moralizing posture toward the protagonist by arguing that in María Eugenia the novelist has realized "a talent for psycho-sociological analysis, carried out with careful, intelligently simple art" ["un acierto de análisis psico-sociológico, hecho con arte esmerado, inteligentemente sencillo"] as she describes "this gradual step-by-step process" that results "in the annulment of her personality and the cease-fire of her rebellion" ["esa graduación, esa dosificación. . . en el proceso de anulación de su personalidad, de claudicación de todas sus rebeldías"].[18] And in response to doubts about the novelist's future (from such critics as Gonzalo Zaldumbide), Carrión states that many believed *Ifigenia* was a disguised autobiography in which the author revealed her innermost secrets; thus they did not expect her to write again. This was not so.

[Though it] was the case of Jorge Isaacs, and very definitely the case of the German writer Remarque . . . nothing of the sort happened [with de la Parra]. . . . Teresa de la Parra, five years after *Ifigenia* . . . gave us her *Memorias de Mamá Blanca*. . . . For her, the writer's writer, . . . Dostoyevski's "sentence" retains its implacable force: Teresa de la Parra will write in order to exorcise her ghosts, and they in turn will reproduce themselves.

[ . . . caso de Jorge Isaacs, caso muy sostenible del alemán Remarque. . . . [19] Nada de eso hubo. . . . Teresa de la Parra, a los cinco años de *Ifigenia* . . . nos regala sus *Memorias de Mamá Blanca*. . . . Y es que para ella, escritora de verdad . . . la condenación de Dostoievsky conserva su valor implacable: Teresa de la Parra escribirá para destruir sus fantasmas, y sus fantasmas se reproducirán.][20]

Despite this critic's response to the previous decade, in his own work he also comes to problematize the feminine, only in a different manner from his predecessors. In passages that are intended to praise, Carrión comments on de la Parra's style.

But sometimes swept away by tropical enthusiasm, she'll come out with a slightly rhetorical passage. . . . She isn't strong enough to stifle or suppress it, and there we see her *sensitive maternal nature*. Right after, as if to beg indulgence for the fault, she rewards us with a few ironic sentences that "knock down" the preceding paragraph. . . . The ghosts Teresa de la Parra destroys when she writes, with a show of elegant *frivolity*, with *compassionate* irony, and, at times, with an *almost masculine hardness*, are other human lives . . . they are also contemporary lives.

[Pero cuando alguna vez, *emportée* por el entusiasmo tropical, le sale un párrafo un poquitín oratorio. . . . No tiene el valor de matarlo, suprimiéndolo, y allí se ve *su sensitiva maternalidad*. Mas en seguida, como para hacerse perdonar la falta, nos ofrece la recompensa de unas frases irónicas que "le toman el pelo" al párrafo anterior. . . . Los fantasmas que Teresa de la Parra destruye al escribir, con una apariencia elegante de *frivolidad*, con ironía *compasiva* y, a veces, con *dureza casi masculina* son las vidas humanas anteriores a ella, las vidas . . . contemporáneas también.][21]

This critic is describing a familiar literary technique, ironic self-referentiality: "Sometimes . . . she'll come out with a slightly rhetorical passage . . . [and] right after . . . she rewards us with a few ironic sentences." Explicating this method in de la Parra's text, though, Carrión relates it to the feminine: "She isn't strong enough to stifle or suppress it, and there we see her *sensitive maternal nature*." Even though this might be considered a positive maternalness (it does not "suppress" or "stifle"), it is

characterized as a "fault," that must "beg indulgence"; that is, it is devalued and therefore de-authorized.[22] Carrión does not explain the author's "elegant frivolity" or "compassionate irony," because they are
accepted simply as cultural attributes of the feminine. On the other hand,
the "hardness" is admired and elicits a clarification: it is "almost masculine."

Carrión's text reveals a rereading of the critical-literary text (the literary
work and its accompanying critical literature) that implies a recognizable
text—that is, the cultural construction of the feminine. This repetition of
the critical text differs in that it explicitly adds the possibility of the masculine to the culturally devalued construction of the feminine. It creates a
dichotomy, a polarization, between the feminine and the masculine. But
this involves a disguised conceptual hierarchy in which one of the terms of
the opposition is privileged: "maternalness" is devalued while "masculine
hardness" is admired. In this rereading, the "signifying energy" of the reduced, recognizable text "becomes unbound, to use Freud's term, through
the process of repetition which is a return, not of the same, but of
difference."[23] It is this return of difference that determines the incomplete
or temporary nature of each rereading.

Writing in the midforties, Pedro Díaz Seijas recalls the comments of
Miomandre with an exclamatory remark that Teresa de la Parra is sincere,
ingenuous, confessional; that "her scenes of exaggerated feminine delicacy
serve, at all times, to scrutinize almost perfectly the sentimental love
psychology of women" ["sus cuadros de ponderada delicadeza femenina,
sirven en todos los tiempos para escrutar de una manera casi perfecta, la
psicología amorosa y sentimental de la mujer"]; and that "she has not been
able to quiet anything felt in her woman's soul" ["no ha podido callarnos
nada de lo que su alma de mujer sintió"], because "when she writes she
gives herself completely in her words" ["cuando escribe se da íntegra en
sus palabras"].[24] Seijas's desire repeats Miomandre's, but in a magnified,
eroticized form. He does not engage in an analytic discourse that responds
to de la Parra's sophisticated, ironic, and subtle prose; rather, he addresses
an empty word toward an Imaginary construction—here, an erotic
object—which describes the novel/novelist according to his own desires.
He later affirms:

> Within the feminine thinking of the times, the wealth of ideas about morality
> and prevailing social customs which Teresa de la Parra expresses with brave de-
> termination is surprising. . . . [But] running through her ideas and convictions is
> the arrogant and inexperienced mind of the adorable María Eugenia Alonso
> . . . . Woman's delicate sensibility often lapses into sentimental musings, thus
> disturbing the balance of reason and intelligence. She then becomes, from a
> theoretical standpoint, a romantic figure who attempts to see everything through
> her own personality.

[En el pensamiento femenino de la época, causa sorpresa el desbordante caudal de ideas que sobre la moral y las costumbres sociales imperantes, lanza Teresa de la Parra, decidida y valiente. . . . Tras de sus ideas y de sus convicciones, va la mentalidad arrogante e inexperta de la adorable María Eugenia Alonso. . . . La sensibilidad delicada de la mujer, cae a menudo en la reflexión sentimental, donde rompe el equilibrio de la inteligencia, asistida de la razón. Y es entonces, para una posición teórica, un ente romántico que trata de verlo todo a través de su propia personalidad.][25]

In absolute conformity with his eroticized image of the feminine, his recognizable text, Seijas is surprised at de la Parra's strength and determination in expressing a "wealth of ideas about morality and prevailing social customs." He belittles this abundance of ideas by associating it with the protagonist of the novel, whom he characterizes ambivalently: she is "arrogant and inexperienced" but "adorable." Reaffirming a romantic ideal of woman, Seijas doubts the author's capacity to think, maintaining that because she is a woman, her "delicate sensibility often lapses into sentimental musings," with the result that "the balance of reason and intelligence" breaks down. Asserting his authority, he assumes a "theoretical standpoint" from which he further devalues the novelist, observing that she is "a romantic figure who attempts to see everything through her own personality."

Clearly, it is Pedro Seijas himself who reacts romantically rather than analytically, as he reduces the protagonist and writer to erotic object and devalues what does not fit into this scheme. One might ask, why, if the intention is to praise the author, has the effect been to diminish her, to subtly revile her? Why this ambivalent discourse?

Psychoanalytic theory shows that a masculine fear of woman, especially the infantile dread of maternal autonomy, has been objectified as contempt for woman. In addition, masculine ambivalence about feminine charms underlies traditional images of the terrible goddess-witches (the Sphinx, Medusa, Circe, Kali, Delilah, Salome), practitioners of the art of duplicity with which they seduce men and rob them of their masculine generative energy.[26] Primordial fear and ambivalence are the fundamental emotions that inform this critical discourse, in which the feminine creator and creation are diminished, eroticized, and delicately repudiated.

Arturo Uslar Pietri, another more insightful, writer of the 1940s, did not see in Teresa "a romantic figure who attempts to see everything through her own personality"; rather, he read the novel as a crisis of the social order, dramatized in the protagonist. "In *Ifigenia* there appears . . . the drama within woman, which is the dramatic heart of the crisis in the social order." ["En *Ifigenia* aparece . . . el drama dentro de la mujer, que es la entraña dramática de la crisis de un orden social."][27] The problematization of the feminine, however, is repeated in an intensified manner.

Teresa de la Parra is one of the most feminine of writers. No one surpasses her in this. *Ifigenia* is a woman-book: attractive, dark, disturbing. . . . In her prose there are sentences, sensual stammerings, the simplest of adjectives, that flaunt their nakedness at us. . . . [Teresa de la Parra] was a "young lady," a *señorita*: that monstrously delicate and complex combination, that flower of the Baroque.

[Teresa de la Parra es una de las escritoras más femeninas. Nadie la excede en este don. *Ifigenia* es un libro mujer: atractivo, oscuro, turbador. . . . En su prosa hay frases, torpezas, simples adjetivos, que son como una incitadora desnudez. . . . Era [Teresa de la Parra] una señorita: ese ser monstruosamente delicado y complejo. Esa flor del Barroco.][28]

It is interesting to note how critical discourse acquires an erotic resonance in relation to the feminine: the woman writer, protagonist, and text are combined and confused into one ambivalent erotic object that is both desired and feared ("attractive, dark, disturbing")—flower and monster simultaneously. In the confusion that he constructs, Uslar Pietri creates a polarization within the feminine itself, into angel (flower) and monster. As North-American feminists explain, there is a long tradition in patriarchal texts that presents resplendent images of submissive women along with negative images incorporating "the sacrilegious fiendishness of what William Blake called the 'Female Will'".[29] Often, this negative image of woman—the monster—does not hide behind the angel, but resides within (in an inferior part of) the angel. Uslar Pietri unconsciously embraces this masculine tradition and from it recovers the paradoxical images that simultaneously characterize woman as angel and monster; thus he speaks of Teresa de la Parra as "a 'señorita': that monstrously delicate and complex combination, that flower of the Baroque." This tendency to idealize and degrade the author comes from an underlying but fundamental ambivalence toward maternal power.[30] Because this kind of explanation belongs to the construct of woman as other, it is difficult to imagine what the critic means when he reiterates that Teresa is a "feminine writer." She herself has difficulties with this label.

Once . . . somebody told me (condescendingly, of course) that my novel *Ifigenia* was full of "femininities." I honestly believed that he meant to flatter me, and I was about to thank him warmly with a smile. But just in time I realized that these "femininities" did not constitute a virtue, but rather a serious defect. So with the same smile with which I was going to thank him for his praise, I thanked him for the advice and assured him that I would never again commit another "femininity." The truth is, I will never be able to correct myself at all, because I still haven't figured out what he meant by that.

[Una vez . . . me dijo uno (con aire de protección naturalmente) que mi novela *Ifigenia* estaba llena de "feminidades." Yo creí sinceramente, que se trataba de un gran elogio, e iba a dar las gracias con la más amable de mis sonrisas. Pero aún a tiempo me di cuenta de que las "feminidades" no constituían una cualidad, sino un grave defecto. Entonces con la misma sonrisa con que iba a dar las gracias por el elogio las di por la advertencia y ofrecí que en adelante no volvería a cometer ninguna otra "feminidad." Lo cierto es, que no podré corregirme nunca, puesto que aún no he logrado comprender lo que quisieron decirme.][31]

In the forties the critical text repeats the problematization of the feminine in a different way: the masculine (which resided before on the surface of the critical discourse, ostensibly to enrich that discourse but which in fact constituted the favored term in the masculine/feminine polarization) disappears. The imaginary construction of the feminine itself polarizes and becomes explicitly ambivalent and erotic, desired and feared. In relation to this, Simone de Beauvoir maintains that woman has been obliged to represent all of man's ambivalent sentiments concerning his inability to control his physical existence—his birth and death. As other, woman comes to represent the contingency of life, this life that is made to be destroyed. She adds that "it is the horror of his own carnal contingency which he [man] projects on her [woman]." This underlying mechanism that Coppélia Kahn has named the maternal subtext keeps the critic from addressing the feminine subject, and it explains the mixture of enchantment and repudiation (devaluation) with which Seijas speaks of de la Parra, as well as explaining the ambivalence of Uslar Pietri.[32]

Even the most distinguished Hispanic-American critics have not avoided using cultural characterizations of the feminine. Each time that these surface as questionable or problematic, the procedure of negation begins. The collective subject (which manages the production and reproduction of culture) defends itself against what becomes conscious; repudiates, discredits, belittles, or attributes it to another.[33] This mechanism comes into play in Mariano Picón Salas's writing during the early fifties.

Many Hispanic-American women, still imprisoned in the most trivial routines and conventions, were waiting for such a message. And *Ifigenia*, unique for its grace and adolescent malice, . . . conquered the entire Hispanic world. It was read simultaneously in Mexico, Bogota, Montevideo, in Santiago de Chile. I knew an elderly Chilean philosophy professor who confessed to me, like one who has committed a delightful sin, that he devoted to the small and fantastic María Eugenia Alonso a moment he had stolen from Kant.

[Muchas mujeres hispano-americanas, prisioneras todavía en las más ñoñas rutinas y convenciones, estaban esperando un mensaje semejante. E *Ifigenia*, obra única por su gracia y su adolescente malicia, . . . conquistó todo el mundo hispánico. Se leía, simultáneamente, en México, en Bogotá, en Montevideo, en Santiago de Chile. Conocí, un viejo profesor chileno de Filosofía que me confesaba como un pecado deleitoso haber dedicado a la pequeña y fantástica María Eugenia Alonso, un tiempo robado a Kant.][34]

Here the feminine, the recognizable text, appears in the very reading of the text. The others—discredited female readers, imprisoned "in the most trivial routines and conventions"—were waiting for "such a message" (i.e., *Ifigenia*). On the other hand, for male readers, who are not prisoners but men dedicated to the important enterprises of life (such as philosophy), "the small and fantastic" protagonist becomes an erotic object with whom one confesses to have committed a "delightful sin" in "a moment stolen from Kant." The ambivalence, drawing attention to itself in simultaneous praise and repudiation of the novel, manifests itself here in the assumption of two different readers—male and female—and two antithetical readings. In a well-regarded essay of 1953, Ramón Díaz Sánchez questions the literary production of the novelist, declaring that de la Parra failed to

> travel [certain] roads. And among them that of love. . . . We find few allusions to this particular path in the books, letters and oral and written memorabilia of Teresa de la Parra, if one excepts her possible fleeting love affair with the Ecuatorian Gonzalo Zaldumbide and the exquisite but painful romance that she describes in *Ifigenia*. . . . It is the presentiment of love . . . that affords her the encounter with Bolívar's dramatic presence. . . . [He] is, then, her teacher in love and for a moment, she converts him into her model. . . . But is this enough? No. It is not. In order for the ideal substance of love to be converted into literary material and intervene in the creation of art, it must first be transmuted into human substance.

> [. . . transitar caminos. Y entre ellos el del amor. . . . Pocas son las alusiones que sobre este particular encontramos en los libros, el epistolario y los recuerdos orales y documentales de Teresa de la Parra, si se exceptúan su supuesto y fugaz noviazgo con el ecuatoriano Gonzalo Zaldumbide y el bello y doloroso romance que describe en *Ifigenia*. . . . El presentimiento del amor . . . es el que le proporciona su encuentro con la huella dramática de Bolívar. . . . [El] es, pues, su maestro de amor y ella lo convierte por un momento en su paradigma. . . . Pero, ¿es esto bastante? No. No lo es. Para que la substancia ideal del amor pueda convertirse en materia literaria e intervenir en una creación de arte, es necesario que se transmute en substancia humana.]³⁵

This critical interest in the most intimate details of the novelist's love life has been frustrated to this day. To determine that de la Parra failed to "love more," that she lacked "vital experience," that she had a prudish attitude toward love, that love never revealed itself to her, that she was in love with love, that she had an obstinate distrust of marriage—to say all this is to create a fabulous monster that masks the real woman. Recently, R. J. Lovera de Sola, in response to Díaz Sánchez, has shown how love and literary creation were opposite currents in the life of Teresa de la Parra.

> There are two facts to consider: her attitude toward love, and the alternatives to her literary vocation. . . . Teresa was not prejudiced against love, but she knew that in her time to marry meant losing her independence. She also knew she would not escape the rude shock that marriage would create for a woman as

beautiful and creative as she was. In this sense her considered observations regarding the tragedy of Delmira Agustini . . . are all too graphic . . . her words, all too significant.

[Se trata de dos hechos: su actitud ante el amor y las alternativas de su vocación literaria. . . . Teresa no tuvo una prejuiciada idea del amor, aunque sí tuvo plena conciencia de que en su tiempo casarse, era perder su independencia y además no se le escaparon los rudos males que crearía a una mujer bella y creadora como ella una unión conyugal. En este sentido son demasiado gráficas sus observaciones sobre la tragedia de Delmira Agustini . . . son palabras demasiado significativas.][36]

But Ramón Díaz Sánchez elaborated the situation to his liking by suggesting that de la Parra could not truly come into her own as a writer until through a "teacher in love," she had actually experienced love in the flesh. This, of course, represents a projection of his own desires and his Imaginary construction of the feminine.[37]

In this decade's criticism, the recognizable text situates the feminine apart from the text, in either the sexual/love experience of the female writer or in the gender of the reader. The feminine appears as a needy entity, implicitly devalued—a discredited reader in need of "such a message," or a belittled creator in need of a "teacher in love'" to realize herself fully in her writing. The privileged masculine, however charged with erotic resonance, is presented as abundant and self-fulfilled. A lucid, superior reader, he makes a delightful parenthesis in his important studies in order to spend some sinful time with the feminine text. The critic's "teacher in love" would offer full realization to the feminine, if only the creator would submit herself to his erotic knowledge.

The young readers of the sixties did not know personally the "attractive" Venezuelan (this seems to have disturbed the analytic faculties of those who wrote during the preceding decades). Significantly, their criticism coincided with the beginnings of an important movement to revalue women.[38] The cultural climate changed gradually in its attitude toward women, and with this change there was a transformation in the conscious cultural construction of the feminine. At the start of the decade, Fernández Paz Castillo commented that Teresa de la Parra introduced a new element to the traditional rural novel and story form: familial intimacy and tenderness. He adds:

[T]he existence of the rustic outskirts of the city was also a charming aspect of the primitive elegance our novelists discarded, and Teresa de la Parra, thanks to the fineness of her feminine spirit, found. . . .
It would be difficult to find in another woman writer a more feminine language. Without affectation, she goes to the heart of things with the fineness of a woman. Despite that, she possesses great Spanish austerity.

[(E)n la existencia de los rústicos aledaños a la ciudad·hubo también un encanto de la elegancia primitiva que desecharon nuestros novelistas y que encuentra, gracias a la finura de su espíritu femenino, Teresa de la Parra. . . .
  Difícilmente podría encontrarse en otra escritora un lenguaje más femenino. Sin rebuscamientos llega al alma de las cosas, con finura propia de mujer. Pero, con todo, tiene una gran sobriedad castellana.][39]

Though this critic reiterates the opinion about de la Parra's femininity—the "fineness of her feminine spirit," her "feminine language"—these distinctions are not associated as clearly with the previous ambivalence or with the (unconscious) intention to eroticize and devalue the work and author. On the contrary, the feminine here is an element that enriches the creation, that is appreciated and valued for its difference: "She goes to the heart of things with the fineness of a woman."

In 1961 Alfonso Rumazo González, evoking de la Parra twenty-five years after her death, was able to modify (in part) the criticism of previous decades that had perceived her work as an autobiographical confession or had confused the author (a woman who published her first book at age thirty-four) with María Eugenia (the eighteen-year-old protagonist of that novel.)[40]

As a writer, she is a late bloomer. Her writing first began to appear when she was thirty. For this reason there are no surprises, no shouts, no gesturing; but rather, the sharp pepperiness in which irony flourishes. . . . She was extremely fortunate to begin at the right time, when the past has become a source and the future harbors no disproportionate hopes, only muted desires. At the age of thirty the true destiny of this serene and smiling woman emerges; and she will be loyal to it to the end.

*Ifigenia, [Las] Memorias [de la Mamá Blanca]*, contain autobiography, but Teresa is fully, uniquely, most sincerely, the same in . . . each of her works, because each is understood and shown through the writer, and with the benefit of the existence and vision of the writer.

[Es una escritora que comenzó tarde; sus primeras páginas aparecen a los treinta años. De ahí que no traigan ni asombro, ni gritos, ni gesticulaciones; más bien el por qué de pimienta en que se nutre la ironía. . . . Fue el bien sumo de empezar a tiempo, cuando ya el pasado vuélvese fuente, y sobre el futuro no se yerguen esperanzas desmesuradas, sino anhelos en sordina. A los treinta años surge en esta mujer serena y sonriente su auténtico destino; y será leal a él hasta el final.

*Ifigenia, [Las] Memorias [de la Mamá Blanca]*, contienen autobiografía; pero Teresa está, plena, única, sincerísima, lo mismo en . . . todos a la vez, porque todos son entendidos y mostrados a través de la escritora, y con aprovechamiento del existir y ver de la escritora.][41]

There is nothing in this critical appraisal that problematizes the feminine, diminishing or devaluing the work of the novelist. In this decade, the feminine returns as a valid entity, valued for what it presents through a particular woman writing. It is as if the Imaginary order that previously limited and impoverished critical discourse on the novel and novelist, now gradually gives way to something closer to symbolic order; as if the worn out recognizable text begins to erase itself by the force of repetition to give way finally to a critical-literary text.

In 1974 Víctor Fuenmayor addressed the relationship between writer and protagonist—one that the preceding criticism misrepresented by referring to the narrative as a confession. He asked: "Does the writer agree with the rebellion of María Eugenia? The relationship between the writer and María Eugenia's story is either very ambiguous or very ambivalent." ["¿Está de acuerdo la escritora con [la] rebeldía [de María Eugenia]? Es muy ambigua o muy ambivalente la relación entre la historia de María Eugenia y la escritora."] In order to clarify finally the situation, he allows Teresa de la Parra to explain.

> In reality, my character María Eugenia Alonso was a synthesis, a living copy of several types of women whom I had seen (at close range) suffer in silence, and whose true depths I wanted to discover, *to let speak* as a protest against the pressure of their environment.
>
> [En realidad, mi personaje María Eugenia Alonso era una síntesis, una copia viva de varios tipos de mujer que había visto muy de cerca sufrir en silencio, y cuyo verdadero fondo me interesaba descubrir, *hacer hablar*, como protesta contra la presión del medio ambiente.][42]

Fuenmayor does address narrative problems that arise in the reading of any literary text. In this manner, his response to previous criticism helps both to erase the Imaginary construction and to give the word to the feminine subject who writes and speaks. The result is a less problematized concept of the feminine, as the critic addresses a literary construction firmly grounded in a textual reality.

In 1981 Orlando Araujo speaks for today's readers of Teresa de la Parra. He responds to previous readings and situates them in their historical and cultural context.

> What was most objected to in her time is what today's reader most appreciates: her irreverence toward the accepted, the irony with which she portrays a city and its inhabitants at a social and spiritual crossroads between the coffee and petroleum industries. . . . In 1924, *Ifigenia* was a true challenge both to the "manners" of the time as well as to genre writing. That a young woman should speak with such freedom and should mock a society that admired and envied her, must have been intolerable to many people of her class and to the literary mediocrities who observed her from afar. . . . Yet there is no bitterness or venom in her

work, no satire, no bad humor: she says things with a smile, or with peals of laughter. . . . and thus she sweeps aside the conceited incompetent who, in her time, administered the word at festivals and conferences.

[Lo que más se la objetó en su tiempo es lo que más aprecia el lector actual: la irreverencia frente a lo consagrado, la ironía con que refleja a una ciudad y a unos habitantes en la coyuntura de un tránsito social y espiritual entre el café y el petróleo. . . . En ese 1924, *Ifigenia* era un verdadero desafío tanto al costumbrismo de la vida como a las letras del costumbrismo. Que una muchacha hablara con tanto desenfado y se burlara de una sociedad que la admiraba y la envidiaba debió ser intolerable para mucha gente de su clase y para la medianía literaria que la miraba desde lejos. . . . No hay, sin embargo, amargura ni venenos en su novela, ni sátira, ni mal humor: hay un decir sonriendo, o riendo a carcajadas. . . y así se va llevando por delante a las nulidades engreídas que, en su tiempo, administraban la palabra en fiestas y congresos.][43]

With the advantage of time since *Ifigenia's* publication, Araujo points out that it was de la Parra's irreverence and irony toward the official position, toward the cultural canon consecrated by custom, that was then so objectionable. That the irreverent words and attitudes might spring from the lips of one of the best families in Caracas, from the lips of a well-to-do "señorita," envied for her refinement and intelligence, was intolerable to her contemporaries. Araujo's reading answers those who gave the first critical response to *Ifigenia*—or, better said, those who orchestrated a chorus against the novel. The earlier criticism that read with condescension, a moralistic and censurous attitude, and an explicit ambivalence or insult, is deconstructed by this new appreciative reading. What actually undoes the earlier reading is the presumption that the Imaginary mode of signification would dominate unequivocally and would impede the possibilities of different modes of signification.

In conclusion, this study of the masculine criticism of Teresa de la Parra has sought to attend to those aspects of the text that are taken for granted without recognition of the range and implications of what they affirm. There exists a level of critical discourse that does not acknowledge the feminine subject who writes in all her complexity nor the feminine text that speaks with all its ambiguity, but it knows only an imago, a cultural construction of the feminine. This constitutes the recognizable text within the critical text. The recognizable text repeated itself each decade but with certain differences: what is constant is the ambivalence and the devaluation of the feminine.

On the other hand, in the seventies the limited recognizable text seems to have exhausted itself in the process of repetition, an occurrence that coincided with both the disparagement of the preceding criticism by the new generation who never knew the "attractive" writer, and the beginnings of a movement to revalue women that brought about a transformation in the cultural construction of the feminine. The new critics began to value the feminine for its difference and to read Teresa de la Parra's work with literary criteria.

So the critical scene progressively has become a reversal of the dramatic textual scene. The novel dramatizes the progressive plundering, crippling, and eventual submission of the protagonist to the demands of patriarchal society. Critics, on the other hand, began by expecting the submission of the novel and novelist to the patriarchal constrictions of the feminine (what they were able to conceive of or admit within feminine writing), but they gradually have given way to a more open reading, in which they begin to address the feminine text as subject.

# Notes

This article was translated from the Spanish by Bernice Hausman, with the collaboration of the author.

1. Velia Bosch, ed., *Teresa de la Parra ante la crítica* (Caracas: Monte Avila, 1980).

2. Jacques Lacan, "The Empty Word and the Full Word," in *The Language of the Self*, ed. Anthony Wilden (New York: Dell, 1975), p. 15.

3. It is important to specify the definition of *imago* as "the unconscious prototypical figure which orientates the subject's way of apprehending others; it is built up on the basis of the first real and phantasied relationships within the family environment. . . . The imago is often defined as an 'unconscious representation.' It should be looked upon, however, as an acquired imaginary set rather than as an image: as a stereotype through which, as it were, the subject views the other person"; J. Laplanche and J. B. Pontalis, *The Language of Psychoanalysis*, trans. Donald Nicholson-Smith (New York: Norton, 1973), p. 211.

4. Jacques Lacan, "Le Stade du miroir comme formateur de la fonction du Je," *Écrits I* (Paris: Seuil, 1966), pp. 89–97; and Shoshana Felman, "To Open the Question," *Literature and Psychoanalysis: Yale French Studies* 55/56 (1977): 5–10.

5. Roland Barthes, *S/Z* (Paris: Seuil, 1970), pp. 3–9.

6. Laplanche and Pontalis, *The Language*, pp. 394–97. It is worth noting that feminist criticism has tended to leave women in the Imaginary, rather than giving her a place in the Symbolic (e.g. Kristeva's early work).

7. Francis de Miomandre, "*Ifigenia* por Teresa de la Parra" (1924), in *Teresa de la Parra: Obra* (Caracas: Ayacucho, 1982), pp. 3–5.

8. Barbara Johnson, "The Critical Difference: BartheS/BalZac," *The Critical Difference: Essays in the Contemporary Rhetoric of Reading* (Baltimore: Johns Hopkins University Press, 1980), p. 5.

9. Quoted by Ida Gramcko, "Teresa de la Parra: Nuestra primera y excepcional escritora," *El Nacional* (Caracas), 23 April 1945, in Bosch, *Teresa de la Parra*, pp. 61–62.

10. Gramcko, "Teresa de la Parra," p. 64.

11. Benjamín Carrión, "Teresa de la Parra," in Bosch, *Teresa de la Parra*, p. 43.

12. Barthes, *S/Z*, pp. 3–16.

13. Lisandro Alvarado, "Una opinión sobre *Ifigenia*," in Bosch, *Teresa de la Parra*, pp. 17–22.

14. Shoshana Felman, "Turning the Screw of Interpretation," *Literature and Psychoanalysis: Yale French Studies* 55/56 (1977): 94–207.

15. Gonzalo Zaldumbide, "*Ifigenia*, de Teresa de la Parra," in Bosch, *Teresa de la Parra*, p. 32.

16. Carrión, "Teresa de la Parra," p. 43.

17. In fact Zaldumbide was in love with de la Parra, which may account for some of his confusion. This will be documented later in the article.

18. Carrión, "Teresa de la Parra," pp. 42–43.

19. In this article, written in 1930, 'Carrión errs in his predictions about the future writing of Erich Maria Remarque (1897–1971). His novel *Im Westen nichts Neues* (1929) was followed by *Der Weg zurück* (1931), *Drei Kameraden* (1937), *Liebe deinen Nächsten* (1941), and *Arc de Triomphe* (1946).

20. Carrión, "Teresa de la Parra," p. 47.

21. Ibid., pp. 39–40; the emphasis is mine.

22. It seems fair to speak also of and devalue the "sensitive maternal nature" of Laurence Sterne, Machado de Assis, Macedonio Fernández, or other writers who use self-referentiality with ironic or parodic intention. Yet critics speak of these writers as "dialogic," "carnavalesque," "revolutionary," and consider them to be the fathers and precursors of the new Latin American novel.

23. Johnson, "The Critical Difference," p. 4.

24. Pedro Díaz Seijas, "La intimidad femenina en *Ifigenia*," in Bosch, *Teresa de la Parra*, pp. 70–72.

25. Ibid., p. 75.

26. Karen Horney, *Feminine Psychology* (New York: Norton, 1973), pp. 133–46; Dorothy Dinnerstein, *The Mermaid and the Minotaur* (New York: Harper and Row, 1976), pp. 124–54.

27. Arturo Uslar Pietri, "El testimonio de Teresa de la Parra," in Bosch, *Teresa de la Parra*, p. 79.

28. Ibid., p. 79.

29. Sandra M. Gilbert and Susan Gubar, "Toward a Feminist Poetics," *The Madwoman in the Attic: The Woman Writer and the Nineteenth-Century Literary Imagination* (New Haven: Yale University Press, 1979), pp. 28–29.

30. Coppélia Kahn, "The Hand That Rocks the Cradle: Recent Gender Theories and Their Implications," in *The (M)other Tongue*, ed. Shirley N. Garner, Claire Kahane, and Madelon Sprengnether (Ithaca: Cornell University Press, 1985), pp. 72–88.

31. Teresa de la Parra, "*Ifigenia*, la critica, los críticos y los criticones" (Paris, 1926), *Obras completas* (Caracas: Editorial Arte, 1965), p. 498.

32. Simone de Beauvoir, *The Second Sex* (New York: Knopf, 1953), p. 138; and Coppélia Kahn, "Excavating 'Those Dim Minoan Regions': Maternal Subtexts in Patriarchal Literature," *Diacritics* 12, no. 2 (Summer 1982): 32–41.

33. Laplanche and Pontalis, *The Language*, pp. 261–63.

34. Mariano Picón Salas, "Cartas de Teresa de la Parra," in Bosch, *Teresa de la Parra*, p. 90.

35. Ramón Díaz Sánchez, "Teresa de la Parra o la ansiedad del camino," in Bosch, *Teresa de la Parra*, pp. 103–105.

36. R. J. Lovera de Sola, "Un aspecto de la vida de Teresa de la Parra," *El Nacional* (Caracas), 4 December 1978. Because of the way this article is signed, it is not possible to know whether the author is female or male.

37. The critics' direct or indirect involvement in Teresa's love life no doubt further affected their critical reading (misreading) of her work. For this reason it is interesting to note that Ramón Díaz Sánchez's preoccupation with the loves of

Teresa was probably influenced by a letter Gonzalo Zaldumbide, an earlier critic, sent him. It reads: "Teresa was the woman I loved the most deeply in my life. There is nothing in my recollection of her that clouds or alters her memory. Her life was pure clarity in my eyes. She was infinitely kind and her intelligence was such that, understanding all, it forgave all" ["Teresa fue la mujer que más profundamente he amado yo en mi vida. Su recuerdo no tiene en mi memoria sobra alguna que la empañe o la altere. Su vida es la más diáfana a mis ojos. Su bondad fue infinita y su inteligencia tal, que todo lo perdonaba porque todo lo comprendía"]. And in 1965, in an interview published in Caracas, in *El Nacional* (26 January, sec. C, p. 7), the octogenarian Zaldumbide concludes his praise of Teresa with these words: "Make of it what you will. I loved her as I have loved no one!" ["Añada a esto lo que usted quiera. ¡La amé, como a nadie he amado!"] However, in a 1957 interview, Teresa's sister María suggests the presence of a love greater than that of Gonzalo in the life of her sister, but avoids giving specific names. Nélida Galovic Norris could find out nothing from friends and relatives about Teresa's love life. See "The Successful Years: A Critical Appraisal of Teresa de la Parra" (Ph.D. diss., University of California, Los Angeles, 1970). Teresa de la Parra never married.

38. It took almost twenty years for this reevaluation of women to begin to manifest itself in tangible ways within official institutions. See Rosario Hiriart's comments on the acceptance of women into the Spanish and French Royal Academies. Rosario Hiriart, "Estudio preliminar," *Más cerca de Teresa de la Parra (Diálogos con Lydia Cabrera)* (Caracas: Monte Avila, 1983), p. 21.

39. Fernández Paz Castillo, "Teresa de la Parra: Una Caracas suave y lejana," in Bosch, *Teresa de la Parra*, pp. 112–14.

40. As the French critic Philipe Lejeune explains, in order to speak of autobiography there must exist an explicit autobiographical pact between the writer and his or her readers. He also states that an autobiographical novel may imitate an autobiography in every way. *Le Pacte autobiographique* (Paris: Seuil, 1975), pp. 14–26.

41. Alfonso Rumazo González, "Teresa de la Parra (A los 25 años de su muerte)," in Bosch, *Teresa de la Parra*, pp. 124–32.

42. Víctor Fuenmayor, "Los federales y la poesía perdida," in Bosch, *Teresa de la Parra*, pp. 164–65. Fuenmayor is quoting a letter written by Teresa de la Parra to an unknown recipient on 29 December 1932 (p. 165).

43. Orlando Araujo, "Sobre *Ifigenia*," in Bosch, *Teresa de la Parra*, pp. 155–56.

# Feminine Space and the Discourse of Silence: Yolanda Oreamuno, Elena Poniatowska, and Luisa Valenzuela

## JANET GOLD

> Escucha ese silencio,
> Es un silencio anclado,. . .
> Escucha ese silencio
> Que se pega a tu carne[1]

Much has been said about the silent or the silenced woman or the woman in search of her voice. In this essay I too will talk about silence, but the silence I discuss is not a silence of absence, of emptiness, or of passivity. I want to explore a silence of presence and fullness. Feminine silence is described as absence because one notices only the surface of a gesture, a look, or a text, and fails to attend to the language of the interior. One must listen for both the richness and the barrenness of silence, since what appears to be a whisper may be the echo of a laugh, or a scream transformed. Feminine silence often masks vulnerable interiors or hides secret spaces. Its message may be "Room for Rent," but it may also say "Caution," "Danger," "Do Not Disturb," "Woman at Work." Strategies for creation and expression are as many and varied as we are; it is enriching to sense them, to admit them, to articulate them.

As I read "Valle alto," "De noche soy tu caballo," and "La felicidad," knowing that these three texts were written by women, I experience what Marguerite Duras calls "an organic, translated writing. . . translated from blackness, from darkness".[2] Duras refers not to any product of a woman's pen but rather to specifically "feminine literature". Such writing is "organic" because it comes from the compost of dark, fertile, interior space, translated because it is born from silence rather than from a tradition of articulation.

Much of women's writing imitates the established literary discourse of its time, with varying levels of success and varying degrees of experimentation within the given parameters. But some women have written from a different point of departure. They begin with themselves, with interior spaces and silences, and transform this wordless knowledge into a written reality. Obviously, this writing is not based on a theoretical platform, for theory carries with it a particular discourse, its own "already formed language."[3] This kind of women's writing is rather a "violent, direct literature" translating the silence of the "wild country" of feminine space.[4] Women write from silence when they bring forth from the undifferentiated the words and rhythms and structures that articulate their inner realities through a new discourse.

Consequently, this "feminine" literature perhaps can be best understood and appreciated if we approach it not from a critical/theoretical platform, but from within ourselves. If one listens to the text rather than talking at it, it becomes a conversation among women seeking to define and refine the tools of narrative. My reading of these stories is intended to be such a conversation, and its starting point is recognition, intuitive appreciation, pleasure. These stories show women who survive, who confront loneliness, isolation, fear, and death; and from their inner resources they create what they need to sustain themselves. Whether erotic fantasy, interior monologue, or memory, the resources from which they draw come from their very center.

Each of these three stories has as its protagonist an ostensibly silent woman; but I hope to demonstrate the tone, the timbre, and the resonance of their silence. They are silences formed in the deep center, the fertile realm of dreams, of the unconscious, of the womb—they grow from the dark spaces of fear, loneliness, and captivity. In all of the stories, the narrator has situated her writing in relation to the silence of her own darkness. The "empty" spaces (which, paradoxically, are the generators of form) upon which the protagonists draw are discourse made corporal, a presence that encompasses and forms even as it threatens to destroy. This presence finds very different expression in each of these stories, but the common substance is unmistakable: images of solitude, death, or imprisonment point out the silence and darkness of this space, as well as its possibilities. These are stories about human loneliness, woman and nature, desire, dreams, and power, but they are also about the physicality of language; they are about the female space of creativity. They are about the silence and the fertile darkness that haunt our lives, into which we try in so many ways not to fall, but whose existence is life itself because with it we know and from it we create.[5]

The protagonist of Yolanda Oreamuno's "Valle alto" [High valley] is an unnamed woman traveling alone in a foreign country.[6] She begins this episode of her journey at the bus station of an anonymous city. Her intended destination, her motives for traveling, her origins? We know only that she is alone, that she feels she must arrive at her destination before nightfall, and that she is preoccupied with some unarticulated concern.

The opening paragraphs begin with physical descriptions that correspond to inner realities as much as to external conditions. The city is sterile, dry, and unbearably bright. Its lines are angular, there is no wind, and the clouds, pregnant with water, are painfully close to the city, yet it doesn't rain. The air is full of a disquieting vibration. In this city, the woman is estranged and desperate: the elements are all wrong. We sense that she has been traveling for a long time, searching for a way to break out of loneliness. The next morning, the woman wakes up and discovers she is in a narrow bed in a country inn, alone, unable to recall how she got there. She begins and ends in loneliness and emptiness, but what is significant is what happens on the way to her destination.

Between loneliness and loneliness lies temporary union. The woman experiences respite from solitude, breaking through her loneliness and her existential aridity by creating (or living) a beautiful and sensual erotic fantasy. The elements are now perfect: she shares a cab with a handsome stranger; she sits in the back seat where she observes him unnoticed; the car breaks down in the middle of nowhere; she and the perfect stranger begin walking together. Nature is now in complete sympathy with her senses and desires, and when the long dry spell is finally broken by a rainstorm, she and the stranger make perfect love. Every step in her fantasy reveals a stronger identification between nature and the couple, so that as they near the moment of physical consummation it becomes clear that their communion is sanctioned by the elements: "How natural it seemed, under the burning blanket of heat, to be walking down an unfamiliar road with a man whose name she didn't even know!" ["¡Qué natural le parecía, bajo el cobijo ardiente del calor, ir por un camino raro con un hombre cuyo nombre ignoraba!"] (p. 132). From the dark silence of her being the woman has created an erotic fantasy in which all of nature participates. For the duration of her fantasy, "only two things were awake, her imagination and her body" ["Todo estaba inerte: sólo había dos cosas despiertas, la imaginación y el cuerpo"] (p. 134). She muses on the embraces of nature—vines clinging to trees, moss-covered roots. She identifies herself and her lover with the flower and the seed, with the dry earth absorbing the rain. She becomes the vine, the root, the orchid, the female animal; because "human beings, on a night like this, stopped living as separate entities, and became part of the whole of nature" ["Los seres humanos, en una noche así, dejaban de existir como unidades aparte, y pasaban a constituir parte del todo natural"] (p. 134).

If the story opens and closes with sterile alienation and disorientation, then the body of the text is just that—an actual physical presence, a fertility rite in the woman space. Her fantasy satisfies her desire for union, if only temporarily, because it is her creation and therefore her union with her dark silences. The woman exhibits two very different personalities during the story. In the city, and again at the inn the next morning, she is passive, disoriented, and somehow one-dimensional. During her adventure/fantasy, on the other hand, she becomes increasingly assertive, creative, poetic, and at peace. Her erotic fantasy is a breathing space, a stop along the road of her lonely life's search or journey, that integrates her with herself, with man, and with all of nature.

The protagonist of Luisa Valenzuela's "De noche soy tu caballo" [At night I am your horse] is in a similar situation in that she finds herself alone and in need of a dream or fantasy to sustain her.[7] She also is alienated, although in a significantly different way. While the world of "Valle alto" essentially is mythical and the isolation is individual, Valenzuela's story is situated in the social-political reality of torture and terrorism. At the end of the story the reader learns that the protagonist is in jail. She has been tortured but has refused to disclose information about her lover, an anti-government activist who has eluded all efforts to capture him. The harshness of her isolation poignantly contrasts the nature of her dream/memory. From the solitude of her cell she remembers the sensual experience of her last contact with her lover. Because he is sought by the police he is forced to go to her only at night (in her dreams?), to conceal his whereabouts, to leave while she is sleeping, and never to tell her where he's been or what he's done. She remembers tenderly the treasures he brought with him that night—a bottle of rum and a Brazilian record; she recalls her desire to sink into happiness and not to worry about the ugly possibility of their danger; she mentally repeats the way he looked into her eyes and remembers the passion and tenderness of their lovemaking. The contrast between her memory and her present situation is startling. The way her lover surprised her with a visit, waking her in the middle of the night, and the sensuality of what occurred between them, contrasts sharply with the arrival of the police later that same night: "Their hands mauling me, their voices insulting me, threatening me, the house torn upside down" ["Las manos de ellos toqueteándome, sus voces insultándome, amenazándome, la casa registrada, dada vuelta"] (p. 108). In jail she denies her lover in order to save him, denies that he was with her, claims he's abandoned her, that she hates him, until she is not sure (or so the reader is led to believe) if he really did visit her that night, if they really did make love so beautifully, if there really was a bottle and a record.

The erotic, in the form of memory/dream, is both illusion as well as the strongest bond with a reality outside the woman's cell. The story questions reality in a fundamental way: How can the cruel presence of her torturers, who represent repression on a personal as well as on a national or even global scale, be more real than the memory of a few sensual hours she may or may not have spent with her lover? Is pain more real than pleasure? Is the present more real than the past? The bottle and the record are artifacts of another dimension, reminders of levels or spheres of reality that coexist. Since the text leaves the reader in doubt as to whether she actually was with her lover, it is not essential to know if she is sustained emotionally on a fantasy or on an actual memory. What is significant is her capacity to reinvent tenderness and sensuality out of the darkness of her pain and the silence of her refusal to cooperate with the police.

In both "Valle alto" and "De noche soy tu caballo" the protagonists exist within the woman space upon which they draw to create worlds in which they can survive when confronted with a dehumanizing reality. Similarly, place and space exist in separate spheres in "La felicidad" (Happiness) by Elena Poniatowska.[8] The place is a bedroom; the protagonist is a woman. The action is the creation of discourse to fill the dark and silent space in which the woman finds herself after she and her lover have made love. Their lovemaking has left him exhausted and he is falling asleep. She, on the other hand, has been stimulated rather than drained, excited with the realization that her chance to break out of human solitude is slipping away. She had hoped that love—its caresses, myths, and reassurances—would conquer death and loneliness. But coitus has come and gone, he is slipping away from her into sleep, and she sees herself moving farther and farther from the bliss of union that eroticism had promised.

The rhythm of "La felicidad" is an urgent rush to fill empty space. This can be interpreted on one level as an unsatisfactory sexual experience. She begs him not to fall asleep and leave her behind, but he does; so she will get up, get dressed and go walking "until she is exhausted" ["hasta quedar exhausta"] (p. 100). His lovemaking has left him sweetly spent, while she remains unsatisfied and will have to fend for herself. On another level, more abstract perhaps, yet equally intense and immediate, her response to their lovemaking may be a reaction to having glimpsed the dark silence of the existential void. Ecstasy has brought her to the edge of rationality, and she is afraid to face this vision alone. The need for reassurance and tenderness after orgasm is acute. She has exposed her most fragile being to him, she has denied her autonomy, and now she is frightened. She needs him to stay with her and to help put herself back together. She wants to believe that this terrible longing and separation are not the deepest reality.

Her interior monologue (it is addressed to her lover, but we never hear his response) is an attempt to capture a moment and to stretch it out in time and space. Words become the continuation of ecstasy. They are sensual because they comfort, cajole, and caress; they reassure her, fool her into thinking she has conquered death and human solitude. The monologue is one long sentence that tumbles headlong, scarcely stopping for breath. It is a veritable orgasm of words: the mind races with the passion of physical union, and the discourse repeats the rhythm. As Claudine Herrmann remarks:

> Time and space respond to the mind's rhythm, which is at one with the biological rhythm of pulsation such as the circulation of the blood or nervous response. . . . Time and space no longer participate in the artificial continuity imposed by social life, but in a reality that is simply that of intimate life.[9]

A quality shared by all three of the stories discussed here is that of figuration rather than representation. In *The Pleasure of the Text*, Roland Barthes distinguishes between these two modes.

> Figuration is the way in which the erotic body appears. . . in the profile of the text. . . . The text itself, a diagrammatic and not an imitative structure, can reveal itself in the form of a body. . . . Representation, on the other hand, is *embarrassed figuration*, encumbered with other meanings than that of desire: a space of alibis (reality, morality, likelihood, readability, truth, etc.).[10]

By adopting the form of the erotic fantasy, Oreamuno in "Valle alto" absents her text from the space of alibis. Both the protagonist and her lover remain anonymous, as do the valley and the country inn. In addition, the woman is a traveler in a foreign country thus locating the erotic outside of the boundaries of familiar restrictions, placing it in the sensual realm of the exotic. The text acquires its figuration through the identification of the woman and the man with the all-embracing forces of impersonal nature. Their embrace is carefully timed to coincide with the rhythms of a higher order.

> The man, who could have had her already, if he wanted, had not touched her. Because he, one with the earth, with the storm and the tree, was obeying the greater harmonies of nature's concert, and would bend over her when the branch bowed beneath the weight of the rain, neither before nor after.

> [El hombre, que ya podía tenerla, si quería, no la había tocado. Porque él, uno con la tierra, con la tormenta y el árbol, sólo obedecía los grandes acordes del concierto natural, y se inclinaría sobre ella cuando se inclinara la rama bajo el peso del agua, no antes ni después.] (p. 135)

Valenzuela's text also avoids representation by combining pain and pleasure, waking and dreaming realities. The woman tells her story amid the convergence of these various realities. Rather than reducing her text to a denunciation—of political repression, of police brutality, of woman as victim or sexual object (although certainly these denunciations are there and should be considered)—Valenzuela expands the text to include contradictory elements of the woman's experience. She does this by beginning with the doorbell ringing in the night; what ensues may be oneiric. The man who enters has the marks of an exciting dream character, a conspirator, a deliciously dangerous lover. He is unwilling to speak of anything he has done, or tell her where he has been. "What good would it do you to know what I've been up to? It's better for you not to know" ["¿De qué te sirve saber en qué anduve? Ni siquiera te conviene"] (p. 106). They drink a bottle of rum. Inebriation and its illusions throw additional shadows on a situation already in a twilight zone. She refers to her lover as Beto, although she adds: " . . . I know that's not his real name but it's the only one I'm allowed to say out loud" [" . . . sé que ése no es su verdadero nombre pero es el único que le puedo pronunciar en voz alta"] (p. 107). When she is awakened again, this time by the phone, she assumes it is Andrés, or, rather, "the one we call Andrés" ["el que llamamos Andrés"] (p. 107). But it's a trick; it's not Andrés at all. (Yet why should it have been since there is no character really named Andrés?) Or is it that she's still somewhat asleep and can't distinguish the voice? Or is the man they call Andrés really a stool pigeon? Who is to be trusted? Which is the most real of these possibilities? If one chose to unravel the lies from the near-lies, the misrepresented from the unrepresented, conceivably, the representational version could be produced. But that would be another story. Valenzuela's text, by refusing to locate itself either in an ephemeral imagination or in a concrete prison, embodies both of these possibilities and so transcends either one. The space of the text is at once the undifferentiated darkness of silence and the materialization of articulated possibilities.

The figuration of "La felicidad" is produced largely by its rhythm, which gives the story a frantic, prayer-like quality that keeps the text from being representational. The woman's need to verbalize happiness pushes her forward; her fear of losing what she has named pulls her back. Frantic ambivalence, combined with the attempt to draw her lover into her with words, to fill their bed with her desire, creates a suffocating embrace with its discourse of repetitions, affirmations, pleas, its panting use of commas stringing together an endless invocation to happiness.

The nonrepresentational quality of these texts is due also to the fact that they are not descriptions or views of external realities; they are self-contained, self-controlled creations of the will. They do not conform to what Chantal Chawaf describes as the traditional narrative style that summarizes and measures distances.[11] Rather, they represent the woman space in dialogue with itself. There is no other real dialogue in these stories. When conversation appears it is remembered, desired, or invented, part of a theater of the imagination. Each narrator, finding herself adrift, fashions a life preserver from her own being that buoys her through the storm. Yolanda Oreamuno's protagonist contrives an erotic fantasy; Luisa Valenzuela's determinedly guards the treasures of her memory; Elena Poniatowska's talks her way to sanity.

Most significant in these stories is that each appears to be told from the center, from an internal point of departure dangerously close to darkness. Each narrator draws from the resources of her self, attempting to recreate the center, to use it as raw material to transform her experience. All three texts both represent and inhabit a woman's inner space. Although "Valle alto" is narrated in the third person, this need not prevent recognition of the interior landscape from which the erotic dreamscape is constructed.

It is this locus, this interior reservoir, both tangible and ephemeral, that as a woman reading a woman I recognize. As the flesh of its discourse enfolds me I find myself in a deep familiar place. My center communicates with the center transformed of these texts and my reading (dialogue) becomes a (re)-creation of myself. The woman center proves to be not empty or passively waiting to be filled, but rather the generator of images, the teller of tales, and a source of strength, as well as the space within which women may spend time with themselves.

## Notes

1. Eunice Odio, "3", from *Territorio del alba*, collected in *Open to the Sun. A Bilingual Anthology of Latin American Women Poets*, ed. Nora Jácquez Weiser (Van Nuys, Calif.: Perivale Press, 1979), p. 150. Weiser's translation of the lines quoted: "Listen to that silence / It's an anchored silence / . . . Listen to that silence / sticking to your flesh."

2. Marguerite Duras, "From an Interview," in *New French Feminisms*, ed. Elaine Marks and Isabelle de Courtivron (New York: Schocken, 1981), p. 174.

3. Ibid.

4. Ibid., pp. 174–75.

5. Although the temptation to speculate is great, my purpose is not to attempt a definition (and thereby a reduction) of that irreducible female voice so many are curious about, but rather to posit a personal reading of three women's texts, foregrounding my current intuitions regarding "the feminine." I consequently do not equate "woman space" with an actual physical space, nor "darkness" with irrationality in a manichean conceptualization; but I am experimenting with a departure from logocentric criticism to blend the personal, the poetic, and the feminine in a critical discourse that is to be read for itself as well as for its commentary on other texts.

6. Yolanda Oreamuno, "Valle alto," in *El cuento costarricense*, ed. Seymour Menton (Lawrence: University of Kansas Press, 1964), pp. 126–35. Subsequent citations from this story will be made parenthetically. Translations of the text into English are my own.

7. Luisa Valenzuela, "De noche soy tu caballo," in *Cambio de armas* (Hanover, N.H.: Ediciones del Norte, 1982), pp. 105–109. Subsequent citations from this story will be made parenthetically. Translations of the text into English are my own.

8. Elena Poniatowska, "La felicidad," in *De noche vienes* (México: Grijalbo, 1979), pp. 95–100. Subsequent citations from this story will be made parenthetically. English translations of the text are my own.

9. Claudine Herrmann, "Women in Space and Time," in Marks and de Courtivron, *New French Feminisms*, pp. 168–73.

10. Roland Barthes, *The Pleasure of the Text*, trans. Richard Miller (New York: Hill and Wang, 1975), pp. 55–56.

11. Chantal Chawaf, "Linguistic Flesh," in Marks and de Courtivron, *New French Feminisms*, pp. 177–78.

# Words between Women: Victoria Ocampo and Virginia Woolf

## BERNICE L. HAUSMAN

## 1. Introduction

Victoria Ocampo (1890–1979) was a wealthy Argentine feminist who defied cultural restrictions against women to assert herself as an influential publisher, editor, translator, and writer. She founded and underwrote the literary journal *Sur* [South], promoted the translation of European and North American literature into Spanish, and encouraged Latin American writers. Although she herself wrote hundreds of essays and some fiction, Victoria Ocampo more often is considered a patron of literature than a literary critic or writer. However, even a cursory reading of her critical work reveals another Victoria, whose approach repudiated traditional, patriarchal notions of appropriate literary criticism in order to express her experience as a woman reader.

Like many avid readers, Victoria Ocampo had a few particular writers of whom she wrote most frequently and after whom she modeled herself as a writer and critic. Among her favorite literary people were Rabindranath Tagore, T. E. Lawrence, Aldous Huxley, and Virginia Woolf. Ocampo's relationship to Woolf differed from her relationships to other writers, because she identified with Woolf both as a writer and as a woman. In her writings about Woolf and her work, Ocampo emphasizes Woolf's treatment of the feminine and of women's relationship to literature; she was one of Virginia Woolf's first feminist readers. As feminist documents, her critical essays chart the relationship between a woman writer and her feminist reader. Their relationship—a metaphorical room where they spoke to each other away from the company of men[1]—exemplifies how two women writers may encounter each other and alter the terms of literary discourse.

Ocampo and Woolf met in 1934, at the London opening of a Man Ray photography exhibition. Images, reflections, portraits, and photographs were to weave in and out of their personal relationship, which lasted until Woolf's suicide in 1941. The themes of mirroring and reflection are documented in their correspondence and in Ocampo's "testimonies" as well as in her explicitly literary works on Woolf.

Ocampo consistently used Woolf's texts to identify and clarify her image of herself. Over and over she defined and differentiated: "In this we are the same, in that different." Since women always have defined themselves within a hierarchy that separates and judges according to masculine values, it has never been easy to say "I am this, she is that" and to leave the statement unfettered, plain, the two sides equal. While Ocampo acutely felt and expressed her differences from Woolf, the body of her work on Woolf is impressive in its insistent identification with text and author, its determined belief that Woolf's texts could lead to an understanding of the self as woman, and its sustained pursuit of the author through her text. Ocampo was able to gain access to Woolf by asserting her difference from the Englishwoman; instead of allowing patriarchal definitions to identify and hierarchize her difference, she used it as a powerful feminist tool to explore her relationship to writing and texts.

## 2. Theoretical Beginnings

Before I begin my study of Ocampo's essays on Woolf, I would like to introduce the paradigm that has helped me to formulate my ideas about the (textual) relationship between these two women. The paradigm is that of the mirror or the concept of the mirror as it relates to women writers and literary production. I develop it through a reading of mythology, fairy tales, and feminist theory—discourses within which mirrors and mirroring circulate as metaphors for creation and contemplation. Needless to say, mirrors are also significant within the "real" life experience of many women, and this experience will be called into the discourse of feminist literary theory.

In the story of Echo and Narcissus,[2] Narcissus, looking into the pond, sees his image reflected on the surface of the water and falls in love with that image. Recognizing himself in the reflection, he expresses sorrow and confusion before he dies, and in this expression lies the paradigm of man-the-artist: inspired by the sight of his own image, man speaks. In the same story, however, Echo loses her power to speak as punishment for saying too much at the wrong time; Juno condemns her to repeat the last words she hears. In effect, Echo mirrors through speech what is spoken to her and loses the power to generate original text. She can only reflect the words of the male artist and, in her silence, becomes the mirror through which the male voice speaks. Thus, while mirroring is a metaphor available to all artists, representing the act of relating their work to the established literary tradition, it may have different consequences for female, as opposed to male, artists. The story of Echo and Narcissus suggests that the male artist expresses himself at the expense of the female, for whom mirroring signifies the endless repetition of male-generated texts.

As Echo becomes an aural "mirror"—reflecting back to Narcissus his own speech—women become mirrors for men within patriarchal society: denied selfhood, women are expected to reflect the personhood of men. At the same time, however, women also try to find themselves *within* mirrors, using them to evaluate themselves within the community of women, seeing in them patriarchy's vision of the "real woman." The mirror is a prewritten text, speaking the patriarchal language and inscribed with patriarchal values: in it "woman" is "written," and to it women must attend in order to reflect adequately what is already there. It is easy to become convinced that the text resides within the body, making the physical self the object of one's artistic energy; dissatisfied with her reading of the image in the mirror, woman believes she must rewrite herself rather than fix the mirror. Thus, woman's body becomes the artistic object, the object of her artistic energy; the making of oneself into a work of art has been the creative project for women within patriarchy, and consequently, women's texts largely have been private, personal, and connected to the body. (Indeed, when this is not the case, the woman writer is criticized for writing outside her "sphere.")

In *The Madwoman in the Attic*, Sandra Gilbert and Susan Gubar use a specular paradigm to construct a feminist poetics; in their analysis, the patriarchal mirror entraps woman and leaves her speechless. In the Snow White tale, the stepmother/queen is "a plotter, a plot-maker, a schemer, a witch, an artist, an impersonator, a woman of almost infinite creative energy, and self-absorbed as all artists traditionally are." Notable for her relationship to a mirror that speaks the voice of patriarchy pitting her against her stepdaughter, the Queen dies dancing *silently* in her hot iron shoes.[3] Mary Elizabeth Coleridge, in "The Other Side of the Mirror," writes of meeting an alternative, nonpatriarchal self who has "no voice to speak her dread." But, according to Gilbert and Gubar, "she has an invincible sense of her own autonomy, her own interiority . . . women themselves have the power to create themselves as characters, even perhaps the power to reach toward the woman trapped on the other side of the mirror/text and help her to climb out."[4] To change the mirror's function, the imprisoned woman must free herself to create new texts that mirror women not according to an image defined by men but according to women's vision of themselves. This task is no less than an appropriation and an inversion of the patriarchal mirror.

The new text, distorting and re-forming patriarchal reflections of "woman", is still a mirror. The woman reader who writes may respond to it with another text, revolutionizing the role of the mirror (text) in women's relationships by using it as a tool for response and creation (rather than as a gauge with which to measure and judge). As a model for literary discourse independent of—or, at least, displaced from—patriarchal expectations, the metaphor of the text-as-mirror *between* women, constitutive of relationship rather than value, is one that, without naming it as such, Victoria Ocampo used in her critical essays on Virginia Woolf.

## 3. Real and Literary Meetings: "Carta a Virginia Woolf" [Letter to Virginia Woolf]

When Louise Bernikow described "two women alone in a room,"[5] she could have been peeking into the living room of Virginia Woolf's house at Tavistock Square, December 1934. There, Ocampo and Woolf had their first interview. The following month, Ocampo wrote "Carta a Virginia Woolf" in which she describes the visit and responds to Woolf's ideas about women and writing. The letter was published in the first volume of Ocampo's *Testimonios* [Testimonies] as a public response to their meeting (Woolf apparently did receive a copy—in translation; see letter 2977 of *The Letters of Virginia Woolf*, p. 365). Ocampo begins the essay as if she were peering through a window, watching the English writer and her Argentine admirer converse. She uses this perspective to emphasize the historical significance of the meeting and then moves into her own voice to speak directly to Woolf.

"The two women look at each other. They have different gazes." ["Estas dos mujeres se miran. Las dos miradas son diferentes."][6] Two women writers, alone in a room. Different gazes, same gesture. They speak about what it is like to be a woman writer. For Ocampo, this means she must differentiate her experience from Woolf's: "one backed by a formidable tradition; the other with a void at her back" ["la una adosada a una formidable tradición, la otra adosada al vacío"]. Ocampo also says: "I would like to state publicly, Virginia; 'Like most uneducated south american [*sic*] women, I like writing. . . .' And this time, the word 'uneducated' must be pronounced without irony." ["Desearía confesar públicamente, Virginia; 'Like most uneducated south american [*sic*] women, I like writing. . . .' Y esta vez, el 'uneducated' debe pronunciarse sin ironía"] (pp. 10–12). Both Woolf's original statement—"Like most uneducated Englishwomen I like reading"—and Ocampo's revision are ironic because both women were privately educated and were very well read writers. Woolf established her difference from masculine literary tradition, and Ocampo follows her by asserting her South American identity as a point of difference between herself and the Englishwoman.

All the articles collected in this volume . . . testify to my hunger. To my hunger, so authentically Latin American! In Europe, as I said to you a few days ago, it seems you have everything but hunger.

[Todos los artículos reunidos en este volumen . . . son una serie de testimonios de mi hambre. ¡De mi hambre, tan auténticamente americana! Pues en Europa, como le decía a usted hace unos días, parece que tiene todo, menos hambre.] (p. 11)

This point of difference—Ocampo's South American hunger—is a locus of rich, creative possibility, and with it she claims a place for herself within a literary world that previously had none for an Argentine woman writer.

The body of "Carta a Virginia Woolf" discusses Woolf's *A Room of One's Own*. Ocampo's discussion of Woolf's ideas moves from agreement toward revision and rearticulation. Ocampo consistently revises Woolf's analysis of women's relationship to writing and challenges Woolf with her own experience as a reader. In this way she "mirrors" Woolf with a difference, establishing a dialogue between women about women and writing. She asks, for example, that Woolf acknowledge her privileged position as an educated Englishwoman. She also argues for a less critical, more passionate approach to women's writing. Questioning Woolf's opinion that Charlotte Brontë writes too angrily and defending the expression of passionate emotion in literature, Ocampo writes, "Do you think, for example, that the *Divine Comedy* was written without a trace of resentment?" ["¿Cree usted, por ejemplo, que la *Divina Comedia* haya sido escrita sin vestigios de rencor?"] (p. 14). Accord and revision are integral to the establishment of a constructive, nurturing, and challenging dialogue. This is the project of the "Carta": to answer the mirror, to shape a text so that it both reflects and comments upon Woolf's writings.

The strength and energy of the essay emanate from Ocampo's insistence upon difference and her articulation of that difference. It is a difference that does not separate or isolate the two women but rather enhances and enriches their relationship. Difference has not been a viable mode of being for women within patriarchy: it has meant evaluation, judgment, hierarchy. (If Snow White is beautiful, then the stepmother/queen is not so beautiful, and a fatal competition results.) By asserting her difference from and solidarity with Woolf, Ocampo revises the way women speak to each other within patriarchal society. The discussion no longer is mediated by the male voice of the mirror (as in Snow White), and women do not compete to be the most favorable (i.e., feminine) in men's eyes. Rather, they articulate difference as equals, accepting difference as integral to their identities as women and as writers. Difference is transformed from a liability to an empowering and creative force.

Ocampo's approach celebrates the subjectivity of the writer; she infuses her work with personal anecdote, emphasizing the interconnectedness of literature and life. "Carta a Virginia Woolf" begins a dialogue between two literary women with Ocampo establishing herself as a woman who responds to a text by maintaining and defending her difference. In this way, she revises the stakes of literary discourse, as a feminist.

## 4. Feminist Ideas: "La mujer y su expresión" [Women and Expression]

Ocampo's feminist perspective is integral to her literary methodology.[7] Her feminism involves a specific relationship between the personal and the political, which in turn informs her perspective on literature: her ideas about women's expression, her approach to male writers, and her expectations of women artists. For Ocampo, insertion of the personal woman into the masculine arena is a political act.

In her essay "La mujer y su expresión" (originally a radio broadcast), as in "Carta a Virginia Woolf," Ocampo promotes dialogue as a way to revise the masculine mirror text. The mirror, like masculine literary discourse, has been monologic, and in order to transform it, women must engage it in dialogue. She believes that women's discourse already admits such interruption and she asks women to break into and transform the masculine monologue. She links expression to self-consciousness and self-realization: "the knowledge that is most important to a person is that which has to do with the problem of self-realization" ["el conocimiento que más importa a cada ser es el que atañe al problema de su autorrealización"].[8] This project is difficult, however, because "women in general, and South American women in particular, are not at all prepared to achieve that victory. They do not have the necessary instruction, freedom, or tradition" ["lo mal preparada que está actualmente la mujer en general y la sudamericana en particular para alcanzar esta victoria. No tiene ni la instrucción, ni la libertad, ni la tradición necesarias"] (p. 282). The vision Ocampo offers of women working together to create this tradition draws heavily upon her ideas about women's maternal nature and its relationship to artistic expression.

Characterizing woman-as-mother as "saintly" because she perfects herself as an example (a work of art) for her children, Ocampo writes: "The artist attempts to create perfection outside the self, the saint within the self" ["El artista trata de crear la perfección fuera de sí mismo, el santo en sí mismo"] (p. 276). This characterization of women's expression as limited to the perfection of herself as an exemplar is the cornerstone of her analysis of the patriarchal prohibitions against feminine artistic endeavors. Ocampo argues that women need freedom to choose their expressive form; and freedom, in the realm of written expression, is intimately linked to the development of a woman's literary tradition and aesthetic.

In order to develop that tradition, Ocampo reevaluates women's maternal intelligence and expertise and calls upon women to use their talents for the future of women artists. In this way, she turns the paradigm inside out. "It is this maternal attitude toward the future of feminine humanity that must sustain us today" ["Es este sentimiento de maternidad hacia la humanidad femenina futura el que debe sostenernos hoy"] (p. 284). This future depends upon women who, taking up their conventional nurturing role (in other words drawing upon their tradition as caretakers of the world's future generations), will commit themselves to the development of a women's artistic tradition now.

The force of Ocampo's feminism comes from her insistence that feminine values and talents be inserted into dominant masculine culture. Her ideas are part of a feminist position that has been and continues to be a common perspective in the women's movement: since women's values, talents, and expression are repressed by patriarchal domination, the feminist project is to re-place feminine culture into the mainstream. Speaking from a self-defined personal voice is therefore a political act because it defies the masculine proscription against speaking the feminine personal in the masculine public. Ocampo inserts herself into the masculine literary world by celebrating her personal, female self, and answering the male literary monologue; she speaks to the mirror, inviting dialogue and a revision of public, male discourse.

Woolf herself was not always considered a political feminist. Naomi Black, in "Virginia Woolf: A Life of Natural Happiness," documents Woolf's political involvements and asks "why then, was she so long considered only a feminist in a personal sense, and why was she later believed to be committed only to limited forms of equality, to androgyny, or to female separatism?"[9] Black asserts that the misunderstanding of Woolf's political ideas was caused in part by her own misrepresentation of herself and her politics. The main reason, however, was the misinterpretation of the feminist project that Woolf outlines in her overtly political writings. Black's assessment of Woolf's feminism is pertinent because it contributes to an understanding of Ocampo's political ideology.

Black differentiates social feminism from equal rights feminism, which in Woolf's time was embodied in the women's suffrage movement. Social feminists "reversed the [biological] argument so that innately womanly qualities became the justification for a public role for women."[10] Black defines Woolf's feminist analysis as a subtle variant of social feminism, stating that "her assessment of the domestic female realm was more com-

plex than the usual social feminist ones . . . her rationale was . . . closer to
the argument of today's feminists."[11]

Ocampo's social feminism, though different, has a similar foundation.
For her, reformation of society has more to do with the integration of
separate male and female spheres than the radical redefinition of masculine
and feminine qualities. Ocampo's analysis is less subtle than Woolf's and
far less sophisticated in its indictment of patriarchy, but its energy derives
from the same political roots: it calls upon a feminine sensibility to reform
the inequities and excesses of the masculine world. Her perspective on
literature is based on her feminism and depends upon the insistent assertion of the personal "I" in her readings.

## 5. *A Room of One's Own*: Women's Relationship to Text and Emotion

In her gloss on poverty and wealth as related to literature and creativity,
Ocampo emphasizes a major point of *A Room of One's Own*. Woolf's
book, while speaking broadly to the issue of "Women and Fiction," concentrates on women's poverty (relative to men's wealth) and laments the
effect of this poverty on women's writing. She does not, however, hesitate
to criticize and evaluate women writers.

> The woman who wrote those pages [Charlotte Brontë] had more genius in her
> than Jane Austen; but if one reads them over and over and marks that jerk in
> them, that indignation, one sees that she will never get her genius expressed
> whole and entire.[12]

There is much disagreement among contemporary feminist literary critics
about what Woolf means in her characterization of anger as out of place in
a literary text. It seems that Woolf perceives anger as an intrusion upon the
scene of writing: "She left her story, to which her entire devotion was due,
to attend to some personal grievance. . . . Her imagination swerved from
indignation, and we felt it swerve" (p. 76). She argues that the effect of
women's poverty upon their literature is to disrupt the "natural flow," to
disrupt the talent that creates the sentence, to impede the genius at work.
Women who attend their personal anger while writing will write imper-
fectly.

In Woolf's eyes, the oppression of women has had a disastrous effect on
their writing. She blames the context of the woman writer for the errors in
her text. On the other hand, Woolf does not allow sympathy for the
woman writer's circumstance to interfere with her evaluation. The result is
a unique critical form; in locating the cause of a text's flaws within the

writer's circumstance and not her person, Woolf integrates a feminist analysis of the woman writer's material existence with an analysis of her artistic work.

Ocampo's responses to *A Room of One's Own* touch upon these issues of poverty, creativity, anger, and expression. She defends Brontë, however, sensing that Woolf's valuation of a calmness in writing is inappropriate to women's condition and unmindful of the qualities of great literature. She defends Brontë because "by defending her cause I defend my own. If only perfection is moving, Virginia, there's no doubt I've lost before I start." ["Defiendo su causa, es la mía que defiendo. Si sólo la perfección conmueve, Virginia, no cabe duda que estoy perdida de antemano."] The difference between Austen and Brontë, she suggests, "is a matter of differences of character" ["se trata de diferencias de carácter"] ("Carta" 14).

Ocampo identifies strongly with these women writers ("In an environment similar to that of Charlotte Brontë and Jane Austen a hundred years ago, I began to write and live; similar, Virginia, but worse." ["En un medio semejante al que pesaba sobre Charlotte Brontë y Jane Austen, hace más de cien años, comencé yo a escribir y a vivir; semejante, pero peor, Virginia."] ("Carta" 16) and this identification motivates her defense of Brontë's indignant "interruptions." It also helps to identify herself as a woman writer, within the context of Woolf's vision.

> And if, as you expect, Virginia, any effort, no matter how small helps to accelerate the birth of a form of expression that as yet has not found the right temperature for blossoming, let my effort join that of so many women, known and unknown, who have worked for such a goal.

> [Y si, como usted espera, Virginia, todo esfuerzo, por oscuro que sea, es convergente y apresura el nacimiento de una forma de expresión que todavía no ha encontrado una temperatura propicia a su necesidad de florecer, vaya mi esfuerzo a sumarse al de tantas mujeres, desconocidas o célebres, como en el mundo han trabajado.] ("Carta" 17)

Woolf and Ocampo differ in their analyses of women writers and the role of anger in a written text because they locate themselves within their own texts, and in relation to the texts they discuss, differently. Both are women writers, both relate stories that include their personal experience, both are avidly feminist in their purpose and presentation, but their involvement with the texts they analyze is different. Woolf remains outside the experience of the texts she reads, while Ocampo places herself within the experience of the text. Ocampo becomes emotionally involved and committed to the spirit of the text; Woolf stands distanced from, although not unaffected by, that level of experience.

In *A Room of One's Own* Woolf presents a variety of scenes in which she is the primary character: herself attempting to enter the library at "Ox-bridge University," lunching at the men's college, dining at the women's college, snooping in the Reading Room of the British Museum. Woolf tells a dramatic story of her investigation of the relationship between women and fiction and wealth. This story-telling mode distances her from the text—possibly a natural result of the lecture style she adopts—and makes her primary commitment to her own text, rather than to the texts of which she speaks. On the other hand, Ocampo's essay, while, like Woolf's, is directed at an audience, is less concerned with its own creation—with *telling*—than with its argument for and with another text.

Woolf's personal anecdotes frame the telling of her story—the story of women's relationship to literature and wealth. Ocampo's self-reflexive remarks keep her essay centered upon the person of the writer and the subjectivity of her experience. Woolf chooses the conventional structure of the personal essay to relate her feminist ideas, while Ocampo uses a private literary form made public. The modes complement each other as representational strategies, as each takes a position against a literary tradition that excludes women's voices. Both revise the patriarchal mirror text: Woolf by maintaining the frame and altering the reflective surface; Ocampo by stepping outside the frame and substituting a mirror of a different sort. These two revisionary modes affect the kind of oppositional gestures each writer can make, and how closely each adheres to the masculine tradition.

Woolf's more traditionally structured essay (as compared to those of Ocampo) reflects the fact that her attack on masculine literary discourse both replicates and repudiates the patriarchal norm. She utilizes a particular representational strategy in her criticism that contains the emotional intensity within the form of her writing. Despite this deference to literary conventions, the men in Woolf's circle disliked her most overtly feminist text *Three Guineas* because, as Joanna Russ comments, "Although crammed with facts and references, it has the wrong *style*; it is personal and sounds unscholarly. . . . That is, the tone is not impersonal, detached, dry enough—in short, not patriarchal enough—to produce belief."[13]

Ocampo also uses specific stylistic strategies to challenge the literary tradition, but she writes with less deference to that tradition than Woolf. Her personal voice dominates the forms of her address, and she speaks more intimately about her own experience. Her literary writings deviate more radically than Woolf's from the traditional forms of literary criticism and, as a result, have not been accepted by that tradition. Ocampo's impassioned defense of her experience as a woman reader is the foundation of her interpretive strategy, and it leads her to write about literature in a form she calls "testimony."

It would be reductive to conclude that Woolf is a consummate, cool, English essayist while Ocampo is a passionate, expressive, Latin artist—

reductive and certainly racist. It is more useful to understand how Woolf and Ocampo counterreflect each other's textual self-representations; each seems to express the unconscious desire of the other's text; each speaks the silenced voice of the other. Ocampo's texts embody the passion raging behind Woolf's measured words, while Woolf articulates the order that seeks to impose itself on Ocampo's fluid, ranging prose. Woolf's limited adherence to literary conventions earned her a measured amount of honor and respect as a writer and critic. In her response to Woolf, Ocampo mirrors what patriarchy has chosen not to see and what Woolf herself buried within her essay: emotion at the scene of writing.

## 6. Response to *Orlando*

If, as J. J. Wilson asserts, Woolf's *Orlando* is an antinovel—"a work 'deliberately constructed in a negative fashion, relying for its effects on omitting or annihilating traditional elements of the novel, and playing against the expectations of the past' "[14]—then Ocampo's *Virginia Woolf, Orlando y Cía* [Virginia Woolf, Orlando and Company] is an antiliterary essay, deviating from the expected form and playing against "the expectations established in the reader by the (essay) form and the conventions of the past."[15] And just as the introduction to *Orlando* (the "Writer's Preface") alerts the reader to the "hoax" of the text, the opening paragraph of Ocampo's essay warns the reader that the text may be altogether different from what he or she may expect.

> I am going to speak to you as the "common reader" of Virginia Woolf's work. I am going to speak to you of the image I retain of her. Don't expect to hear pure literary criticism; you'll be disappointed. My encounter with the author of *Orlando* has reassured me once again that—among other things—nothing I have imagined of woman, dreamed for her, defended in her name, is false, exaggerated or vain. And in thinking of Virginia Woolf, I cannot forget it for one moment.
>
> [Voy a hablarles a ustedes como "common reader" de la obra de Virginia Woolf. Voy a hablarles de la imagen que conservo de ella. No esperen ustedes oír crítica literaria pura; se decepcionarían. Pues el encuentro con la autora de *Orlando* me ha traído una vez más—entre otras cosas—la certidumbre de que nada de lo que había yo imaginado de la mujer, soñado para ella, defendido en su nombre, es falso, exagerado ni vano. Y al pensar en Virginia Woolf, no puedo olvidarlo ni un momento.][16]

Ocampo thus mirrors the "antinovel" with an "anti-essay."

Woolf resurrected the term "common reader" from Dr. Johnson, publishing two volumes of essays entitled *The Common Reader*. Ocampo identifies herself as a common reader of the preeminent twentieth-century common reader—Virginia Woolf herself. Ocampo defines the common reader as one who "differs from the critic and the scholar in that he or she reads exclusively for pleasure and without having to worry about communicating knowledge. The common reader does not have a method, only a passion: reading" [". . . difiere del crítico y del erudito en que lee exclusivamente por placer y sin preocupación de tener que transmitir sus conocimientos. No tiene un método sino una pasión: la lectura"] ("Orlando y Cía," p. 46). (She formulates this definition from Woolf's, which appears in the introduction to the first *Common Reader*.) As a common reader, Ocampo allies herself with Woolf at just the point that the (traditional) reader expects her to speak *about* Woolf.

Reading as a common reader and speaking about Woolf's person as well as her work leads Ocampo to warn her listeners that the lecture (the essay was an address) will not be "pure literary criticism." Those who expect the traditional literary response to Woolf will be disappointed. This warning, implied in the verb *decepcionar*, brings up the theme of deception and its relationship to literature. (Ocampo later recalls the theme in her discussion of *Orlando*, tying together men's relation to women and to literature and exposing their similar, and thus suspect, origins.) This warning suggests that Ocampo plans to tinker with expectations that lead to a narrow concept of literary criticism. Her claim also implies the radical nature of her reading: it has the power to affect her ideas and feelings about women in the world. And by stating her own "deception" forthrightly, Ocampo subverts any accusation that she deceives without warning, making the "anti-essay" utterly undeceptive.

The other significant aspect of this opening paragraph is the degree to which Ocampo identifies with Woolf and the way that she moves from this identification to an avowal of solidarity with all women. The passage moves from "the author of *Orlando*' ["la autora de *Orlando*"] to "woman" ["la mujer"] and conflates the two, making Woolf the embodiment of all women. This conflation is connected to another; that of author and text. Ocampo states that she will present the work of Woolf as well as images of the author herself. She adds that an encounter with *Orlando's* author convinces her of the potential of all women. Locating textual meaning in the author's intention is not new, but this imagined encounter with the author of the text and the consequent spiritual meeting with all women, is an added twist.

Ocampo's involvement with the texts and characters she discusses is illustrated by her brief treatment of *Mrs. Dalloway*. Describing Clarissa Dalloway's response to the comment that she resembles her mother while wearing a gray hat and walking in a garden, Ocampo writes:

The past has just entered the present for her, but much more sharply than when present was only present. . . . There are these two details: the gray hat and the fact of walking in a garden, these create for her now the powerful sense of memory's presentness. . . Virginia Woolf knows that the emotion and anguish will not well up in Clarissa's heart from something important and abstract, so to speak (her resemblance to her mother), but rather from something insignificant and concrete (the gray hat that she wore, her walk in the garden).

[El pasado acaba de entrar para ella en el presente, pero de un modo mucho más punzante que cuando no era sino presente. . . . Son estos dos detalles: el sombrero gris y el hecho de caminar por un jardín, los que crean hoy toda la poderosa actualidad del recuerdo . . . Virginia Woolf sabe que la marea de la emoción y de la angustia no subirá en el corazón de Clarissa por algo importante y abstracto, por decir así (su parecido con la madre), sino por algo insignificante y concreto (el sombrero gris que llevaba, su paseo en un jardín).] (p. 13)

The original text in *Mrs. Dalloway* reads:

She looked tonight, she said, so like her mother as she first saw her walking in a garden in a grey hat.
And really Clarissa's eyes filled with tears. Her mother, walking in a garden! But alas, she must go.[17]

Ocampo is so connected to Clarissa's experience that she takes it upon herself to explain the character's motivations. She identifies with the text, argues for it, going even deeper than the text itself cares to plunge. She becomes co-author of the text, entering the mirror, breaking through the traditional separation of text and critic, mirror and woman, to recreate the original writing. What at first might seem an excessive critical liberty also may be construed as a radical revision of textual boundaries and of the "passive" role of the (female) reader.

Ocampo continues this identification with the text in her lengthy discussion of *Orlando*, in which she retells the story, highlighting what she perceives to be its most important points. These tendencies—her identification with the analyzed text and its characters, and her retelling of the story— help to explain her phrase "nothing I have imagined of woman, dreamed for her" ["nada de lo que había yo imaginado de la mujer, soñado para ella"]: the "para" is an ambiguous preposition that identifies Ocampo with the "ella," dreaming for and with her. When Ocampo tells Orlando's story, *with* Woolf, she tells her own story and the story of all women. This mirroring allows her to insert herself into the scene of literary discourse, to read her life into the text, and to redefine a text, allowing it to describe her own experience. It is a way of reflecting and revising the original work and a bold act that creatively reformulates the critical project.

Ocampo places *Orlando* squarely within the chronological development

of Woolf's work. Unlike most critics who emphasize "*Orlando*'s enigmatic
or idiosyncratic nature,"[18] Ocampo describes the text's passage "from
novel to poem, from reality to fiction, from humor to lyricism, from irony
to ecstasy, from one century to another as if it were the easiest thing in the
world" ["de la novela al poema, de la realidad a la ficción, del humorismo
al lirismo, de la ironía al éxtasis, de un siglo a otro como si fuera el juego
más fácil del mundo"] (pp. 17–18). Asserting that for both Proust and
Woolf, time is "the principal persona on stage" ["el principal personaje
puesto en escena"], she goes on to say: "This preoccupation with time
comes to take shape, to materialize, in *Orlando*" ["Esta preocupación del
tiempo llega a tomar cuerpo, a materializarse en *Orlando*"] (p. 15). Ocampo presents *Orlando* as a work that is part of the whole of Woolf's oeuvre,
expressing themes congruent with her other works; in other words, it is a
characteristically Woolfian text.

In her discussion of the novel, Ocampo specifically attends to themes of
gender and literature; although she does not articulate it explicitly, she
evidently considers *Orlando* a text concerned with men, women, and their
relationship to writing. In the beginning she pays lip service to the commonly held idea that *Orlando* is "about" Vita Sackville-West, but since she
leaves this topic quickly and never returns to it, one can assume that she
did not consider it to be of significance. The thread that Ocampo follows is
that of a writing person and literary character; she is interested in how
Woolf describes the writer from the sixteenth to the twentieth century and
how this writer comes to be a woman.

In following the story of Orlando through the centuries, Ocampo also
traces the corresponding attitudes toward writers and artists. She describes
Orlando as one driven to read and write, who lives passionately within and
for literature, even though it is not "proper" to his station in life. She
identifies closely with his love for literature and eloquently describes the
nature of this passionate involvement. Ocampo allies herself with Orlando
and opposes the cultural expectations of his time. In her depiction of him
as one at odds with society, she is describing herself as a woman writer.

Things seem to have changed a great deal since then, and the story of these
outdated customs makes us laugh. It is important to remember that if they have
changed for men, they have scarcely begun to change for women. All women
who have written have repeated in one way or another Jane Austen's gesture of
hiding her manuscript under a piece of blotting paper when visitors or servants
entered the room.

[Las cosas parecen haber cambiado mucho desde entonces y nos hace sonreír el
relato de estas costumbres de trogloditas. Conviene advertir que si han cambiado
para los hombres, apenas empiezan a cambiar para las mujeres. Todas las que
han escrito han hecho, de uno o de otro modo, el gesto de Jane Austen ocultando

su manuscrito bajo un secante cuando los visitantes o los criados entraban en su cuarto.] (p. 26)

As a patron of literature in the seventeenth century, Orlando pays a quarterly sum to a certain Nicholas Greene and invites the poet to his home—only to be the subject of his next sharply satirical poem. Ocampo notes, "women and literature, one after another, have deceived Orlando profoundly" ["La mujer y la literatura, una tras otra, habían decepcionado profundamente a Orlando"] (p. 29). This statement is perhaps the most subtle and ironic in the entire essay; in it, Ocampo expresses not only her interpretation of the story but, more significantly, offers an astute observation about how men perceive their relationship to both women and literature. It echoes a few of Woolf's opening remarks in *A Room of One's Own*:

> The title women and fiction might mean . . . women and what they are like; or it might mean women and the fiction that they write; or it might mean women and the fiction that is written about them; or it might mean that somehow all three are inextricably mixed together.[19]

Women and literature are fictions that deceive men even as they are created by men; when the fictive woman takes pen in hand and writes herself, she must contend with this tangle of deceptions. Ironically, Ocampo's statement masks a complex relationship between the male reader/writer and his fictions, and alludes to Woolf's belief that men's fictions about women affect the fictions women write. Ocampo's statement ("Women and literature, one after another, have deceived Orlando profoundly") is a mirroring of Woolf—a telescoping of a group of related concepts into one sentence that reflects back to Woolf the way her "fictions" mirror her own theoretical work.

When the seventeenth century becomes the eighteenth, Orlando becomes a woman, waking from a seven-day stupor during which she is visited by Chastity, Purity, and Modesty. She returns home after adventures with gypsies, and it is only on the boat to England that, in skirts for the first time, Orlando really feels that she is a woman. In discussing Orlando's growing self-awareness as a woman, Ocampo notes: "Women are not naturally obedient nor chaste nor perfumed nor adorned with jewels, they only become so by submitting to the most exasperating discipline" ["Las mujeres no son naturales ni obedientes, ni castas, ni perfumadas, ni revestidas de adornos, y que sólo llegan a serlo sometiéndose a la más molesta disciplina"]. Women must hide their charms (ankles, for example) beneath skirts; "practically the only right left to her was to serve tea to these gentlemen, asking if they preferred with cream or not" ["El único derecho que le había quedado, o poco menos, era el de servir el té a esos señores preguntándoles si les gustaba claro o cargado"] (pp. 30–31).

Characteristically, Ocampo discusses this section of the novel in order to prove a point outside the text. She justifies Orlando's anger.

Orlando sees men denying women the most minimal instruction for fear that one day women will laugh at them, and she sees them, at the same time, devoted to and submissive before the whims of the most shameless, the most idiotic women, all because they wear skirts.

[Orlando ve a los hombres rehusando a las mujeres la más mínima instrucción por miedo de que un día se rían de ellos, y los ve, al propio tiempo, entregados, sometidos a los caprichos de las más desfachatadas, de las más tontas por el hecho de llevar ellas faldas.] (p. 33)

Ocampo speaks here of her own life, identifying with Orlando's experience and entering that very experience with her own emotion and impulse. The story is about Orlando, the motivating sentiment written in Woolf's text, but the emotion that carries the passage is Victoria Ocampo's. She represents what she believes to be the feminist import of Woolf's tale by identifying its meaning with her own experience.

The nineteenth century brings dampness and fog to London, and marriage for Orlando. She also publishes her poem "The Oak Tree," which she has carried at her breast for centuries. She writes a coded telegram to her husband (busy rounding Cape Horn in a thunderstorm), and Ocampo comments "It too is in a way, a coded message, and the most penetrating one of the book" ["Es también en cierto modo un mensaje cifrado, y el más penetrante del libro"] (p. 39). This implies that what is most significant, most "penetrating," also may be the most elusive. By not deciphering the message, Ocampo mirrors Woolf's enigmatic text, and encodes her own elusive message.

Toward the end of the essay, which goes on to discuss other works by Woolf, Ocampo tries to imagine another writer creating *Orlando*: Colette.

Rather, let's not even try to imagine it: I should never have chosen her. The marvellous sensuality of this Frenchwoman lies at the opposite of what characterizes and distinguishes Virginia Woolf's mode of sensibility, of spirituality.

[Mejor dicho, no tratemos de imaginárnosla: nunca la hubiera elegido. La genial sensualidad de esa francesa está en el otro polo de lo que particulariza y singulariza el modo de sensibilidad, de espiritualidad de Virginia Woolf.] (p. 43)

In this statement, Ocampo explains her choice of Woolf as a model by articulating Woolf's difference from Colette. This choice is crucial to her literary project, because her essay mirrors Woolf's text. In the comparison between Woolf and Colette, Ocampo names Woolf as a literary mother, defines the tradition she chooses to mirror, and establishes her own literary heritage.

In her analysis of *Orlando*, Ocampo traces the sensibility of the woman writer throughout the centuries. (If, as Woolf suggests in "Women and Fiction," "there was no continuous writing done by women before the eighteenth century,"[20] then the predecessor of Orlando the twentieth-century woman writer must have been a sixteenth-century boy.) *Orlando* establishes a women's literary tradition and suggests that an alternative to masculine literary discourse would not mirror the masculine tradition but would be defined by the openness of the writer to cross fertilization of gender. Ocampo, in concentrating her critical energy on *Orlando*, defines her own project as a reader: to revise the terms of literary discourse by attending to the implications of gender in literature.

## 7. Fathers and Husbands in *A Writer's Diary*

In 1953 Leonard Woolf published *A Writer's Diary*, a one-volume collection of excerpts from Virginia Woolf's extensive diaries. Upon publication of this volume, Ocampo wrote *Virginia Woolf en su diario* [Virginia Woolf in her diary], a book-length meditation on Woolf's life and writings that draws heavily upon—but does not confine itself to—*A Writer's Diary*. Ocampo emphasizes the profound effects of men's censorship of women's writing, and the various forms that censorship can take, by discussing Leonard Woolf's editing of his wife's diaries, and the influence of Sir Leslie Stephen upon his daughter. She also relates the circumstances of Woolf's death, re-viewing the situation from Woolf's perspective and recognizing a purpose in the act. Throughout her book, Ocampo allows Woolf's experience, as represented in the diary, to guide her pen.

Leonard Woolf included in *A Writer's Diary*:

> practically everything which referred to her own writing. I have included also three other kinds of extract. The first consists of a certain number of passages in which she is obviously using the diary as a method of practising or trying out the art of writing. The second consists of a few passages, which, though not directly or indirectly concerned with her writings, I have deliberately selected because they give the reader an idea of the direct impact upon her mind of scenes and person, i.e. of the raw material of her art. Thirdly, I have included a certain number of passages in which she comments upon the books she was reading.[21]

Victoria Ocampo objects to Leonard Woolf's expurgation of the text. She believes he has intervened to alter and repress his wife's diaries. He maintained that "The diary is too personal to be published as a whole during the lifetime of many of the people referred to in it,"[22] but Ocampo does not consider this sufficient reason to suppress a text. She argues against Leonard Woolf's extensive editing, repeating his own rationale in order to subvert it.

The living have a right to a kind of respect that is not accorded the dead. Something disturbs me about this point of view, for if living people are less indifferent to public opinion than dead people, they are also better equipped to defend themselves.

[Los vivos tienen derecho a un género de respeto que no se estila con los muertos. Algo me choca en este punto de vista, pues si un vivo es menos indiferente a la opinión pública que un muerto, está mejor pertrechado para defenderse.][23]

What surfaces throughout *Virginia Woolf en su diario* is Ocampo's anger that Leonard Woolf has interfered with her access to Woolf by manipulating the text of her diaries. Ocampo considers her textual access to Woolf crucial to their relationship. She senses the suppressed text through the gaps of the published excerpts.

The omissions have not been marked by ellipses in order not to make the reading into an obstacle course: they had already invaded too much terrain. This is a great bother, for readers stumble at every turn over barriers all the more obvious to the sensibility for being whisked out of sight, for being purely latent, like an illness that offers no more symptoms than a vague malaise.

[Las omisiones no han sido señaladas con puntos suspensivos para no hacer de la lectura una carrera de obstáculos: habían invadido demasiado terreno. Esta preocupación molesta, pues el lector tropieza a cada instante con vallas tanto más manifiestas a la sensibilidad cuanto que están escamoteadas, puramente latentes, como una enfermedad que no ofrece más síntoma que un vago malestar.]

Ocampo's second chapter attempts to explain Woolf's comments about her father. The entry for 28 November 1928 begins:

Father's birthday. He would have been 96, 96 yes, today; and could have been 96, like other people one has known: but mercifully not. His life would have entirely ended mine. What would have happened? No writing, no books;—inconceivable.[24]

Ocampo responds: "Here readers pause perplexed. They want to know more. They want to know why. The omission is flagrant. What is there behind this reflection?" ["Aquí el lector se queda perplejo. Querría saber más. Querría saber por qué. La omisión es flagrante. ¿Qué hay detrás de esa reflexión?"] (p. 21). In this statement she addresses two issues: the silencing power of the father and the editorial intervention of the husband.

Ocampo describes Leslie Stephen as a tyrant, concerned only with himself; but she adds:

If it is certain that Leslie Stephen imposed a good number of Victorian taboos on his family, he also gave his daughter the freedom to read any of the books in his library, a pretty intellectual attitude.

[Si es cierto que Leslie Stephen imponía buena cantidad de tabúes victorianos a su familia, les daba a sus hijas entera libertad para leer cualquier libro de su biblioteca, actitud bastante intelectual.] (p. 26)

Unable to explain the specific nature of Stephen's oppression of his daughter Virginia, Ocampo refers to the fathers of Elizabeth Barrett Browning and Charlotte Brontë, two Victorian men notorious for repressing their talented daughters. Although she denies Stephen's similarity to these two, Ocampo suggests by association that it is in the nature of fathers to silence their daughters (or at least to try). Since the expurgated diary does not offer an explanation of Woolf's comment "No writing, no books;—inconceivable," Ocampo can only believe that some pertinent information concerning Woolf's relationship to her father was suppressed by Leonard Woolf. She suggests that the connection between the silencing effect of the father and the editorial censorship of the husband is not arbitrary, nor insignificant.

Joanna Russ's *How to Suppress Women's Writing* helps to illuminate the issue at hand; she discusses the discouragement to women artists:

In 1881 Leslie Stephen, the father of Virginia Woolf, wrote of George Eliot that she has "a certain feminine incapacity for drawing really masculine heroes." Virginia Woolf's husband, Leonard, married to a literary artist and extremely supportive of her and her work, could nonetheless remark to Modern Language Association past president Florence Howe, when she was past thirty, "Why does a pretty girl like you want to waste her life in a library?"[25]

Russ cites Jane Marcus concerning Leonard Woolf's direct censorship, revealing that not only did he suppress "some of his wife's feminist and socialist writings" but he obscured her connections to left-wing journals and groups of working women.[26]

It is clear from Russ's discussion that certain kinds of writing routinely are edited out of women's texts and that both Leslie Stephen and Leonard Woolf displayed various forms of the masculine bias that works to suppress women's writing. Ocampo understood Leonard Woolf's censorship to be related to the oppressive influence of Leslie Stephen. The effect of both men is to distort the feminine mirror text, and according to Ocampo, censorship is the profound effect of men on the texts of women.

However, it is not always men who are the agents in this process. It is easy to see how Woolf could turn on herself, editing out the harsher sentences of her own work, and criticizing anger in the work of others. Thus, while her male friends (Keynes, Forster, her nephew Quentin Bell) and her father and husband responded negatively to her feminism—Berenice Carroll writes: "The response of men in (Woolf's) own circle was cool, uncomprehending, or openly hostile" to *Three Guineas*[27]—Joanna Russ documents Woolf's own ambivalent and contradictory relationship to anger and its expression, demonstrating how unresolved the issue was in her work.

Russ approaches the topic of anger in Charlotte Brontë's work in much the same way that Ocampo defends Brontë in "Carta a Virginia Woolf." In response to Mary Ellmann's comments about Brontë, Russ writes "I believe that Ellmann is made uneasy by Brontë because the direct expression of female anger makes her uneasy (*the anger in her book* [*Thinking About Women*] *is disguised by irony and mockery . . .*)."[28] The same comments could be made about Woolf: her dislike of Brontë's anger and the transformation of anger into irony within her own text. Russ calls this kind of censorship the "double standard of content," by which women's writing is criticized (and suppressed) for content that goes uncensored in men's texts.

In "Carta a Virginia Woolf," Ocampo objected to Woolf's own censoring tendencies. Sensing the suppressed voices within Woolf's texts, she spoke for their legitimacy, mirroring voices *within* the texts. Her emphases on censorship, editing, and criticism, while appearing to be the result of an intense, personal response to the texts, make up an integrated argument about the nature of masculine censorship and the suppression of women's writing. In *Virginia Woolf en su diario*, Ocampo's anger toward Leonard Woolf is not a personal grudge but an example of the anger of women in general directed at the masculine oppression of feminine expression.

## 8. Conclusion

In her response to Ocampo, Woolf sometimes took the role of mentor: "I'm so glad you write criticisms not fiction . . . I hope you will go on to Dante, and then to Victoria Okampo [*sic*]. Very few women yet have written truthful autobiographies. It is my favorite form of reading (I mean when I'm incapable of Shakespeare, and one often is)."[29] This comment reveals an essential interaction between two writers: the exchange of experience, values, and advice from mentor to student, model to apprentice (what the stepmother never gave to Snow White). It unites Woolf and Ocampo in one cause—that of speaking of truth as women—and represents the kind of encouragement Ocampo as a writer did not often receive from the literary world.

When a woman asks another woman to write the truth about her life, it is not a simple task. Woolf wrote:

> [T]elling the truth about my own experiences as a body, I do not think I solved. I doubt any woman has solved it yet. The obstacles against her are still immensely powerful—and yet they are difficult to define. . . . Indeed it will be a long time still, I think, before a woman can sit down to write a book without finding a phantom to be slain, a rock to be dashed against.[30]

Two women alone in a room ask to hear the truth of the other's life. They want to know what women say about themselves.

Ocampo's writings about Virginia Woolf demonstrate how a woman writer models herself after and distinguishes herself from another woman writer. This is a critical issue for all women writers, who must contend with an oppressive literary tradition. In her feminist essays, Woolf established that women's relation to fiction does not reside simply in the text. Ocampo then brought her own experience into the scene of literary discourse, asserting the truth of her life as testimony to the lives of literary women. Both women engage in a critical discourse that is conscious of the reading and writing context.

The mirror paradigm works both textually and contextually, helping to explain how women writers and their texts relate to each other. It also demonstrates how women can transform their relationship to literary tradition by redefining its function in their own terms. In her critical essays, Ocampo came to mirror Woolf's writing without using their differences competitively. Her work on Woolf marks the beginning of an integrated feminist literary approach, based on a general feminist theory and applied toward the analysis of women writers.

As Ocampo began to conceive of the feminine subject as witness, she offered her experience as evidence of the textual experience (reading), thereby grounding her reading in its extra-literary context and bringing an analysis of her experience into literary discourse. She remained acutely aware of her emotional responses to literature and acknowledged their validity by refusing to recognize a reading that ignored the passionate and spiritual elements of a text. Her faith in her own experience makes Victoria Ocampo's texts compelling documents and identifies them as models for contemporary feminist criticism. Her writings are full of strength, energy, and daring—qualities to which women do not have consistent access because they are generally associated with masculinity.

As a writer and critic, Victoria Ocampo has been overlooked by the "serious" literary establishment; yet she formulated an alternative approach to criticism. Open to the experience that a text offered, she attempted to give voice to the silenced and maligned expression of women, and she steadfastly defended her subjectivity as a reader. In studying her ideas, I have come to appreciate her practice of feminist reading that values the reader's response to both text and context, as well as her refusal to separate the two. Victoria Ocampo, as a literary mother, offers the contemporary feminist reader not only a fresh perspective on Virginia Woolf but also an opportunity to initiate her own project of mirroring and textual production.

# Notes

1. Louise Bernikow, *Among Women* (New York: Harper and Row, 1981), p. 10.

2. Ovid, *Metamorphoses*, trans. Rolfe Humphries (Bloomington: Indiana University Press, 1955), pp. 55–73.

3. Sandra M. Gilbert and Susan Gubar, *The Madwoman in the Attic: The Woman Writer and the Nineteenth-Century Imagination* (New Haven: Yale University Press, 1979), pp. 38–42.

4. Ibid., pp. 15–16.

5. Bernikow, *Among Women*, p. 10.

6. Victoria Ocampo, "Carta a Virginia Woolf," in *Testimonios*, 1st ser. (Madrid: Revista de Occidente, 1935), p. 9. Subsequent references will appear in the text.

7. For a more extended discussion of Ocampo's feminism, please see Amy Katz Kaminsky, "Women and Feminism in Victoria Ocampo's *Testimonios*," in *Proceedings of the Sixth Annual Hispanic Literatures Conference*, ed. Juan Cruz de Mendizábal (Indiana University of Pennsylvania, October 1980), pp. 69–85.

8. Victoria Ocampo, "La mujer y su expresión," in *Testimonios*, 2nd ser. (Buenos Aires: Ediciones Sur, 1941), p. 281. Subsequent references will appear in the text.

9. Naomi Black, "Virginia Woolf: A Life of Natural Happiness," in *Feminist Theorists*, ed. Dale Spender (New York: Pantheon, 1983), p. 310.

10. Ibid., p. 302.

11. Ibid.

12. Virginia Woolf, *A Room of One's Own* (New York: Harcourt, Brace & World, 1929), p. 72.

13. Joanna Russ, *How to Suppress Women's Writing* (Austin: University of Texas Press, 1983), p. 75.

14. M. H. Abrams, *A Glossary of Literary Terms* (New York: Holt, Rinehart and Winston, 1971), quoted in J. J. Wilson, "Why is *Orlando* Difficult?", in *New Feminist Essays on Virginia Woolf*, ed. Jane Marcus (Lincoln: University of Nebraska Press, 1981), p. 174.

15. Wilson, "Why is *Orlando* Difficult?", p. 174.

16. Victoria Ocampo, *Virginia Woolf, Orlando y Cía* (Buenos Aires: Ediciones Sur, 1938), p. 7. All subsequent references will appear in the text.

17. Virginia Woolf, *Mrs. Dalloway* (New York: Harcourt, Brace & World, 1925), p. 267.

18. Wilson, "Why is *Orlando* Difficult?", p. 170.

19. Woolf, *A Room of One's Own*, p. 3.

20. Virginia Woolf, "Women and Fiction," in *Women and Writing*, ed. Michele Barrett (New York: Harcourt, Brace, Jovanovich, 1979), p. 43.

21. Leonard Woolf, Introduction to *A Writer's Diary*, by Virginia Woolf, ed. Leonard Woolf (New York: Harcourt, Brace & Co., 1953), pp. viii–ix.

22. Ibid., p. vii.

23. Victoria Ocampo, *Virginia Woolf en su diario* (Buenos Aires: Ediciones Sur, 1954), p. 14. Subsequent references will appear in the text.

24. Virginia Woolf, *A Writer's Diary*, p. 135.

25. Gordon S. Haight, ed., *A Century of George Eliot Criticism* (Boston:

Houghton Mifflin, 1965), p. 144; Florence Howe, "Literacy and Literature," *PMLA* 89, no. 3 (1974), p. 438; quoted in Russ, *How to Suppress Women's Writing*, p. 12.

26. Jane Marcus, "Art and Anger," *Feminist Studies* 4, no. 1 (February 1978), pp. 93–94; quoted in Russ, *How to Suppress Women's Writing*, p. 74.

27. Bernice Carroll, "'To Crush Him in our own Country': The Political Thought of Virginia Woolf," *Feminist Studies* 4, no. 1 (February 1978), p. 99; quoted in Russ, *How to Suppress Women's Writing*, p. 73.

28. Russ, *How to Suppress Women's Writing*, p. 95; emphasis added.

29. Virginia Woolf, *The Letters of Virginia Woolf*, vol. 5, ed. Nigel Nicholson and Joanne Trautmann (New York: Harcourt, Brace, Jovanovich, 1979), letter #2966.

30. Virginia Woolf, "Professions for Women," in *Women and Writing*, p. 62.

# Moving Selves: The Alchemy of *Esmero* (Gabriela Mistral, Gloria Riestra, Rosario Castellanos, and Gloria Fuertes)

## HARRIET S. TURNER
### (Essay in Homage to Joaquina Navarro)

On an island off the New England coast, a small, fragile outpost known as the "little gray lady of the sea," Lydia Coffin stitched a rhyme into her sampler.

> Plain as this Sampler was,
> as plain we find
> Unletter'd, unadorned the Female Mind.
> No fine ideas fill the Vacant Soul,
> No graceful colouring animates the Whole.
>
> With Close Attention carefully inwrought
> Fair Education prints the pleasing Thought
> Inserts the curious lines on proper Ground
> Compleats the Work and scatters Roses round.[1]

This nineteenth-century poem is a distinctively feminine piece of writing. It differs from a masculine text not simply in characterization ("the Vacant Soul"), point of view ("as Plain we find"), theme ("Fair Education"), or the obvious gender link to stitchery, handcrafts, and household arts. Lydia Coffin's words also imply that the "Female Mind" inhabits a space different and apart from masculine thinking. With respect to this space one paradox is evident: the text of the sampler depicts consciousness—the mind's process of sensing, visualizing, and reflecting, as "Fair Education prints," "inserts," "compleats," "scatters." Yet the female mind is configured as something caught and completed as a work. The contrast creates a kind of kinesthetic image: the sampler stitches together stasis ("Vacant Soul") and movement (printing, inserting, completing). It projects duality—a self split and differentiated, empty and full, past and present, blank-eyed and graced in color. The nominalized, inert soul occupies space; it is located in past time, framed in reflection. The verbal, animated self, moving in a continuous present, appears to contravene spatial limits. Yet that moving self is also bound, held in a frame, circumscribed within the rounded perfection of a complete work.

The rhyme's kinesthesia denotes a formerly frozen, vacant state becoming free, animated, and shaken loose, like unbound hair from a bun. Thus movement inserts a covert, "curious," reflexive line into the sampler. Here, a self-consciously framed text appears to turn upon itself. The female mind, empty and plain, a conspicuous nonentity with no fine ideas and no coloring, comes into color, movement, and being at the precise moment when movement itself is stopped. The female mind acquires life when the work is "compleat"—stitched in cloth, pinned to its frame, hung on the wall.

Simple poetic devices reiterate artistic circularity and stasis of this rhyme. Alliterative rhyming sounds, the distinct, visual pattern of two divided stanzas stitched as one design, the rounded shape of roses—these motifs represent closure. Closure, further pressed by repetitive, rhyming sounds, occurs as words open the mind, filling it, as "Fair Education" prints the thought, alters perception, leads the mind out of itself. Fair education releases the stored energies of its etymon *exducere* in the moment that it prints the thought and inserts the line that frames the female mind. Movement and mind stop just as the reader, like Lydia Coffin, takes part in them by stitching, by reading and reflecting upon what is "compleat."

The sampler, by elaborating the paradox of a dual space, textual and pictorial, inside and outside, configures a tenace. It circles the female mind as circular, unified figures ("roses round") cause the mind to flower, make it move. In that movement, the female mind bends back upon itself to stop and take note of its journey. Thus it stands stitched both as a divided, split thing and as a unified entity—something at one with itself, something one and two at the same time. It defies space, jumping out of its frame in the moment that it remains clasped and closed within that space. It displays the paradox of reflexive movement and spatial limits, and thus appears as something confined, yet powered with inner energy defined as female.

Lydia Coffin's sampler, a visual and verbal artifact, places education and the Female in a relationship tinged with irony. Can a mind, so spatially conceived and confined, participate in movement, engage in reflection? Can something passive, printed with thought, turn upon itself and pursue the paradoxical potential of its own differentiation? In short, can it jump out of the frame? Eunice Odio, contemporary woman poet from Costa Rica, affirms this transformational power of the female mind.

> But I can open myself like a flower
> and jump down from my eyes to see me
> open to the sun.

[Pero puedo abrirme como una flor
y saltar desde los ojos para verme
abierta al sol.][2]

Active and receptive, dynamic and constrained, something intact and self-contained, yet something self-conscious and contemplative—Eunice Odio's female mind, like Lydia Coffin's flowers, adopts a reflexive stance that leaves it, in spite of its completion, curiously unfinished and open to the sun.

In this way the sampler conveys a mixed message, consonant with its dual spatial plane and reflexive impulse. On the one hand, it hangs on the wall as an emblem of accomplishment, exalting the spirit in roses scattered round. On the other hand, it is a sample, an intimation of what might come to pass, warning future, educated female minds. Their pleasing thoughts and animated colors may remain inert and apart, framed on the wall, dishonored and devalued, notwithstanding the glory of those red roses scattered round.

The southern shore of Lydia Coffin's little island points directly to Spain. "Spain: 3000 miles" says a giant compass, *la rosa de los vientos*, painted on the side of a store that fronts on Main Street, cobblestoned since whaling days. In late summer of 1958, that compass made me think about the sampler's close, inwrought stitches and red roses scattered round and how they connected to my education at Smith College during a time of cross-purposes, like the cross-stitch of the rhyme. At Smith, my Spanish professor Joaquina Navarro encouraged me to spend my junior year in Spain. At the time my Spanish wavered. Sentences sagged and my pronunciation was poor. However, day by day, for two years, I pressed my English articulations ever closer to Professor Navarro's native Castilian. She spoke a Spanish even Spaniards would envy—quick, vibrant, full of fire—*fino, suave, matizado*. In that language she printed a pleasing thought that, down to this very hour of writing, has served unfailingly to support visions and scatter roses.

You ask, "what distinguishes Hispanic culture from your own, from the culture we live in here, in this country?" For me the basic difference is a question of *esmero*—a quality of mind or disposition of the spirit that enables a person to make something out of nothing. It means to find just the right touch, the right word or, even more significantly, to know when to say nothing. *Esmerarse en el trabajo*—to take infinite pains with a certain task: this means to use care, utter concentration, so as to achieve a perfect result; it means to work in an enlightened way, with feeling, yet with propriety, whether we iron a blouse, write a letter or show respect, to one's self as well as to others. Such sensitivity is quite delicate, even illusory. It partakes of vision, of a certain sense of expectancy, *esmero*. It's what makes possible the experience of *otherness*, for it requires a reflexive stance toward things, which links our immediate, tangible reality with a longing for eternity.

When we bind a book, lining the cover with *esmero*, with utter care, the new look—shiny, thickened, firm—appeals to us immediately. The essential thing, however, is that we've made the book last longer; now it has staying power, like a faithful friend. In Spain, where material goods are still scarce, a careful, even frugal, touch becomes a matter of survival. For in the end—and I want to be clear about this—we sense the presence of the Good only as a fleeting, fragile thing. Our view, at heart, is theological in implication, best expressed by Calderón when he defined life as a dream, a frenzy, an aberration. Here in the United States, land of plenty, everything tends toward waste, whereas for us, to slow down, take care—*esmerarse en el trabajo*—is to pay homage to things, espy that spark of quicksilver in them that shines momentarily. Isn't it precisely *esmero*—attention brought down close, on bended knee—what inspires the *Odes* of Pablo Neruda, what draws the map of their inner fire? *Tomato, suit, artichoke, onion*: these simple things find themselves transformed by the *alchemy of esmero*. Now they stand exalted, illuminated from within, leafed out in all the splendor that the smallest detail confers.

So there you have it. What's waiting for you out there in Spain? Nothing less than the supreme possibility of otherness, a dynamic already stored as energy in the painstaking study of language itself. I do believe that to speak or write another tongue teaches us to re-live words, to understand them for what they really are: signs, metaphors in themselves which denote, in García Lorca's marvellous phrase, "the leap on horseback taken by one's imagination." In Spain you'll take the leap, becoming other than yourself without forsaking, for a moment, the person you really are, in other words, the person you want to be, now and forever and in fullest measure.[3]

This essay in homage to Joaquina Navarro offers a gloss on her words, as I remember them, recast in my own words. The notion of *esmero*, when linked to language learning, suggests the definition of a different critical space: one set between two things—two texts, two languages or geographical areas, two genders or times. A spatial sense of paradoxical in-between-ness hones self-perception to a fine point; it also conceives of education as a process of consciousness that sets that self in motion through the transformational power of speech—what might be called the alchemy of *esmero*. As a student, I learned this from Joaquina Navarro. As a teacher, I relearned it from my Oberlin students who have practiced their own alchemy of *esmero* in translating from Spanish to English.[4]

My purpose is to focus on the link between space, self, and the female mind by comparing certain poems by Hispanic women writers to Lydia Coffin's New England sampler. Gabriela Mistral (Chile), Gloria Riestra and Rosario Castellanos (Mexico), and Gloria Fuertes (Spain) wrote poems that, in differing ways, render the self as subject and object of its own contemplation. These writers defined, as did Lydia Coffin, word and world in a distinctly feminine way. Like the sampler's rhyme, their poems display a covert kind of reflexivity that links the articulation of self to a text that, while rooted in spatial limits, nonetheless remains conspicuously mobile. This reflexivity "changes places" to change meaning, reversing highs and lows, insides and outsides. Thus each poem represents what J.

Hillis Miller has called "the linguistic moment"[5]—that place or point in a poem where word and world cross in a self-reversing or metaleptic movement that separates constituent parts of the observing self so as to re-invent them as a new poetic persona. In the process, the poem is made to reflect upon its own nature as poetic text.

Here I would contend that this kind of reflexive stance—curious and covert, partial and elusive—takes root in the poet's perception of gender, of a female mind clasped within a masculine environment. In her poem "Soneto de la muerte I" [Sonnet of death] Mistral symbolizes that environment as a "frozen niche," while Riestra, in her poem "Soledad" [I am alone], merely alludes to it as "world" ["mundo"]—an exterior, undifferentiated space where she does not belong. In "Soy una y estoy sola" ["Woman"], Fuertes configures such an exterior, gravitating spatial presence as absence—alienation, inattention, absolute negation. Castellanos, in her hymn to "Una palmera" [A palm tree], designates that space as "the dark country of man" ["el país oscuro de los hombres"].

In each composition a moving self takes shape within, over, or against the masculine space. The sense of a reborn, rising persona becomes consubstantial with verbal articulation and the recovery of speech. Thus poem and personal identity stand reviewed as a kind of fictional experiment that raises the writing self, transforming it, much as the ancient science of alchemy sought to change base metal to gold. In these poems, the writing self plunges powered by its split between self as subject and self as object. It operates and is defined as continuous re-vision, asserting the visual aspect of poetic design—image, stanza division, length of line, patterns of rhyme. As a visual piece, the writing self stands, as it were, only to "jump down from its eyes to see itself open to the sun"; it is a transparent sign, a transparent lily ["lirio transparente"] in Gloria Riestra's image, inside the poem and outside of it, simultaneously transfigured as two-in-one. Private and intact, the writing self nonetheless remains linked to someone or something outside of itself. Thus it changes places to become, in essence, selfless, a form of compassion or otherness [otredad].

Gabriela Mistral's "Soneto de la muerte I" keynotes this reflexive dynamic in several respects. Merely by the use of a pseudonym at the time of public presentation in 1914[6] she conveys in this poem the tensions of being a female writer. Mistral did not sign her poetry with her own name because, according to Langston Hughes, "as a young teacher she feared, if it became known that she wrote such emotionally outspoken verses, she might lose her job."[7] Instead she invented another name, another persona replete with other worldly and masculine associations: Gabriela, alluding to the archangel and annunciator Gabriel, also to the Italian modernist poet, Gabriele d'Annunzio; and Mistral, name of the Mediterranean sea wind and of the Provenzal poet, Frederic Mistral.

The revision discloses irony in this gender "cross-over" of Mistral's writing self. Until the recent publication of two bilingual anthologies of poetry by Latin American women, Mistral's poems had received recognition only because they appeared to conform to female stereotypes.[8] Male critics pointed to the merit of her "feminine" themes—"love of God, nature, the mother, the world's just causes, the humble, persecuted, suffering, and forgotten" ["amor a Dios, a la naturaleza, a la madre, a las buenas causas del mundo, a los humildes, perseguidos, dolientes y olvidados"]. Aesthetic appreciation focused on her "great sensibility" ["gran sensibilidad"].[9] Scant attention was paid to meaning and to how that meaning technically was achieved.

Other qualities of Mistral's poetry are noted in a curious way. For example, in their widely used anthology, Enrique Anderson-Imbert and E. Florit single out as a chief virtue Mistral's poetic "vigor," suggesting that vigor—a sinewy sort of cerebral strength celebrated by Huidobro in his famous dictum[10]— was distinctly a property of the male mind. Mistral's vigor was, according to Florit and Anderson-Imbert, "more the vigor of a poet than a poetess" ["vigor de poeta más que de poetisa"].[11] Thus it seems that the adoption of a masculine pseudonym did nothing to deflect injurious criticism. Not surprisingly, Mistral's "crazy women" poems ["Locas mujeres"] and other works of hers went unrepresented in most anthologies. Nor did critics take note of Mistral's anger in the exclamations of the short lyric poem "I Have No Solitude" ["Yo no tengo soledad"], published in Ternura [Tenderness] (1924). In that poem, anger mixes subversively with maternal impulses. In "Lluvia lenta" [Slow rain], Mistral evokes a distilled anger, a bitterness dripping-slow like rain that drills into the soul. It is nothing less than a cosmic affliction that women alone must bear and about which men—secure and sheltered in the home, childlike in their comfort, ignorance, and privilege—know nothing. "Within the home, men / do not feel this bitterness, / this cargo of sad water / sent from on high." ["Dentro del hogar, los hombres / no sienten esta amargura, / este envío de agua triste / de la altura."][12] Man as mothered child— Mistral's maternal instinct harbors suppressed outrage.

Gabriela Mistral's "Soneto de la muerte I," published in Desolación [Desolation] (1922), takes root in autobiographical experience.[13] The occasion was the suicide of a young love, a railroad worker who shot himself in 1909. His untimely death prompted the writing of her sonnet, which plays with the ideas of word and world to cheat time and death on their own terms. In order to banish time, Mistral invokes temporality in her verse, stressing rhyme and alliteration. In order to transcend death she manipulates death-related images—dust, slumber, moonlight, and earthly imprisonment. Her aim is to exploit a system of paradoxes in a reflexive way; that is, she fabricates out of death-words an opposite word-world of immediacy and vitality that overlaps her "I" and "Eye" in a linguistic moment of self-critique.

### Death Sonnet I

I'll take you from the icy niche where they placed you,
lower to the humble, sunny earth.
They didn't know that's where I'll die,
we'll sleep in the same bed.

Gently, a mother with her sleeping son,
I'll lay to bed in the earth.
It will be all softness for your body,
a cradle for a crying child.

Then I'll sprinkle rose-dust and earth,
and your spoils, almost weightless, will remain
imprisoned in the moon's blue cloud of dust.

I'll leave you, singing my beautiful revenge—
because no one's hand will drop to the secret depth
to contest your fistful of bones.

—Translated by Marti Moody, 1979

[Soneto de la muerte I

Del nicho helado en que los hombres te pusieron
te bajaré a la tierra humilde y soleada
Que he de dormirme en ella los hombres no supieron,
y que hemos de soñar sobre la misma almohada.

Te acostaré en la tierra soleada, con una
dulcedumbre de madre para el hijo dormido,
y la tierra ha de hacerse suavidades de cuna
al recibir tu cuerpo de niño dolorido.

Luego iré espolvoreando tierra y polvo de rosas,
y en la azulada y leve polvareda de luna,
los despojos livianos irán quedando presos.

Me alejaré contando mis venganzas hermosas,
¡porque a ese hondor recóndito la mano de ninguna
bajará a disputarme tu puñado de huesos!]

The opening quatrain of the sonnet establishes a double context of selves
and spaces. Worldly spaces are high and outside, in frozen niches and
nameless men—"los hombres," pall bearers or grave diggers, aloof, alien,
unfeeling. Countering the niche of the uncaring masculine hand are inner,
female spaces, filled with voiced realities as the poet speaks to the dead
youth, now somehow "alive" and in secret collusion with her. Inside-
outside, height and depth, warmth and cold, soft earth and hard stone
work, white light and maternal darkness, silence and speaking, empty

spaces filling as a single mind faces collective ignorance: these opposites partake of a directional movement in the sonnet. This movement expresses a psychic and conceptual reality that is higher in value. Like the body placed in the frozen niche, words are placed so as to draw the eye from the outer edge of the sonnet into its inner recesses, spelling out a new space that is placed lower but is higher in worth.

In this way, the rigorous form of the sonnet—its strict pattern of lines and syllabic count—appears to frame, like the frozen niche, an inner, opposite linguistic reality; an internal "poem," as spatial oppositions of high and low, inner and outer, make movement itself intrinsic to meaning. From the first quatrain to the second and from there to the tercets, connotations of "high" and "outside" begin to function rhetorically. They impose a sense of emotional distance whereas, "inner" and "low" foreshorten and connect. Placement, then, elicits a reading that reverses the moral identity of "high" and "low": "low" becomes "high"—blessed and warm, open and female—whereas "high" descends in value, standing aloof and arched, a cold, masculine frame.

In this way, the divisions of the sonnet allow a choice between world—a high, frozen niche—and *word*—spoken comforts, embedded in an earth mother, sunk low but flung forward and high for contemplation as the poetic part of the sonnet. Here is the linguistic moment, the place where language turns inward to focus on itself, a writing self now divided between the whole of the high sonnet form and the transformational power of images in the lower parts of the second quatrain and first tercet. This turning point quickly draws a circle on death, effacing its frozen niche: earth becomes a pillow, a shared resting place, and death itself a dreaming sleep. Rather than bury the body, the poet lays it to bed with maternal gentleness, countering the alien and indifferent placement in the niche. Earth becomes a cradle receiving the body, with *encabalgamientos* in lines 7 and 8 that create a sense of rhythmic rocking. The dead body becomes a sleeping son, a crying child, so that time tips backwards. It unravels at the moment of burial, pointing back to life's source, the moment of birth. Enclosure in the womb and in the poem is absolute. The sonnet gives birth to the dead love and to the writing self.

One last gesture—scattering earth over the grave—completes the linguistic transformation. In the other world, high and outside, this act represents closure as earth covers coffin, sealing off and weighting down. Now Mistral uses earth to relieve weight, compel movement, and infuse darkness with light, color, and aroma.

> Luego iré espolvoreando tierra y polvo de rosas
> y en la azulada y leve polvareda de luna
> los despojos livianos irán quedando presos.

At this point, movement, not rest, controls the sonnet. Mistral's use of the future progressive tense and her stress on inner rhyme—alliterative, liquid *l*'s, alternating with the assonance of open vowel sounds in *a* and *o* ("la azulada y leve polvareda de luna")—mark time, pulsing the lines. They change the static moment of burial into birth, the timelessness of death into the temporal flow of living.

In this way, midpoint in the sonnet, inner and low words transform a high and outside world. They engender a poem within the classical sonnet form. The poem or part of the whole divests the sonnet itself of weight and oppression; it has, in effect, divested death of its frozen niche, its lock on life in the moment that earth becomes dust—rose dust, ascending and mingling with moon dust to make an airy bed for the weightless remains of the beloved. Within her sonnet Mistral has inserted lines and "scattered roses," releasing her beloved as she recreated him, as well as her own writing self, her own innermost poetic persona. Again highs and lows, in- sides and outsides cross and reverse in this mobile image of earthbound remains that ascend to the sky. High now implies something sublime and represents union, not separation, as earth dust and moon dust mingle and as darkness and light become one. Oneness overtakes two, even with re- spect to poetic meter. As the sonnet progresses, the outer pattern of the sonnet rhyme scheme (abab, abab, cdc, cdc) recedes, giving way to the waving, pulsing sounds of inner lyric lines. Assonance, ascendance, and alliteration prevail over rhyme.

The closing tercet links the dual structure of sonnet frame and inner poem to the perception of a divided self—a mind that becomes the object of its own contemplation. Now the poet sings of "beautiful revenges." What are these revenges? One represents the victory of word over world; another affirms life over death; another refers to that division between the whole (sonnet) and part (inner poem). This inner poem (the first tercet) depicts the poet's imagined persona. The unconventional syllabic count of those alliterative lines and its stumbling pace traces a sense of a self unhing- ed, displaced, and divided. This self is contemplated as object as the poet engages in re-vision, viewing herself slightly crazed, swaying tipsily, scat- tering rose dust over a moonlit grave.

In the closing tercet, this dancing, unhinged self declares still another revenge—one against her own gender. "¡La mano de ninguna / bajará a disputarme tu puñado de huesos!" Like her own sonnet that contains an inner poem, Mistral as female mind contains within her poetic persona opposing selves, as maternal caress ["dulcedumbre de madre"] crosses with the defiance of a jealous lover. Death assures her of that final revenge against the future: only she can possess her beloved. In this way, poem and persona, each a divided entity, stand at cross-purposes, informing the text obliquely with an aspect of self-critique. That critique results from a secret tension between the one and the other. In "Soneto de la muerte I" this self-referential, confessional aspect is covert, partial, and deeply embedded in poetic form. It finds an explicit voice in "La otra" [The other], another autobiographical poem published three years before her death, in *Lagar* [Wine press] (1954).

"La otra" is masculine in character. It is wayward and driven ["andariega"], to recall the definition of Octavio Paz for "the bad woman" ["la mujer mala"].[14] "La otra" is exalted in ambition, unfeeling like the frozen niche, dry and spiny, hard as stone, obdurate and flaming proud, highflying like the hungry eagle.

> One of my selves I killed.
> I did not love her.
>
> She was a flaming, spiny flower,
> high on the mountain;
> she was parched and burned;
> she never drank.
> . . . . . . . . . . . . .
> I left her to die,
> ripping away my own flesh.
> She perished like an eagle
> left to starve, alone on high.
> . . . . . . . . . . . . . . . . . . . . . .
> If you cannot, then,
> just forget her.
> I've killed her. You
> kill her, too!
>
> —Translated by Lori Rubinstein, 1987

> [Una en mí maté.
> Yo no la amaba.
>
> Era la flor llameando
> del cactus de montaña;
> era aridez y fuego;
> nunca se refrescaba.
> . . . . . . . . . . . . . . . .
> La dejé que muriese,
> robándole mi entraña.
> Se acabó como el águila
> que no es alimentada.
> . . . . . . . . . . . . . . . .
> Si no podéis, entonces,
> ¡ay!, olvidadla.
> Yo la maté. ¡Vosotras
> también matadla!]

"La otra" expresses Mistral's paradoxical, moving self, a divided identity that both affirmed and plagued her to the end. On the one hand, she sought to suppress her masculine traits by invoking, over and over, that "dulcedumbre de madre" of the "Soneto de la muerte I." On the other hand, *la otra* inevitably is present in every poem. Mistral sees her dancing in the first tercet of "Soneto," singing sweet revenges in the second, printing thought and inserting the lines, quite literally, of "La otra." In effect, *la otra* is the writing self, writing the very poem that calls for her own effacement. The poem itself encapsulates its own linguistic moment, that place where poem and persona cross in a self-reversing, double cross, creating in the one a tension between two that remains unresolved. "Soneto de la muerte I" (completed in 1909, published in 1922) and "La otra" (1954) configure at beginning and end Mistral's moving self, raised as a continuous revision, reflexive and reflective, in the "Work compleat."

A divided self also moves in the poetry of Rosario Castellanos (Mexico). As in Mistral's sonnet, the notion of space—high and low, inside and outside—frames a dual perception of the female mind in movement. Two poems from her book *El rescate del mundo* [*The Rescue of the World*] (1952) exemplify this notion: "Atardece en la playa" [Evening on the shore] spells out the image of a drifting, divided "I" ["yo dividida"], whereas "Una palmera" [A palm tree] raises up the redemptive image of two united in oneness.

Evening on the Shore

Evening on the shore. Darkness doubles
within the swelling waters.

Over the sand quicken fiery flames
—a broken, brilliant star—
spiking the night with silver spurs
whipped on by the wind.

And I, a self divided, move
between banks of water and flame,
half bitten and bloodied by taciturn fish
half bloodied in flames, fiercely torn in two.

—Translated by Lori Rubinstein, 1987

[Atardece en la playa. En el río madura
una profunda noche duplicada.

Sobre la arena late
—como una estrella viva y desgajada—

una hoguera que el viento apresura, clavándole
sus espuelas agudas y plateadas.

Yo, dividida, voy como entre dos orillas
entre el fuego y el agua:
mitad sangre, mordida de taciturnos peces
y mitad sangre rota de fiera llamarada.]

Glimpsed from a distance, in reflected surfaces, Castellanos's "yo dividi-da," like García Lorca's mirror images,[15] appears upside-down. As an in-verted star torn from the heavens and thrown into flame, her life spark glints darkly on the sand and swims in a swollen, tumbling sky, overturned as a reflected image in the river's "profunda noche duplicada." The moving self implodes. It has become an inscape, a mirror image held inside nature, brought down from the sky, overturned in water, dispersed and direction-less, in wind-blown flames; fire and water are cruel and hostile environ-ments. Drifting between "dos orillas", this "yo dividida" is a devoured thing, splintered and shredded, a mirage twice removed from the source of light. Light and life die, flaming white in metallic fires and streaking red in blood in "Atardece en la playa."

Conversely a re-invented, integrated, verbal self emerges in Castella-nos's hymn to the female mind in "Una palmera."

> Lady of the winds,
> heron of the grasslands,
> when your waist is swaying
> you make a song.
>
> Expression of prayer
> or prelude to flight,
> the heavens pour themselves drop by drop
> into your cup.
>
> From the dark country of men
> I have come to kneel and contemplate you
> Poetry
> high, rare, unadorned.
>
> —Translated by Frances Richard, 1987

> [Señora de los vientos,
> garza de la llanura
> cuando te meces canta
> tu cintura.
>
> Gesto de la oración
> o preludio del vuelo,

en tu copa se vierten uno a uno
los cielos.

Desde el país oscuro de los hombres
he venido a mirarte de rodillas,
alta, desnuda, única,
poesía.]

Upward movement overtakes downward drift; things once set low, rise; darkness gives way to light; inscape becomes escape; and a "yo dividida" stands transfigured in the image of the rising palm. "Una palmera" prints the thought and inserts the lines in a way that enables the poet to create a poem that becomes its own self, *poema-persona-palmera*. The poem is a place of communion and transubstantiation; the leafy fronds trace out a cupped, holy space, newly created between earth and sky, where three converge into one—an exalted, female image of trinity.

From below, "desde el país oscuro de los hombres," Castellanos as lyric speaker contemplates the palm. It represents *poesía*; it traces her poem and reflects to the contemplative eye of the poet her best self. In effect, poet and *palmera* stand as mirror images for one another: the palm rises, the poet ascends from a dark netherworld; the palm gestures in a religious movement of worship and prayer, and the poet kneels in reverence; the palm sings, whistling at the waist and the poet voices a song of praise. Poetic design confirms this dual identity of poet and palm. The swaying rhyme, assonant and alliterative, the cupped images and alternation of long and short lines print thought as pattern and pattern as idea—*poesía*. In turn, *poesía* equates *poema*, *palmera*, and *poeta*. Castellanos reviews the self as she writes the poem and contemplates the whole as *palmera*—"alta, desnuda, única, / poesía." For her, this trinity is a redemptive image, the hope of the future, *el rescate del mundo*.

Within the self-referential poetic of Gloria Fuertes (Spain), word by definition, is world, poem is *persona*, and history is her story, *Historia de Gloria* [Story of Gloria] (1983).

> When you finish reading this book
> —or whatever it is—,
> this Poetry
> —or whatever it is—
>
> Within you will have perched a miracle
> —or whatever it is—,
> you have relaxed a few minutes
> and "entered" into Gloria*
> without ever having to die.
> *(into Gloria Fuertes)

—Translated by Lori Rubinstein, 1987

[Al terminar de leer este libro
—o lo que sea—,
esta poesía
—o lo que sea—
en ti se habrá posado un milagro
—o lo que sea—,
te has distraído unos minutos
y has "entrado" en la Gloria*
sin necesidad de morirte.]
    *(en la Gloria Fuertes)

In *Historia de Gloria*, the even, bare diction—that voice a "dry stick" ("palo seco")—of the poem "Woman" ("Soy una y estoy sola"), displays a reflexive dynamic expression of value, uniting *ética* and *estética*.

Woman

I'm one and I'm alone.
No call, no visit.
I was left without tobacco,
without hands and without wine
suffering like crack-dried earth.
Sundown, long and deep.
I'm one and I'm alone.
The rain soothes me
(Now, poetry is beside me)
Now we are two, poem.

—Translated by Jenifer Lee

[Soy una y estoy sola
Soy una y estoy sola
No ha llamado ni vino.
Me quedé sin tabaco
sin manos y sin vino
sufriendo a palo seco.
Tarde larga y profunda.
Soy una y estoy sola.
La lluvia me serena
(y está la poesía junto a mí)
ya somos dos, poema.]

Commenting on her translation, Jenifer Lee writes:

This poem is like "Sola moro" in that it is a celebration of "self." The images in the progression are very common, which is characteristic of Gloria's work. The theme is also a very common one for her. This poem seems to be divided into equal parts. The first four lines create the image of a woman who . . . has stopped her life to sit and wait. This kind of aloneness is empty and yearns for company. There is no solace or escape (tobacco or wine). In fact she is paralyzed by it, "sin manos." The second half is a realization that she is not missing anything at all. Her company is her poetry. Because poetry originated from herself, she can control it. It is a complement. The last line of the poem asserts the speaker as a separate entity—"somos dos." This second kind of aloneness is filled with inspiration: "She will begin to dialogue with her solitude, to get used to it and to her shadow, to joke about it so as, finally, to accept it as a faithful friend that inspired her verse" ("[E]mpezará a dialogar con su soledad, a acostumbrarse a ella y a su sombra, a burlarse de ella para, finalmente, aceptarla como fiel compañera inspiradora de sus versos.")[16]

Conceived in the very movement of the reading eye—"ya está la poesía junto a mí"—the poem becomes the writing self and each the other's company in solitude, or *soledad*. Simple devices—the use of the copulative "y," parallel construction of "no. . . ni," internal rhyming and a syllabic count evenly distributed in each line—divide each line into halves. In turn, as Jenifer Lee notes, the poem itself is divided into two equal parts, upper and lower. In this way, division traces a pattern of reciprocity and reconciliation; paradoxically, something divided (another "yo dividida") stresses equipoise, the oneness of two, distinct but equal, parts. That is, the oneness of *poema* and persona achieved through a dialectic of presence and absence, blank page and written poem, of the sense of "I" accompanied by "eye," takes shape only as equality becomes a basic premise. Inserted into its own curious, inwrought, self-reflexive line is the implication that dualities coexist only when both partake of each other in equal shares. Such a value seems intrinsic to the female mind. Here, Jenifer Lee's comment on her translation of the title is instructive: "The 'one' in line 1 and 7 [is] very important because it creates a feeling of unity. To keep the feminine quality of 'one' the title was changed to simply 'Woman'" (p. 10). Her one, two-syllabled noun as a title fits the two-in-one wordplay that the poem offers between *soledad*, gender, and the idea of equality.

In "Soledad" [I am alone] by Gloria Riestra (Mexico), the link between aloneness and space, and re-vision and self-invention, acquires a distinctly moral and metafictional edge. As Robert Scholes notes with respect to one of Borges's tales, in Riestra's poem "idea and pattern, and the idea *of* pattern, dominate our vision."[17] The idea of pattern not only makes visible the privilege of a narrating or writing self but displays that privilege as conscious choice. Choice divides the poem and prints the thought of *soledad* in two ways, causing that key word to gloss itself, to bend back upon itself and become a "self-text," one and two at the same time.

I am alone

A whirlwind of celestial birds are mine
Yes, world, I am very alone.

Alone, from the thick grove, down-below
From the scattered clouds, below.
Are, perhaps, even the stars below?

And from the beaming sun, my home,
My solitude is of transparent lilies,
Of heavenly crystals.

And higher still . . .
I am one; alone!

—Translated by Naomi Eigner, 1985

[Soledad

Con mi huracán de pájaros celestes,
sí, mundo, estoy muy sola.

Sola, de la arboleda para abajo
de las errantes nubes para abajo,
tal vez de las estrellas para abajo
¡Qué soledad la mía!

Pero del sol arriba, donde vivo,
mi soledad de lirios transparentes,
de cristales celestes.

Y aún más alto . . .
¡Qué soledad la mía!]

From *Soledad sonora* (1950)

The poem represents an act, an identity and a state of consciousness that are in their essence analytical, imaginative, and moral. The term analytical refers to the sense of something that has been separated into constituent pieces and parts. Here is a moving self evoked forward and back within a continuous present; here are stepped or terraced spaces, oriented on a vertical axis, up and down—"abajo," "arriba," "y aún más alto." There is the self apart, hugging a hurricane of beating birds; and there is the self accompanied, winged, transparent, filled with light.

The pieces and parts of the poem, organized into a poetic design of lines and spaces, cause idea and pattern to interface and become a single imaginative construct. This deliberately imagined text drastically alters the semantic environment of the key word *soledad*. Now the process of reading becomes part of the poem, part of what it is about, extending that "aboutness" to itself so that subject and object, self and *soledad*, the "I" and the "eye," are one, yet differentiated. In effect, they are moving selves that, like mirror images, reflect one another in a linguistic moment of pure transparency, as the meaning of *soledad* changes from aloneness to the dazzling plurality of transparent lilies. This quality of transparence, as defined by David Walker, causes meaning to inhere "not in any externally projected drama but in the drama of sensibility that is enacted as one reads it."[18]

In this sense, one may assign a moral character to the kind of self-contemplation that takes place in Gloria Riestra's poem. It represents the willed triumph of self-invention in the face of radical aloneness, apartness, abandon, *soledad*. Acting as "I" and "eye," as both speaker and reader, the poet gathers *soledad* into herself and flies, jumping out of time and space even as she remains fixed forever within them and in the "Work compleat." Her reflexive, doubled identity thus equates perception and the poetic act enabling the poem to become the instrument of its own meditation. Now, truly, word has become world: *soledad* and self are dwelling places and space transmutes to a sign, acquiring a singular, linguistic transparency. *Soledad*, turning in on itself, flowers as "mi soledad de lirios transparentes." By definition these transparent lilies are plural, harmonied, and sublime. They represent the very essence of two-in-oneness that is three, another re-invented trinity echoed in the book's title of three-syllabled, two words about one concept—*Soledad sonora* [Sonorous solitude]. Moving selves and Joaquina Navarro's alchemy of *esmero*: from Lydia Coffin's red roses to Gloria Riestra's transparent lilies I find power, astride two languages, to "jump down from my eyes to see me open to the sun" ["saltar desde los ojos para verme abierta al sol"].

## Notes

1. Lydia Coffin's sampler (71–62i) is the property of the Peter Foulger Museum, Nantucket, Mass., and is reproduced courtesy of the Nantucket Historical Association.

2. The lines by Eunice Odio, written 12 June 1946 (Granada, Nicaragua) preface the introduction to *Open to the Sun. A Bilingual Anthology of Latin American Women Poets*, ed. Nora Jácquez Weiser (Van Nuys: Perivale Press, 1979), p. 1. Weiser's anthology, the first of its kind, features translations by her former students at Oberlin College.

3. Joaquina Navarro's words in Spanish as I remember them, adding some words of my own:

Me preguntas, ¿qué distingue mi cultura, la hispánica, de ésta, la que vivimos en este país? Y te diré que para mí, la diferencia esencial tiene que ver con el esmero, temple o disposición de ánimo que sabe hacer mucho con poco, encontrar el toque preciso, la palabra exacta, sobre todo, callar a tiempo. *Esmerarse en el trabajo* significa poner sumo cuidado en ser cabal y perfecto, hacer cualquier cosa con cariño, acierto y lucimiento—planchar una blusa, escribir una carta, respetarse a una misma para respetar a los demás. Delicadeza, sensibilidad, ilusión, o sea, el esmero, que hace posible la experiencia de *otredad*, actitud reflexiva que une lo más inmediato y palpable con el ansia de eternidad.

Si empastamos un libro, forrándolo con esmero, nos complace su nueva identidad táctil, vistosa, particular y sin embargo, lo esencial es que el libro dure más, que sea, forrado con esmero, fiel y consecuente con nosotros. En España, donde todavía escasean los bienes, un trato *esmerado* ya es cuestión de sobrevivir. Al fin y al cabo—y hay que poner esto muy en claro—sentimos la presencia del Bien como cosa frágil, transitoria, errante. Es una actitud en su raíz teológica, precisada para siempre por Calderón, cuando afirmó la vida como sueño, frenesí, ilusión. Aquí en Estados Unidos, país de la abundancia, todo convoca al derroche, mientras que para nosotros, *esmerarse por las cosas* es rendirles homenaje, captar por un instante ese azogue que resplandece en ellas. ¿No es el esmero lo que potencia las odas de Pablo Neruda, lo que hace posible su milagrosa radiografía? Tomate, traje, alcachofa, cebolla: el poeta los ha pasado por la secreta alquimia del esmero y ahí quedan exaltados, iluminados minuciosamente en todo el esplendor de su verdad.

Eso es todo. ¿Qué te espera en España? Pues nada menos que la gran posibilidad de otredad, vivencia que anida, íntima, en el esmerado aprendizaje de la lengua. Creo que, al hablar y escribir en otro idioma, vivimos la palabra nuevamente. La entendemos tal cual es realmente: signo, en sí mismo metáfora, que representa, según la frase celestial de García Lorca, "un salto ecuestre que dé la imaginación" (Lorca, *Obras completas* [Madrid: Aguilar, 1963], p. 69). En España darás ese salto, llegarás a ser otra, sin dejar de ser la que eres, es decir, la que quisieras ser, por fin y para siempre y en toda su plenitud.

4. Here I want to acknowledge the work of my students at Oberlin College, notably poems translated by Ruth Flanagan, Emily Goldman, Lori Rubinstein, Jennifer Collins; the two poems translated by Naomi Eigner, Jenifer Lee, Frances Richard, and Lori Rubenstein included in the text; and Jessica Brown's senior honors thesis, titled "The Art of Translation" (*summa cum laude*, Oberlin College, 1984). Marti Moody's translation of the "Soneto de la muerte I" was published in Nora Jácquez Weiser's anthology. Carol Maier and I are responsible for translations not otherwise attributed.

5. In his preface J. Hillis Miller writes: "This is a book . . . about moments of suspension within the texts of poems, not usually at their beginnings or end, moments when they reflect or comment on their own medium. I call this suspension the linguistic moment. It is a form of parabasis, a breaking of the illusion that language is a transparent medium of meaning" (*The Linguistic Moment* [Princeton: Princeton University Press, 1985], p. xiv).

6. For documentation of origin, number, and dates of publication of the Mistral sonnets, see Raúl Silva Castro, "Notas sobre los *Sonetos de la muerte I* de Gabriela Mistral," *Hispanic Review* 30 (1965): 57–62. He accounts for seven extant sonnets and suggests that four remain unknown, bringing the total to eleven, the number indicated in the title of a sonnet that appeared in Gastón Figueira's book, *De la vida y la obra de Gabriela Mistral* (Montevideo, 1959). With respect to the publication of the first three sonnets Silva Castro writes: "The three 'Sonetos de la muerte I', for which Gabriela Mistral was awarded a prize in December 1914, in a poetry competition in Santiago de Chile, were probably written in 1909, the same year that Romelio Ureta took his life." ["Es probable que los tres 'Sonetos de la muerte I' que Gabriela Mistral vió premiados, en el mes de Diciembre de 1914, en unos Juegos Florales de Santiago de Chile, fueran escritos en 1909, el mismo año en que se quitó la vida Romelio Ureta."] (p. 62)

7. Gabriela Mistral, *Selected Poems of Gabriela Mistral*, trans. Langston Hughes (Bloomington: Indiana University Press, 1957), p. 9.

8. See Weiser, *Open to the Sun*; and Mary Crow, ed., *Woman Who Has Sprouted Wings: Poems by Contemporary Latin American Woman Poets* (Pittsburgh: Latin American Literary Review Press, 1984).

9. Silva Castro, "Notas," p. 57.

10. "We are in the heaven of nerves. / Muscles hang, / like mementos, in museums; / but this does not mean we are less strong: / True vigor / resides in the head." ["Estamos en el cielo de los nervios. / El músculo cuelga, / como recuerdo, en los museos; / mas no por eso tenemos menos fuerza: / El vigor verdadero / reside en la cabeza."] Vicente Huidobro, "Arte poética," in Enrique Anderson-Imbert and Eugenio Florit, eds., *Literatura hispanoamericana*, 2nd ed. (New York: Holt, 1970), 2:258.

11. Anderson-Imbert and Florit, *Literatura*, 2:229.

12. Gabriela Mistral's poem "Lluvia lenta," the poem "Soledad," by Gloria Riestra, and "Una palmera," by Rosario Castellanos, are cited from Joseph Silverman and Luis Leal, eds., *Siglo XX* (New York: Holt, 1968), pp. 32, 149, 133. Mistral's "Soneto de la muerte I" and "La otra" are taken from Anderson-Imbert and Florit, *Literatura*, 2:231, 235–36. Castellanos's poem "Atardece en la playa" is taken from *El rescate del mundo* (México: Chiapas, 1952).

13. Silva Castro, "Notas," p. 57.

14. Octavio Paz, *El laberinto de la soledad*, 2nd ed. (México: Fondo de Cultura Económica, 1973), p. 35.

15. García Lorca's poem "Canción de jinete," offers visual, mirrorlike images of stars, spurs, and flaming *hogueras* similar to those of Castellanos's poem: "Night digs its spur / into black flanks'/ driving stars. / . . . In the black moon, / a cry! and the bonfire's / long horn." ["La noche espolea / sus negros ijares / clavándose estrellas. / . . . En la luna negra, / ¡un grito! y el cuerno / largo de la hoguera."] Federico García Lorca, *Obras completas* (Madrid: Aguilar, 1963), p. 377.

16. Jenifer Lee, "HERSTORY. Gloria Fuertes as Seen through her Poetry (Poet and Woman)," unpublished portfolio of translated poems, Oberlin College, 1985. Lee quotes from the introduction by Pablo González Rodas, ed., *Historia de Gloria* (Madrid: Cátedra, 1983), p. 10.

17. Robert Scholes, *Elements of Literature* (New York: Oxford University Press, 1978), p. 176.

18. David Walker, *The Transparent Lyric* (Princeton: Princeton University Press, 1984), p. xii.

# The Language of Treasure:
# Carolina Coronado, Casta Esteban, and
# Marina Romero

## NOËL VALIS

### Prologue to Marina

Women writers, declared Carolina Coronado[1] in 1862, are a luxury. "What does my name matter?" she asked. "The name of a woman writer can be suppressed in contemporary literature without producing the slightest ripple on the calm horizons of art, because as writers we are the lush outgrowth of the nineteenth century. . . ." ["¿Qué importa mi nombre? Puede suprimirse el nombre de una escritora, en la literatura contemporánea, sin que su mengua produzca la menor turbación en el sereno horizonte del arte, porque las escritoras somos una exuberancia del siglo XIX. . . ."][2] Absence is a woman's name, Carolina seems to suggest. And yet terms like "exuberancia" and "lujo" are strange coins to express depreciation of the feminine.

Even stranger are the circumstances in which these words appeared: in a prologue ostensibly written to introduce Ventura Ruiz Aguilera's elegiac remembrances of his young daughter Elisa. Indeed, such tender regard for a dead child—characteristic of the nearly morbid adoration of children often felt by the secularized nineteenth-century European bourgeoisie— might be taken for the maternal cries of a middle-class *poetisa* in the throes of ritualizing the sacredness of family. "In effect," says Carolina, "our first impression upon reading this small collection of verses is that a woman has written them. Their deep tenderness, the minute description of the beloved object, the tenacity of memory, the insistence on exacerbating such recollection, the bitter devotion with which the Virgin is invoked, and above all, the ingenuousness of certain details seem appropriate to a woman, to a mother." And then almost triumphantly she notes:

> Do you know why they couldn't be the verses of a mother? Because mothers, even when they are poets, do not sing of their children's death. . . . A mother

falls mute, I assure you. . . . [W]hen our children die, we possess only one form for expressing our grief: silence, an unbroken and eternal silence! . . ."

[En efecto, la primera idea que ocurre al leer esta pequeña colección de versos, es que los ha escrito una mujer. Su honda ternura, la minuciosa descripción del objeto amado, la tenacidad de sus recuerdos, la insistencia en exacerbarlos, la piedad amarga con que se invoca a la Virgen, y, sobre todo, la ingenuidad de algunos detalles, parecen propios de una mujer, de una madre. ¿Sabes por qué no podrían ser versos de una madre? Porque las madres, aunque sean poetisas, no cantan la muerte de sus hijos. . . . La madre calla, yo os lo juro. . . cuando éstos mueren, no tenemos sino una forma para expresar nuestro dolor; ¡el silencio, el silencio nunca interrumpido, el silencio eterno! . . . ] (Prologue pp. xvi–xvii)

Notice how neatly Carolina has inverted her terms, at first out of luxuriance, feminine redundance, but then out of silence, feminine significance. One can't help wondering what has happened to the other poet, Ventura Ruiz Aguilera, in this prologue. By the time she returns to him in her concluding remarks, he somehow has been diminished in size; for in writing of a mother's grief, Carolina implies, his own store of emotion is simply not equal in intensity to a woman's. Thus, writing is subtly seen as inferior to sentiment, or as the Extremaduran writer observes, the poet is born in order to interpret a mother's suffering: "Si hay que interpretar el dolor de una madre, para eso ha nacido el poeta" (Prologue, p. xvii).

In case the reader doesn't understand the ironic point she is trying to make, Coronado concludes by saying:

She was his only daughter, and he has lost her, and this is of all sorrows the greatest. For this reason, I have torn from my book the title of a poem which had less right to it than this one dedicated to mourning a child, and I have transported it here, calling the unnamed work of my unfortunate friend THE SORROW OF SORROWS.

[Era su única hija, y la ha perdido, y éste es de todos los dolores el mayor dolor. Por eso, arrancando de mi libro el título de una poesía, que no tenía tanto derecho a llevarlo como éste dedicado al duelo de una niña, lo he transportado aquí, llamando a la obra sin nombre de mi desgraciado amigo EL DOLOR DE LOS DOLORES.] (Prologue, pp. xvii–xviii)

But of course in naming the poet's work with a title from one of her own poems ("Despedida a mi hermano Angel. El dolor de los dolores"), Carolina cleverly asserts a subtext that in essence is the theme of her prologue: womanly superiority embodied in feeling as the source and strength of Ventura's (or other male writers') poems.

Now this certainly is not what Ruiz Aguilera had in mind. He begins his *Elegías* (subtitled "El dolor de los dolores") by saying: "Mothers, with children / in the grave, / And soul submerged / in eternal mourning; / I shall spread my wings, / And to console you / seek your hearth: / *I am your tears.*" ["Madres, que tenéis hijos / en el sepulcro, / Y el corazón cubierto / De eterno luto; / Yo tenderé mis alas, / Y a consolaros / Iré a vuestros hogares: / *Yo soy el llanto.*"] (Ventura's emphasis).[3] Here the poet as paternalistic provider supplies the verbal expression of maternal tears. He is less the interpreter than the giver of sentiment. Carolina's prologue, on the other hand, subtly subverts Ventura's message by suggesting that what seems genuinely feminine in his poetry—the tenderness, tenacity of memory and so on—is in reality a mere simulacrum. For Coronado the feminine, above all as embodied in maternal feeling, surpasses the verbal.[4]

Ventura only can approximate what has already been given to women: the sorrow of sorrows. In giving her title to Elisa's father, Carolina inverts traditional feminine dependence on male support. Thus the *exuberancia* or lush foliage of the woman writer becomes a protective bower shading Ventura's verses. By prefacing and naming his work, Coronado assumes the status of patron; in this way she reverses the negative notion of the woman writer as a useless luxury by giving that luxury value. And since the patron of luxury is the endowment, it is beautifully ironic that Ruiz Aguilera should unwittingly underline Carolina's patronal presence in an epigraph taken from one of her poems: "My shadow departs, but I remain" ["Se va mi sombra, pero yo me quedo"].

"What does my name matter?" Carolina asked. It matters a great deal. By using depreciation as a gently ironic form of feminine appreciation, Coronado enhances her own individual worth. She does so, however, at the risk of being misunderstood; for what reader of the nineteenth century would have taken her statement of feminine superfluity as other than the truth? And was not sentiment a woman's domain? Yet Carolina suggests something quite different; when she deliberately confuses accepted ideas of what constitutes *lo femenino*, she is saying, in effect, that the feminine is not an object of definition.[5] It is a value. Ventura cannot experience a mother's tears, he can only imagine them. But such value only can be seen in relation to other things. That is, what is necessary is an act of denomination, of designating value through naming. One could say that bestowing a name upon womanly sentiment—"the sorrow of sorrows"—constitutes the writer's dowry in the dual sense of the word; for the dowry represents not only a woman's goods or estate but a natural talent as well. Thus Carolina's endowment—closely related etymologically to the dowry—is in reality that inner luxury of self stored within, slowly, painfully accumulating in silence. It is, in a word, treasure.

## The Poetics of Assay: A Second Prologue

But silence doesn't weigh very much in the scheme of things. Indeed, rather than the familiar heaviness of silence one should speak of its weight-lessness in women's lives and writing.[6] Feminine inconsequence is shown graphically in an anonymous, nineteenth-century *romance de señoras* titled "El peso de los hombres, y mugeres" [The balance of men and women], in which the winged male figure of time puts both sexes on the scale, only to find that "man for his firmness, / dropped very quickly, / and woman stayed high up; / but not to worry / for she is frivolity itself" ["que el hombre por su firmeza, / cayó con mucha presteza, / y la muger quedó en alto; / y esto no dé sobresalto / pues toda ella es ligereza"].[7] (Appropriately, an illustration accompanies the verses.) This lightness/weight opposition firmly associates value with heaviness ("firmeza" as solidity) and insignificance with lightness ("ligereza"). Moral attributes correspond perfectly to physical ones.

Yet, as Milan Kundera comments, Parmenides thought lightness was positive and weight negative, unlike Beethoven, for whom a "weighty resolution" was much to be desired. Characteristically provocative, Kundera opts for irresolution, noting that "the only certainty is: the lightness/weight opposition is the most mysterious, most ambiguous of all [opposites]."[8] This is significant, because considering the feminine as value is a notion fraught with difficulties. It depends not only on who is tipping the scales, but on what substances are being weighed. How is one to judge silence? The sacredness and supremacy of sentiment over the verbal must be measured against the possible inacceptability of voicing certain themes and feelings. In other words, if Carolina can only express the "sorrow of sorrows" as the subtext for a larger text, Ruiz Aguilera's *Elegías*, then one again faces the ambiguities and contradictions of feminine inadequacy and dependence.

Even after accounting for the conventions of romanticism[9] and the vicissitudes of biography (Carolina's loss of a child in 1854) in understanding silence and sentiment as interchangeable values, one is still left with the rueful ironies of self en-gendered muteness as a strange form of writing in spite of itself. Does a woman write against herself? So it would appear, judging from Carolina's comments about her own poetry.

I am not a writer. I wrote poetry from the moment I knew how to speak; I stopped writing from the moment I learned to be silent, and those voices which from time to time were heard like the muted echo of a subterranean stream the traveler hears in the silence of the night cannot serve as a solid critical foundation for making judgments about my poetic gifts. Those echoes escaped my silent, resigned soul against my will.

[Yo no soy literata; hice versos desde que supe hablar; dejé de hacerlos desde que aprendí a callar y esos tonos que de tiempo en tiempo se han escuchado como el eco sordo del arroyo subterráneo que oye el viajero en el silencio de la noche, no pueden servir de base al crítico de buena ley para fundar un juicio

> sobre mis facultades poéticas. Esos ecos se han escapado de mi alma resignada y silenciosa contra la voluntad mía.][10]

Carolina is right. The critic cannot understand her poetry solely on the basis of her "voices" or "echoes"; she must also attend to her silence. What an extraordinary vision of silence she must have encountered in catalepsy! Certainly those periodic lapses into a deathlike state of quietude help to explain her fear of burial, documented in her refusal to allow neither husband nor daughter to be interred below ground. Thus the horror of heaviness and silence are entwined intimately through mutual association with death.

Carolina's buried soul—that "subterranean stream"—relates to the notion of weight as a sign of mortality. In the prologue to Ventura's *Elegías*, she declares that "children are not dead bodies; they evaporate, turn into rays of light, cross the ethereal sphere and rise to heaven. . . ." ["Los niños no son cadáveres; los niños se evaporan, se vuelven rayos de luz, cruzan el éter, y suben al cielo. . . ."] (p. xii). Later she comments that Ventura's "verses possess such refined cruelty turned against their very creator, that I am uncertain whether the object has been to write or commit suicide" ["tienen estos versos tal refinamiento de crueldad contra su mismo autor, que dudo si su objeto ha sido escribir o suicidarse"] (p. xiv). I suspect Coronado has misinterpreted Ruiz Aguilera here. The last poem of his *Elegías* clearly suggests the traditional role of catharsis that the writing process often plays. He writes: "Here, the cemetery!. . . / There, the sea. . . the world! / The court is this, / impure morass / calling me / with tumultuous voice" ["¡Aquí, el cementerio!. . . / ¡Allá, el mar. . . el mundo! / La corte es aquella, / cenagal impuro, / Que me está llamando / Con voz de tumulto"] (p. 53). And the last two lines read: "For I return to the sea, / for I return to the world!" ["Que yo al mar vuelvo. / ¡Que yo vuelvo al mundo!"] (p. 54).

For Carolina writing is not cathartic but cataleptic. Consider the case of dead children. Coronado cannot bear the thought that a child should possess the heaviness of death. Thus she pushes away the unacceptable thought by thinking of heaven. More importantly, she endows the dead child with lightness, an incredible airiness, with the effect of dematerializing the body and leaving behind the spirit that is, for the poet, the real child. Behind the kitsch of religious sentimentality lies a very real fear—the fear that a dead child may be, after all, nothing but an inert body subject to decay. Kitsch is that aesthetic ideal that, as Milan Kundera suggests, "excludes everything from its purview. . . essentially unacceptable in human existence."[11] What distinguishes Carolina Coronado from poetasters of the period who eulogized the deaths of children is her admittance of the word *cadáver*.[12] If writing is suicidal, then there is something inherent in the process of literary creation that leads to a terrible sense of closure through revelation, as though words could lift—and let fall—the tombstone of reality. What Carolina fears is the weight of words, for by writing of her departed dead, she, in effect, buries them a second time. Thus writing becomes a form of death, and her prologue a catafalque for the (eventual) interment of Elisa. The only relief for Coronado is that she will not be responsible for burying her; but of course she did not give birth to her either.

The alternative to the suicidal impulses of writing is silence, or burying the body within the poet's very soul. The morbid suggestiveness of this thought is exemplified anecdotally by Coronado's insistence that her dead husband be left *corpore insepulto* in the family chapel during the remaining twenty years of her life. Every night she would take leave of "el silencioso," or "the silent one," as she referred to him, by the balcony connecting bedroom and chapel.[13] The gesture, obscurely anthropophagous in nature, becomes a resurrectional act, in which death is denied and sentimental commitment renewed nightly. Carolina's homage to her husband beautifully illuminates how the body as feeling is incorporated within the womanly self through the generative impulse. Thus the treasure of sentiment is transformed into the weightlessness of silence, akin to what Kundera calls the "lightness of being." But such conversion only can be transacted through the corporal heaviness of a dead husband. Like the dependency relationship established between Coronado's prologue and Ventura's *Elegías*, this one too is contingent upon a larger text, in which a woman's name becomes a significant subtext in measuring the contradictory values of lightness/weight.

The hoarding of treasure within the body—or the body-within-the-body—becomes literal negotiation when naming takes on added value. As Simón Palmer has observed, "that male support was essential is confirmed by noting how many women writers placed between their first and second last names a 'de,' which clearly indicated their marital status." ["Que el apoyo masculino era esencial se observa al comprobar cuántas colocaron entre el primer y segundo apellidos un 'de', que indicaba a las claras su estado civil."][14] A woman's name may be her only dowry as a writer. But such patronage of self runs the risk of debasement when the value of the feminine acquires an exact bill of denomination. Nowhere is this more apparent than in the desperate case of Casta Esteban y Navarro (1841–85), the widow of Gustavo Adolfo Bécquer. By the time Casta published her only book in 1884, Gustavo's reputation as the quintessential romantic poet of Spain had already been established.[15] Unfortunately, he left her in straitened circumstances financially, a condition the widow meant to remedy with the sale of her book *Mi primer ensayo* [My first essay].[16]

Casta's venture was an utter failure. The volume apparently received no critical attention at the time, and subsequent interest in her work has been centered largely on her status as Bécquer's widow. *Mi primer ensayo* is not a well-written book. Composed of twelve pieces ranging from the romantically sentimental to the sketch of customs, it is at best the uneven and untutored attempt of a novice writer, as the awkward and confusing subtitle—"Colección de cuentos con pretensiones de artículos" [A collection of stories with aspirations of being articles]—suggests. Bécquer scholar Rica Brown bears down heavily on the "atrocious vulgarity" of the book ["una cursilería atroz"]. Indeed, she "would have preferred it had never been written, out of respect for the poet, first of all, and second, because [the work] reveals not only intimate sorrows but the meanness of the author's spirit" ["preferiríamos que no lo hubiese escrito, por respeto al poeta, primero, y segundo, porque revela no sólo dolores íntimos, sino la mezquindad del alma de quien lo escribe"].[17]

Other readers have doubted Casta Esteban was capable of writing such a book.[18] After all, she couldn't spell and her knowledge of grammar was limited, an argument that ignores the fact that nineteenth-century women were often educated at home or even self-taught. And institutional learning nearly was always rudimentary for females.[19] Carolina Coronado, Fernán Caballero, and Rosalía de Castro displayed similar defects and omissions of formal instruction.[20] Martínez Cachero simply calls Casta a "non-writer" and a "distressed woman" ["una persona no escritora, una atribulada mujer"], while labeling his article, "Bécquer's Widow, Writer."[21] The critic can't have it both ways. One cannot blame the author for the book's flaws and then accuse her of being too ignorant and too ordinary to write such an ordinary book. Casta was a very poor writer, but she was a writer.

What Casta Esteban lacked was a dowry, that inner luxury of self that Carolina Coronado could afford to spend in silence. How keenly Casta must have felt her insufficiency as a woman writer is painfully evident from the title page, with the author's name printed as "Casta Esteban y Navarro, Viuda de Gustavo Adolfo Bécquer." And she signs herself "the widow of Gustavo A. Bécquer" a second time at the end of the dedication.[22] In the balance of men and women Bécquer's widow weighed very little, though one can imagine how the scale must have settled a fraction lower with the addition of Gustavo's signature. At any rate it is clear that Casta's treasure consisted of her dead husband's writerly fame, thus making it possible for her to cash in literally with the name "viuda de Bécquer," a signature that legitimized her writing efforts. Certainly too she must have been aware that in the economics of writing, prose was worth (i.e., sold) far more than poetry.[23]

For many readers such economic dependency upon the value of naming may forever relegate Casta Esteban to the dusty subbasement of remaindered and forgotten books. Thus it is not surprising that one of the narrations should be called "Historia de un pobre duro" [The story of five miserable pesetas], the pecuniary peripeteia of a five-peseta coin—also the price of *Mi primer ensayo*, incidentally—as it passes into various hands. The same pen would write, with the cynicism of the disillusioned romantic, in "¿Existe el amor?" [Does love exist?]: "today, in an age of enlightenment, the best love note is one from the Bank. Money, health, peace and tranquillity are the facts of real life at its most positive" ["[H]oy, en el siglo de las luces, el mejor billete de amor es un billete de Banco. Dinero, salud, paz y sosiego son los elementos de la vida real y positiva"] (p. 223). Devotees of Bécquer who roundly condemn the incompatible Casta for making the poet miserable are missing the point. For surely the weight of unhappiness fell just as heavily on the widow dragging along the esteemed corpse of her husband for years. Yet, surprisingly, aside from the use of his name, she mentions Bécquer only twice in *Mi primer ensayo*: once to cite from the *rima*, "Hoy la tierra y el cielo me sonríen" ["Today heaven and earth smile upon me"] (p. 83); and again, epigraphically, from "Las hojas secas" [Dead leaves], for "Historia de un pobre duro." However, Bécquer's indirect presence is felt throughout the book, if only in the form of a negation. For Domínguez Bordona, Casta's frequently aggressive anti-romantic stance is symptomatic of the disdain she held for Gustavo's ideals: "Casta Esteban was not kind to the memory of her husband" ["No fue Casta Esteban piadosa con el recuerdo de su marido"].[24] That *Mi primer ensayo* also represented the wounded feelings of Casta herself simply does not occur to him.

But how else does one explain the bitterness of phrases like this one: "A woman seeks to deceive a man and the man believes he's deceived the woman, and both are themselves deceived" ["La mujer pretende engañar al hombre y el hombre cree engañar a la mujer, y los dos a la vez son engañados"] (p. 221). Elsewhere she speaks of marriage as "the tomb of love" ["la tumba del amor"] (p. 48) and love as a "poisonous liquid fate offers us in a golden cup" ["el amor es un líquido emponzoñado que la fatalidad nos brinda en copa de oro"] (p. 223). And finally she likens the male to an image more commonly associated with the female: "Man is like the spider who tirelessly weaves his thick web, only to catch the unsuspecting, careless fly falling into his trap" ["El hombre es cual la araña que teje y teje su tupida red sin descanso, para en su día cazar a la imprudente y cándida mosca que a su paso toque"] (p. 11). Then, mixing metaphors and grammar with sublime confidence, she repeats a phrase seen in another passage: "A man offers us his poison in a golden cup, and once drunk, the results are inevitable; after he has satisfied his appetite, he throws us aside calling us the weaker sex and emptyheaded!" ["El hombre nos brinda su veneno en copa de oro, y una vez bebido, sus resultados son inevitables, y después de satisfecho su apetito, nos arroja de su lado llamándonos ¡sexo débil y cabezas sin sentido!"] (11).

The only original note in Casta's invective is her extraordinary vehemence. What is of interest, however, are the specific circumstances in which these last sentences are inserted. By that I refer less to the truth of biography (not at all to be discounted, as the reader surmises here and elsewhere), than to the text itself. Casta's most strident statements of female resistance to male influence are contained in an introductory essay entitled "Dos palabras a mi sexo" [A few words to my sisters] (pp. 9–19). Significantly, she signs this section "La autora" [the author], and not "the widow of Bécquer."

"Dos palabras a mi sexo" should be read in conjunction with the dedication "A la Excma. Sra. Marquesa del Salar" (pp. 5–7). Quite frankly she tells how she herself paid for publication of the book as a "last recourse to protect myself against poverty and hunger . . ." ["como último recurso para defenderme de la miseria y del hambre . . ."] (p. 6). A few lines later she says:

I made my small boat out of the meager materials from my head. The only thing I needed was a grand and imposing figure, as a captain for my tiny ship, whose name would save it from certain shipwreck, and at once I thought of Your Excellency, not for how much your name would be worth to me, but because I knew that your soul had suffered like mine . . . thus a powerful magnet carried my grief to yours.

[Construí mi pequeño buque con el escaso material de mi cerebro, y sólo me faltaba una figura grande y elevada, que a modo de capitán de tan mezquina nave, la salvara con su nombre de un seguro naufragio, y al punto me acordé de V. E., no por lo mucho que me pudiera valer su nombre, sino porque sabía que su alma sufría como la mía . . . así un poderoso imán llevó mi dolor al suyo.] (p. 6)

It is evident from this *dedicatoria* that Casta Esteban understood the value of a name. Whether she succeeded in gaining concrete support from her aristocratic patroness is not known. Of greater interest is her feminization of a traditionally masculine image, the ship captain, in what constitutes a reversal of gender-related values. Here, a woman's name—her worth in the social and economic spheres—represents authority, with the power to direct and, most significantly, to save. But like Carolina, Casta also underscores the superiority of feminine sentiment expressed through suffering.[25] Read another way, a woman's grief—here, identified by specifically naming the Marquesa del Salar—is transformed into a saving device, a "powerful magnet" unifying and thereby rescuing the foundering female body or vessel.

The value Casta Esteban places on naming the feminine is fully confirmed in what could be called a second prologue, "Dos palabras a mi sexo." Men and women, she declares, never can be friends. Sexual roles and custom invariably make theirs a relationship of subjection. Women, on the other hand, possess strength in friendship. She writes enthusiastically, "long live female unity, created by women themselves!" [" ¡Viva la unión de la mujer, creada por la mujer misma!"] (p. 17). To make her point she elaborates a long chain of mothers in history and letters, which culminates in citing verbatim Sor Juana's "Hombres necios que acusáis" ["Foolish men who accuse"]. "These," she says, "are our mothers." But then she adds: "We are also the daughters of Carthage's invincible soldiers, Numancia's unconquered warriors. . . etc. etc." ["Estas son nuestras madres, y también somos hijas de los guerreros invencibles de Cartago, de los guerreros invictos de Numancia. . . . etc. etc."] (p. 16). The list of male benefactors, or "fathers," is much shorter and reads like a primer on Spanish patriotism, stressing courage and talent. Casta's "mothers," on the other hand, include the best and the worst of women in history, mixing virtuous Roman matrons with the Messalinas of iniquity. Her point seems to be that in the very naming of such mothers and daughters she creates a circle of unity characterized almost exclusively by the virtue of being feminine. These too are her patrons. Thus her prologue is both a plea for women's independence through the strength of feminine solidarity and a morale booster for Casta's desperate circumstances.

Casta Esteban's startling feminist posture must be balanced against the demands of self-interest and the realities of her disadvantaged position. The prologue—like Carolina Coronado's ironic self-effacing assertion of feminine superiority—is built on a structure of unequal supports. On the one hand, Bécquer's widow marks off a zone of independence by constructing a feminine tradition of precedence and patronage. On the other, she does so precisely as "Bécquer's widow." Just as Carolina's prologue is but a subtext for Ventura Ruiz Aguilera's larger text, so Casta's "Dos palabras" and indeed all of *Mi primer ensayo* are predicated on a larger text, Gustavo Adolfo Bécquer himself (and indirectly, her list of male forebears).[26] Thus independence is bound paradoxically by the superior strength of subordination. Independence is the lesser text.

Such ironies come about through an inversion of value itself. When Carolina declares that women writers are a luxury, she suggests a dual use of the term. First she implies a woman's soul possesses intrinsic value for its richness of sentiment. Thus the value of the feminine refers to a woman's identity as such. Her silence becomes the deepest mark of that value. By transferring her inner fund of feeling to the printed page, the woman writer turns the virtual into the material, which for Coronado ultimately represented a "killing transaction." Value then becomes a commodity, not a creation (that is, the body-within-the-body or the quickening of silence).

For Casta Esteban, however, silence meant starving to death, and writing was a literal defense against dying. The widow of Bécquer saw clearly that she was a "name," a commodity. By signing herself "la viuda de Gustavo Adolfo Bécquer" she took the conscious step of marketing herself and her book as pieces of merchandise.[27] In this way she objectified herself as an extrinsic value with no ultimate significance beyond what the market will pay. Given such economic realities, *Mi primer ensayo* gains in meaning as a luxury item, a sign of the past century's "démocratisation du luxe."[28] Casta's prologue, in which she allies herself with a long line of women exemplifying precedence and patronage, can be seen as a form of self advertisement. The presence of other women in her text becomes a component in the marketed creation of a writerly self with the result that the feminine as intrinsic value is also exploited as literary merchandise. The

Stumbling subtitle aside, *Mi primer ensayo* indeed is aptly named. As an essay, it represents not only Casta's first literary attempt or experiment but it is her first rehearsal in fabricating an authorial self as well. Beyond the meanings of practice, exercise, and performance, the word *ensayo* in Spanish also points to a third signifier: the *assay*. Once again the question of value arises. In the *dedicatoria*, Casta writes to her wished-for patroness: "If I succeed in pleasing you with my insignificant handiwork, I will see my efforts recompensed with interest. . . . " ["Si logro agradarla con *mi pobre producción*, veré recompensados mis desvelos *con usura*. . . ."] (p. 7, italics added). How does one judge the worth of a book that the author herself calls a "*pobre producción*" and whose sole vantage is to garner interest, as the telling phrase, "*con usura*" indicates? When placed upon the scale, poor Casta as commodity/creation is found wanting.

And in the end: the same silence? Surely not. Coronado could not bear to objectify in words the bodies of those she loved, preferring to nurture silence as the weightless antidote to the heaviness of mortality. Words accumulated against her will. But in writing against self, she also struggled against the body. To write meant to turn the body inside out, naming the treasure within. But the creative act when made corporal becomes a commodity. In the most pathetic of cases, it becomes Casta's little boat, the vessel, which is herself, cruelly exposed to the tides of supply and demand. When the essay turns into a form of *assay*, naming assumes an even more urgent function in women's writing: that of de-sacralizing the hidden unity of body and self. Such violation of the unspoken identities between self and body forces the woman writer out of herself, out of the rich silence that has become the body-within-her-body. But her silence lacks gravity, hence the feeling of inadequacy, of uncertainty, that arises when she is weighed against the sheer corporality of male writing.[29] Thus a husband's cadaver or the elegiac verses composed for a dead child can represent the unbearably heavy corpus of a male tradition that wrenches the body from self in

e act of writing and turns the writer into a digger of graves, or of buried
asure.[30] Writing then becomes necrology, making widowhood a sign for
e intolerable weight of dead signatures, the emblem of male-empowered
gitimacy. What then does a woman's name matter?

## The Poetry of Deprivation

t these are not romantic times—decidedly not. Nor should I indulge in
rofitable acts of commiseration and complaint. Talking about inade-
icy has the unfortunate effect of magnifying it, the feeling of insufficien-
iccupying ever larger tracts of empty land. I began this essay as a note of
olusage; women writers are a luxury, but the notion of luxury in West-
society is an ambivalent value, simultaneously suggesting great price
great uselessness. Hence it is not surprising to find in women's writing
ious forms of self-depreciation, ranging from the subversively symbolic
arolina Coronado) to the openly negotiable (Casta Esteban y Navarro).
either case, a woman writing must capitalize on what she owns as a
writer, all the while operating under the understanding that her dowry is
not entirely her own. In other words, until recently, she had to reconcile
two kinds of possession, one internal and the other from without: her talents, or dowry, and her self as luxury item. Awareness of a larger possession inevitably creates a blank zone of insufficiency, a lack that has made
women's literature in some ways shadowless. "My shadow departs," Carolina Coronado wrote, "but I remain." ["Se va mi sombra, pero yo me
quedo."] This lack of a shadow has to do with a tradition based on lightness, that unbearable lightness of inconsequence and silence.

There is, however, another side to this, the second part of Carolina's
sentence: "but I remain." Coronado's insistence on her persona, left tanta-
lizingly undefined, is in a dual sense serenely biographical. First, because
the poem was a response to her contemporaries' 1848 homage to her at the
Liceo Artístico y Literario of Madrid.[31] Those same contemporaries had
mistaken a cataleptic episode for her death in 1844.[32] "Although it may
seem to you, my friends, that I hide myself, / because yes, it is deception
. . . Never! . . . I couldn't. . . ." ["Aunque os parezca, amigos, que me
escondo, / porque es engaño, sí. . . ¡Nunca! . . . ¡No puedo! . . ."][33] The
poet's seemingly artless sincerity should not sidetrack one from the subtle
and converging dualities of body and spirit, that blurred waver between
absence and presence.

Carolina simply refuses to be buried. Thus in the most profound sense of
the word, biography assumes what could be termed a bodily function in the
poet's writing life. The vacuum women writers have felt—in themselves,
outside themselves—can be conceived as a physical ache for a part of the

body that doesn't yet exist. To fill that vacuum, or biographical insufficiency, requires an account of one's personal treasure. The investment of biography in women's writing turns the narrative account into embodiment, the totality of a woman's presence in the form of a tangible gift. It is, in a word, a statement of value. Thus the richness of such writing emerges paradoxically out of a lack, which may be expressed as uncertainty or as inadequacy. In this context, feminine insufficiency acquires a peculiar relevance, painful but illuminating, as a part of the compelling dead zone that is the poetry of deprivation.

## "Still Marina" / "Marina todavía"

"Give me, oh Lord, / something to wrest / my body from nothingness." ["Dame, Señor, / algo que arranque / mi tronco de la nada."] With these lines of despair Marina Romero ended her book *Sin agua, el mar* [Without water, the sea] (1961).[34] This poem about emptiness once more raises the question of sentiment in women's writing. This is a subject that women for much of the twentieth century sedulously tried to avoid in their writing. Fearing the kitsch of sentimentality, a woman writer ran the risk of unsexing her voice. This fear of disclosing that inner luxury of self is sad proof of feminine dependence on male approval. It doesn't seem to matter that kitsch, as Kundera gently reminds us, "is an integral part of the human condition."[35] The modern woman writer has shunned it as synonymous with feeling itself. One cannot help thinking of the contortions to which sensibility was subjected stylistically in writers like Gertrude Stein and Djuna Barnes (without forgetting either biography, or that such aesthetic mascarades were a part of the modernist period). Even Carolina Coronado, steeped in romantic values, inverts womanly sentiment by suggesting that a male writer also, Ventura Ruiz Aguilera, is capable of weeping the tears of a disconsolate mother. But of course for Carolina this was evidence of the obvious superiority of feminine feeling. Dependence on a male context, however, made her position as a writer mere prologue to what followed. How then does a woman writer overcome such subjugation, without sacrificing her self?

It must be through writing itself. So I have been thinking as I read once more the poetry of my teacher, Marina Romero. I have come to it, round about, with veiled reluctance. In the guise of scholarship I found myself postponing the inevitable reencounter after so many years. Other women—Carolina Coronado, Casta Esteban y Navarro—made claims and spoke up, quietly the one, stridently the other. I was puzzled that I should have prepared myself for this reunion with Romero by moving backward into the past. There were of course larger aims behind this essay: I wanted

to see the flow of feminine experience, that storehouse of womanly treasure without which I could not hope to situate Marina Romero's poetry.
Nevertheless, I also suspected unwillingness to meet with an old self. De-
ferring the moment, I avoided the clash of disparate personas. After all, I
knew Marina Romero. I could see a small woman, carefully arranged white
hair, hands opening like the leaves of a prayer book, the veined serenity of
the rose and the book enduring the same space. This meant that I could see
myself at age twenty, sitting in the front row of her classroom at Douglass
College, waiting for mystery to unfold. At age forty that young waiting
seems a kind of radiance, untutored and vulnerable. Twenty is waiting, a
form of lateral experience. What one doesn't see is the continuousness of
that lateral view. Whatever I saw or read in Marina Romero at this point
was filtered by a double lens, creating a dual physical biography. Clearly,
the insistent object I was pursuing, the value of a woman's writing life, only
could be approached through indirection and allusion. But the sense of
biography eluded me precisely because I was looking aslant, keeping my
distance. In a word, I was refusing to come to terms with sentiment.

This reluctance to disclose feeling—otherwise praised as that luxurious
inner provision of self—lies at the heart of women's writing, paradoxical as
this sounds. When sentiment is undervalued, fear and inadequacy descend,
making a poem seem hesitant, uncertain. The sense of person is diminished. An old self dies, is buried. The body becomes a carrier of disease,
the slow corruption of feeling. So Romero writes:

To time / they keep adding days. / Words unconnected / to memory. / Suddenly
/ you find yourself / with youth grown / in the little bit of body / to support it /
Everything so small: / body, / time, / memory . . . / So small life. . . .

[Al tiempo / se le van echando días. / Palabras extrañas / a la memoria / De
pronto / se encuentra uno / con la juventud crecida / en lo poco del cuerpo / que la
alienta. / Todo tan pequeño: / el cuerpo, / el tiempo, / la memoria . . . / Tan
pequeña, la vida. . . .] (Poem 25, *Sin agua*, p. 21)

Just as the numbered poems of *Sin agua, el mar* are given in descending
order, so the process of diminishment follows its logical course in this
book, culminating in the intense vision of nothingness as seen in the third
to last poem.

Without water, / the sea. / Without time, / the clock. / Without air / the sigh. /
Without heat / this cold, / this emptiness / without sea, / without time, / without
air, / this emptiness.

[Sin agua, / el mar. / Sin tiempo / el reloj. / Sin aire / el suspiro. / Sin calor / este
frío, / este vacío / sin mar, / sin tiempo, / sin aire, / este vacío.] (p. 51)

The preposition "sin" [without] functions anaphorically here—and as a leit motif throughout the poetry—suggesting desolation and deprivation so extreme that words and sentence structure are reduced to their minimum expressivity.

One of the ways Romero stresses her sense of dispossession in *Sin agua, el mar* is through ironic juxtaposition with the notion of plenty. Her first poem for example begins: "Almost lost, for having found myself so much, / between the devil and the deep six / I live in the non" ["Casi perdida, de encontrarme tanto, / entre la espada y la pared desvivo"] (p. 9). In spare, restrained language, abundance—"de encontrarme tanto"—is negative, pointing to the suffocating weight of the self, which can only be lived by unliving (*desvivir*). Elsewhere, she writes, "They say I'm lucky, / and I'm not complaining. / My shoes always shine. / I have another pair and another, / so many, / that it's a problem / setting them all on the road" ["Dicen que tengo suerte, / y no me quejo. / Me brillan siempre los zapatos. / Tengo otros y otros, / tantos, / que es un problema / dárselos al camino"] (p. 45). I have bread every day and lots of friends, she goes on to say, reiterating in the end: "That's why I'm not complaining" ["Por eso no me quejo"]. The simple effect of accumulation makes the poem somewhat self-deprecatory, because it operates by default on the principle of a missing referent. In Poem 6, the gesture of adding distinct personalities becomes an exercise in incongruity: "that simple sum / of two plus two / makes five" ["esa sencilla suma / de dos y dos / son cinco"] (p. 47). The numbers will not add up. And finally, in Poem 4 she reaches the sum of sums: "I keep on adding / well, / I think, / all the yesterdays. / Figures / rush at me / numbers / are lost / truths / are all mixed up. / So many zeros! / On which side?" ["Yo voy sumando / bien, / creo, / todos los ayeres. / Se me agolpan / las cifras, / se me extrañan / los números; / se me confunden / las verdades. / ¡Tantos ceros! / ¿De qué lado?"] (p. 50). Numbers in Romero's poetry are based upon a strange mathematical assumption: the more you add, the less you get. Thus the notion of plenty is converted into the bitter poetry of subtraction.

Likewise, I had to shift into reverse through her work, looking at two books in particular, *Presencia del recuerdo* [Presence of memory] (1952) and *Midas. Poema de amor* [Midas. Love poem] (1954), in order to reach the bleakness of the *non* in *Sin agua, el mar*. But moving backwards has governed the overall design of this essay. One moves backwards when writing about writing because the self can only see relationships in retrospective. In this sense, writing itself tends to eulogize over its subject as memory. Only the thinking pen pushes forward, fixing flourishes and signing documents as proof we've really been here.

What is left is the "presence of memory," as Marina Romero understands it. "The tenacity of memory, the insistence on exacerbating such recollection," as Carolina Coronado remarked when she subtly undefined *lo femenino*, produces a poetry in which sentiment becomes a form of possession and possession an impossible space. Marina writes: "Long space, suspension in the time of your waiting. / Weightless present. / Arrival, / and your absence made flesh" ["Largo espacio, / suspensión en el tiempo de tu espera. / Ingrávido presente. / Llegada, / y tu ausencia hecha carne"].[36] The play between absence and presence, redolent of the Salinian paradox—the book is dedicated "to the memory of Pedro Salinas"—becomes a metaphoric high wire act in another poem, "Reloj de sol" [Sun dial]: "Suspended in time / like the acrobat child / on the wire" ["Suspendido en el tiempo / como acróbata niño / en el alambre"] (p. 51). But of course the state of being suspended—of being weightless—is impossible to sustain, because the poet cannot really inhabit it. When she remembers herself, it is as something she possesses—"I have myself" ["me tengo a mí"] ("Una Carta" [A letter], p. 17)—but situated in an empty present; "everything so without space / and so apart / so without, like yesterday" ["todo tan sin espacio / y tan aparte, / tan sin como el ayer"] (p. 17).

Possession—having, wanting—runs obsessively throughout *Presencia del recuerdo*. A poem is cut "like the possession / of a day" ["como la posesión / de un día"] ("El poema" [The poem], p. 12). The sea exists "without me / but not mine" ["ya mar sin mí, / pero no mío"]. And in the same poem, "a small grief" ["un pequeño dolor"] needs to be gathered "in beauty / and to make it belong, / and not borrowed" ["recogerlo en belleza / y hacerlo poseído, / y no prestado"] ("En Ibiza, al mar" [In Ibiza, by the sea,], p. 14). In "Momento de siempre" [Moment of forever], the poet possesses a bird or a flower for an instant ("I possessed you for a moment" ["te poseí un momento"] but a memory forever, even though it never "reaches" her present ("Memory, / in your moving away / from this present of mine / and not arriving . . . / I have you forever" ["Recuerdo, / en tu alejarte / de este presente mío / y no llegar . . . / te tengo siempre"], p. 23). The paradox of possession through memory is reiterated when she writes: "If I were to lose you forever, / Still, I would find you, / beyond the leaf / and the stream, / in my murmur alone / on the other side / of this world of voices" ["Si te perdiera para siempre / así, te encontraría, / más allá de la hoja / y del arroyo, / en mi murmullo sólo, / al otro lado / de este mundo de voces"] ("Paradoja" [Paradox], p. 53). The passionate intensity of her possessive remembering is heard clearly in such concluding phrases as "eternally mine" ["eternamente mío"] and "ardently absorbed in me, / mine alone" ["afanosamente adentrado, / mío sólo"] (p. 54).

When the memory is lost, possession is cut off. Thus, "Cuando no sepa tu nombre" [When I no longer know your name], one of the loveliest poems in *Presencia del recuerdo*, stresses the intimate connections between a name and possession: "When your name is / completely new to me, /

then, I will have lost you" ["Cuando tu nombre me sea / completamente nuevo, / entonces, te habré perdido"] (p. 55). The act of naming is for Romero, as it was for Carolina Coronado and Casta Esteban, an implicit declaration of principles. In naming, the poet creates the jointures fundamental to her universe: the very notion of relationships. The writer's voice is predicated on the presence of the other, unnamed yet specific as the "tú" to whom she writes. (In at least one instance she is precise, writing "To Pedro Salinas.") For its intimacy and sense of shared identification, such a relationship is, in essence if not in truth, that of two lovers, a relationship that receives fuller development in *Midas. Poema de amor*. This is naming at its most self-absorbed: "for in this same circle / we are the same center." ["que en este mismo círculo / somos un mismo centro."] ("Un mismo centro" [The same center], p. 84) But such fusion of identities only comes about because the other is "mine, only mine" ["mío, tan mío"] (p. 84). Naming is a form of possession, and the absent lover in *Presencia del recuerdo* is the self-created image possessed through and in memory.

But without the other, what of Marina? (If I forget, will love remember?) The poet's sense of ownership extends to that "same center" twice over. That is, it exposes a disturbing dependency on a larger presence, one that gives title to the book itself and ultimately engulfs the poet in a painful awareness of her own insufficiency. Thus that feminine dependency, observed earlier in Carolina Coronado and Casta Esteban y Navarro, becomes internalized in the guise of a ghostly lover. Sentiment becomes a trap for the woman writer. Her greatest possession, feeling is also a burden of incalculable heaviness, a subjection of the self to obligatory shadows.

Experience then becomes abbreviated, what the poet calls "este no florecer" (p. 44), an unstoppable nonflowering. "Why not the rose in bloom?" ["¿Por qué no rosa llena?"] (p. 19), she asks in "A una rosa cortada" [To a cut rose]. When experience is cut short like the rose, words become uncertain, their scent fades. A question expects no answer, as in the poem "¿Cómo?" [How?]: "How to begin / with the morning a blank?" ["¿Cómo empezar / con la mañana blanca?"] (p. 61). "How to forget," she says later, "an uncertain word?" ["¿Cómo olvidar / una palabra incierta?"] And she ends with this line: "How to know / where the dawn?" ["¿Cómo saber / en dónde está la aurora?"] (p. 62). (Emily Dickinson asked the same question in "Will there really be a morning?").

Romero shortens feeling by reducing verbs to their infinitive. Concision in her poetry does not lead to plenitude, as it does, for example, in Jorge Guillén, hence the significance of a title like "Posible plenitud" [Possible plenitude]. She begins: "You can be happy / with a pain, / yes, / when you swallow air / and the wrinkle in a dress / doesn't matter" ["Se puede ser feliz / con un dolor, / sí, / cuando se bebe el aire / y no importa / la arruga de un traje"] (p. 68). And she ends: "You can be happy / beyond yourself, / in the intimate contours / of eternal things" ["Se puede ser feliz / más allá de uno mismo, / en un contorno íntimo / de las cosas eternas"] (p. 69). Thus a sentence begins deceptively with a quiet statement of apparent affirmation ("Se puede ser feliz"), only to be leavened with qualifying remarks of ironic reduction. You can be happy, she suggests, when it doesn't matter anymore. The very title, at once contradictory and tentative, anticipates the impossible space of Marina Romero's poetry, that space that offers the uncertain, tender gesture of the incomplete act, the wish expressed through personified absence. "You can be happy / with an absence," she says. ["Se puede ser feliz / con una ausencia."] (p. 68) But then fulfillment—lived experience—is postponed indefinitely. Thus she writes in another poem, preparing herself for exultation: "Tomorrow / I will live the rose" ["Mañana, / yo viviré la rosa"] ("Dádiva" [Gift], p. 71).

The ironic attempt to live beyond oneself merely confirms what the poet already knows: to transcend self is impossible, in some respects undesirable. Marina's ambivalence toward the oppressive yet necessary selfness of experience is symbolic of the unsuspected trap of sentiment. Poetry can come about only residually, as the remains of experience. But what of experience foreshortened? And can writing compensate for the unspoken loss? Marina Romero's poetry reflects the radical insufficiency of memory as an agent of resurrection. The weight of mnemosyne—*presencia del recuerdo*—turns mortuary when the writer recreates herself through a second shadow. "Why," she asks at one point, "do I go without thinking to your shadow?" ["¿Por qué / sin razonar / voy a tu sombra?"][37] Yet Marina herself is shadowless: "an intimate present / of dense felt, / of a single me / without shadow" ["un íntimo presente / de afelpada materia, / de un yo solo, / sin sombra"] ("Niebla" [Mist], *Presencia*, pp. 30–31). The present is "opaque," filled with "a tenuous borrowed light" ["opaco / de tenue luz prestada"] (p. 30). Poetry, then, lies somewhere between the plush inertia of presentness and the lightness of being. But the real point of reference is memory. The present merely borrows its light, just as words can rely only on the past. For the woman writer, however, writing what she remembers has often been accomplished by leaning on someone else's memory.

Writing in this way becomes even more of a vicarious experience. Carolina Coronado's rejection of burial—her desire for resurrection, whether of husband or a dead child—also can be viewed from underneath as repressed necrophilia. Casta Esteban y Navarro's exploitation of her dead husband's name is necrophagous. A similar though significantly more subtle pattern of latent anthropophagy emerges in Romero's passionate need to have the other "afanosamente adentrado, mío sólo" (*Presencia*, p. 54). In this way she internalizes her longing by metaphorically swallowing the lover within, so that they are "the same center" (*Presencia*, p. 84). Thus possessiveness—the obsession with memory as owned experience—becomes the thing possessed, the treasure that is stored in the body. Feeling, then, becomes synonymous with the loved object; sentiment—the body-within-the-body—is ingested as *bios*, or biography. In this, I have recreated in feminist terms—and it is ironic—the recurring myth of woman as man-eater. Writing can be conceived as a reverse process of gestation, in which the dead lover, husband, child, is given birth once more, inside.

But there is something freakish in this feminized version of the Frankenstein story, because the relationship between creator and creature is inverted. Ultimately it isn't the thing created, but the woman writer herself who is placed in a state of dependency. The result is a strange form of alienation from her own writing, as though the words were not really hers. The text objectifies a private resource, turning creation into commodity. The struggle to write in a woman artist may arise in part out of a deep reluctance to relinquish what is uniquely hers, out of fear of the ensuing emptiness. Once written, the thing possessed becomes preterite, lost. Thus Marina writes of her solitude: "Here am I, / and that light, / and that color, / and that lost song. / Is it enough?" ["Aquí yo, / y esa luz, / y ese color, / y esa canción perdida. / ¿Basta?"] ("En esta soledad" [In this solitude], *Presencia*, p. 67). How that single question—"¿Basta?"—hangs bleak and isolated, suspended over loneliness.

But the awareness of insufficiency grows with dependency. "It was only your voice," Marina writes, "clinging to my flesh, / an inner torrent / of roses in anguish." ["Era sólo tu voz / agarrada a mi carne, / chorro interno / de rosas en angustia."] ("Sólo tu voz" [Only your voice], *Presencia*, p. 45) The suffering contained in such remembering has its roots in a prior dependency, as the poem "La palabra" [The word] reveals. "Afraid of saying it / like everyone else," she begins ["Miedo de decirlo / como todos"] (p. 72). "Afraid of your getting tired," she goes on ["Miedo de tu cansancio"]. "Afraid emptiness / will gather my words / and they will float / eternal, / without rest, / in a bottomless limbo." ["Miedo de que el vacío / recoja mis palabras / y se queden flotando / eternas, / sin reposo, / en un limbo insondable"] (*Presencia*, pp. 72–73). The feeling of feminine inadequacy could not be clearer in these lines of uncertainty and anxiety.

This same feeling acquires an intense physical concreteness in *Midas* (1954).

> You will drown my dimensions
> when you turn your back on me
> and you are tangible
> without your flesh.
> Visitor of amnesia
> you will erase my body
> inhabited only
> by sighs,

and my exact hands
will touch your freezing
roads of tenderness.
On my shoulders your invited
dream of absence,
and in my trembling the anxiety
of not having learned you.

[Ahogarás mi dimensión
cuando me vuelvas la espalda
y te me quedes tangible
sin tu carne.
Visitante de olvidos,
me borrarás el cuerpo
habitado tan sólo
de suspiros,
y mis manos precisas
te palparán helados
caminos de ternura.
En mis hombros tu sueño
invitado de ausencia,
y en mi temblor el ansia
de no haberte aprendido.]

(Poem 31, p. 51)

In Poem 43, she writes: "Oh my small body / incapable of holding you, / undertow of my bones / who could deny you!" ["¡Ay mi cuerpo pequeño / incapaz de amarrarte, / resaca de mis huesos / quién pudiera negarte!"] (p. 67). And finally, this ultimate reduction of body and spirit: "I keep on getting smaller / without your support / like a cut out / paper silhouette / like a pine needle, / unthreaded / without its center. . . ." ["Me voy disminuyendo / sin tu respaldo como una recortada / silueta de papel / como una hoja de pino, / aguja deshebrada / sin su centro. . . ."] (Poem 36, p. 57). Within the implicit desire to be all for the lover lies the progressive deterioration of a woman's self. "El ansia / de no haberte aprendido" is Marina's confession—the feminine equivalent of the manly failure of nerve—that somehow she has not been pleasing, has not measured up as a woman. Even her body was insufficient, she suggests. Indeed, it is as a body that she diminishes, painfully disappearing into the very paper that documents her fading away. Her absent partner erases her corporal presence in one poem, and in another, she slips into a paper profile, losing the physical sense of person. A process of uncreation subjects the poet to her eventual disappearance, making her body an unwanted thing and turning Frankenstein into the creature, just before vanishing among the ice floes of chilled indifference.

"Ahogarás mi dimensión," Marina writes. Memory oppresses, suffocating the poet with the lover's heaviness. Sentiment, when it assumes the physical form of possession, can be destructive, burying the very body from which it springs. Perhaps for that reason Carolina Coronado preferred to hide her sentiment, giving it the name of silence. Casta Esteban y Navarro, on the other hand, chose to exhibit what treasure she possessed, but at her own (material and emotional) expense. Marina Romero seems to have realized the risk, judging from the poem "Dádiva" [Gift] (*Presencia del recuerdo*). "You have to give / the light its treasure" ["Hay que dar / a la luz su tesoro"] (p. 70), she begins, playing as well with the other meaning of "dar a luz" as giving birth. "Throw out memory / from the dark room / and the badly spoken word; / forget the agony / of unending trains / and rigid stations" ["A tirar el recuerdo / de habitación oscura / y palabra mal dicha; / a olvidar la agonía / de trenes inconclusos / y de estaciones yertas"] (p. 70). Instead, she says: "Fill my hands / and heart with stars / and give them to the wind / in open caress!" ["¡Que me llenen las manos / y el corazón de estrellas / para darlas al viento / en abierta caricia (!)"] (p. 71). The traditional imagery of light and dark in this poem carries other values as well. Treasure is diaphanous, weightless, while memory must be thrown like unspeakable trash out of darkness. This move toward lightness and openness through self-divestment continues as a significant countermotif in her next book of poetry, *Midas. Poema de amor*.

The gleam of treasure, as the title suggests, radiates throughout *Midas*, beginning with the very first poem: "Gold, / these long fingers / of mine, / as soon as your memory touched them" ["Oro, / estos dedos largos, / míos, / en cuanto los tocó tu recuerdo"] (p. 9). Instead of disappearing from Marina's poetry, memory undergoes a conversion, as the monetary image of the Midas myth makes clear. The act of remembering transforms the poet herself, turning her into literal treasure.[38] This metaphoric investing of the body with a coat of gold is in effect the poet's endowment, Marina's capital outlay in herself. In other words, the authority of self—her golden (in)vestment—earns full value only when some implicit assessment is attached to it. The Midas touch, then, turns Marina into pure gold and, in the process, converts sentiment into a value through corporal investment. Thus feeling once more becomes embodied as treasure, as in Carolina Coronado and Casta Esteban y Navarro. But by literally incorporating feeling into her text the poet also must contend with the heaviness of the image created, with the conversion of treasure into treasury. Like the myth she has exploited, to be worth one's weight in gold can prove to be undigestible.

The Midas story also recalls another part of this essay: the notion of possession, suggested in the material inertness of gold. At work in this reelaboration of an old image are two principles playing against each other: conversion as lightness and possession as heaviness. *Midas* displays an object lesson in enchantment. The swift metamorphosis releases the poet from the cloth of material constraints, just as the mythical king must have felt an initial exultation upon seeing how he could change physical reality into the shape of his desire—upon knowing, that is, the power of imagination. But enchantment never entirely satisfies the human spirit, perhaps because ultimately it represents an untenable space: the space of possession. One imagines in order to possess a thing more fully, but to do so, one must dispossess oneself of some deeply held part from within. To imagine, in this sense, means to let go part of the treasure, to expect deprivation. The result of this inner depletion of self—this emptying of the body's inner resources—is the creation of another body, the Midas figure verbally reencarnated. Yet the woman poet doesn't really let go: she reabsorbs the body inside, in an attempt to become the possessor possessed. In Romero's poetry, the golden shape of Midas is Marina herself. Sentiment—the-body-within-the-body—in assuming a verbal form, still clings to its physical origins, refusing to leave its place of birth.

But above all, this is remembered feeling, worth its weight in gold. How does the poet get around the heaviness of an old possession? She must start inventing again. "Reality not yet invented," writes Marina, "and arriving / new, / still without a name" ["Realidad aún no inventada / y al llegar, / nueva, / todavía sin nombre"] (*Midas*, p. 12). To write, she must find names for things. But to name is, of course, a form of repossession, as Romero suggests in these lines: "And when you come to me / new born and without your shadow, / with my words, I alone, / shall possess you" ["Y cuando te me acerques / naciente y sin tu sombra, / con mis letras, yo sola, / te tendré poseído"] (p. 19). But the poet can only recreate when the original name or experience, "is already opaque / is full of people" ["Tu nombre ya está opaco, / está lleno de gente"] (p. 18). In other words, the burial must have taken place, the name like a niche having been filled in and slowly darkening. In starting over—new, without a shadow—Marina privileges poetic invention as a resurrectional act over memory's entombment.

But the lightness of creation implied in the notion of verbal metamorphosis—the writer as alchemist—cannot be sustained, because the poet continues to hoard her treasure of remembered feeling. Release only can be provisional; this becomes clear in the last lines of *Midas*: "Outside myself, / beating out of synch / I've given you new life. / Now you are forever / created in my words, / and no slow drop / can free you" ["Como una enajenada / palpitando a destiempo / te he dado nueva vida. / Ya quedas para siempre / creado en mi palabra, / y no habrá lenta gota / que logre emanciparte"] (p. 80). Enchantment has turned into enchainment, and verbal resurrection of the other into unending possession. "So love, when it has gone," Djuna Barnes once wrote, "taking time with it, leaves a memory of its weight."[39] Similarly, that heaviness of feeling settles like the "slow drop" of these lines into the poet's alienated heart, and maladjusted time—which is also a non-time, a *des-tiempo*—beats uselessly against memory.

These last words read against the backdrop of the remaining poems in *Midas* reveal that emancipation is in truth unwanted, because it means poetic erasure for the writer herself. Proclaiming memory's manumission puts the owner of retrospect at risk. Her property is endangered, openly set upon the auction block of publication as a commodity, a finished product ready to sell. On both public and private accounts, such frontal exposure offends. The poet's greatest possession becomes her greatest shame, a sign of inadequacy and dependence. Slave and owner are one in much of women's writing: the inner luxury of self that women possess is, in turn, possessed by someone else, the trace of otherness informing memory and word. Women's literature cannot be understood without the retrospective presence of the other: Carolina's grieving male poet, Casta's dead husband, Marina's ghostly lover. Similarly, one's old self—historically, emotionally—is revealed by moving backwards into real time and the surrogate of memory. By shifting into reverse, as I have done throughout this essay, I've opted for a writing of subtraction, stripping away the feminine self and making deprivation apparently her sole virtue. But do not be deceived —"Never!. . . I couldn't!", Carolina declared on her own behalf. "My shadow departs," she said, "but I remain."

Carolina's beautifully modulated phrase of balanced presence and absence is illustrative of the way women have asserted self through the diction of reticence. This same lateral view is unveiled subtly in these lines from *Midas*.

> How to escape the obscure
> obsession of your soul
> for a "not to love you"
> clean of your memory?
> I will cover this name
> with a false pseudonym
> resisting your presence,
> extinguishing your trace,
> and for me, if I can,
> Still Marina,
> but to leeward of your destiny.
> And, who knows!
> some day . . .
> like Lazarus . . .
>
> [¿Cómo esquivar la oscura
> obsesión de tu alma

> para un no quererte
> limpia de tu recuerdo?
> Me cubriré este nombre
> con un falso seudónimo
> resistente a tu encuentro,
> apagando tu rastro,
> y para mí, si puedo,
> Marina todavía,
> pero al socaire
> de todos tus destinos.
> Y, ¡quién sabe!,
> algún día . . .
> como Lázaro . . . ]
>
> (Poem 8, pp. 20–21)

Earlier I spoke of the poet's disappearance from her poetry, but it is clear from this poem that only her shadow departs. Marina herself remains, tentative and uncertain, hiding her real self under another name. Even in the bleakest of her poetry, found in *Sin agua, el mar*, Marina remains, refusing to be buried—hence the significance of the ambiguous reference to resurrection with the word "Lazarus" ending the poem. Ambiguous because it isn't certain who or what is to rise again, or when. But plainly, Marina's persona resists writing necrology in these lines.

In naming herself, however hesitantly, the poet asserts the value of a woman's writing life, thus answering Carolina's non-rhetorical question, "What does my name matter?" That her response comes roundabout— "Me cubriré este nombre / con un falso seudónimo"—is unsurprising, indirectly reflecting the long tradition of disguised authorship in women's writing. That she answers from the "leeward side" merely confirms the oblique direction taken in the assertion of self, already doubly layered with a false pseudonym of deceptive redundancy. Nor should one discount an alternate reading of the phrase, "al socaire de," as "enjoying the protection of," which contributes further to the ambiguous tonalities of the poem. Most significantly, the poet constructs her feminine self in relation to otherness; for, despite her resistance, the trace of alterity remains, poised elliptically in "Lázaro," the last word of the text. Gender questions aside, this open ending also points to a possible regeneration of the poet's self. But the poem does not define that self. Indeed, writing as a resurrectional act suggests not only divestment of the old self but an implicit lightness as well. The richness of women's writing, arising as it does, paradoxically, out of biographical insufficiency, also suggests that one cannot define what, in the long run, only can be subtracted—what can only be understood as lightness, the unbearable lightness of being.

# Notes

See also "Marina Romero," pp. 11–12.

1. Carolina Coronado (1820–1911) attained considerable popularity in Spain in the 1840s and 1850s as a woman writer of romantic, intimate poetry (*Poesías*, 1843, with expanded editions in 1852 and 1872, the last an extremely rare one). Even after her poetic voice became muted and sporadic, she was reprinted in newspapers and anthologies for many years afterward. See Antonio Porpetta and Luzmaría Jiménez Faro, *Carolina Coronado (Apunte biográfico y Antología)* (Madrid: Ediciones Torremozas, 1983), for further background. After I finished this essay, I ran across two new studies on Coronado: Isabel María Pérez González, *Carolina Coronado* (Badajoz: Departamento de Publicaciones, Diputación Provincial, 1986); and Gregorio Torres Nebrera, ed., *Carolina Coronado: Treinta y nueve poemas y una prosa* (Extremadura: Editora Regional de Extremadura, 1986).

2. Carolina Coronado, Prologue to *Elegías y Armonías. Rimas varias*, by Ventura Ruiz Aguilera, 3rd ed. (Madrid: Imprenta, Estereotipia y Galvanoplastia de Aribau y Compañía [Sucesores de Rivadeneyra], 1873), p. ix. Subsequent references will appear in the text.

3. Ruiz Aguilera, *Elegías y Armonías*, p. 19. Subsequent references will appear in the text.

4. Coronado wrote in 1857: "Without a child a woman's life is unbearable" ["Sin un niño la vida de la mujer es insoportable"]. Quoted in María del Carmen Simón Palmer, "Escritoras españolas del siglo XIX o el miedo a la marginación," *Anales de Literatura Española* (Universidad de Alicante), no. 2 (1983): 480.

5. Critics conventionally see Coronado's poetry as sublimely feminine, "una sostenida aria de feminísima melodía" (Gerardo Diego, "Primavera de Catalina [sic] Coronado," *Boletín de la Biblioteca de Menéndez Pelayo* 38 [1962]: 401), without questioning the basis for such a view. Ironically, her first publication in 1839 ("A la palma") was praised for its "original and manly thinking" ["pensamientos originales y viriles"]. Quoted in Porpetta and Jiménez Faro, *Carolina Coronado*, p. 18.

6. For the effects of silence on women writing, see Tillie Olsen, *Silences* (New York: Delacorte Press, 1979); and Adrienne Rich, *On Lies, Secrets, and Silence* (New York: W.W. Norton, 1979).

7. Isabel Segura, ed., *Romances de señoras* (Barcelona: Altafulla, 1981), p. 53.

8. Milan Kundera, *The Unbearable Lightness of Being*, trans. Michael Henry Heim (Boston and London: Faber and Faber, 1985), pp. 8, 5–6, 33.

9. See Russell P. Sebold, *Trayectoria del romanticismo español* (Barcelona: Editorial Crítica, 1983), chap. 1.

10. Carolina Coronado, *Poesías*, ed. Julio Cienfuegos Linares (Badajoz: Arqueros, 1953), pp. 20–21.

11. Kundera, *The Unbearable Lightness*, p. 248.

12. Neither is Ventura Ruiz Aguilera exempt from such sentimentalizing over the death of a child. See, for example, "A la memoria de Jesús Rodríguez Cao," pp. 112–13. His notes to *Elegías y Armonías* contain several references to dead children and to *coronas fúnebres*, or poetic garlands, composed in their honor (pp. 315–17). I found several examples listed in the card catalogue of Madrid's Biblioteca Nacional.

13. Porpetta and Jiménez Faro, *Carolina Coronado*, p. 38.

14. Simón Palmer, "Escritoras españolas," pp. 478–79.

15. Rica Brown, "La fama póstuma de Bécquer: Nuevos datos," *Revista de Filología Española* 52 (1969): 525–35.

16. For more information on Casta Esteban y Navarro and her literary fortunes, see J. Domínguez Bordona, "Un libro de la viuda de Bécquer," Separata of *Revista de la Biblioteca, Archivo y Museo* (Ayuntamiento de Madrid) (Madrid: Imprenta Municipal, 1926); and, especially, José María Martínez Cachero, "La viuda de Bécquer, escritora," in *Studia Philologica. Homenaje ofrecido a Dámaso Alonso*, vol. 2 (Madrid: Gredos, 1961), pp. 443–57.

17. Rica Brown, *Bécquer* (Barcelona: Aedos, 1963), p. 160.

18. Martínez Cachero, "La viuda de Bécquer," pp. 455–56.

19. Geraldine M. Scanlon, "Revolución burguesa e instrucción femenina," in *Nuevas perspectivas sobre la mujer*. Actas de las Primeras Jornadas de Investigación Interdisciplinaria (Madrid: Universidad Autónoma de Madrid, 1982), pp. 163–73.

20. Diego, "Primavera de C. Coronado," p. 401.

21. Martínez Cachero, "La viuda de Bécquer," p. 449.

22. Casta Esteban y Navarro, *Mi primer ensayo. Colección de cuentos con pretensiones de artículos* (Madrid: Tipografía de Manuel Ginés Hernández,1884), p. 7. Subsequent references will appear in the text.

23. Rachel Bowlby, *Just Looking. Consumer Culture in Dreiser, Gissing and Zola* (New York and London: Methuen, 1985), p. 9.

24. Domínguez Bordona, "Un libro," p. 5.

25. Later, she also says that whatever literary value her book might have derives from being "drenched . . . in that pure and crystalline water the eyes distill, [when] overwhelmed by grief . . ." ["empapados . . . en ese agua pura y cristalina que destilan los ojos, embargados por el dolor . . ."] (p. 73).

26. Not surprisingly, Casta's narratives follow the schema of male *costumbrista* writers like Mesonero Romanos and Larra, and the romantics, Espronceda and Bécquer. Like Fernán Caballero and other women writers of the period, she assumes the voice of a male narrator. Only in "La Romería de San Isidro en Madrid" does she identify herself by stating,"I am not a daughter of Madrid, not that it matters . . ." ["No soy hija de Madrid ni creo me haga una gran falta . . ."] (p. 189), but she makes no further use of gender in the story.

27. For a useful discussion of the book as modern commodity see Bowlby, *Just Looking*, chap. 6; "Culture and the book business."

28. Bowlby, *Just Looking*, p. 68. See also Emile Zola, *Au Bonheur des Dames* (1883; Paris: Fasquelle, 1971), p. 92.

29. Monroe Z. Hafter also makes note of Coronado's "insecurity about her reception as a woman writer in Spain." See his "Carolina Coronado as Novelist," *Kentucky Romance Quarterly* 30 (1983): 416, note 7.

30. Susan Gubar points to another form of bodily sacrilege in which "the creation of female art feels like the destruction of the female body. Because of the forms of self-expression available to women, artistic creation often feels like a violation. . . ." Thus writing is produced "through a painful wounding, a literal influence of male authority" ("'The Blank Page' and the Issues of Female Creativity," in *The New Feminist Criticism*, ed. Elaine Showalter [New York: Pantheon Books, 1985], p. 302). Inquiry into the relationship between feminine creativity and the body has grown in recent years, particularly within French feminism. For an overview see Ann Rosalind Jones, "Writing the Body: Toward an Understanding of l'Écriture féminine," in Showalter, *The New Feminist Criticism*, pp. 361–77.

Also of interest is Susan Rubin Suleiman's anthology of readings, *The Female Body in Western Culture* (Cambridge: Harvard University Press, 1986).

31. Torres Nebrera, *Carolina Coronado*, pp. 12, 160–61.

32. Pérez González, *Carolina Coronado*, pp. 47–51.

33. Porpetta and Jiménez Faro, *Carolina Coronado*, p. 81.

34. Marina Romero, *Sin agua, el mar* (Madrid: Agora, 1961), p. 55. Subsequent references will appear in the text.

35. Kundera, *The Unbearable Lightness*, p. 256.

36. Marina Romero, *Presencia del recuerdo* (Madrid: Insula, 1952), p. 11. Subsequent references will appear in the text.

37. Marina Romero, *Midas. Poema de amor* (Madrid: Insula, 1954), p. 26. Subsequent references will appear in the text.

38. Romero's use of gold as an image of self recalls Emily Dickinson's poem "It was given to me by the Gods" (*The Complete Poems of Emily Dickinson*, ed. Thomas H. Johnson [Boston: Little, Brown and Co., 1960], p. 218), in which "gold is her metonymic name for the wealth which is her poetic gift" (Helen McNeil, *Emily Dickinson* [New York: Virago/Pantheon, 1986], p. 68). I have found stimulating and marvellously accidental similarities between my own essay and McNeil's provocative study of Emily Dickinson, which was recommended to me by Carol Maier after she had read my manuscript. McNeil then led me to Lewis Hyde's *The Gift*, an imaginative inquiry into the nature of creativity and art as a "gift," functioning in "two 'economies,' a market economy and a gift economy" (*The Gift. Imagination and the Erotic Life of Property* [1979; New York: Vintage Books, 1983], p. xi). But it is the "gift economy" alone that is essential to the artist. Thus, Marina gives "the light its treasure" in "Gift"; and Dickinson criticizes the economics of literature by saying that "Publication—is the Auction" (*Complete Poems*, ed. Thomas H. Johnson, p. 348; see also McNeil, *Emily Dickinson*, p. 68). This has been seen vividly enacted in the case of Casta Esteban y Navarro.

39. Djuna Barnes, *Nightwood* (1936; Boston and London: Faber and Faber, 1985), p. 182.

# Contributors

MARYELLEN BIEDER is Associate Professor at Indiana University. The author of *Narrative Perspective in the Novels of Francisco Ayala* (1979), she has published widely on Pardo Bazán, Galdós, Goytisolo, Concepción Gimeno de Flaquer, Mercè Rodoreda, and other writers. She is currently working on late nineteenth-century Spanish and Catalan women novelists.

DEBRA A. CASTILLO is an Associate Professor in the Department of Romance Studies at Cornell University. Her publications include *The Translated World: A Postmodern Tour of Libraries in Literature* (1984) and numerous articles on modern Spanish, Latin American, and British Commonwealth literature. She is editor of *Diacritics* and assistant to the editor of *Anales Galdosianos*.

ELSA KRIEGER GAMBARINI received the Ph.D. from Yale University, was an assistant professor of Latin American literature at Yale, and is currently training as a Jungian analyst. She has published widely in this country and abroad on the Latin American short story.

JANET GOLD is completing the Ph.D. at the University of Massachusetts at Amherst. In 1988, she received a Fulbright to do research in Honduras. She has published and given papers on Spanish and Spanish American women writers.

BERNICE L. HAUSMAN is currently working on an interdisciplinary Ph.D. in "Feminist Studies and Critical Theory" at the University of Iowa. She received her B.A. from Yale University in 1985, where her senior essay, the original version of "Words between Women," was awarded the Steere Prize in Women's Studies.

AMY KATZ KAMINSKY, a feminist critic who has written widely on Spanish and Latin American literature, is Associate Professor of Women's Studies at the University of Minnesota. Her most recent work is *Flores del agua*, an anthology of Spanish women writers from 1400 to 1900.

273

SUSAN KIRKPATRICK is Professor of Spanish and Comparative Literature at the University of California, San Diego. She has published *Larra: El laberinto inextricable de un romántico liberal* and articles on Larra, Valle-Inclán, Fernán Caballero, and Galdós. In 1986–87 she was awarded a Guggenheim Fellowship, which resulted in *Las Románticas: Women Writers and Subjectivity in Spain* (University of California Press, 1989).

LINDA GOULD LEVINE is Professor of Spanish at Montclair State College, where she also teaches Women's Studies. She is the author of *Juan Goytisolo: la destrucción creadora* (1976); a critical edition of Goytisolo's *Reivindicación del Conde don Julián* (Cátedra, 1985); and co-author with Gloria Waldman of *Feminismo ante el franquismo: entrevistas con feministas de España* (1980). She has published numerous articles on Spanish and Latin American women writers.

CAROL MAIER is Professor of Spanish at Kent State University, where she is associated with the Institute for Applied Linguistics. Her work in Women's Studies has appeared in *Letras Femeninas*, *Translation Review*, and *Third Woman*, and her translations include poetry by Ana Castillo and fiction by Carmen Martín Gaite. She has also translated *With Dusk*, by Octavio Armand (1984), and *Written on a Body*, by Severo Sarduy (forthcoming). Among her current projects is a reading of Valle-Inclán's aesthetics from a feminist perspective.

ELIZABETH J. ORDÓÑEZ is Associate Professor of Spanish at the University of Texas at Arlington. She has published numerous articles on contemporary Spanish narrative by women and has recently begun to reread Pardo Bazán and other precontemporary women writers in light of current feminist theory. Also interested in minority and ethnic literature, she has published articles on Chicana literature and narrative texts by ethnic women.

JANET PÉREZ, a member of several editorial boards, is Paul Whitfield Horn Professor of Classical and Romance Languages at Texas Tech University. She taught previously at the University of North Carolina at Chapel Hill, Queens College / City University of New York, and Duke University. In addition to earlier books on Ortega y Gasset, Ana María Matute, and Miguel Delibes, more recently she has published *Gonzalo Torrente Ballester* (1984), *Novelistas femeninas de la postguerra española* (1983), and *Contemporary Women Writers of Spain* (1988). Her articles on the contemporary novel, essay, and theater have appeared in *Hispania*, *Romance Notes*, *Hispanófila*, *Revista de Estudios Hispánicos*, *Cuadernos Hispanoamericanos*, *World Literature Today*, *Estreno*, *Revista Canadiense de Estudios Hispánicos*, *Hispanic Review*, and various other journals.

MARCI STERNHEIM has taught in Yale College and at Wesleyan University. She currently is the Special Assistant to the Secretary of Yale University. She has received an NDFL Title VI Graduate Fellowship for study in Mexico, as well as a Woodrow Wilson National Fellowship grant in Women's Studies for her dissertation entitled "Baroque/Avant-Garde/Neobaroque: The Poetry of Sara de Ibáñez."

HARRIET S. TURNER, Professor of Hispanic Studies at Oberlin College, is a specialist in the novel and short fiction of nineteenth-century Spain and of contemporary Latin America. Her publications include essays on Unamuno and Borges, Rulfo and García Lorca. Currently she is writing a book on the problem of deception and authenticity in the novels of Galdós and Clarín.

NOËL VALIS (Ph.D., Bryn Mawr College) is Professor of Spanish at the University of Michigan. She has published *The Decadent Vision in Leopoldo Alas* (1981), *The Novels of Jacinto Octavio Picón* (1986), *Leopoldo Alas (Clarín): An Annotated Bibliography* (1986), and an annotated edition of Pereda's *Bocetos al temple* (forthcoming). Her articles on Clarín, Galdós, Fernán Caballero, Ana María Matute, Ray Bradbury and Borges, the Latin American novel, painting and realism, Emilia Pardo Bazán, etc., have appeared in *Novel*, *MLN*, *Romanic Review*, *Hispania*, *American Spectator*, *Bulletin of Hispanic Studies*, and other journals. She is currently working on the connections between late romanticism, women writers, and *lo cursi* in nineteenth-century Spain; and a translation of Pedro Salinas' *Víspera del gozo*.

TERESA VILARÓS-SOLER is Assistant Professor of Spanish at the University of Wisconsin-Madison. She has published several articles, some of them on authors from nonmainstream literatures, such as Ausias March and Gonzalo R. Mourulho. She is currently at work on a feminist interpretation of Benito Pérez Galdós's novels.

# Index